D0298273

THE COLD WAR

MARTIN WALKER

THE COLD WAR

And the Making of the Modern World

FOURTH ESTATE · *LONDON*

First published in Great Britain in 1993 by
Fourth Estate Limited
289 Westbourne Grove
London W11 2QA

ISBN 1–85702–004–9

Typeset by York House Typographic, Ltd
Printed in Great Britain at the University Press, Cambridge

Contents

What does this sudden uneasiness mean,
and this confusion? (How grave the faces have become!)
Why are the streets and squares rapidly emptying,
and why is everyone going back home so lost in thought?

Because it is night and the barbarians have not come.
And some men have arrived from the frontiers
and they say that barbarians don't exist any longer.

And now what will become of us without barbarians?
They were a kind of solution.

C. P. Cavafy, 'Waiting for the Barbarians'

Preface

This book is the story of its author's life. I was born into the crucial winter of the Cold War, when the blizzards which devastated the Europe of early 1947 forced the dispatch of a plaintive but historic appeal to Washington. The Durham coalfields near my birthplace, just decorated with the defiant signposts, 'These pits now belong to the People', had frozen solid, along with the nation's railroads and the docks. Six million men, almost a third of the workforce, were laid off. Although nominally a time of peace, the rationing of food was more severe than it had been at the height of Hitler's unrestricted submarine warfare. Exhausted by war, impoverished by peace, Britain belatedly acknowledged that the burden of Empire and of Europe's defence was no longer to be borne, and asked the Americans to take over the support of Greece and Turkey.

It was to be a long mission. I was just starting to toddle when the American atomic bombers were first stationed in Britain. My elder daughter will soon be old enough to have children of her own, and the bombers are still there, along with the American troops on the Rhine. As Senator Pat Moynihan once observed, 'This is the stuff of Roman legions.'

The Cold War has been the constant, implacable condition of the vast demographic wave of the children who were born as the soldiers of World War Two came home to a bitter, uncertain peace. Now that we think it is over, and that the nuclear shadow may at last be passing, and that two members of that generation are now President and Vice-President of the last and lonely superpower, we have to make sense of what the Cold War has been, and how it has shaped us and the uncertain new world ahead, and what it has left behind.

By accidents of geography, of nationality, and then of profession, I find that a remarkable portion of my life has been spent as a curious and usually bewildered non-combatant in the various parts of the Cold War's far-flung front lines. My first memory of a newspaper is reading an account of the mistreatment of British prisoners of war in the Korean conflict. In 1956, at a primary school in the north of England, I published my first newspaper, a rude wall-poster whose headline dealt with the Suez crisis. I remember the prime minister Harold Macmillan visiting my grammar school just after his return from a summit with Nikita Khrushchev in Moscow, and recall my disappointment that he was not wearing the white fur Cossack's hat in which he had looked most dashing in the newspapers. In the Cuban missile crisis of 1962, I took part in my first school debate, arguing with adolescent passion that the Americans must withdraw their missiles from Turkey to save Britain from annihilation.

And yet it seemed natural that, with a father and four uncles who had served in the Royal Air Force during what we still call 'the war', I should join the RAF section of the Cadet Corps, wear a boy-sized uniform each Friday, undergo my pilot's training and accept the duty of being liable to serve as a reservist in time of war. Military service seemed inevitable, part of the condition of a nation that was constantly ready to stand to arms. The odd contradiction of attending Ban the Bomb marches while learning how to fly through the RAF, and making my first visit to the USA through a Nato scholarship for young air cadets, caused no anguish. Opinions were one thing: the reality of national readiness was quite another.

My first visit to the Soviet Union was made in the Easter vacation of 1968, part of a National Union of Students tour. It took us through West Berlin at the time of the Rudi Dutschke riots, through Warsaw as the students battled the security police by the Copernicus statue, and to Moscow and Leningrad where we found Russian students much like ourselves. And so were the students of Prague, thrilling to that extraordinary Spring which spoke of Socialism with a human face, and the students of Paris at their barricades. It was only later, at demonstrations against the Vietnam War at Harvard and in Washington in 1969 and 1970, that I came to understand the self-indulgence of us Western Europeans, not faced with the threat of conscription into an odious war which faced the Americans, and the different but grim menace of civilian life which loomed over my Polish and Russian friends.

It was in that realisation – that the Western Europeans who had begun after 1945 as the Cold War's hostages and had by the late 1960s become its beneficiaries – that this book had its origins. My profession as a journalist has provided endless opportunities to study the Cold War's erratic progress at close hand. Covering the Portuguese revolution of 1974, where a Nato ally seemed for a moment to be tottering into the socialist camp, the strange absence of Soviet influence and aid for an enthusiastic Communist Party emerging from the underground helped explain the superpower stasis which had been agreed for Europe. Just as the West had not moved to the relief of Hungary in 1956, of Czechoslovakia in 1968, of Poland in 1970 and 1981, the Soviets did not exert themselves as Portugal and Spain hauled themselves from their fascist past.

In 1979, newly married and on an extended honeymoon, my wife and I found ourselves in Iran as the Ayatollah's rule consolidated, and then in Afghanistan. We drove from Pakistan through the Quetta Pass to Herat, which had just been retaken after a burst of liberation which had seen a hundred Soviet military advisers and their families slaughtered, and their heads paraded through the town on pikes. In Kabul, the night sky was electric with the tracers of the gunships. The Khalq and Parcham factions of the Afghan Communist Party were at war, the Soviet advisers were joining in, and I had to defy the curfew to chase down some bottled water for my wife, stricken with dysentery. We left through the Khyber Pass on the last civilian convoy.

But not for the first or the last time, I confronted the terrifying irony that while my press card and passport paraded my neutrality, my skin made me indistinguishable from a hated Russian – or in other places at other times, from an equally loathed American imperialist. At a road block in southern Ethiopia in 1975, just after the fall of Haile Selassie, my harmless library card for the British Museum reading room, which carried no name but only some ominous colour-coded symbols, almost got me shot as an American spy. Dodging Moroccan armoured columns with the Polisario guerrillas of the Western Sahara in 1977, or being held at gunpoint by Colonel Gadafy's troops in Libya in 1981, the role of the Cold War proxies of the Third World was brought sharply home. We were all white outsiders, trying to impose our will, or our order, on places where the locals found our presence unwelcome.

Then in Brazil to make sense of the Latin American debt crisis, the awesome, unfolding powers and vulnerabilities of global finance began to grip my imagination in a way that has never ceased. Covering the travails of the Mitterrand government in France in 1983, as a leading European power tried for the last time to enact a programme of social reform in defiance of the economic orthodoxies, the new power of the global market to override the measures for which electorates had voted became bluntly clear. In the following year, I was asked to reopen the *Guardian* bureau in Moscow, and found myself covering not only the peaceful revolution of Perestroika, but the inability of even a centrally planned autarky to escape the disciplines of this global economic system.

As we left Moscow, the Soviet foreign ministry spokesman, the urbane and affable Gennady Gerasimov, who had served as a correspondent in New York, bade me farewell, raised a glass and toasted my departure 'from one declining superpower to the other'. To have covered both Moscow and Washington during the long drawing down of the Cold War has been an extraordinary privilege, and profound thanks are due to Peter Preston, the editor of the *Guardian*, and all my colleagues at that newspaper. The *Guardian* was founded in 1821, as the voice of the booming new industrial city of Manchester. Its birth in the first industrial revolution, its dependence on the first multinational trading system which developed around cotton, may explain why this book is not simply a diplomatic history, but ranges far beyond the usual structures of power and alliances to explore the underlying tectonic shifts in the world's economic system.

Acknowledgements are also due to a number of other organisations and publications which allowed me to explore my developing theories about the Cold War as history. The distinguished American diplomat Bill Maynes, whom I first knew when we were both Congressional fellows of the American Political Science Association, working on Capitol Hill in 1971, has been an outstanding editor of *Foreign Policy*. He and Tom Omestad encouraged me to write on America's role in the world for that august quarterly. Mr Sherle Schwenninger has been a splendid editor of *World Policy Journal*, and maintained a sprightly liberal tradition in American thinking about foreign affairs, in spite of the prolonged intellectual hegemony of conservatism and *realpolitik*. I am grateful to them, and to Mr Peter Doyle and Robert Guttman of *Europe* magazine, the publication of the European Community in the United States, who asked me to explore some of the longer-range implications of the world after the Cold War.

Both the International Press Institute and the Committee to Protect Journalists invited me to return to Moscow for conferences and research trips which proved more than useful. The new journal *Demokratizatsiya*, produced jointly by Moscow State and the American University, invited me on to their editorial board and to chair some of the sessions on democratising the KGB. This resulted in a detailed advisory memorandum for President Boris Yeltsin and, for this book, some unusual insights into the role of intelligence in the Cold War.

Thanks are also due to the Canadian Institute for International Peace and Security and the Czechoslovak Institute for International Relations in Prague, and to Canada's Parliamentary Committee for

Foreign Affairs, who invited me to give papers on European security after the Cold War, some themes of which found their way into this book. I am also grateful to Dr Michael Hogan, editor of *Diplomatic History*, for inviting me to concentrate my thoughts on the latest flurry of books in the newly emerging field of post-Cold War studies.

There has been in recent years a golden age of contemporary history studies in US–Soviet relations and in the Cold War, as archives creak open, memoirs are published, and an entire generation of gifted scholar–journalists has been unleashed. The notes to this book record my debt, and the debt of anyone writing in this field, to Richard Barnet, Dr Michael Beschloss, Kai Bird, Sid Blumenthal, Abe Brumberg, David Calleo, James Chace, Stephen G. Cohen, Ray Garthoff, Patrick Glyn, Ed Hewett, Walter Isaacson, Bob Kaiser, Walter LaFeber, Michael MccGwire, Don Oberdorfer, and Strobe Talbott, to name only those whose books have been kept closest to hand. To many of those named, I am also grateful for insights gained in discussions and conversation, as well as their work in print. And a great debt is also due to Dr Kenneth Courtis, perhaps the leading Western expert on the Japanese and East Asian economies, for his advice and insights, and to the indispensable Dr Georgi Arbatov of Moscow.

Any merits this book may have stem from the way that I have been able to clamber on to the shoulders of these and other scholars, and use their work to try and see the global experience of the Cold War from a slightly different and sometimes wider point of view. All the errors and misjudgements are, of course, my own.

The greatest debt is due to my family, who put up with my long absences and distractions and encouraged and sustained me throughout. My wife Julia has shared many of the experiences, from Afghanistan to Moscow and Washington, and helped me make sense of them, while our daughters Kate and Fanny embody the life and promise that comes after the Cold War. This book is dedicated to them, in the hope that they will know an even longer and more productive peace.

Martin Walker,
Washington DC

Introduction

> Two things of opposite natures seem to depend
> On one another, as a man depends
> On a woman, day on night, the imagined
> On the real. This is the origin of change.
>
> *'Two Things', Wallace Stevens*

The history of the Cold War has been the history of the world since 1945. Communications and missile technology required the Cold War's proxy battle zones to girdle the entire earth and its satellites to orbit above. The Cold War was truly a global conflict, more so than either of the century's two world wars. South America and sub-Saharan Africa, continents which had been largely spared the earlier struggles, were sucked into its maw. Turks fought in Korea, Algerians fought in Vietnam, Cubans fought in Angola, and American and Russian schoolchildren, whose lessons had been interrupted by nuclear air-raid drills, grew up to die in Saigon and Kabul.

For all its economic and psychological burdens, and despite the appalling consequences in those parts of the developing world where the superpowers fought their wars by proxy, the Cold War had one great merit: it became an institution, marked by a kind of warped stability and an evolving code of acceptable behaviour, which helped spare humanity the devastation of a Third World War. The Cold War was also the first total war between economic and social systems, an industrial test to destruction. Victory became clear when the Soviet economy in the 1980s cracked under the strain of devoting an ever-larger proportion of gross national product (GNP) and research resources in the vain attempt to keep pace. The West prevailed because its economy proved able to supply guns as well as butter, aircraft-carriers *and* private cars, rockets as well as foreign holidays for an ever-increasing proportion of its taxpayers.

The West developed a peculiar mix of free enterprise and state investment, which generated an unprecedented synergy between private prosperity and defence-orientated public spending. The US Inter-state Highway Network was originally funded under a National Security Act, to speed evacuation of the cities under the threat of nuclear attack, and to facilitate the movement of troops. The surge in US college education after the 1950s was equally funded and justified in terms of national security: the need to catch up with a Soviet adversary which had put the first Sputnik into orbit in 1957, and the first man into space four years later.

In the course of the Cold War, the US became what Senator Daniel Patrick Moynihan has dubbed 'the National Security State', with a vast standing army, a global intelligence network, and a military–industrial economic complex whose booming factories helped spur the post-war growth of California and the Southern states, transforming the industrial and political geography of America.[1] When the Cold War began, the population of California was not quite five million, and Presidential candidates usually hailed from the traditional industrial states or the Atlantic seaboard, with their commercial and ethnic links to Europe. When it ended, the population of California was over thirty million, and it provided more than one in ten of US Congressmen elected in 1992. In Richard Nixon and Ronald Reagan, the new economic superstate of the west had already provided two Presidents.

The economic impact of the Cold War also played an incalculable role in the shaping of the modern economic world. The Cold War was the strategic rationale behind the Marshall Plan and the unprecedented US investment in Western Europe's post-war economic recovery. American aid and later US private investment force-fed the German economic miracle. And for four decades, the US garrison of 300,000 men in West Germany pumped dollars into the local economy and acted as a bridge which facilitated Europe's exports to America. It was the returning US servicemen who made the Volkswagen Beetle the first foreign car to make dramatic inroads into the vast American market.

America's Cold War defence budgets also pumped investment into the now booming economies of the Pacific Rim. Japan's economic miracle can be dated with some precision to the effect of the Korean War, when Japan became the main base for the US war effort. Japan was the rest-and-recreation centre for troops on leave, as well as the beneficiary of the constant flow of pay to the permanent US naval, Marine and Air Force garrisons on Japanese bases. Recovering from the devastation of World War Two, Japanese industry geared up to supply the non-lethal requirements of the US forces, the ports and warehousing centres, the medical equipment and maintenance facilities, the watches and radios and souvenirs the troops took home.

In the 1960s, the US war in Vietnam had a much wider impact across Asia. Japanese Hondas and stereos and radios packed the PX stores on the American bases. The hotel boom of Bangkok followed the Thai capital's designation as a main rest-and-recreation centre. Singapore's dockyards, suffering from the withdrawal of Britain's attenuated fleet, found new customers in the US Navy. Hong Kong's reputation as Asia's duty-free shopping centre was consolidated by the US troops.

The old British Empire had a saying, 'Trade follows the Flag', and America's global deployments of the Cold War fulfilled that prescription to a degree which can be traced in the booming Asia and Western Europe of today. Those booms would probably have happened anyway; the Marshall Plan and the long watch on the Rhine, the Korean and Vietnam wars certainly intensified that process. Above all, they accelerated the dramatic expansion of world trade which helped the American and broader Western economies to the prosperity which was the root of their eventual triumph over the enclosed and far less commercial Soviet system.

At the same time, the American garrisons in Europe and Asia brought with them their music, their cigarettes, their cars and films and Coca-Cola. The sudden shock of American popular culture which hit Europe with the GIs of World War Two was deepened and consolidated by the continued global presence of Americans in the Cold War. It was a soft and seductive form of power whose effect was all the more potent for being subliminal; witness the irony of European students demonstrating furiously against the Vietnam War to the rhythms of rock 'n' roll, or the Kremlin inveighing against America's cultural imperialism as Pepsi went on sale alongside the black-market Levi jeans on Moscow street corners. Even Aeroflot's pilots had no choice but to study English, the language of the world's commercial airways.

The deeper changes which the Cold War brought to the Soviet Union were less immediately apparent. Stalin had imposed a national security state of an incomparably more ruthless and intrusive kind, long before the Cold War began. But the climate of confrontation permitted this repressive system and the militarisation of society to assume a life and a political force of its own, almost irrespective of the efforts at thaw and reform by Stalin's successors. Each time the Soviet leaders tried to redirect their economy towards the production of more consumer goods, the demands of the arms race forced them back into the military–industrial bunker. Khrushchev's demobilisation of a million men in 1957 not only won him the sullen enmity of the officer corps, but the attempted reduction in the defence budget had to be reversed to meet the new American challenge of the Polaris submarines and the Minuteman missiles. Kosygin's economic reforms after 1964 were aborted largely because of the General Staff's demands for a Soviet navy and a strategic nuclear parity to redeem the defeat in the Cuban missile crisis.

An awful symbiosis emerged between the main actors of the Cold War, a rhythm of escalation between the Pentagon and the Soviet strategic rocket forces, and a long secret war between the KGB and the CIA which helped make the spy thriller into the distinctive cultural genre of the period. The two sides became locked into the roles of hero and villain in one another's morality play, as two distinct theories of social and political organisation believed they were grappling for nothing less than the inheritance of the planet.

Had anything like this civil war of the human race ever happened before? There are some intriguing historic parallels: the long twilight struggle of the Roman Empire against the barbarism without and social decay within; the still uncompleted Kulturkampf between Christendom and Islam. Indeed, Dean Acheson, the American Secretary of State during the Cold War's most intense years, observed in his memoirs:

> The threat to Western Europe seemed to me singularly like that which Islam had posed centuries before, with its combination of ideological zeal and fighting power. Then it had taken the same combination to meet it: Germanic power in the east, and Frankish in Spain, both energized by a great outburst of military power and social organization in Europe. This time it would need the added power and energy of America, for the drama was now played on a world stage.[2]

The Europeans claim with justice that they are a great civilisation, consistently cultured and uniquely creative. Their peoples developed the newspaper and the novel, the symphony and the opera, the portrait and the oil painting, the factory and the stock exchange, the parliament and the election. The world has paid a stiff price for this European contribution; Europe also invented the concentration camp and the nation state organised for war. The Europeans at their grandest justified their colonial empires as bringing the benefits of civilisation and Christianity to savage shores and dark continents wracked by tribal strife. But in fact, the fractious European tribes have consistently proved to be the most aggressive and warlike, vicious and even genocidal of all the earth's peoples.

The endemic wars of Europe in the past millennium have been of two broad kinds: wars of ideology, about what other men and women are allowed to believe: and wars of succession and the balance of power. The Cold War, for the first time, combined both of these characteristics of the European mode of war. It was about the balance of power, a war of the German succession, and at the same time it was an ideological confrontation. The Cold War was fought about the fate of Europe, and by the two great successor states of the European tradition, the United States and the old Russian autocracy reborn as the Soviet Union through the ideology of Communism. It was thus the last and greatest of Europe's civil wars.

So while the Cold War became a death struggle between economic and social systems, it was also an internecine strife that was located squarely within the Western intellectual tradition. For all the attempts to portray the Soviet Union as a semi-Asian state, as 'the East', the Soviet side mobilised behind the banner of a classically Western ideology which had been drawn up in the British Museum, based on Marx's studies of the industrial revolution in England, and refined in the political stirrings of the new working class of Germany and France. In purely ideological terms, the confrontation of the Cold War was an extreme version of the continuing political debate between conservative and social democratic parties across Europe. It was a fatally exaggerated form of the ongoing choice between organising societies on a collective or on an individual basis, which is part of the common political vocabulary of North America as well as Europe.

The Revolution of 1917 was launched as an attempt to develop a new kind of collectivised society, an idealist and even utopian bid to replace the tsarist autocracy with a new and fairer and more democratic political vision. But it was also an attempt to modernise and indeed to Westernise a largely peasant and backward land. Communism was the West, in all its furious and industrialising energy, a twentieth-century version of that earlier Westernising process which Peter the Great had imposed upon the virtually feudal Russia of the early eighteenth century. It was no historical accident that launched the Bolshevik Revolution in that city of St Petersburg which the enlightened despot had built and named after himself, and which was to be renamed Leningrad after the Bolshevik leader.

The vision of utopia was marred from the beginning by a ruthless civil war between Reds and Whites. British, French, Japanese, Czech and American troops spasmodically intervened against the Bolsheviks. And the Bolsheviks responded with the deliberate policy of state terror, to secure their grip. Launched by Felix Dzherzhinsky's Cheka, the reliance upon the secret police was to become characteristic of a regime which had begun with fine intentions. But the terror only developed into a characteristic and encompassing feature of the Soviet state under Stalin, and it assumed its full horror after Hitler's Nazi Party came to power in Germany in 1933. The Great Purges were justified in the name of national security as the totalitarian twins of Germany and Russia spent the pre-war years in a curious rehearsal of the Cold War. Stalin's party rivals and the Red Army generals were tried and condemned as German spies. The two systems fought by proxy in the Spanish Civil War, and enjoyed their own calculated phase of *détente* to devour Poland and the Baltic states before Hitler's catastrophic plunge into war in 1941.

It is never easy to argue with success, and the Soviet victory over Nazism not only established Stalin squarely in the heart of central Europe, it also established the grim methods of Stalinism as a tried and tested system which his successors found it difficult to change. Stalin's ruthlessness had industrialised the country, won the war, established a defensive glacis which guaranteed that the German threat would not revive, and crushed domestic dissent. The spasmodic attempts at internal reform and international *détente* by Stalin's heirs always laboured under this dreadful inheritance. The industrial and defence and security establishments which Stalin had built into the very structure of the state were not only durable at home, they also fuelled a constant suspicion and military response in the West. With hindsight, the eventual collapse of the Soviet system may appear to have been inevitable, a deliberate control and suppression of human creativity which was doomed to enfeeble the state's economic and eventually military potential. It did not always seem that way.

Whittaker Chambers, the former Communist agent in the United States who became the main witness against Alger Hiss in the US House of Representatives Committee on Un-American Activities, said that in changing his allegiance, he felt he had joined the losing side.[3] When Khrushchev said, 'We shall bury you', many in the West took it literally.[4] When Communists seized power in China, and when the first Sputnik seemed to herald a Soviet technological lead in 1957, the West tasted the prospect of eventual defeat. And after America's strategic reverse in Vietnam was followed by widespread opposition in Western Europe to deploying new Cruise and Pershing missiles, the most likely outcome of the Cold War seemed to be a kind of stable draw, an endless and uneasy peace of grudging coexistence.

The militarised vocabulary of the Cold War leads us too easily to talk of the West's victory and the Soviet defeat. In reality, the end of the Cold War was just as much a Soviet decision to redirect their frustrated energies to a new challenge, a decisive and still unresolved confrontation with their own internal problems and structures. In legal terms, the Soviets did not plead guilty, but *noli contendere.* In human terms, everyone won, and it was the Cold War itself which lost. It had endured long enough to become more than simply a way of life, rather a structure and defining context within which world events took their warped shape. Americans, Russians, Europeans and eventually the rest of the world became its prisoners, hostages to the nuclear balance which the world's leading economies strained themselves to maintain.

But at the same time, the Cold War became a form of global insurance against catastrophe, a system of political control which prevented local wars from getting out of hand. A stabilising paradox emerged in which smaller nations pursued their own policies and conflicts in the shadow of the superpowers, but the price of US or Soviet support and arms supplies was a surrender of an important aspect of their sovereignty to the strategic priorities of Moscow and Washington. The superpowers did not permit, because they dared not risk, a regional conflict developing into a total war. That constraint is now being removed, just at a time when smaller powers from India to Israel have developed their own nuclear capacity, and the missile technology to deliver the warheads which were once the monopoly of the superpower condominium. The defeated Soviet Empire has crumbled into the component parts which tsarism assembled and which Stalin welded into a gruesome homomorph, half Gulag and half tank. The familiar dangers of the Cold War have ended; the unknown perils of its aftermath lie in wait.

Chapter 1

1945: Yalta to the Bomb

> Yes, Russia is a Sphinx. Exulting, grieving
> And sweating blood, she cannot sate
> Her eyes that gaze and gaze and gaze
> At stone-lipped love for you, and hate.
> Get you all gone to Ural fastnesses.
> We clear the ground for the appalling scenes
> Of war between the savage Mongol hordes
> And pitiless science with its massed machines.
>
> *'The Scythians'*, Alexander

On 4 February 1945, with victory in sight and their armies poised to invade the German heartland, the leaders of the Grand Alliance met at the ancient Black Sea resort of the Tsars to agree the design for the post-war world. The site was carefully chosen. In a Soviet Union ravaged and exhausted by the German invasion, the old Livadia summer palace was a rare and relatively unspoilt sanctuary. Built for Tsar Nicholas in 1913, Livadia was the centre of a complex of palaces along the lovely Crimean shore, where the Soviet leaders could assert and display their inheritance of an older Russian empire.

Stalin himself took over the Koreis palace of Prince Yusupov. Winston Churchill and his British delegation were housed in the Vorontsov palace, some twelve miles away. Its stately park was dotted with 'stone wives', statues of women that had been recovered by archaeologists from the graves of the twelfth-century warriors of the steppes. Living women were also a feature of Soviet hospitality. Field Marshal Lord Alexander recalled having to ask 'a sort of female valet, dressed in a kind of nurse's uniform' to sleep outside his room, where she had evidently intended to spend the night.[1] Rank has its privileges. The American delegation was housed in the Livadia palace itself, in conditions of such crowding that sixteen colonels had to share a single room with the bedbugs.[2]

The Yalta conference was hailed at the time as a new and hopeful departure in human events. At the final caviare dinner hosted by Stalin on 8 February, in a toast to Churchill and Stalin, President Roosevelt said he felt the atmosphere between them 'was that of a family'. Stalin said he was convinced that 'our relations in peacetime should be as strong as they had been in war'. Ever the orator, Winston Churchill replied that he 'felt we are all standing on the crest of a hill with the glories of future possibilities before us'. For Harry Hopkins, Roosevelt's closest adviser and his special envoy to other heads of state, 'We really believed in our hearts that this was the dawn of the new day we had all been praying for.'[3]

It was a grim day for the German city of Dresden. At a meeting on the first day of the Yalta conference with the British and American chiefs of staff, the Soviet deputy chief of staff General Antonov asked for air support to stop German reinforcements being moved to the Soviet front. He asked in particular for the transport centres of Berlin, Leipzig and Dresden to be 'allotted to the Allied air forces'. From the night of 13 February until the morning of 15 February, waves of some twelve hundred British and US bombers devastated Dresden. When it ended, 39,773 people were officially registered as dead. Another 20,000 are believed to have been burnt beyond recognition as corpses. 'Who knows the number?' says the inscription at Dresden cemetery.[4]

The destruction of Dresden is the clearest reminder that when the Big Three met at Yalta, the most destructive war of history was still being fought. By 1945, fifty countries had joined the Allied cause, including Guatemala and Liberia, and mobilised sixty million people into their armies. At least ten million of them died, although the figures for China and the Soviet Union remain vague. A comparison of the pre-war against the post-war Soviet census suggests that the combined civilian and military death toll was close to twenty-five million, but that would include the monstrous toll of Stalin's Gulag. Nine countries, including Albania and Thailand, had joined the cause of the Axis and mobilised some thirty million troops, and at least six million of them died. The civilian casualties, from starvation and disease and bombing and death camp, were higher than the military, as half the globe was sucked into the maw of a vast, industrialised war machine, whose American factories alone spewed out 296,000 warplanes, 86,000 tanks and 11,900 ships.[5]

So Yalta's diplomatic negotiations and the dispositions of the postwar world were made amid the brutal urgencies of military decisions designed to bring about the agreed war aim of Germany's unconditional surrender. And it was that very war aim which contained the roots of the Cold War. Unconditional surrender, when Hitler was able to keep his armies fighting to the last bunker in Berlin, meant the destruction of everything which made up the German state. Germany's armed forces, its system of internal government and communications, its economy and its food and distribution systems, were all to be devastated by the final surrender in May 1945. By the end of the war, Germany was a humanitarian disaster and a political and military vacuum which the victorious Allies had to feed and fill.

They were ill-equipped to do so. They had another war to fight and win, against Japan in the Pacific. The three allies also faced the end of the war in Europe with different, and potentially incompatible, strategic objectives. Stalin wanted security, a Germany that could never threaten to invade Russia again, as it had done twice in the past thirty years, and a wide defensive belt of friendly territory in Eastern Europe, just in case. 'Friendly', in this context, meant ready to subordinate their national sovereignty to Soviet interests. In practice, this meant client states with Soviet-style governments, protected by a secret police and with a state-controlled economic system that would not allow the emergence of a prosperous middle class. Such property-owners, said Karl Marx's orthodoxy and Stalin's suspicions, would inevitably seek an independent political role to match their economic weight.

Stalin's entirely rational objectives threatened the policy Britain had adopted in Europe since the days of the Kaiser, of Napoleon, of the Sun King Louis XIV and even of the Spanish Armada in the sixteenth century: to ensure that no single power dominated the European continent, as Stalin now threatened to do. The Americans wanted peace and trade, an amicable and democratic new order in Europe. But they also wanted to bring their troops home from Europe as fast as possible, partly because of the immediate priority of the war against Japan, and partly because Congress was impatient. 'Two years would be the limit,' Roosevelt told a silently watchful Stalin, and an appalled Churchill.[6] 'If the Americans left Europe, Britain would have to occupy single-handed the entire Western portion of Germany. Such a task would be far beyond our strength,' Churchill noted privately.[7] The crushing of Germany created an opportunity which only Stalin seemed able to seize.

At that moment, the hitherto barely foreseen results of the war crystallised. Nominally a victor of the Grand Alliance, Britain's victory was Pyrrhic, bought at a price so high that its role as a Great Power could no longer be sustained. This meant that the cardinal principle of British policy thereafter would be to maintain an American military presence in Europe. The alternative would be Soviet domination of a hollow continent in which Britain was too weak to play its traditional role of the balancing power.

This was the nightmare that Churchill had dreaded in the early summer of 1944, when the Soviet armies were racing into Poland and the Balkans. 'The Russians are drunk with victory and there is no length to which they may not go,' he had written to his foreign secretary, Anthony Eden.[8] To forestall too sweeping a Russian occupation, the British pressed – not for the last time – for a swift invasion of Germany in the hope of reaching Berlin before the Soviet armies. In September 1944, British and American airborne forces were parachuted across the Rhine at Arnhem in one of the boldest failures of the war. Churchill flew to Moscow the following month, in the hope that the traditional diplomacy of realism could secure what the paratroopers had failed to win.

At 10 pm on 9 October, Churchill met Stalin in the Kremlin and said, 'How would it do for you to have ninety per cent predominance in Rumania, for us to have ninety per cent of the say in Greece, and go fifty-fifty about Yugoslavia?' Churchill sketched out the figures on a sheet of paper, adding 50–50 for Hungary, and 75–25 in Bulgaria (in Stalin's favour). Stalin 'took his blue pencil and made a large tick upon it, and passed it back to us'.[9] The British Foreign Office memorandum of the conversation also records that Stalin accepted that Britain after the war would be 'the leading Mediterranean power'.[10] The famous sheet of paper contained no reference to Germany or Czechoslovakia, nor to Poland, the country for which Britain had gone to war in 1939, but which had become in Churchill's eyes a hopeless cause. Just before he left for Yalta, Churchill confided to his personal secretary: 'Make no mistake, all the Balkans, except Greece, are going to be Bolshevised, and there is nothing I can do to prevent it. There is nothing I can do for Poland either.'[11]

The promise of Allied victory in 1944 led to almost a year of mutual suspicion, which the Yalta conference was intended to resolve. Stalin suspected that Britain and America were plotting a separate peace with Germany, precisely in order to fend off Soviet domination of central Europe.[12] Stalin's motives in halting his armies on the outskirts to Warsaw, to watch the rising of the Polish Home Army crushed by German troops, aroused British and American contempt, mixed with the belief that Stalin wanted the German slaughter to create a political vacuum in Poland that could be filled by his Communist clients. Western diplomats begged for landing and refuelling rights at

Soviet-held airfields, to allow its aircraft in Italy to supply the besieged Polish resistance. Until it was too late, Stalin refused. 'It was the toughest talk I ever had with a Soviet official,' US Ambassador Averell Harriman recalled.[13]

Warsaw's agony in 1944 threw into question the fate of liberated Europe after the war. In public, there were protestations of Allied solidarity. In private, Churchill's fears of Soviet ambition were becoming widespread among American officials too. 'There was no time when the danger from the Soviet Union was not a topic of anxious conversation among officers of the State Department,' recalled Louis Halle, of the Policy Planning Staff. 'And by the winter of 1944–5, as the day of victory approached, it became the predominant theme in Washington.'[14] It was also the main concern of American diplomats and military attachés in Moscow, whose direct experience of the Kremlin made them markedly more suspicious of Soviet intentions than their political masters back home. In September, Ambassador Harriman wrote to the White House: 'Unless we take issue with the present policy, there is every indication the Soviet Union will become a world bully.'[15] Harriman's chief adviser, George Kennan, later to be celebrated as the father of the policy of containment, set down in that autumn of 1944 what was to become the basic principle of Western policy towards the Soviets for a generation. Kennan stressed the need 'to determine in conjunction with the British the line beyond which we cannot afford to permit the Russians to exercise unchallenged power'.[16]

For Churchill, and for his generals, and for an influential group of American officials if not for President Roosevelt, the battle lines of the future were already being drafted before Yalta, as the simple geography of Soviet military occupation defined a new political reality in Europe. Stalin evidently agreed, telling the 1944 military mission from Yugoslavia that: 'This war is not as in the past; whoever occupies a territory also imposes on it his own social system. Everyone imposes his own system as far as his army has power to do so. It cannot be otherwise.'[17] Roosevelt and his high command differed. On the eve of the Yalta conference, the US and British chiefs of staff met in Malta to plan the next phase of the attack on Germany. This provoked one of the most bitter Allied disputes of the war. The British urged again a swift armoured spearhead to occupy Berlin, while from Italy another assault should seek to take Vienna and Prague before the Red Army could create tomorrow's political facts on today's battlefields. The Americans point-blank refused, insisting that they would not take casualties for political reasons. General George C. Marshall, the army chief of staff, said that if the British plan were adopted, he would recommend to the supreme allied commander in Europe, General Eisenhower, that he had 'no choice but to ask to be relieved of his command'.[18]

So the Yalta gathering opened with each of the Big Three at odds with the other, in an atmosphere of suspicion, and facing the divisive issue of the kind of European future their victory over Germany would produce. The intimacy of Anglo-American relations, during the war against Germany and later in the long confrontation against the Soviet Union, was by no means guaranteed as the Big Three met at Yalta. It was no part of Roosevelt's war aims to restore the pre-war British Empire, and he told Stalin privately at Yalta that he thought Hong Kong should be returned to the Chinese, or internationalised as a free port.[19]

The last of the wartime conferences, Yalta was also the first of the post-war summits, and this duality of character helps explain Yalta's subsequent grim reputation. Immediately hailed around the world as a landmark in human history, and read aloud to cheers in the US Senate, the communiqué of the Yalta summit gave little hint of the furious denunciations it would later attract. The main tasks of the conference were to agree on plans to end the war in Europe, to win the war against Japan in Asia, and then to settle the broad outlines of the peace. There was much give and take. Stalin agreed to Britain's insistence that the French also be allowed an occupation zone in Germany, after Churchill said that without French power, Britain did not feel able to contain the western front of Germany alone.[20] Difficult issues, like the amount of German reparations, and the number of votes the Soviet Union would have at the future United Nations, were put off to the new structure of regular meetings of foreign ministers.

For the British and Americans, the immediate object was to secure a firm promise and a date for Soviet military support for the final phase of defeating Japan. The plans of General Douglas MacArthur assumed Soviet support to hold down the Japanese armies on the mainland, while British and American forces invaded Japan's home islands. The Soviet pledge to join the war in the Far East was secured when an overnight note from President Roosevelt to Stalin, hurriedly translated over breakfast by Andrei Gromyko, promised to grant Stalin his booty of the Kurile Islands and Sakhalin.[21] This was a classic example of horse-trading between Great Powers, sitting oddly with the grand principles of high-minded international behaviour which Woodrow Wilson had made characteristic of American diplomacy.

There was much high-mindedness at Yalta, but the most ruthless *realpolitik* was deployed to ensure that the Red Army would spill some of the blood required in the final defeat of Japan. The idealism was reserved for the agreement to establish the United Nations, and in the document on the future of the liberated territories which was to be at the heart of the subsequent debate about the blame for the Cold War.

Since this is the text upon which all future accusations of Soviet betrayal and bad faith were made, it is worth quoting at length. The Americans pressed for this Declaration because of political pressure at home, focused above all on the fate of Poland, and backed up by the votes of some seven million Polish-Americans. The Declaration on Liberated Europe started by repeating the principles of the Atlantic Charter: 'The right of all peoples to choose the form of government under which they will live, the restoration of sovereign rights and self-government to those peoples who have been forcibly deprived of them by the aggressor nations.' The crucial paragraph went on:[22]

> To foster the conditions in which the liberated peoples may exercise these rights, the three governments will jointly assist the people in any European liberated state or former Axis satellite state in Europe where in their judgment conditions require: (a) to establish conditions of internal peace; (b) to carry out emergency measures for the relief of distressed peoples; (c) to form interim governmental authorities broadly representative of all democratic elements in the population and pledged to the earliest possible establishment through free elections of governments responsive to the will of the people; and (d) to facilitate where necessary the holding of such elections.

This read well, and Roosevelt was much relieved by this apparent Soviet concession, but the wording was essentially meaningless. 'Democratic elements' meant one thing to Stalin, and quite another to Winston Churchill, who observed wryly at Yalta that he was the only one of the Big Three who could be ejected from office at any time by the votes of his own people.[23] Churchill was right: unless death intervened, an American President had a tenure of four years. 'Free elections' and 'the will of the people' were elastic phrases. This was a document designed to paper over differences, after Stalin had made the point brutally clear. 'Mr Churchill had said that for Great Britain the Polish question was one of honour and that he understood, but for the Russians it was a question both of honour and security,' Stalin said, according to the American transcript. 'Throughout history,

Poland had been the corridor for attack on Russia . . . It was not only a question of honour for Russia, but one of life and death.'[24]

Behind Stalin's words lay the reality of the war still raging, and of centuries of Russian history. Through Poland had come Hitler's tanks, and a generation before that, Kaiser Wilhelm's armies had taken the same route to the Peace of Brest-Litovsk which had wrenched the Baltic states and the Ukraine from the beleaguered Bolsheviks. A century earlier, Napoleon had followed the Polish route to take and burn Moscow in 1812. The century before that, it had been the turn of the Swedes, and the century before them, the Poles had occupied the Kremlin. Russia, a country without natural boundaries like France's River Rhine, or Britain's twenty-one miles of Channel, or America's wide ocean moats, had been invaded by each of its neighbours.

Stalin's obsessive fear of attack was obvious to Churchill, who had supported the British invasion of Lenin's Russia in 1919, arguing the need 'to throttle the infant Bolshevism in its cradle'. American troops had joined that abortive massed attack by the capitalist world upon the young Communist state, along with French, Polish, Czech and Japanese forces. This evidence of history led Stalin to insist on keeping the Red Army's territorial gains as a matter of national security, whatever the Western powers might say, and so did the Communist ideology he still professed. As Lenin had put it, in words which Western anti-Communists seldom tired of reciting: 'As long as capitalism and socialism exist, we cannot live in peace; in the end, one or the other will triumph. A funeral dirge will be sung either over the Soviet Republic or over Capitalism.'[25]

Churchill had few illusions about the fate of Poland, or the form of Europe that would follow the Yalta summit. Roosevelt had many, and expressed them to an enthusiastic joint session of Congress on his return to Washington on 2 March. Roosevelt's optimism helped deepen America's subsequent disillusion, as Stalin's definition of an independent, democratic Poland turned out to be very different from that Roosevelt hoped he had achieved. 'The Crimean Conference ought to spell the end of the system of unilateral action, the exclusive alliance, the spheres of influence, the balance of power, and all the other expedients that have been tried for centuries, and have always failed,' Roosevelt told Congress, in terms which echoed Woodrow Wilson's pious hopes of a seemly new international etiquette after the First World War.[26] The first critique came within a month, in *Time* magazine, in the form of a viciously elegant fantasy. It was written by

Whittaker Chambers, the former Communist agent turned conservative who would later be chief accuser for the crusades of Congressman Richard Nixon and Senator Joe McCarthy against Soviet agents in the US government. Called 'Ghosts on the Roof', the essay imagined the spirits of the last Tsar, Nicholas II, and his wife, sitting on the roof of the Livadia palace and eavesdropping on the negotiations. His admiration for Stalin mounting as the Soviet leader secured strategic advantages and conquests for Russia that the tsarist empire had never achieved, the Tsar declared that he too will become a Communist.[27]

Chambers had a point. By the end of the European war, Soviet dominance of Eastern and central Europe was a military fact, embracing a political reach of which the Tsars had only dreamed. The Red Armies had advanced to a hundred miles west of Berlin, had occupied the eastern halves of Austria and Czechoslovakia, including Vienna and Prague, and dominated the Balkans. The Yalta conference had promised to give Russian warships easier access to the Mediterranean through the Dardanelles, a strategic goal the Tsars had never reached, and also recovered the position in the Far East that tsarist Russia had lost after their humiliating defeat by Japan in 1905. It was a vast extension of the Soviet empire to be held down, and all that the world had learned about the means of Soviet domestic control in the 1930s suggested that their regime would not be pretty. Even before Yalta, Harriman warned from Moscow of 'the institution of secret police who may become involved in the persecution of persons of truly democratic convictions who may not be willing to conform to Soviet methods'. And as Roosevelt was addressing Congress, the State Department was reading the cables from Bucharest, describing how Andrei Vyshinsky, the Soviet deputy commissar for foreign affairs, interpreted the spirit of Yalta. Visiting the Romanian capital, Vyshinsky stormed into the King's study, slammed his fist on the table and demanded a new, pro-Moscow government. When the King of Romania demurred, noting that the Yalta agreement guaranteed free elections, Vyshinsky looked at his watch. 'I will announce the new government in exactly two hours and five minutes,' Vyshinsky snapped, and stalked out, slamming the door so hard the plaster cracked.[28]

The immediate victims of Yalta were the Soviet prisoners of war, many of them Ukrainians or Balts or other unwilling members of Stalin's empire, who had been persuaded to take up arms on Hitler's behalf against the Red Army. But they were not the only prisoners transferred to Stalin's grim mercies by the US and British forces. Civilians and ordinary POWs, Jews from the concentration camps and an unknown fraction of the displaced persons who wandered the devastation of post-war Europe, were caught in the implacable net. The loathsome business of forcing them back into Stalin's arms at gunpoint provoked suicides among the hapless prisoners, and near-mutinies among the appalled British troops. But with British and American POWs still inside the Soviet zone, and British and American lives to be saved by securing Soviet support for the last campaign against Japan, the orders and priorities from London were clear.[29]

The next victims of Yalta were American illusions. Within days it became clear that Stalin's promise of democracy and independence in Poland did not include any serious political role for the Polish government-in-exile which had spent the war in London. 'We began to realize that Stalin's language was somewhat different from ours: "Friendly neighbours" had an entirely different connotation to him,' Harriman recalled. 'I am outraged,' he cabled back to the White House in March, when the Russians refused to let American medical teams into Poland to treat and evacuate American prisoners of war. On 3 April, Harriman reported that the Polish talks had degenerated to breaking point, and asked to come home. Harriman planned to take with him an eight-page memorandum drafted on 21 March, which could not have been more bluntly phrased: 'Unless we wish to accept the 20th century barbarian invasion of Europe, with repercussions extending further and further in the East as well, we must find ways to arrest the Soviet domineering policy . . . If we don't face these issues squarely now, history will record the period of the next generation as the Soviet age.'[30]

In the final days of his life, Roosevelt seemed to agree. At Warm Springs, receiving one of Harriman's angry telegrams after lunch, Anna Hoffman reported that the dying President slammed his fists on his wheelchair and declared, 'Averell is right. We can't do business with Stalin.'[31] But Roosevelt's last reply to the Moscow Embassy on 12 April called for more conciliation, and he died that day. His policy, however, of refusing finally to believe the worst of his Soviet comrade-in-arms would outlive him for some time.

The new President Harry Truman came into office with little preparation for foreign affairs, and his one striking comment on relations with the Soviet Union had been made in the week Hitler invaded in 1941: 'If we see that Germany is winning we ought to help Russia, and if Russia is winning we ought to help Germany, and that way let them kill as many as possible although I don't want to see Hitler victorious under any circumstances.'[32]

Truman's education in Soviet policy was to be equally blunt. On his second day as President, Truman was given a report on the international situation by Secretary of State Edward Stettinius, which warned him: 'Since the Yalta conference the Soviet government has taken a firm and uncompromising position on nearly every major question.'[33] He was also delivered a solemn report drafted for Roosevelt on 2 April by the wartime intelligence agency, the Office of Strategic Services. The first warning that the future security of the United States was at stake, as well as the fate of Poland, it said: 'Russia will emerge from the present conflict as by far the strongest nation in Europe and Asia, strong enough, if the United States should stand aside, to dominate Europe and at the same time to establish her hegemony over Asia . . . In the easily foreseeable future Russia may well outrank even the US in military potential.'[34]

The warnings could hardly have been clearer. But Harriman was to make them even harsher, returning from Moscow to press his views on the new President. He began by convincing the President's top advisers. Over dinner with Navy Secretary Forrestal on 19 April, Harriman stressed that 'the outward thrust of Communism was not dead, and that we well might have to face an ideological warfare just as vigorous and dangerous as Fascism or Nazism'. The next day he gave a special seminar for the senior officials at the State Department, to warn: 'The Soviet Union, once it had control of bordering areas, would attempt to penetrate the next adjacent countries . . . This issue ought to be fought out insofar as we can with the Soviet Union in the present bordering areas.'[35]

From that meeting in the State Department building just west of the White House, Harriman strolled across to see the new President. With him came the Secretary of State Stettinius, the veteran Moscow diplomat Chip Bohlen, and Under-Secretary Joseph Grew. But it was Harriman, fresh from Moscow, embodying not only the vast wealth from the family railroad fortune but the mantle of Roosevelt's wartime alliance with Stalin, who dominated the meeting. It was a crucial moment, the chance for Harriman to convince the innocent new President that the pledges given to Roosevelt at Yalta were being broken. He began with that dark phrase he had crafted in Moscow – 'the barbarian invasion of Europe'. But Harriman knew that what Truman needed was not just warnings, but practical policy advice. A new and more realistic basis was needed for working with the Russians, a tough policy that made it clear there were benefits available for cooperation, and penalties for hostility.

Truman, a veteran of the horse-trading way of Senate politics, seized at once upon the thought of bargains. He could not expect to get one hundred per cent from the Russians, he said, but on the big issues he expected to get eighty-five per cent, and Poland would have to be resolved under the principles agreed at Yalta. 'I intend to tell Molotov that in words of one syllable.'[36]

On 23 April, Truman convened a long and crucial briefing in the White House by his Russian experts. This was the moment when the balance in American policy began to shift, away from Roosevelt's wartime trust, to Truman's post-war suspicion. The briefing took place immediately before Truman's meeting with Soviet foreign minister Vyacheslav Molotov, who was on his way to San Francisco for the first UN meetings. Stalin had only agreed to send Molotov as a gesture to Roosevelt's memory, and it was to be Truman's first confrontation with the Soviet leadership. The preliminary meeting of the Americans was attended by the men who had run the war from Washington, Roosevelt's intimates, and Truman was still, if not awed, then deeply respectful of their collective wisdom. He was surrounded by Roosevelt's war cabinet: Colonel Henry Stimson, the Secretary for War; General Marshall; Admiral Leahy; Secretary of State Stettinius; Navy Secretary Forrestal; with Harriman and the US military attaché to Moscow, General John Deane.

The meeting was the more important because, just ten weeks after Yalta, Roosevelt's old war cabinet no longer shared a consensus. Stettinius began by reporting the previous evening's meeting at the State Department with Molotov and the British foreign secretary, Sir Anthony Eden. 'Great difficulties had developed over the Polish question,' and they had continued at a further meeting that morning, Stettinius went on. It was now clear that the Russians were trying to force their own puppet government upon Britain and the United States. President Truman, saying that relations with Moscow had so far been 'a one-way street', asked the rest of his advisers for their views.

The Russians had always kept their word 'in the big military matters', said Stimson. The real veteran of the cabinet, Stimson warned against 'a collision', and voiced his 'fear we are rushing into a situation where we would find ourselves breaking our relations with Russia'. Forrestal disagreed, warning that Poland was not the only breach of Yalta; Bulgaria and Romania were going the same way. Harriman said the issue was plain, whether 'the US should be a party to Soviet domination of Poland'. Properly and firmly handled, Harriman went on, this need not lead to a break with Russia. Admiral

Leahy spoke of the agreements made at Yalta, and said he was sure the Russians would never permit free elections in Poland. Stettinius then read aloud the Yalta declaration which Stalin had signed.

General Marshall said he leaned to Stimson's view, for the military reasons which had weighed so heavily at Yalta. A breach with Russia could delay their entry into the war against Japan 'until we have done all the dirty work'. Truman returned to what he saw as the core of the issue – 'the execution of agreements entered into between this government and the Soviet Union'. Seeing the meeting was swinging his way, Harriman spoke up again. He agreed with Stimson that the military agreements which Russia had kept were 'decisions it had already made for itself, but on other military matters it was impossible to say they had lived up to their commitments'. Harriman was then followed by his ally from the Moscow Embassy, General Deane, who spoke of his own experience in the Soviet capital, and advised, 'if we were afraid of the Russians we would get nowhere; we should be firm when we were right'. Truman, just twelve days into office, said cautiously that he would follow the views of the majority.[37]

The hard-line views which Harriman brought with him from Moscow had won. The new policy had begun, and later that day, it was slammed on to the table before the Russians for the first time. Molotov entered the Oval Office, accompanied by Ambassador Gromyko, to be told bluntly by Truman of his 'deep disappointment' that the Yalta agreement on Poland was not being met. Citing opinion in Congress and American public opinion, Truman then gave him a message for immediate delivery to Stalin, which warned that the failure to fulfil the Yalta agreement 'would seriously shake confidence in the unity of the three governments'. As Molotov went into a long reply, Truman intervened four times, each time more sharply, stressing 'there was only one thing to do, and that was for Marshal Stalin to carry out that agreement in accordance with his word'.

'I have never been talked to like that in my life,' protested Molotov.

'Carry out your agreements, and you won't get talked to like that,' snapped Truman. And in Gromyko's account: 'Quite unexpectedly, still in the middle of our talk, Truman suddenly half rose and gave a sign to indicate that our conversation was over, in effect breaking off the meeting.' In retrospect, Gromyko thought, Truman's 'stridently pugnacious' attitude could be explained only by the knowledge that the United States now had the atom bomb. In fact, it was two days later that Colonel Stimson first briefed the new President of 'the most terrible weapon ever known in human history, one bomb of which could destroy a whole city'.[38]

Through Soviet eyes, the new American stance was alarming and suspicious. Stalin's fears deepened three weeks later, when Truman celebrated the German surrender on 5 May by shutting off the Lend-Lease shipments to Britain and to Russia, so brusquely that some ships turned around in mid-ocean. After howls of outrage from London and Moscow, Truman softened the policy. But when his personal envoy Harry Hopkins met Stalin in Moscow on 27 May, Stalin growled that if this was 'designed as pressure on the Russians in order to soften them up it was a serious mistake'. Stalin went on to complain that the US–British decision to allow France to join the post-war Reparations Commission was 'an insult', since France had 'opened the frontier to the Germans'. And on Poland, Stalin cited the text of Yalta as implying that the other Allies had agreed that the pro-Soviet provisional government should be the basis for the new regime: 'No other understanding of the Yalta agreement was possible. Despite the fact that the Russians were a simple people, they should not be regarded as fools, which was a mistake the West frequently made.'[39]

Worse was to come. When Harriman had suggested to Truman that the policy of firmness could be backed up by the carrot of American economic aid in return for cooperation, he had in mind the Soviet application for American credits of $6 billion* for post-war reconstruction. The request had been made by Molotov in January 1945 and put off for later by the Americans. It had been mentioned again at Yalta, and again without an American response. As if embarrassed by the American silence, the Soviets did not raise the matter again until August, when their troops were already fulfilling the Yalta agreement by fighting the Japanese in Manchuria, and were told to Moscow's disbelief that the Americans could find no trace of their financial request. In fact, it seems to have been lost when the records of the Foreign Economic Administration were transferred to the State Department. Accident it may have been; after the rows over Poland, it did not look that way to the Russians.[40]

Stalin might have been relieved to learn that the British, too, felt that they were suddenly being treated shabbily by their American ally. The British were equally worried by the interruption of Lend-Lease in May, and their fears were confirmed when Truman cancelled the programme altogether just eight days after the Japanese surrender in August. Bankrupt after sustaining over two years of war alone, and being forced to sell all British holdings in America, Britain had

* In this book, 'billion' is used to mean '1,000 million' and 'trillion' to mean '1,000,000 million'.

assigned its leading economist, John Maynard Keynes, to handle the delicate financial negotiations. He initially faced an American Treasury Secretary, Henry Morgenthau, whose policies were to reduce Germany to an agrarian economy, and 'to move the financial centre of the world from London and Wall Street to the US Treasury'.[41] Morgenthau was removed in Truman's first cabinet reshuffle in July 1945, possibly because he had favoured 'a concrete plan to aid them [the Russians] in their reconstruction period'.[42]

Even with the advocacy of the formidable Keynes, who brought personal experience of the 1919 Treaty of Versailles to the post-war financial talks, the British were appalled by the American positions. There was a mood of something close to betrayal, that the loyal British ally was being plundered while she was down, among both Churchill's government and the Labour government under Clement Attlee which replaced it after the general election in July.

The US had supplied its British ally some $27 billion in Lend-Lease items of food and munitions, and Britain had sent the US some $6 billion in reverse Lend-Lease goods. Under the final deal, Britain had to pay another $650 million in cash to settle the account. To pay that, and to pay for food imports while its economy was still mobilised for war, Britain needed a loan of $3.75 billion. This was agreed, at what Britain felt was an unfriendly 2 per cent interest rate over fifty years. Worse still, this followed the Bretton Woods conference on the future global economy which established the dollar as the world's main reserve currency, freely convertible into gold, pushing the pound sterling into second place. This was not only a blow to British pride, it also burdened the pound with an international trading responsibility which it simply could not sustain without American economic support. To get the American loan, the British were forced to agree to ratify the Bretton Woods deal in full, and to make sterling freely exchangeable against the dollar within a year. In practice, this meant that the British were forced to open up their protected colonial markets, their main hope of export growth and long-term recovery, to American competition. This was done as a deliberate act of US policy, in sharp contrast to the later generosity of the Marshall Plan. 'We loaded the British loan negotiations with all the traffic the market could bear,' reported Will Clayton, the American negotiator.[43]

The political effect of these technical economic arrangements upon Anglo-American relations was appalling. Before the year was out, it was dubbed in Parliament 'an economic Munich', and the Americans were accused of using their economic muscle to take over Britain's protected markets in the colonies. 'Selling the British Empire for a packet of cigarettes,' sneered Tory MP Robert Boothby, noting that such terms of settlement were usually reserved for defeated enemies. Even *The Economist*, a traditionally pro-American weekly, noted: 'It is aggravating to find that the reward for losing a quarter of our national wealth in the common cause is to pay tribute for half a century to those who have been enriched by the war.'[44]

At the same time, Truman simply repealed the joint authority for nuclear weapons which Roosevelt had agreed with Churchill when British scientists were first assigned to the Anglo-American-Canadian Manhattan Project. Again, the Americans claimed to have lost their copy of the accord the two men had signed on 19 September 1944, which said 'full collaboration . . . for military and commercial purposes should continue after the defeat of Japan'.[45] In June, Churchill sent a photograph of his own copy, but it did little good. Under Congressional pressure, Truman signed the McMahon Act into law the following year. This effectively barred the United States from sharing atomic secrets with anyone, even the British who had begun the research.

Nor was Truman eager to tell the Soviets about it. On 16 July, the eve of the Potsdam summit, the news was flashed to Truman that the first atom-bomb test in New Mexico had proved successful. Further news had to wait another five days, for the first detailed report reached Berlin by courier. It took Stimson an hour to read aloud to his President the news that the bomb had 'far exceeded most optimistic expectations and wildest hopes of the scientists'. Truman, Stimson recalled, was 'tremendously pepped up',[46] so much so that a baffled Churchill later asked whatever had come over the President. Only the next day did Churchill understand, when Stimson read to him the report from New Mexico. Three days after that, on 24 July, Truman 'casually mentioned to Stalin that we had a new weapon of unusually destructive force'.[47]

What Truman did not say to Stalin was that earlier in the day he and Churchill and their chiefs of staff had sat around a table in the gloomy dining-room of No. 2, Kaiserstrasse, and agreed to drop it on Japan by 10 August. Gunpowder and electricity were meaningless by comparison, Churchill had observed. 'The atomic bomb is the Second Coming – in Wrath.' The first had been bad enough, the evidence of the power of conventional bombing in the devastation of Berlin all around them. It had stunned Truman, who scribbled almost random names of ruin and war's horror into his diary after his first sight of Berlin: 'I thought of Carthage, Baalbek, Jerusalem, Rome, Atlantis, Peking . . . of Scipio, Rameses II, Sherman, Jenghiz Khan.' What none of the men sitting around that table in Kaiserstrasse could have known was that the room in which the atomic decision was first taken had only weeks before been witness to an older horror; ten weeks of gang rape by Soviet troops upon the daughters of the German publisher Gustav Müller-Grote. It had been his house, and he and his grandchildren had been beaten and made to watch, until the family had been evicted to make way for what Truman called his 'Little White House'.[48]

As Truman, Stalin and Churchill met at Potsdam, in the old Hohenzollern palace just outside the ruins of Berlin, the tensions between the wartime allies were becoming acute. This was not a replay of Yalta, in which personal appeals to wartime loyalty could carry much weight. Already, America's wartime leader had been replaced. Before the Potsdam conference was complete, Churchill had been voted out of office and replaced by Attlee, and the assertive role in the British delegation was now taken by the new foreign secretary, the veteran trade-union boss Ernest Bevin.

The negotiations over the outstanding issues of Poland and the other Eastern European countries proved difficult and divisive. As the new Secretary of State James Byrnes reported to the three leaders on 28 July: 'The US has unfortunately found that if it agrees with the Soviet delegation, the British delegation does not agree, and if it agrees with the British, then the Soviet disagrees.'[49] Potsdam papered over some cracks, on reparations and the decision to treat Germany as an economic unit, rather than as zones. But the mistrust which followed Yalta was not allayed, and it now festered in the transformed environment of the nuclear age.

Whatever Truman may have thought about Stalin's bland reaction to his low-key reference to the new weapon, it came as no surprise to the Soviet leader. In Ottawa on 9 July, a week before the New Mexico test, one of the British physicists on the project, Dr Alan Nunn May, met his contact, Colonel Zabotin, of the Soviet Embassy to Canada. He gave Zabotin '162 micrograms of Uranium 233, in the form of acid, contained in a thick lamina'. From Klaus Fuchs, another of the British scientists in the Manhattan Project, the Russians knew precisely what kind of weapon was being developed, and that the final manufacturing on the bomb was being carried out.[50]

The pressure was now on Stalin. The evening after Truman's casual remark, Stalin ordered Molotov to cable the chief Russian nuclear scientist Kurchatov to accelerate the work on the Soviet bomb project. Stalin then personally cabled Beria, the secret-police chief, with the same instruction.[51] In Bulgaria and Romania, the establishment of pro-Soviet governments was accelerated, and the pressure on Turkey began to permit the passage of Soviet warships through the Dardanelles. Although Stalin had agreed to withdraw Soviet troops from northern Iran by February 1946, preparations began for their reinforcement, along with the formation of a separatist movement in the Iranian province of Azerbaijan. Truman was 'worthless', Stalin confided to Nikita Khrushchev.[52] But the pace of events in the Far East was about to pass Stalin by.

The atom bomb was dropped on Hiroshima on 6 August, and the Soviet Union had yet to fulfil its Yalta promise and declare war upon Japan. Soviet troops were poised and straining at the leash to invade Manchuria, but the Chinese government was still prevaricating on the precise terms on which it would invite the Soviets to join the war. This was deliberate. Now that the Americans had the war-winning bomb, the need for Soviet allies, so powerful at Yalta, had passed. Byrnes, the Secretary of State, had already urged Truman to force the Japanese surrender without Soviet participation if possible. Stimson and General Marshall saw little point in further diplomatic efforts to bring in the Soviets now that the US had the war-winning weapon. From the Moscow Embassy, Harriman helped the Chinese delaying tactics.[53]

Aware that they faced a race against time if any of the spoils of war were to be won, the Soviet Union declared war on 9 August, the day the second atom bomb fell on Nagasaki. Two days later, when the Japanese offered to surrender, it was Stalin's turn to delay, hoping to bargain for Soviet influence over post-war Japan. The Allies should first 'reach an agreement' on the commanders and structure of the occupation, Molotov told Harriman just before dawn. 'I reject it in the name of my government,' Harriman retorted, without bothering to check with Washington.[54] Stalin dropped it, but noted sourly that the joint Allied occupation agreements that were in force in Vienna and Berlin were not being extended to the Russians in Tokyo.

'They [the USA and Britain] wanted to take advantage of the results of the war and impose their will not only on their enemy, Germany, but on their ally, the USSR as well,' Khrushchev concluded.[55] The Soviet view was understandable, and in Britain, in the American Embassy in Moscow, in the State Department, the OSS and among Truman's top military advisers, Khrushchev's suspicions were justified. But Truman's subsequent actions make it clear that the Roosevelt tradition of trust was not entirely dead. First, there is clear evidence of American demobilisation. The US Army numbered over eight million men at the time of Japan's surrender. Within the month, the GIs were being processed out of the army at the rate of 15,000 a day, 100,000 a week. By 1948, the army had been slashed to 554,030.[56] This was hardly evidence of aggressive intent. Second, there was intense debate in Truman's cabinet over whether or not to share the scientific secrets of the atom bomb with the Russians.

In the month after the atom bombs fell on Japan, Colonel Stimson went to his cabin in the Adirondacks to grapple with the new moral problem, to which he finally felt the only solution was the principle he had learned at the Skull and Bones club of Yale: 'The only way to make a man trustworthy is to trust him.' These were the closing words on the long memorandum, on the need to share with Russia the bomb's secrets, that he took to Truman on 12 September. 'If we fail to approach them [the Soviets] now, and merely continue to negotiate with them, having this weapon rather ostentatiously on our hip, their suspicion and their distrust of our motives and purposes will increase,' it argued. Stimson had already submitted his resignation, knowing that Secretary of State Byrnes was heading for a new meeting with Molotov, and 'wished to have the implied threat of the bomb in his pocket'. Truman persuaded Stimson to stay on until the next cabinet meeting on 21 September, when it would be the only topic on the agenda.[57]

After Stimson spoke, the new Under-Secretary of State Dean Acheson took up his argument: 'The advantage of being ahead in such a race is nothing, compared with not having the race.' Treasury Secretary Fred Vinson differed: military secrets should not be shared. The bulk of the cabinet agreed with Vinson. Truman, who had heard similar sentiments from the Congressional leaders, stressed they were 'not discussing the question of giving the secret of the bomb itself to the Russians or to anyone else, but the best methods of controlling bomb warfare and the exchange only of scientific information'.[58] Faced with a divided cabinet and watchful Congress, Truman devised the politician's compromise of an Atomic Energy Commission. The scientific principles were secrets no longer; they could be shared. But what he later called 'the know-how of putting it together' could not.[59] This was not Stimson's grand gesture of trust; but nor was it the Kremlin's image of the capitalist class warrior bent on atomic domination.

But if Soviet intelligence had access to the papers being drafted in the office of the joint chiefs of staff at the Pentagon, their worst suspicions would have been justified. In a paper entitled 'Strategic Vulnerability of Russia to a limited air attack', the JCS produced in October 1945 a plan to destroy twenty of the largest Soviet cities with atomic bombs. They included Moscow, Leningrad, Gorky, Tashkent,

Baku and Novosibirsk, although interestingly not Kiev in the Ukraine, apparently because it had been so devastated by the conventional war just ended. Military staffs are constantly producing contingency plans; that is their job. The importance of the 'Strategic vulnerability' paper should not be overrated, but the fact remains that just ten weeks after the end of World War Two, US military planners were contemplating the targets of World War Three.[60]

The choice of targets was explained as 'mixed industrial areas containing the highest proportion of research and development, specialized production facilities and key government or administrative personnel'. The strategic rationale of the Pentagon staff was spelt out with chilling clarity; these targets 'would exploit the maximum capacities of the weapon, produce the quickest, most direct and certain effects on Russia's immediate offensive capabilities, and achieve greatest impact against her latent offensive power'.

The great question remains: who was to blame for the Cold War? American revisionist historians have put the blame on their own side, on the determination to consolidate and extend US economic dominance, or at least on the distinct change of policy that came with Truman's inheritance of the White House. Post-glasnost Soviet scholars have pinned the responsibility squarely on Stalin and his imperial ambitions. Neither answer is persuasive. Leaders of great powers, amid wars and negotiations and the constant press of events, are seldom able to devise a coherent plan, or to apply it.

The Soviet Union had an ideology which gave the capitalist West ample cause to be nervous, and Russia had a history which mandated a suspicion of its neighbours. The implicit tensions in their relations might have been eased, as President Roosevelt had believed, by American goodwill. But Roosevelt died, and Truman had to prove himself fit to fill those giant shoes. Truman took the best advice on offer, and with the exception of Stimson and Wallace, the bulk of his cabinet, his diplomats and his Soviet experts urged him to be firm. Harriman, although he later claimed to have been on Roosevelt's side of the argument all along, certainly helped to steel Truman's resolve and intensify his suspicions in the crucial first days after he inherited the White House. It is just possible, had Roosevelt lived, and had there been no stricken Europe between them, no Western European Allies still festooned in embarrassing colonial entanglements, and in a most prickly pride, that the Cold War might not have got under way. But Roosevelt was dead, the Americans had the monopoly of the bomb and Europe sprawled between the victors, to be occupied, rescued or fought over.

The real culprit was the dreadful logic faced by both sides when they confronted the problem of what was to be done with defeated Germany. The dilemma was plain: to ensure that it could not start a third European war, but also to treat it fairly enough so that German resentment would not explode dangerously in the future, as it had done after the Treaty of Versailles in 1919. For Stalin, that meant occupation, and a defensive zone for the Soviet Union throughout Eastern Europe. For the West, it meant de-Nazification, free enterprise and stable democratic institutions, with the emphasis often on the stability rather than the democracy. But the problem of Germany, where both sides were prepared to be ruthless, led inevitably to the problem of Poland, where the West was touched by honour and sentiment and by domestic political considerations. Britain had gone to war for Poland in 1939, Polish pilots had tipped the balance in the Battle of Britain and Polish troops had fought loyally alongside the Allies in Italy and in France. And in the USA, Polish-Americans commanded seven million votes.

Roosevelt's admirable hopes for a post-war settlement based on the wartime Grand Alliance depended upon the maintenance of trust, which withered in the bitter disputes over Poland in that pre-nuclear summer between the conferences of Yalta and Potsdam. But Germany and Poland were only the most dramatic aspects of the much larger problem of Europe. Unconditional surrender meant Germany laid waste, Britain exhausted, France and Italy demoralised, and the whole continent of Europe prostrate. 'There is complete economic, social and political collapse going on in central Europe, the extent of which is unparalleled in history unless one goes back to the collapse of the Roman Empire,' John J. McCoy, Stimson's chief aide at the War Department, wrote to Truman on 23 April.[61]

Only Russia and the United States were in a position even to begin to grapple with the challenge. Neither one, it was soon clear, was prepared to let the other impose their different solutions: Sovietisation on the one hand, and the Marshall Plan on the other. The age-old issue of the control of Europe which had sucked Britain into so many interventions since the days of Churchill's ancestor, the first Duke of Marlborough, was beyond Britain's capacities. The Americans inherited the responsibility, and the role. And Europe's age-old question of the balance of power blended swiftly into the ideological struggle between capitalism and Communism. The two incompatible approaches to the problem of Europe were to become the competing visions of the wider Manichean struggle between the two mutually uncomprehending camps.

Chapter 2
Containment

They that dig foundations deep,
Fit for realms to rise upon,
Little honour do they reap
Of their generation.

'The Proconsuls', Rudyard Kipling

Hindsight imposes blinkers as well as perspective. From the viewpoint of the 1990s, there are few things harder to comprehend than the extraordinary popularity in the West by 1945 of 'Uncle Joe' Stalin and the heroic Red Army. For the American public, immune behind the Atlantic barrier, and for the British behind the Channel, there was something epic about the way the Red Army had borne the brunt of the fighting against Hitler's Wehrmacht, reeled back to the Volga, recovered at Stalingrad and fought their way back to Berlin. Until the US and British troops invaded Italy in 1943, they were facing only four divisions of German troops, while the Red Army grappled with more than two hundred.

Even for many conservatives, the pre-war memories of the evils of Communism had been redeemed by the blood the Red Army had shed in four years of war. The King of England presented a sword of honour to the fortress-city of Stalingrad. The British troops scrawled 'Joe for King' graffiti on Europe's ruined walls. And when he returned from victory in Europe, General Dwight Eisenhower solemnly assured Congress 'nothing guides Russian policy so much as a desire for friendship with the United States'.[1]

As wartime allies, the Russians were hailed as 'one hell of a people, who look like Americans, dress like Americans and think like Americans', by the later passionately anti-Soviet *Life* magazine.[2] This prime American weekly of its day, with a circulation of four million in the United States and another 317,000 abroad, went on to describe Stalin's secret police, the NKVD, as 'a national police similar to the FBI'.[3] Luce's business magazine *Fortune* ran an opinion poll in 1943 which found 81 per cent of the respondents agreeing that the US should work with Russia as equal partners in the coming peace.[4]

Look magazine ran an approving cover on 'A Guy Named Joe', which made Stalin into a friendly fellow: 'He knows Arctic meteorology, Leatherstocking Tales, soap and war.' He was also 'among the best-dressed of the world leaders, making Churchill in his siren suit look positively shabby'. *Collier's* magazine ran a special issue, 'What Kind of Country is Russia Anyway?' Neither socialist nor Communist, the magazine concluded, but 'a modified capitalist set-up . . . [moving] . . . toward something resembling our own and Great Britain's democracy'.[5]

America's political best-sellers of the day, *Mission to Moscow* by the former US Ambassador Joseph Davies and Wendell Wilkie's *One World*, contained breathtakingly indulgent accounts of Stalin's regime. Davies affirmed that in the show trials of Stalin's purges in the 1930s, 'justice had indeed been done'. Walter Lippmann, the most respected figure in American journalism, assured his readers that these two books were the most admirable studies of the Soviet Union on offer.[6]

The trust in Stalin which Roosevelt displayed at Yalta, and which Truman did not finally abandon until the year after the war's end, was not only widespread; it was a powerful political force. With 907,000 members in France by the end of 1945, and 1,771,000 in Italy, the Communists were the largest party in each country. The numbers swelled with the momentum and the respect that came from having been the spearhead of the French Resistance and the Italian partisans.[7] On 26 May 1946, in the last free elections Czechoslovakia was to hold for another forty-four years, the Communists won just over 35 per cent of the vote. This was more than twice as many votes as the next largest party, led by the veteran President Eduard Beneš.[8]

For many Europeans, the wartime feats of the Red Army blended with the still bitter memories of capitalism's failures during the Great Depression and the mass unemployment of the 1930s. In Britain, Churchill was swept from office in the general election of 1945 because the Labour Party's promise of a welfare state and a planned economy seemed to guarantee no return to those conditions. Central planning and state control had won the war, went the Labour Party argument of 1945. Now they could win the peace. 'To me, as to millions of others, Soviet behaviour after the war came as a bitter disappointment. We had thought, as Bevin told the Labour Party Conference in 1945, that "Left could speak to Left",' recalled Denis Healey, a Communist as an Oxford undergraduate in the 1930s, who went on to become the most pro-Nato defence secretary of the 1960s Labour government.[9] At Britain's 1945 election, some Labour candidates were introduced with passionate pleas for an Anglo-Soviet alliance.[10]

The speed with which Stalin's popularity was transformed into fear and contempt was a most remarkable swing of public opinion, and it is striking that the Soviet Union should on repeated occasions have provoked dramatic shifts of Western opinion. It happened in August 1939, when Stalin signed the Non-Aggression Pact with Hitler, the prelude to the German–Soviet partition of Poland. It happened again in 1956, when the invasion of Hungary devastated what was left of pro-Soviet opinion in the West, and in August 1968 with the invasion of Czechoslovakia, and again in December 1979 with the invasion of Afghanistan. On each occasion, a long and partially successful 'peace offensive' from Moscow was ruined by the sight of a great power asserting the prerogatives of its own security by sending its troops into the territory of a small neighbour.

And yet the Soviet Union was not just another great power, defending its interests with a mixture of force and diplomacy in the classic manner of international affairs. It could act with the selfish logic of the breed, signing the sphere-of-interest agreement with Churchill to carve up the post-war Balkans, just as Tsar Alexander I had sat with the Emperor Napoleon on a raft on the Niemen river to carve up Europe between them. But Stalin's USSR was also seen in the West as something different and more menacing, a unique and implacable ideology in arms, threatening to expand. This shift in perception took place among the governing establishments in both London and Washington in the last weeks of 1945 and the first two months of 1946. In the course of one hundred days, the West's view of the Soviet Union changed from an assumption that the Russian bear was up to its old tsarist tricks of dominating Eastern Europe and thrusting to the Dardanelles, into a conviction that the West was being conscripted into a new crusade. The syntax and vocabulary switched from the traditional lexicon of the balance of power to a language altogether messianic.

One American diplomat, George F. Kennan, played a remarkably powerful role in bringing this about. A shy, erudite and formidably intelligent man, Kennan had been a member of the first team of American diplomats to open diplomatic relations with the Soviet regime, and was to become, briefly, the US Ambassador to Moscow at the height of the Cold War. He was by no means an instinctive democrat. In the course of one of his periodic depressions, Kennan in

1938 drafted a book explaining why 'benevolent despotism' in America was to be preferred to the shrill disorders of democracy, and its core was the need for 'the very extensive restriction of suffrage in national affairs'. Immigrants, blacks and women (Kennan dubbed them 'frivolous') were to be denied the vote. From his earliest experiences of the Soviet state, Kennan in 1931 was writing of Soviet Russia as 'unalterably opposed to our traditional system, there can be no possible middle ground or compromise between the two . . . the two systems cannot even exist in the same world unless an economic cordon is put around one or the other of them.'

Kennan's bleak views were deepened by his experience of the purge trials of pre-war Moscow, and found some oddly Freudian roots. 'Nations, like individuals, are largely the product of their environment, and many of their characteristics, their fears and neuroses, as well as their abilities, are conditioned by the impression of what we may call their early childhood.' Russia's early childhood, Kennan noted, was the experience of the Mongol yoke. And it is difficult to escape the conclusion that Kennan's own gloom about Soviet Russia was linked to his own capacity for unhappiness. An intensely private, moody and introspective man, Kennan praised his Norwegian wife for 'the rare capacity of keeping silent gracefully. I have never seen her disposition ruffled by anything resembling a mood.'

A clever analyst, and deeply read in pre-Revolutionary Russian culture, Kennan was not a man to strike up much rapport with the Soviet officials with whom he dealt, far less to make personal inroads into the suspicious and hostile world of Moscow under Stalin's terror. Ironically, for the influence he was to wield on US–Soviet relations, Kennan had begun his diplomatic career in 1933 by recommending that 'We should have no relationship at all with them'. He did not like the Russians very much, or at least those workers and peasants in whose name the Revolution had been launched. On a visit to the Black Sea resort of Sochi, he confided to his diary:[11]

> Had the fathers of the Revolution really imagined that once the upper and middle classes had been kicked out of these watering places, the members of the proletariat would move in and proceed to amuse themselves gracefully and with taste? Did they really fail to foresee that such simple people would make pigsties of these hotels and villas, would have no appreciation for sky and air and mountain scenery?

As Ambassador Harriman's resident Soviet expert in the Moscow Embassy, Kennan's sombre and hostile views began increasingly to set the tone of Harriman's cables. Kennan despised the Yalta agreements as 'the shabbiest sort of equivocation', and mused about the possibility of Britain and the United States negotiating a separate compromise peace with Germany. In the post-Yalta summer of 1945, Kennan proposed the obvious solution for a man with such authoritarian leanings, to 'divide Europe frankly into spheres of influence, keep ourselves out of the Russian sphere and keep the Russians out of ours'. From his desk at the State Department, his former Embassy colleague Charles Bohlen retorted: 'Foreign policies of that kind cannot be made in a democracy. Only totalitarian states can make and carry out such policies.'[12] The history of the following year, whose tone was to be set by Kennan's famous long telegram, was to show how far democracies could be changed into accepting just such 'totalitarian' solutions.

In the months after the Potsdam conference, there was plenty of evidence for those who assumed that Stalin was conducting Russia's traditional expansionist policies. The foreign ministers of the Big Three met in London in September, and 'failed to agree on anything'. Britain's Ernest Bevin told his officials: 'Our relations with the Russians about the whole European problem are drifting into the same condition as that in which we had found ourselves with Hitler.'[13]

Bulgaria and Romania followed Poland in establishing servile pro-Soviet governments. Bulgaria did so with an improbable 88 per cent vote for the Fatherland Front, in elections which American diplomats insisted were rigged.[14] Another foreign ministers' meeting was held in Moscow in December, just as pro-Soviet forces in northern Iran seized control, and declared a new national government of Azerbaijan, which immediately granted the Soviet Union oil-drilling rights. The *New York Times* reported that Soviet troops had kept the Iranian army inside its barracks.[15]

On the following day, the same newspaper reported an intensified war of nerves against Turkey, with *Pravda* and *Izvestiya* announcing claims on Turkish territory by Soviet Georgia. This came against the background of an alarming buildup of Soviet divisions, with 200,000 troops in Bulgaria, and twelve divisions on Turkey's eastern frontier. The Soviet Union was pressing for open access for its warships through the Dardanelles, and for refuelling and repair facilities which sounded ominously like the nucleus of a naval base.[16]

In Washington, where the daily press reports and diplomatic cables began to take on the drumbeat of impending war, this was more evidence of the Kremlin's drive to expand and conquer. From the Soviet point of view, this was all balance-of-power politics as usual.

The Soviets had already swallowed their exclusion from the Allied governments in Italy and in Japan, although in justice Stalin could claim as much right to a voice in administering these defeated enemies as the United States was claiming in the governments of Eastern Europe.

As Molotov insisted, they were in Eastern Europe simply collecting the spoils they had been promised by Churchill in 1944, and ratified at Yalta and Potsdam. In the Dardanelles, they were pushing for the right of access to the Mediterranean, which had been a foreign-policy goal since the eighteenth century, and which Truman had acknowledged at Potsdam. In Iran and Turkey, they were pushing their traditional influence on the southern border. And they were doing so in a defensive mood. As Alexander Sokolov argued in *Novoye Vremya*, the Moscow current-affairs weekly, it all began with the US control of the atom bomb, which 'altered the views of some foreigners who formerly advocated international collaboration . . . [but now] . . . attempt to use the atom bomb in the game of international power politics'.[17]

The Soviets were playing the game as they had always understood it, from the classic experience of European diplomacy; push for advantage where one can, relax the pressure where one must. The war of nerves on Turkey had been relaxed on 2 November, when the Turkish government accepted the principle that Soviet warships had free rights of passage through the Dardanelles. When the US Secretary of State Byrnes came to Moscow in December to complain of the new regimes in Romania and Bulgaria, Stalin and Molotov accepted the American proposals to change their composition with little demur.[18] The following year, they were to back down in Iran as well.

Moreover, the Soviets felt aggrieved that their gestures of ideological concession were repeatedly ignored in the West. The Communist International, the organisation which subordinated all foreign Communist parties to Soviet authority, had been formally wound up in 1943. It had been done in terms which explicitly accepted that there were now various national routes to socialism, because of 'the deep differences of the historic paths of development of various countries'. The closing resolution of the Comintern said the organisation 'has been outgrown by the growth of the working-class movement, and by the complications of its problems in separate countries and has even become a drag on the further strengthening of the national working-class parties'.[19]

For the party faithful, including its leaders in Poland, Czechoslovakia, Bulgaria and other Eastern European countries, this acceptance of 'differences of historic paths' was to be taken seriously. The leader of the Greek Communist Party, Nicos Zachariades, returned from the Dachau concentration camp seriously seeking to cooperate with the British 'protectors', until the British backed the purge of the left by the right-wing government of Admiral Voulgaros. Bulgaria's Giorgi Dimitrov stressed that his country 'would not be a Soviet Republic'. Poland's Wladysaw Gomuka argued, in a theoretical journal intended for party members, not for the West, that 'the dictatorship of the working class, and still more of a single party, would be neither useful nor necessary'. The opening of the Czech party archives in 1968 found internal party documents from 1946 which make it clear that these were also the official views of the party leader, Klement Gottwald, who informed the central committee in September 1946 that: 'Comrade Stalin told me that experience has demonstrated, and the classics of Marxism–Leninism teach that there is not just the one path, through Soviets and the dictatorship of the proletariat.'[20]

An entire school of theory about the unique nature of the new peoples' democracies of Eastern Europe, where private property coexisted with state control of heavy industry, and Communist parties coexisted in pluralism with social democrats and peasant parties, was developed by the Soviet economist Eugene Varga, and published in Moscow.[21] 'It is possible to have political rule by the working people even while the outward forms of parliamentary democracy are still maintained,' Varga argued. His school did not flourish long. The 'outward forms' were to be viciously savaged in the party politics of Poland, Bulgaria and Romania, and in 1947, a deliberate process of political destabilisation and intimidation forced the collapse of the Smallholders Party government in Varga's Hungary. In March 1947, Varga came under criticism in *Pravda*, and by the following year his institute was closed.

The free elections of 1945 in Hungary had resulted in the Smallholders Party winning 57 per cent of the vote, followed by the United Front of Communists and Social Democrats with 34 per cent. The *New York Times* correspondent reported seeing less election day intimidation than in the machine politics of New York City.[22] For most of 1946, Varga's theory of a different and democratic path to socialism had at least some basis in reality. Varga even raised (if only to dismiss) an interesting parallel with Britain, where the new Labour government had established a not dissimilar economic system, nationalising the railway companies, the coalmines and the steel industry, and was building a state health service.

By 1947, these fledgeling hopes that a non-Soviet form of government might develop in Eastern Europe, with mixed economies and parliamentary pluralism, were to be stubbed out, victims of the greater confrontation in which they were to be pawns. And in the light of that confrontation, and the ruthlessness which with Soviet rule was later applied, the dreams of 'separate paths to socialism' looked worse than naïve. But in the heady days of 1946, after the defeat of Fascism and the thrill of liberation, idealism was in the air. And a degree of guarded trust in Moscow's intentions was not always betrayed. In one of the Soviet borderlands, where the intensity of Cold War confrontation was less sharp, the government of Finland was able to establish a slowly increasing independence from Moscow, with a mixed economy and free institutions.

The last chance of such a political compromise for the countries of Eastern Europe died in the final weeks of 1945, just at the moment when the American Secretary of State Byrnes felt he had succeeded. Stalin and Molotov had accepted his insistence that the governments in Romania and Bulgaria be widened to include more opposition ministers and non-Communists, and Byrnes said he felt that US diplomatic recognition could now be extended to them. The Turkish crisis was easing. Stalin easily approved Byrnes's proposal for a UN commission on control of atomic energy. Byrnes, a former Supreme Court justice and veteran Senator who had been senior to Truman in the US Senate, was convinced he had reached a breakthrough, re-establishing Roosevelt's wartime understanding with the Soviets.

His diplomats thought Byrnes had lost his senses. The entire US legation staff in Romania threatened to resign at this 'sell-out'. From the Moscow Embassy, Kennan wrote of 'fig leaves of democratic procedure to hide the nakedness of Stalinist dictatorship'.[23] In Washington, the Republican Senate leadership was up in arms at the thought of sharing atomic secrets with the Soviets. The *New York Times* complained that nothing had been settled on Turkey and Iran, and Truman was incensed at the lack of consultation with the White House before Byrnes reached his agreements. Truman abruptly ordered Byrnes to cancel his plans for a radio broadcast on his diplomatic breakthrough until the Secretary of State reported back to the President in person. Truman called Byrnes into the Oval Office on 5 January 1946, and in cold anger read aloud the text of a letter he had drafted, a letter which has been seen as the real start of the Cold War:[24]

> At Potsdam we were faced with an accomplished fact and were by circumstances almost forced to agree to Russian occupation of eastern Poland, and that part of Germany east of the Oder river by Poland. It was a high-handed outrage. There isn't a doubt in my mind that Russia intends an invasion of Turkey and the seizure of the Black Sea Straits to the Mediterranean. Unless Russia is faced with an iron fist and strong language, another war is in the making. Only one language do they understand – 'How many divisions have you?' I do not think we should play compromise any longer. We should refuse to recognize Rumania and Bulgaria until they comply with our requirements; we should let our position on Iran be known in no uncertain terms . . . and we should maintain complete control of Japan and the Pacific. We should rehabilitate China and create a strong central government there. We should do the same for Korea. Then we should insist on the return of our ships from Russia and force a settlement of the Lend-Lease debt of Russia. I'm tired of babying the Soviets.

Truman subsequently described this letter in his memoirs as 'the point of departure of our policy'. It was not. It represented merely the high point of the first phase of Truman's evolving perception of the Soviet threat, the culmination of his growing suspicion that Stalin was determined to expand as far and as fast as the Red Army would permit. But the entire memorandum with its sweeping geographical references, its grandiose strategic positions, is couched in the vocabulary of the balance of power. And this was the vocabulary of a permanent American overseas commitment and an unending military expenditure which would prove difficult to sell to a US Congress and a fast-demobilising American public still thrilling to the novelty of peace.

The real point of departure came in the following month, when Truman's anger at the Soviet skill at tilting the balance of power gave way to the Manichean vision of a war between good and evil. It began with the elections to the Supreme Soviet, and Stalin's traditional eve-of-poll speech. Stalin knew there was no prospect of an American financial loan, that Lend-Lease was over, and that his other hopes of economic recovery were blocked by the British and American opposition to his requirements for reparations from Germany. Stalin also knew that Truman had failed to ratify Byrnes's promise to extend diplomatic recognition to Bulgaria and Romania. So the West's observers in Moscow expected that Stalin's speech would be bitter, and heard what they wanted to hear.

'The war was the inevitable result of the development of world economic and political forces on the basis of modern monopoly capitalism,' Stalin began. 'The capitalist system of world economy harbours elements of general crises and armed conflicts, and hence, the development of world capitalism proceeds not in the path of smooth and even progress but through crisis and the catastrophes of war.'[25]

This was boilerplate Marxism–Leninism, and Stalin went on to say that the World War Two alliance had assumed 'an anti-fascist and liberation character'. He said in vague and general terms that

> the unevenness of capitalist development usually leads in time to a violent disturbance of equilibrium, that group of capitalist countries which considers itself worse provided than the others with raw materials and markets usually making attempts to alter the situation and repartition the spheres of influence in its favour by armed force. The result is the splitting of the capitalist world into two hostile camps and war between them.

But Stalin did not attack the USA and Britain by name, nor did he say that a post-war slump in the capitalist West would pave the way for socialism. He warned that the need to rebuild Soviet industry would call for longer delays in consumer goods; for more five-year plans devoted to heavy industry. But if Stalin's speech was predicting international tension, the text is clear that it would be within the capitalist world, rather than against the Soviet Union.

This was not how the speech was reported in the United States, where *Time* magazine said it was 'the most warlike pronouncement uttered by any top-rank statesman since V-J Day'. Justice William Douglas told the US Naval Secretary Forrestal that this was 'the declaration of World War Three'.[26] The State Department's Paul Nitze, another Wall Street banker who entered government with the war and was to become one of the high priests of arms control, went to see Forrestal to warn him that this was Stalin's 'delayed declaration of war on the United States'. Others were less alarmed, instead rather baffled by Soviet behaviour, and by its increasing reluctance to cooperate in any international forum, including the economic systems of the World Bank and International Monetary Fund. Accordingly, the State Department and the US Treasury cabled the US Embassy in Moscow, asking it to shed some light on the background to Stalin's speech and the real motives of Stalin's foreign policy.

The cables went to Kennan, in charge of the Embassy since Harriman's departure. He was ill and depressed and thinking of resignation because his eighteen months of warnings about Stalin had gone unheeded. This was his chance. He dictated a 5,540-word cable which became known to history as the Long Telegram, and it struck Washington like a thunderbolt.

Carrying the official stamp 'not subject to condensation', it was forwarded in full to Byrnes, to Under-Secretary Dean Acheson, and then to Navy Secretary Forrestal who printed hundreds of copies for circulation throughout the Washington establishment. All State Department officers were sent a copy, and one of them noted:[27]

> It came at a moment when the Department, separated by circumstances from the wartime policy toward Russia, was floundering about, looking for new intellectual moorings. Now, in this communication, it was offered a new and realistic conception to which it might attach itself. The reaction was immediate and positive. There was a universal feeling that 'This was It', this was the appreciation of the situation that had been needed.

'USSR still lives on antagonistic "capitalist encirclement" with which in long run there can be no permanent peaceful co-existence,' Kennan's telegram began in the clipped syntax of the original cable.

> At bottom of Kremlin's neurotic view of world affairs is traditional and instinctive Russian sense of insecurity.
>
> Russian rulers have always feared foreign penetration, feared direct contact between Western world and their own, feared what would happen if Russians learned truth about world without or if foreigners learned truth about world within. And they have learned to seek security only in patient but deadly struggle for total destruction of rival power, never in compacts and compromises with it.

So argued Kennan, seeking the roots of Stalin's policies far back in Russian history. But then Kennan struck the new theme, that Stalin and his Communist predecessor, and thus presumably Stalin's heirs, would also be different and worse than even the most purblind of Russian Tsars, because on to the neurosis of old Russia was added the fanaticism of a new creed.

> Marxist dogma, rendered even more truculent and intolerable by Lenin's interpretation, became a perfect vehicle for sense of insecurity with which Bolsheviks, even more than previous Russian rulers, were afflicted. In this dogma, with its basic altruism of purpose, they found justification for their instinctive fear of outside world, for the dictatorship without which they did not know how to rule, for cruelties they did not dare to inflict, for sacrifices they felt bound to demand. In the name of Marxism they sacrificed every single ethical value in their methods and tactics . . .

Thus Kennan went on, defining the threat as the combination of the most brutal of great powers with the more ruthless of ideologies. Kennan's concept was to become the new orthodoxy of the West, and from the beginning, he nailed it to immediate diplomatic reality by forecasting the war on many fronts that the West now faced.

In the Western powers

> efforts will be made to hamstring measures of national defence, to increase social and political unrest, to stimulate all forms of disunity . . . poor will be set against rich, black against white, young against old, newcomers against established residents etc.
>
> Violent efforts will be made to weaken power and influence of Western powers [on] colonial, backward or dependent peoples. On this level, no holds will be barred.
>
> Where individual governments stand in path of Soviet purposes pressure will be brought for their removal from office.
>
> In foreign countries Communists will, as a rule, work towards destruction of all forms of personal independence – economic, political or moral.
>
> Everything possible will be done to set major Western powers against each other. Anti-British talk will be plugged among Americans, anti-American talk among British. Continentals, including Germans, will be taught to abhor both Anglo-Saxon powers.
>
> In general, all Soviet efforts on unofficial international plane will be negative and destructive in character, designed to tear down sources of strength beyond reach of Soviet control . . . we have here a political force committed fanatically to the belief that with US there can be no permanent modus vivendi, that it is desirable and necessary that the internal harmony of our society be disrupted, our traditional way of life be destroyed, the international authority of our state be broken, if Soviet power is to be secure.

This was more than a call to arms, it was an invitation to a life-and-death struggle in which there would be no quarter given on either side. The confrontation with this implacable force of evil could not even be conducted on logical terms, since Kennan went on to argue that Soviet policy 'is seemingly inaccessible to considerations of reality in its basic reactions'. It did not even believe in the existence of objective truth: 'This government is actually a conspiracy within a conspiracy; and I for one am reluctant to believe that Stalin himself receives anything like an objective picture of the outside world.'

But having electrified Washington with this nightmarish spectre, Kennan offered a rationale for an American policy to confront it – 'the problem is within our power to solve – and that without recourse to any general military conflict'.

'Impervious to logic or reason, it is highly sensitive to logic of force' was his first argument; Western resolve could hold the line. Second, the Soviets were 'by far the weaker force'. Third, the 'success of Soviet system, as form of internal power, is not yet finally proven'. Finally, the West's own capacity for growth and self-improvement was the crucial bulwark against the terrible enemy – 'World communism is like malignant parasite which feeds only on diseased tissue'. Although the concept of 'containment' was not to be elaborated as the West's policy until Kennan published his anonymous article in *Foreign Affairs* the following year, its lineaments were already clear. The West had the physical and moral resources to resist Communism, and to outlast it, if it could only summon the political cohesion and will.[28]

Kennan's telegram was circulating in Washington as another crisis was brewing over Soviet troops and ambitions in northern Iran. They were eventually to withdraw, but when they bluntly refused to do so on 1 March, this implicit threat to the oilfields of the Middle East appeared to confirm Kennan's darkest forebodings. For the energy-sufficient USA, this was a matter of important strategic interests. For Britain, it was close to economic life and death. From 1945 to 1950, the Anglo-Iranian oil company generated $1.125 billion in profits, and paid more in taxes on its profits to the British government than Iran received in royalties.[29] The time was fitting for the delivery of the British echo to Kennan's telegram, and it came from the most respected voice of the day, Winston Churchill. No longer prime minister, but still the embodiment of the bulldog, Churchill travelled with Truman to the President's home state to deliver what became known as the 'iron curtain' speech on 5 March 1946.[30]

'From Stettin in the Baltic to Trieste in the Adriatic, an iron curtain has descended across the continent,' Churchill warned, citing territory and political influence, in the classic terms of European diplomacy. 'All are subject, in one form or another, not only to Soviet influence but to a very high and increasing measure of control from Moscow.' But Churchill then went on to endorse Kennan's argument, that this was a rampant ideological threat, even more than the predictable expansion of a great power.

> Far from the Russian frontiers and throughout the world, Communist fifth columns are established and work in complete unity and absolute obedience to the directions they receive from the Communist centre. Except in the British Commonwealth and the United States, where

> Communism is in its infancy, the Communist parties or fifth columns constitute a growing challenge and peril to Christian civilisation.

The fame this speech and phrase acquired has obscured the fact that it was not well received in public at the time. While Truman had endorsed Churchill's sentiments by sitting alongside him, applauding and nodding during the delivery, Truman later told reporters he had not known what Churchill was going to say, and replied 'no comment' when they pressed him for a reaction. The American press was critical of Churchill's suggestion of an alliance, 'a fraternal association of the English-speaking peoples'. To Walter Lippmann, the leading commentator of the day, the speech was an 'almost catastrophic blunder', the leftist *Nation* dubbed it 'remarkably inept'. The *Wall Street Journal* assumed Churchill was seeking an Anglo-Saxon alliance against the Soviet Union, and disapproved: 'The country's reaction to Mr Churchill's Fulton speech must be convincing proof that the US wants no alliance, or anything that resembles an alliance, with any other nation.'[31]

If the American press was less than impressed, Churchill was speaking precisely the language of US officialdom. The week after his speech, the Joint Chiefs of Staff at the Pentagon forwarded to the White House a solemn strategic appraisal of the implications of the Iranian crisis which concluded: 'The defeat or disintegration of the British Empire would eliminate from Eurasia the last bulwark of resistance between the US and Soviet expansion . . . Militarily, our present position as a world power is of necessity closely interwoven with that of Great Britain.'[32]

The sheer pace of events now became a factor in the way that official Western opinion was hardening against Stalin. It was barely two months earlier that Truman had snapped at Byrnes that he was 'tired of babying the Soviets'. The Kennan telegram had since given Truman a rationale, Churchill had provided a ringing phrase, and the Pentagon furnished a strategic argument. Events then moved even faster. The day the Pentagon report was completed, there were two reactions in Moscow. The first came from Stalin, and the second was the British Embassy's own version of Kennan's telegram. Stalin's response came in an interview with *Pravda*, saying that Churchill's speech was 'a dangerous move, calculated to sow the seeds of dissension among the Allied states'.[33] Stalin had two main points to make: the first was offensive, that Churchill embodied British imperialism and a racist supremacy as odious as that of Hitler's Nazis; and the second defensive, that the Soviet Union's role in Eastern Europe was misunderstood.

'Mr Churchill sets out to unleash a war with a racial theory,' Stalin went on. 'The English race theory leads Mr Churchill and his friends to the conclusion that the English-speaking nations, as the only superior countries, should rule over the rest of the nations of the world.' Then came Stalin's defence: 'What can there be surprising about the fact that the Soviet Union, anxious for its future safety, is trying to see to it that governments loyal in their attitude to the Soviet Union should exist in these countries?'

Stalin's reaction in turn provoked Britain's acting Ambassador (and later Ambassador to the United States), Frank Roberts, to draft his own three equivalents of the Kennan cable. They followed one upon another, on 14, 17 and 18 March, landing back on Ernest Bevin's desk in London as a coordinated salvo. Less doom-laden that Kennan, Roberts was much cooler in his key conclusions: 'There is infinitely less danger of sudden catastrophe with the Russians than with the Germans . . . [and] . . . they do not call for open conquest and least of all for the launching of a war of aggression, except possibly for limited aims.'[34] But the same apocalyptic note was there, as Roberts warned: 'It may even be asked whether the world is not now faced with the danger of a modern equivalent of the religious wars of the 16th century, in which Soviet communism will struggle with Western social democracy and the American version of capitalism for domination of the world.'

Even more striking for what it says about the attitude of mind in the West's Moscow Embassies as the Cold War got under way was a brief passage on the Russian national character. Kennan had written bitterly of the Russian historical legacy, and of his dismay at the behaviour of the proletariat in the Black Sea holiday resorts; Roberts went further, suggesting 'a fundamental streak of laziness, indiscipline and inefficiency running through the Russian people, who must be constantly kept up to the mark if they are to preserve their position in the world'. This was the authentic British voice of the imperial proconsul, complaining of the feckless ways of his charges. Add this to Kennan's historicist gloom, and it is clear that the Western establishments were getting some odd, as well as hostile, perspectives on the nature of the Soviet threat from their representatives in Moscow.

By the end of March, just a year after Yalta, the new, combative approach had taken hold in Washington and London. But it was only an approach, an attitude based on reaction to what was seen as Soviet aggression, and which now was sustained by the intellectual cohesion of Kennan's telegram. It had not yet become a coordinated policy, and far less was there a readiness to develop a military alliance, or even to sustain and develop the West as one loose economic unit. There was little political will for rearmament; the British were already desperately overstretched to maintain the garrisons of Empire, reintroducing conscription in October 1946. The Americans, and to a lesser degree the British, were inspired to be negative, to block Soviet moves, rather than to build something more positive in response.

But the new firmness was clear in March 1946 in Truman's insistence in what he called 'a blunt message' that Soviet troops leave Iran. Truman's threat, backed up by Britain, was to join a formal Iranian complaint in the United Nations; it had no teeth. The joint chiefs had made it clear they could contemplate military action in Iran 'only in the event of mobilisation for general war'.[35] But the Soviets, apparently sensitive to assembled opinion at the UN, withdrew.

Heartened by this success, Bevin and Byrnes, the British and American representatives at the council of foreign ministers meeting in Paris in April jointly blocked every Soviet proposal. The Soviets would not be allowed to join a four-power control system over the Ruhr; they would not be permitted large reparations from Germany and its former allies; Yugoslavia's claim on Trieste was rejected; and most ominously from the Soviet point of view, Byrnes pressed for something new, the removal of all trade preferences across Eastern Europe.

To the Americans, this demand for 'equal economic opportunity', which they repeated at the next foreign ministers' session in June, was wholly routine. The objective of 'the enjoyment by all States . . . of access on equal terms to the trade and raw materials of the world' had figured in the original Roosevelt–Churchill Atlantic Charter of 1941.[36] But for the Soviet government, this American call for 'the open door' was suddenly interpreted as something close to a declaration of capitalist war by other means. The new Soviet Ambassador in Washington, Nikolai Novikov, drafted his own version of Kennan's long telegram in September 1946.[37] It stressed that

> the countries of Europe and Asia are experiencing a colossal need for consumer goods, industrial and transportation equipment etc. Such a situation provides American monopolistic capital with prospects for enormous shipments of goods and the importation of capital into these countries – a circumstance which would permit it to infiltrate their national economies. Such a development would mean a serious strengthening of the economic position of the US in the whole world and would be a stage on the road to world domination by the US.

By the time he wrote this cable, Novikov certainly knew of the sacking of Vice-President Henry Wallace, one of the few voices in Truman's cabinet calling for moderation and a return to President Roosevelt's wartime alliance with Stalin. Novikov did not know that the suspicions of Truman's White House had already moved on to a new stage. In July 1946, Truman had asked his aide Clark Clifford to draft a speech, the keynote of a campaign to educate the American public in the nature of the Soviet threat. Clifford asked his assistant George Elsey to prepare the draft, and Elsey consulted Kennan. The final version was handed to Truman on 24 September, and Truman asked for all ten copies to be given to him and kept under lock and key, saying, 'This is so hot, if this should come out now it could have an exceedingly unfortunate impact on our efforts to try to develop some relationship with the Soviet Union.'[38]

'If we find it impossible to enlist Soviet cooperation in the solution of world problems, we should be prepared to join with the British and other Western countries in an attempt to build up a world of our own . . . recognizing the Soviet orbit as a distinct entity with which conflict is not predestined but with which we cannot pursue common aims,' the Clifford–Elsey paper argued.[39]

Truman used this theme that 'Conflict is not predestined' in his speech to the United Nations General Assembly the following month, stressing, 'This is still one world, compact and indivisible.' As he left the podium, a delighted Molotov rushed up to shake his hand. On the same day, Stalin announced further cuts of 80 billion roubles in the Soviet defence budget, and an acceleration of demobilisation. Returning the troops to civilian life almost as fast as the United States, the Red Army shrank from the 1945 peak of almost 12 millions to 3 million men by 1948.[40]

These were hopeful signs, and to understand what confounded these signs of mutual hope it is important to realise the economic difficulty which aggravated the ideological and strategic tensions. On the original version of the Novikov cable, released from Soviet archives only in 1990, there are a series of ticks and marks and underlinings, all in the hand of foreign minister Molotov. He underlined the passage about 'the importation of capital', and leaned heavily on the Novikov cable for his speech at the Paris peace conference in October 1946. Molotov's objections to the 'open door', and to the invasion of Western cultural and economic influence this would invite, have an oddly prophetic ring today:[41]

> It is surely not so difficult to understand that if American capital were given a free hand in the small states ruined and enfeebled by the war, as the advocates of the principle of 'equal opportunity' desire, American capital would buy up the local industries, appropriate the more attractive Rumanian, Yugoslav and all other enterprises, and would become the master in these small states. Given such a situation, we would probably live to see the day when in your own country, on switching on the radio, you would be hearing not so much your own language as one American gramophone record after another or some piece or other of British propaganda. The time might come when in your own country, on going to the cinema, you would be seeing American films sold for foreign consumption.
>
> Is it not clear that such unrestricted applications of the principles of 'equal opportunity' would in practice mean the veritable economic enslavement of the small states and their subjugation to the rule and arbitrary will of strong and enriched foreign firms, banks and industrial corporations? Was this what we fought for when we battled the fascist invaders?

In Molotov's eyes, the United States had begun waging its economic war almost as soon as Truman took office, when the Lend-Lease ships were first turned back, and when the Soviet application for trade credits was 'lost' in Washington bureaucracy. In the wake of the Kennan telegram, the first sign of the new American militancy which reached Molotov was a State Department memorandum of 21 February 1946. It warned him that any negotiations on credits would have to take account of compensation claims by American owners for their holdings in the Soviet-occupied areas of Europe and Manchuria. This paper repeated the American insistence on an open door for trade, and said the United States should be consulted and represented on all matters to do with economic reconstruction in Eastern Europe. It also gave notice that the United States wanted to negotiate a Soviet settlement of its debt for Lend-Lease supplies.[42]

There was a degree of innocence in the American position. Funds had been appropriated for the Export–Import Bank, in the expectation that trade credits would be extended to Moscow. But in March 1946, the French premier Léon Blum and his financial adviser Jean Monnet arrived in a Washington still feverishly discussing the Kennan telegram, and they warned that without economic support, their government was likely to fall and be replaced by Communists. The French received the money instead, with $2.7 billion of war debts written off, and an American guarantee of a further $1.3 billion for the French trade deficit. France was rescued in the name of anti-

Communist solidarity, while Poland, Czechoslovakia and Hungary had their credit applications rejected at the World Bank. Secretary Byrnes explained the matter bluntly: 'The situation has so hardened that the time has now come, I am convinced, in the light of the attitude of the Soviet government and the neighbouring states which it dominates, [that] we must help our friends in every way and refrain from assisting those who either through helplessness or for other reasons are opposing the principles for which we stand.'[43]

By the end of 1946, the senior officials in Washington were convinced that they had to contend with an implacable and expansionist Communist state, well-armed, secretly policed, and utterly ruthless, and commanding the resources of client states in Eastern Europe. The senior officials in Moscow were equally convinced they had to contend with an America, supported by Britain and client states in Western Europe, which had its own implacable plan for economic penetration and dominance of the globe. The more each side became convinced of its image of the other, the more they were locked into hostility.

The event which was to seal this hostility into permanence was, ironically, an act of nature. As the suspicions of 1946 hardened into enmity, and as Kennan and Roberts and Novikov established their new orthodoxies in their respective capitals, the weather intervened. The harvest of 1946 was terrible across Europe, and the winter of 1946–7 was the harshest in living memory. The economic crisis in Europe, which had been appalling in 1946, became critical in 1947, and forced the United States to take direct responsibility for the fate of its cold and hungry friends in Europe. Even before a wave of blizzards struck Britain in January, the government had been forced to cut coal supplies to all industries by half. Unemployment rose to six millions, double the peak of the Great Depression of the 1930s, and electricity was limited to a few hours each day. Food rationing was more severe than it had been during the war. The $5,000 million in loans extended by the United States and Canada in 1945 was being exhausted at what the Treasury called 'a reckless and ever-accelerating speed'. Keynes had warned the Americans that this would follow their insistence that the pound be convertible.[44]

Too poor to hang on, but too proud to let go, Britain had clung by its fingertips to the traditional status and commitments of a great imperial power, with its troops and ships stationed around the world. The terrible winter of 1946–7 proved too much, and the commitments had to go. India's independence would have to come within the year, the Palestine mandate would be handed to the United Nations, and the economic and military defence of the eastern Mediterranean would have to be surrendered.

On the gloomy Friday afternoon of 21 February 1947, the British Ambassador's secretary rang the State Department, asking for an urgent meeting with the new American Secretary of State, General George Marshall, the legendary wartime chief of staff. Marshall was out of town, but suspecting what was coming, acting Secretary Dean Acheson arranged to receive a copy of the formal 'blue paper' so that its implications could be addressed by the time Marshall returned on Monday. The British first secretary, Henry Sichel, delivered two documents to Loy Henderson, the State Department's head of Near Eastern Affairs.

'They were shockers. British aid to Greece and Turkey would end in six weeks,' Acheson later recalled. 'The British could no longer be of substantial help in either. His Majesty's government devoutly hoped that we could assume the burden.'[45]

Acheson began a flurry of weekend activity to prepare papers, cost estimates and recommendations, and celebrated on Sunday evening with martinis with Loy Henderson and a toast to 'the confusion of our enemies'. Marshall approved, persuaded President Truman and the War and Navy Secretaries, and on 26 February Truman convened the crucial meeting at the White House with the Congressional leaders who would have to vote the funds. The mid-term elections of November 1946 meant that the Democrats no longer controlled Congress. The Republican Senators and Congressmen, among whom the tendency to isolationism was almost instinctive, would have to be persuaded that the frontiers of US security were now on the Dardanelles. 'I knew we were met at Armageddon,' wrote Acheson, and after Marshall gave a leaden report, Acheson took over. As he recalled:[46]

> These Congressmen had no conception of what challenged them. It was my task to bring it home. Soviet pressure on the Straits, on Iran and on northern Greece had brought the Balkans to the point where a highly possible Soviet breakthrough might open three continents to Soviet penetration. Like apples in a barrel infected by one rotten one, the corruption of Greece would infect Iran and all to the east. It would also carry infection to Africa through Asia Minor and Egypt, and to Europe through Italy and France, already threatened by the strongest domestic Communist parties in Western Europe. The Soviet Union was playing one of the greatest gambles in history at minimal cost.

After the long silence which followed this performance, Senator Arthur Vandenburg, the powerful Republican whose support was required for a bipartisan foreign policy, said to Truman: 'Mr President, if you will say that to the Congress and the country, I will support you and I believe most of its members will do the same.'[47]

This was the birth of the Truman Doctrine, formally spelt out to the joint session of Congress by the President on 12 March. Truman successfully called for $400 million in aid for Greece and Turkey, and for the right to send US troops to administer the reconstruction and train local forces. But far more important for the future was the much wider principle Truman established. He drew a distinction between two worlds, of freedom and coercion, of free institutions against terror and oppression.[48]

> The seeds of totalitarian regimes are nurtured by misery and want. They spread and grow in the evil soil of poverty and strife. They reach their full growth when the hope of a people for a better life has died. We must keep that hope alive. I believe that it must be the policy of the United States to support free peoples who are resisting attempted subjugation by armed minorities or by outside pressures.

The impact of that savage winter of 1947 did not stop with Greece and Turkey. British poverty was serious, France was equally beset, but the western zones of Germany were in the worst plight of all. Divided by the zones of the four powers, and restricted from developing the old nucleus of its heavy industry in the Ruhr, Germany was prostrate, and the cities close to starving. The costs of occupying Germany drained over $300 million from Britain in 1946. The French wanted to annex the Saar as a way to guarantee their coal supplies, and the Soviet government was able to exploit these divisions of Western policy.

For the American zone commander, General Lucius Clay, the solution was plain; the German economy had to be freed from the constraints of occupation. For Truman, this made sense, so long as the Republicans in Congress would agree, and to ensure that they did, Truman asked the former Republican President Herbert Hoover to visit Germany and make his own report. Hoover agreed with Clay, and so did the future Republican Secretary of State John Foster Dulles, who called for expansion of the German economy within a united Europe.[49] That made the policy bipartisan. But the strategic decision to revive, or perhaps unleash once more the German economy, was guaranteed to alarm the Soviet Union. Even some Germans warned that this might be going too far, too fast. 'Russia can point to the enormous damage Germany has already caused, and could do again if rebuilt,' noted Rudolf Kustermeier, the Social Democrat editor of *Die Welt*.[50]

Both the French and the Russians had a veto over changes in Germany as a whole. The reluctant French could be made to agree, through the prospect of further US economic support. The Russians could not, and at the foreign ministers' council meeting in Moscow, Molotov refused to soften Soviet demands for reparations from Germany. But the British and Americans refused to pump support into the Western zone of the German economy if the Russians were simultaneously pumping it out of their zone. Molotov hoped he could block the entire proposal. And since Molotov was conducting these negotiations with General Marshall while the US President was announcing the Truman Doctrine, the division of the world into the free and the enslaved, the Soviet refusal to yield was understandable.

The only Anglo-American alternative was to proceed on their own, dragging the French along, and beginning the process of what was to become the forty-year division of Germany into East and West. The Truman Doctrine, the Dulles speeches and the Hoover report all pointed to a way in which Germany could be rebuilt, while reassuring France and the other Western European countries so recently under German occupation. But even as the awful winter of 1947 gave way to spring, there was no time to waste. US Under-Secretary of State Will Clayton made a swift tour, and reported in May: 'Millions of people in the cities are slowly starving . . . Without further prompt and substantial aid from the US, economic, social and political dislocation will overwhelm Europe.' As General Marshall said in a radio address to the American people after returning from Moscow, 'The patient is sinking while the doctors deliberate.'[51]

Walter Lippmann, dean of American journalists, perceived the inevitable implication. On 5 April, Lippmann's 'Cassandra Speaking' column argued that to fend off a crisis which threatened to 'spread chaos throughout the world, political and economic measures on a scale which no responsible statesman has yet ventured to hint at will be needed in the next year or so'. Three weeks later, Lippmann spelt out the logic that linked the Truman Doctrine to what would become the Marshall Plan: 'After we have discussed the separate needs of Britain, France, Italy and the rest, we should suggest to them that they meet together, agree on a general European program of production and exchange, of imports and exports to the outer world, and that they arrive at an estimate of the consolidated deficit for as much of Europe as can agree to a common plan.'[52]

The Marshall Plan for the recovery of Europe was formally unveiled in a speech at Harvard University on 5 June 1947. Marshall stressed that: 'It would be neither fitting nor efficacious for this government to undertake to draw up unilaterally a program designed to place Europe on its feet economically. This is the business of the Europeans. The initiative, I think, must come from Europe.'[53] Acheson ensured that it did, briefing three British journalists on its importance, and advising them to tell their editors to send full copies of the speech to Ernest Bevin at the Foreign Office. Bevin immediately telephoned Georges Bidault, the French foreign minister, and within two weeks, they and the Russian foreign minister Molotov were all meeting in Paris.

The American press did not see Marshall's speech as quite so important. In the next day's *New York Times*, the first headline read, 'Truman Calls Hungary Coup "Outrage" ', the second headline went on, 'Demands Russians Agree to Inquiry', and only the third headline said, 'Marshall Pleads for European Unity'.[54]

Molotov was invited because the Marshall Plan was designed to seize the moral high ground for the West. The Truman Doctrine speech had made US attitudes to Moscow coldly clear. But if the Marshall Plan were to fail, the Soviet Union should be seen to be responsible. Accordingly, Marshall stressed in his Harvard speech: 'Our policy is directed not against any country or doctrine but against hunger, poverty, desperation and chaos. Its purpose should be the revival of a working economy in the world so as to permit the emergence of political and social conditions in which free institutions can exist . . . Any government which manoeuvres to block the recovery of other countries cannot expect help from us.'

It was the task of Bevin and Bidault to ensure that Molotov understood the political implications of Marshall's phrase about 'free institutions'. But Molotov had come to Paris with more than a hundred experts, including economists, transport and logistics consultants and even nutritionists. Moscow, it was clear, was seriously interested in Marshall's offer, if the terms were right. Molotov began by saying each European country should add up its financial needs, and send the combined list to the Americans. That, retorted Bevin, would be asking for a blank cheque. 'Debtors do not lay down conditions,' Bevin added.

Molotov suspected that like the 'open door' trade policy, the Marshall Plan would be the Trojan Horse of the American dollar, a way to infiltrate the Soviet Union and its sphere of influence in order to destroy it. He suggested that 'only allied countries that had suffered from the ravages of war should participate'. This would exclude both Italy and Germany. Bevin and Bidault said no. Trying to force a decision, Bevin then offered a proposal for a steering committee to draw up a programme for four years, and listing what Europe needed, and what it could provide. Bevin suggested Britain, France and the Soviet Union, and four other European countries should sit on the committee. This was insurance against being outvoted if Communist ministers should block the plan in the French government.

Molotov objected again, saying there 'must be no infringement of the national sovereignty of the European states'. He was then handed a telegram, only partially decoded, straight from Moscow. It reinforced Molotov's hard line; Stalin would not accept common planning, with its implication of American and British economists poring over the Soviet economy. In effect, the Paris conference was over. The Marshall Plan, Molotov finally declared,[55]

> has now served as a pretext for the British and French governments to insist on the creation of a new organisation, standing above the European countries and intervening in the internal affairs of the countries of Europe . . . The European countries will lose their former economic and national independence to the advantage of certain strong powers . . . It will lead to Britain, France and the group of countries that follow them separating from the rest of Europe, which will split Europe into two groups of states.

In this, Molotov was absolutely right. But then Britain and the non-Communist parties in France and the other Western European countries had already chosen their sides. If the Iron Curtain were indeed falling across Europe, then all but the socialists and those to their left knew on which side they preferred to be. On 4 July, two days after Molotov's departure, Bevin and Bidault invited twenty-two European governments, all except Fascist Spain and the Soviet Union, to a wider conference in Paris the following week. The Czechs, Poles and Hungarians all agreed, Bulgaria and Albania expressed interest, and only Yugoslavia and Romania said they would first consult with Moscow.

Moscow cracked the whip. The Czech premier Klement Gottwald and foreign minister Jan Masaryk were summoned to Moscow on 8 July, to be threatened with grim consequences should they go to Paris. Masaryk glumly observed that he had gone to Moscow as the minister of a sovereign state, and returned as a Soviet lackey.[56] Poland, Romania, Yugoslavia, Bulgaria, Albania, Hungary all rejected the invitation, and so did Finland. In retrospect, this has been defined as the moment when the Soviet boot crushed itself into the face of Eastern Europe. At the time, the implications were not so clear.

'Could we risk a complete break with Moscow?' pondered Hubert Ripka, the Czech minister of foreign trade, and a socialist rather than Communist. 'The Soviets might well incite the Communists, in that case, to effect a coup d'état. We were unfortunately unable to expect effective help from the Western powers.' But then Ripka made a different, telling point, citing 'another reason, still more serious. I know that we could not win over the majority of the people for such a policy.'[57]

Ripka was pointing to the uncomfortable truth that whatever the opinions in the White House and Kremlin, many of the people of Europe were still torn. There was as yet no clear division between Communists and non-Communists in Europe. Denis Healey, then the international secretary of the British Labour Party, and by now a firm anti-Communist, spent the year of 1947 attending a series of socialist party conferences across Europe, watching these fraternal parties split between those who wanted to maintain a united front with the Communists, and those prepared to join the liberals and moderate conservatives against the Communists. Eastern Europe was an odd mix of pluralism and putsch. Healey was in Hungary in January 1947 when one of the few Social Democrats in the political police was shot in the back from a Russian limousine. But he also attended the last free conference of Czech social democrats in November of that same year, when the party voted to reject a proposal for fusion with the Communists.[58]

The full weight of Soviet rule did not fall until the following year, with the Communist putsch in Prague in February, and the suicide (or murder) of Jan Masaryk on 10 March. His body was found in the courtyard beneath his window in the foreign ministry. Even in November, Masaryk had few illusions of what was coming, telling an old friend that Czech Communists had already been given orders 'to liquidate their political opposition'.[59] The orders had been given at the first meeting of the Cominform, the Communist Information Bureau, which Stalin launched on 22 September 1946 as a direct response to the Marshall Plan. He convened a conference of the leaders of the Communist parties of Poland, Czechoslovakia, Yugoslavia, Romania, Hungary, Bulgaria, France and Italy, to be the replacement of the unlamented Comintern. This was the formal end of Eastern European hopes of differing paths to socialism.

The report to this extraordinary assembly of European Communists was delivered by Andrei Zhdanov. It contained five main themes. The first was that 'America's aspirations to world supremacy encounter an obstacle in the USSR, the stronghold of anti-imperialist and anti-fascist policy'. The second was that war was not inevitable – 'Soviet foreign policy proceeds from the fact of the co-existence for a long period of the two systems, capitalism and socialism'. The third was that time was not on the West's side: 'World War Two aggravated the crisis of the colonial system, as expressed in the rise of a powerful movement for national liberation in the colonies and dependencies. This has placed the rear of the capitalist system in jeopardy.' The fourth was that 'The Truman Doctrine, which provides for American assistance to all reactionary regimes which actively oppose the democratic peoples, bears a frankly aggressive character.' And the fifth, designed to summon the memory of Nazism, was that: 'The cornerstone of the Marshall Plan is the restoration of the industrial areas of Western Germany controlled by the American monopolies.'[60]

The Italian Communists were stunned by the sharpness of the ideological turn. They were even more dismayed by the attack made by the Yugoslavs upon the Italian and French Communists for not having had the courage to try to seize power in 1945, even though this policy had met with Moscow's approval at the time.[61] The Communists of Western Europe were henceforth conscripted into Soviet service, to be flung as shock troops against the Marshall Plan. As Zhdanov stressed: 'If they are prepared to take the lead of all the forces prepared to defend the cause of national honour and independence in the struggle against attempts to subjugate their countries economically and politically, then no plan for the subjugation of Europe can succeed.'[62]

The result was a wave of strikes, street demonstrations and battles with the police in France and Italy, throughout the winter of 1947–8. Two million workers struck in France on 18 November, the red flag was raised over the Palais de Justice in Marseilles, and the main trade-union body, the Confédération Générale du Travail, formally condemned American aid to France. Parliamentary proceedings were virtually halted, but the government of Robert Schuman stood firm.

The strike called to stop the Paris Métro failed in December, and the wave receded. It lasted longer in Italy, but failed there too, in part because the US and Canadian food aid had begun to arrive in Europe.[63]

But another factor now came into play, the new institutions of national security being established in the United States. On 19 December 1947 the first of them, the National Security Council, held its first meeting in Washington, and decided to use the equally new Central Intelligence Agency to run covert operations in Europe. One of the first directives passed that day, titled NSC 4/A, ordered Admiral Roscoe Hillenkoeter, the new director of Central Intelligence, to use covert methods to prevent a Communist victory in Italy.[64]

The immediate target was the elections of the following year. The methods used included propaganda, disinformation, secret payments to non-Communist political parties, public threats to withhold US aid from a Communist government, and special training and equipment to the Italian armed forces. This was not the beginning of the secret war. That can be dated back to the last days of the war against Germany, when Frank Wisner of the OSS, and later of the CIA, began negotiations with Reinhard Gehlen, the former head of Fremde Heere Ost, the German Army's formidable intelligence department which covered the Soviet armed forces. Gehlen's files and skills and agents were swiftly put at American disposal.

But the Italian crisis represents the first political decision from the White House to launch the secret war. The stakes were recognised to be high. From his new post at the State Department in Washington, Kennan cabled to the US Embassies in Europe: 'Italy is obviously key point. If Communists win election there, our whole position in Mediterranean, as possibly in Europe as well, would probably be undermined.' And if the Communists should win, Kennan recommended US military intervention.[65]

In retrospect, the congealing of the Cold War in 1947–8 was oddly like a series of volleys in a tennis match. The United States opened the service by proposing the Marshall Plan. The Soviets returned the serve by convening the Cominform, and launching the strikes to stop it. The US rushed food to Europe to beat the strikes. Realising their Western European effort had failed, the Soviets responded by establishing firm control in Eastern Europe with the coup in Czechoslovakia. The West's reply was to militarise what had hitherto been an economic relationship with Western Europe. The armed camps began to mobilise under their two opposing banners.

'It really has become a matter of the defence of Western civilisation or everything will be swamped by this Soviet method of infiltration,' Bevin told the British cabinet.[66] The Brussels Defence Pact, of Britain, France and the Benelux countries, was agreed that month. Under its terms, Britain agreed to come to their defence against invasion, and to keep troops in Germany for fifty years. On 12 March, two days after the death of Masaryk in Prague, General Marshall called in the British Ambassador in Washington. 'Please inform Mr Bevin that we are prepared to proceed at once in the joint discussions on the establishment of an Atlantic security system,' Marshall said. Ten months after his launch of the Marshall Plan, the North Atlantic Treaty Organisation was under way.[67]

If the firmness of this Western response came as a surprise to Moscow, a further shock was in store. Unable at first, and later unwilling, to get American credits, and barred from rebuilding its economy through wholesale looting of the western zones of Germany in the name of reparations, Soviet economic recovery was now dependent on whatever resources it could mobilise in its own sphere of influence. Already restive at this, and unwilling to plunge into massive investments in heavy industry, the Communists of Yugoslavia under the wartime partisan leader Marshal Tito began increasing their trade with the West. Yugoslavia also took the lead in proposing a Balkan Federation, which would include a customs union with Czechoslovakia and Poland.

At first, it seemed a routine matter of party discipline. Bulgaria and other Eastern European countries dropped the idea as soon as Moscow complained. But Yugoslavia bridled. On 18 March 1948, hoping to exert sufficient pressure for the Yugoslav party to evict Tito and change the policy, Stalin began to withdraw the Soviet military and economic advisory teams. But Tito, as much a nationalist as a Communist ideologue, began negotiating if not to join the Marshall Plan, then at least to become a fellow traveller. He succeeded. By 1951, the US had supplied Tito with $150 million in civilian aid, and another $60 million in arms.[68]

While the vicious polemics between Stalin and Tito did further damage to what remained of pro-Soviet sympathies among Europe's non-Communist left, the real implication of the Marshall Plan began to unfold. In February, British, French and US officials met in London to discuss a joint plan for the reindustrialisation of their zones of

Germany, treating all three as a single unit. On 7 June, the London Recommendations called on the premiers of the West German provinces, the Länder, to convene a constitutional assembly, which led to the West German state. And on 18 June, the currency reform and the birth of the Deutschmark was announced. The division of Europe was complete, save for the two isolated cities of Vienna and Berlin, still inside the Soviet zone. On 23 June, the Western powers announced that the Deutschmark would also be introduced into their sectors of West Berlin, and on the following day, the Soviets announced their blockade of the city.

Open war, or at least direct military confrontation, was very close. The American General Clay proposed sending US armoured columns into the Soviet zone to clear the roads, a suggestion supported by the fiery British left-wing Labour MP Aneurin Bevan, so much had Stalin lost credibility in the West. The wiser head of Ernest Bevin prevailed, along with the logistical skills of the US Air Force Generals Hap Arnold and Curtis LeMay who recalled how 72,000 tonnes of supplies had been flown over the Himalayas into China during World War Two. And the unprecedented Berlin airlift began. It lasted for eleven months, fed two million people and delivered enough coal to stop them freezing through the winter.[69] An astonishing display of the West's industrial weight and political determination, it also sealed into place the strategic permafrost which was to settle over Europe for a generation.

Not all the aircraft were flying into Berlin. On 18 July, two US Air Force groups of sixty B-29 'atomic bombers', equipped to deliver nuclear weapons, flew into their new British bases. The atom bombs, it later emerged, did not join them until the outbreak of the Korean War in June 1950. Deliberately, however, widespread publicity was given to the bombers' arrival, even though it is doubtful whether the US arsenals contained as many as fifty atom bombs for them to drop, and it is unlikely they would all have been committed to the British-based force.[70] It was all done very briskly and even casually, without any formal treaty.

'Never before in history has one first class power gone into another first class power's country without an agreement. We were just told to come over and "We shall be pleased to have you",' recalled the bombers' commander, General Leon Johnson.[71] That was only a part of the implication of the arrival of the bombers. Although the first

Soviet atom bomb test was not to take place until September of the following year, the nuclear stand-off over a divided Europe had begun.[72]*

* The declassification of parts of the Pentagon's official *History of the Strategic Arms Competition, 1945–72*, in 1993, finally fills in some of the gaps of public knowledge. The atom bombs in Britain, as elsewhere throughout the world, were under the custody of the Atomic Energy Commission, rather than the US armed forces. It was only in July 1950, with the outbreak of the Korean War, that President Truman authorised the storage of eighty-nine sets of non-nuclear components in Britain. The bombs' nuclear cores, the plutonium capsules, were still under the control of the AEC, in accordance with the provisions of the Atomic Energy Act of 1946. These nuclear and non-nuclear components of the bombs were not to be mated together, ready for use, until a full-scale war alert. The Defense Department was first authorised to hold both nuclear and non-nuclear components together in April 1951, when President Truman assigned nine Mark 4 'Fat Man' bombs to the personal custody of General Hoyt Vandenbergh, Air Force chief of staff. Authority to deploy complete warheads to Britain, under USAF custody, was not granted until April 1954. The British, at least, were informed of this. The French were not consulted when President Truman authorised the storage of non-nuclear components at SAC bases in French Morocco in January 1952.[73]

Chapter 3

The Cold War Goes Global – and Comes Home

> Our one task was known;
> Each to mould the other's fate as he wrought his own.
> To this end we stirred mankind till all Earth was ours
> Till our world-end strifes begat wayside Thrones and Powers,
> Puppets that we made or broke to bar the other's path,
> Necessary, outpost-folk, hirelings of our wrath.
>
> *'France', Rudyard Kipling*

The Cold War started in Europe because it was there that US and Soviet troops met in May 1945, over the corpse of Nazi Germany, and discovered that their concepts of Europe's post-war future were dangerously incompatible. Their deepening confrontation spread more slowly to the rest of the world, and without that hostility in Europe might never have spread at all. The United States found itself unhappily but increasingly supporting and then supplanting its European allies' colonial pretensions in Asia and Africa. And Stalin found himself equally glumly forced to support the Chinese Communist Party's successful struggle against the US-backed government of Chiang Kai-shek.

Once under way, once the idea of the Cold War had seized the minds of the leaders in Moscow, Washington and London, it took on a strange kind of creativity, leading them into actions which had never been thought out, but which had far-reaching effect. The American and British plan for post-war Germany had been harsh, to keep the Germans tamed, disarmed, de-Nazified and inhibited from rebuilding their formidable industrial machine. The combination of British poverty and the Soviet threat made that policy redundant within three years of Yalta. Germany had to be rebuilt, at first as an industrial base to help stabilise Western Europe, and then as a full-scale military ally. A similar process developed in Japan.

The initial plan for occupied Japan was to break its will and capacity for future aggression, to disarm the country, to break up the industrial combines, and to inculcate democratic values. The Cold War in Europe, and its spread to mainland China, forced a reassessment. By 9 October 1948, President Truman approved a recommendation from his new National Security Council, which declared that Japan's prosperity was deemed a Western strategic asset, and the policy goal henceforth was: 'To ready democratic Japan for entry into the free world's community of nations as a self-supporting trading partner.'[1]

Once the United States and the Soviet Union began to perceive one another through the prism of the Cold War in Europe, they saw that jaundiced image of the other wherever they looked. The irony was that Europe, the crucible, remained edgily at peace; the vast bulk of the Cold War's fighting and dying took part in Asia, the Middle East, Africa and Latin America. People with brown and black and yellow skins paid thc price of what had begun in Europe as a white men's quarrel. But there was one important parallel between the post-war development in Europe and in Asia; the problems of the peace followed logically from the geographical locations the various armies of the Grand Alliance had reached in the course of winning the war. The defeat of Japan required the wresting of control from the Japanese armies all along the Asian littoral, from Manchuria and Korea in the north, to Burma in the Indian Ocean. And Japan had been fighting two rather different kinds of war. The first, which Japan had been waging against China since 1931, was a classic war of imperial conquest. But the second, which Japan launched in December 1941, was not only an attack on American positions in the Pacific Ocean, it also assumed some of the characteristics of a war of Asian liberation against the European colonial empires in Asia.

The Dutch in Indonesia, the French in Indo-China, the British in Hong Kong, Malaya, Burma and India, and to a degree the Americans in the Philippines, each found that their experience of initial defeat at Japanese hands complicated their subsequent reoccupation. The British had been startled by the success of the Japanese in raising a small army of Indian prisoners of war under Subhas Chandra Bose to fight against them. After the war, the British were to be embarrassed by the hostility of the Indian public to the trial of Bose's men for treason. 'India adores these men,' said Gandhi, while Pandit Nehru, the first prime minister of independent India, hailed their 'passionate desire to serve the cause of India's freedom'. On 8 September, the French began their campaign to recover control of Vietnam from the local Communist resistance led by Ho Chi Minh, by releasing 1,700 Japanese POWs to fight on the French side. The American sense of confusion became acute when Ho Chi Minh began the Vietnamese Declaration of Independence with an approving quotation from the equivalent American Declaration of 1776.[2]

The United States became caught in a contradiction. American anticolonial sympathies may have rested with the local nationalists, with whom in Vietnam, Indonesia and the Philippines they had fruitfully cooperated in the war of resistance against a Japanese occupation whose cruelty swiftly destroyed its initial welcome. But America's crucial allies in Western Europe demanded American support in reasserting control over their old Asian empires. And increasingly as the Cold War deepened they were able to do so not in the name of the old imperialism but in the cause of the new anti-Communism. The USA refused to help the Dutch recover their empire in the East Indies and threatened to withdraw Marshall Aid if the Dutch persisted; was gratified that Britain's Labour government sensibly granted independence to its Indian empire in 1947; but was to be haunted for a generation by the legacy of the French struggle and subsequent defeat in Indo-China. And when Americans followed the French into Vietnam, they were to misapply the lessons of fighting a Communist insurgency which the British had devised in retaining their control of Malaya.

In Europe, because of the Yalta agreements and the positions the Soviet and Western troops had reached in 1945, the Cold War had a static quality. In Asia, because of the civil war in China, and the replacement of the Japanese by the returning European colonialists, the situation became far more fluid and thus intrinsically far less stable. Ironically, both the United States and the Soviet Union had tried to establish stability in China. At the Dumbarton Oaks meetings in August 1944, the Soviets had accepted that Chiang Kai-shek's China would be one of the 'Big Five' members of the United Nations Security Council, with a veto. The next year at Yalta, Roosevelt had persuaded Stalin to agree to treat the nationalist government of Chiang Kai-shek as an ally, even though it had been fighting against Mao Tse-tung's Chinese Communists since 1927. Chiang and Stalin signed a Treaty of Friendship and Alliance in August 1945.[3]

As the war ended in China, it had been assumed by Stalin and the US alike that Chiang's forces would occupy the vast vacuum in northern and eastern China left by the Japanese defeat. Although nominally outnumbered five to one by Chiang's forces, Mao did not agree. The Chinese Communist Party had never enjoyed the wholehearted support of Stalin, and Mao acted under the assumption that he could defeat Chiang and his American supporters, but would have to rely on his own resources. Mao replied to the news of the treaty between Chiang, his civil-war rival, and Stalin, his ideological 'comrade', by telling his troops: 'Relying on the forces we ourselves organise, we can defeat all Chinese and foreign reactionaries.'[4]

China was filled with different armies. The Soviets swept through Manchuria and into northern Korea. The Americans established a naval base at Tsingtao, and by the end of 1945 there were 50,000 US Marines in the country. The British returned to Hong Kong, and Chiang Kai-shek resolved to use his new relationship with Stalin to assert control of the north. Stalin equivocated, allowing the Communists to seize vast stocks of captured Japanese arms, and Chiang's troops became increasingly overextended as they tried to take over the main towns of Manchuria from the Soviet troops. There was sporadic fighting between Chiang's forces and the Communists, and America's General Marshall tried and failed to organise a truce and a coalition government in which Chiang would have the dominant role.[5] The stakes, General Marshall asserted, could hardly have been higher. His mission was to fend off 'the tragic consequences of a divided China and of a probable Russian reassumption of power in Manchuria, the combined effect of this resulting in the defeat or loss of the major purpose of our war in the Pacific'.[6]

Corruption in Chiang's government combined with low morale among his troops and a devastating inflation to weaken what had looked like a commanding position. Newly armed from the Japanese stocks, and with some limited and covert Soviet support, Mao's armies began to win, in spite of Chiang's grudging American support. As President Truman recalled it,[7]

> Chiang Kai-shek decided he was going to occupy North China and Manchuria. General Marshall argued against it, and General Wedermeyer argued against it, but he went ahead. We furnished him equipment, money and a water-lift to Manchuria, and he sent the best divisions he had, well-trained and well-armed, to Mukden. They stayed there until finally the whole thing disintegrated, and they surrendered.

By the end of 1946, it was plain to General Marshall and to President Truman that to save the Chiang government in China, the United States 'would virtually have to take over the Chinese government . . . It would involve the US in a continuing commitment from which it would be practically impossible to withdraw'. In November, the US Seventh Fleet was ordered to withdraw the US Marines. The United States continued to supply Chiang with a total of $2 billion in economic and military aid as the civil war intensified, but with fading hopes that the Nationalist government would endure.[8]

The Cold War in Europe, deepening the conviction in Washington that the West faced a relentless global challenge by Soviet-led Communism, made Mao's advances look far more sinister. Dean Rusk, the deputy Under-Secretary of State for the Far East, and experienced enough to have understood the underlying tensions between Mao and Stalin, still saw it in terms of the spreading Soviet menace: 'Most of us saw Chiang Kai-shek's fall coming, but we were still disappointed when it happened. I saw it as a great tragedy, that the Chinese people, with their tremendous energy and potential, were now wedded to Communist ideology and allied with the Soviet Union.'[9]

There were abundant signs that this was not the case. In April 1949, when the Chiang government fled its working capital of Nanking, most of the world's Ambassadors remained. Only the Soviet envoy joined Chiang in the rout to Canton.[10] Mao proclaimed the People's Republic of China in October 1949, and in December went by train to Moscow, where he remained for two months, while the Sino-Soviet Treaty of Friendship and Alliance and Mutual Help was negotiated and signed. This was seen in the alarmed West as the fusion of a monolithic Communist block, dominating most of Eurasia. China's formal diplomatic recognition in January, while Mao was still in Moscow, of Ho Chi Minh's Vietminh as the legitimate government of a Vietnam still largely under French control, reinforced the Western fears.[11]

But the terms of the Sino-Soviet Treaty were significantly modest. They required the two countries to aid one another in war only in the event of Japanese aggression, or attack by 'any other state which should unite with Japan directly or indirectly in acts of aggression'. The most likely cause of war, an attack upon the Chinese mainland by Chiang's Nationalists from their fortress island refuge of Formosa (Taiwan), with or without US support, was clearly not the kind of conflict which would mandate Soviet support. And since Japan was disarmed, and equipped by the US occupation forces with a constitution which required that it remain disarmed, this was a treaty which did not pledge the Soviet Union to do very much at all.[12]

The revival of Japan came about through three accidents. The first was the decision of General Douglas MacArthur, known as SCAP (Supreme Commander, Allied Powers), to ignore the draconian Morgenthau plan for post-war Japan, and impose his own more lenient scheme. The second unforeseen development was the triumph of the

Chinese Communist Party, which transformed Japan from an occupied enemy into a Cold War bastion, whose need to strengthen its economic base led to the revival of the 'zaibatsu' industrial groups. The third accident was the Korean War, for which Japan was the American military and economic base.

MacArthur was granted extraordinary powers in 1945, which he exercised as a benevolent dictator – on his allies as well as on the Japanese. The Soviets were barred from any governing role in Japan akin to the four-power system in occupied Germany. The British were told that they would no longer command the Australian troops, that the 40,000 British and Commonwealth troops would be made part of the US Eighth Army, and that they too would join the Soviets in the purely consultative councils which MacArthur proceeded to ignore. His own troops were not forbidden to fraternise with the defeated Japanese, but were warned that they faced five years in military prison for striking or slapping a Japanese civilian. The US Ambassador to Japan, William Sebald, was stunned to learn that MacArthur's powers were such that the Ambassador's own cables back to the State Department had to be approved by SCAP.[13]

MacArthur informed the transitional prime minister, Kijuro Shidehara, that all legislators who had been members of militarist parties had to be dismissed from the Diet, the Japanese parliament. The prime minister said that meant the entire cabinet would have to resign. MacArthur said that was fine. The resignations were withdrawn. On 15 September 1945, the liberal newspaper *Asahi Shimbun* suggested in an editorial that the use of the atom bomb on Hiroshima and Nagasaki had been a breach of international law. It was closed for two days, but SCAP began weekly lectures for the Japanese press on the rights and duties of a free press.[14]

MacArthur required a new and democratic constitution. The Japanese government's draft was inadequate, and he wrote his own, an amalgam of British and American practice which established three separate branches of government and a parliamentary democracy. Above all, in Article IX, MacArthur's new Japanese constitution declared that the nation would by fundamental law 'forever renounce war as a sovereign right of the nation . . . Land, sea and air forces, as well as other war potential, will never be maintained.'[15] MacArthur's staff at SCAP included a number of 'New Deal' Democrats who brought their own social-democratic sympathies to the new Japan.

The Communist Party was legalised, and trade unions encouraged. In October, two months after the surrender and just one week after the demobilisation of the Japanese army, SCAP issued a directive which abolished all controls on religious, political and civil liberties, and gave women the vote for the first time. Land reform split up the great estates and gave the land to peasants. Informed by the 'New Deal' theories of the 1930s, MacArthur and his aides imposed a liberal constitution and social revolution on Japan. And they did it in a spirit remarkably free of wartime vengeance. Whereas in the US zone of Germany almost one in four of the population was 'screened' for de-Nazification, in Japan barely three per cent of the Japanese population went through similar procedures.[16]

MacArthur's early rule sought to fulfil the spirit of the idealist Atlantic Charter in whose name the Allies claimed to have fought. But he established political freedoms in desperate economic circumstances. Japan had suffered many fewer casualties than Germany in the war: 1,270,000 military dead, and at least another 670,000 civilians, of whom 138,890 died at Hiroshima alone. The figures are in dispute. Japanese estimates of civilian dead range up to two million. The Japanese economy had, however, been devastated. While Germany had coal and iron ore in the Ruhr, the Japanese islands had few raw materials for industry. The week after he arrived in Tokyo, MacArthur cabled back to Washington for 3.5 million tonnes of food. When Washington delayed, MacArthur sent a second dispatch: 'Give me bread or give me bullets.'[17]

At the end of 1945, Japanese industrial production was just 16 per cent of the level in 1940. With so little economic activity beyond the subsistence level, few taxes could be collected. The eleven great families, who had traditionally owned the giant zaibatsu, were forced to trade in their stocks for non-negotiable government bonds, and the salaries of the new managers were sharply restricted. In 1945, industrial production fell by 64 per cent. In 1946, it fell by a further 38 per cent. The year 1947 saw the first signs of recovery, with a 15 per cent increase, but from such a desperately low base that industrial activity was still just half of what it had been in 1934.[18]

To try to keep some industry alive, MacArthur scrapped the initial plans for reparations: to dismantle 1,100 Japanese plants and remove them to allied countries. It was not enough. When the first moderate socialist government was elected in 1947, there were just four days' supply of rice in the government warehouses. The growth of the Communist Party led to industrial militancy, and on 1 February 1947 a general strike was called. Already under criticism in the US press and Senate for introducing socialism to Japan, MacArthur banned the strike, and began to change course.[19]

For once in the post-war Japan he ruled, the new policy was not MacArthur's decision alone. The echoes of the Cold War in Europe helped impose it, and a retired head of the American Bankers' Association, Joseph M. Dodge, was brought out to Japan to execute the new course. The plans to dissolve the 1,200 firms which had been targeted in the Deconcentration Law, the vehicle to dismantle the zaibatsu, were deliberately delayed by the Japanese, and not pushed by the Americans. Dodge also began working to change MacArthur's ban on foreign investment into Japan. Back in Washington, Dodge had powerful supporters in the US Treasury, which was worried about the costs of MacArthur's policies. The price of sustaining the Japanese economy was rising sharply, from $108 million in fiscal year 1945–6, to $294 million in fiscal year 1946–7.[20]

The new American policy, based upon geo-strategic fear of Communists, was expressed with great frankness by US Army Secretary Kenneth Royall, in a speech to the Commonwealth Club of San Francisco, on 6 January 1948:[21]

> It is clear that Japan cannot support itself as a nation of shopkeepers and craftsmen and small artisans any more than it can exist as a purely agricultural nation. We can expect continuing economic deficits in Japan unless there is some degree of mass industrial production. We are building in Japan a self-sufficient democracy, strong enough and stable enough to support itself and at the same time serve as a deterrent against any other totalitarian war threats which might hereafter arise in the Far East.

As Royall spoke, the civil war in China was still being fought, but the Communists were evidently winning. In Europe, the Marshall Plan was under way. Japan was no longer an isolated group of islands, a problem unto itself and the American occupation. It was part of the global confrontation, taking its place in the West's battle line. Barely a year after the MacArthur constitution had banned a Japanese army, MacArthur was persuaded of the need for a 'jietai', or Self-Defence Force, of initially 75,000 men.

The speed with which America transformed its view about the kind of Japan it wanted can be traced not only to the developments in Europe and China, but also to a rising mood of panic in the United States. 'Our reaction to the fall of China in 1949 was that of a jilted lover,' Dean Rusk commented.[22] It was worse than that. The 'loss' of China was seen as a portent of eventual defeat on a global scale. 'The fall of China imperils the US,' General MacArthur wrote in *Life* magazine. *Time* brooded darkly on 'the red tide that threatens to engulf the world'.[23] The mood is caught in the preamble to the Internal Security Act, widely known as the McCarran Act, which was passed the following year: 'World Communism has as its sole purpose the establishment of a totalitarian dictatorship in America, to be brought about by treachery, infiltration, sabotage and terrorism.'[24]

This was to be the start of a curious pattern in the way that, towards the end of each decade of the Cold War, the West went through a crisis of morale, fearing that it was losing the great struggle. In spite of the formation of the Nato alliance and the steady success of the Marshall Plan in Europe, the loss of China cast a pall over the late 1940s. A decade later, the Soviet technological success with the launch of the first 'Sputnik' earth satellite led to accusations of a 'missile gap'. In the late 1960s, the combination of military setbacks in Vietnam and riots in the USA and across Western Europe and in Japan seemed to portend another going down of the West. And in the late 1970s, defeat in Vietnam combined with economic stagnation, US embarrassment in Iran and the Soviet invasion of Afghanistan to suggest yet another mood of imminent Western defeat.

In such moods, when the cry turns quickly from 'the nation in danger' to 'we are betrayed', democracies can react in uncharacteristic and terrible ways. The moral case for the cause of the West in its ideological crusade had been put simply and eloquently in the Truman Doctrine. He had talked of two worlds, one free, and the other living in fear of the boot through the door in the early hours of the morning. There were tragic times in the West when democratic governments sullied Truman's decent claim by acting in similar, unsavoury ways. The crisis of morale over the loss of China was to be one of the worst such times. It had begun earlier, with the entirely justified fears of spying. Soviet agents were indeed trying to find what they could of the Manhattan Project, and the West's atom-bomb secrets. It would have been extraordinary if they had not. But this was not a simple case of great powers spying upon one another, as they always had. The ideology of Communism, and the West's counter-ideology of freedom, each claimed to supersede the calls of national loyalty among the adherents.

The great difference was that at least in the 1940s, when it still enjoyed the nuclear monopoly, the West had more to conceal, and above all, the Soviets had started to recruit their intelligence networks much earlier. Understanding well how the West worked, the Communist spymasters exerted their greatest efforts, and were to achieve their greatest success, at the great and traditional universities of Oxford and Cambridge in the 1930s. With considerable forethought, the recruiters perceived that clever and ambitious and radical young undergraduates, if caught early, could be made to serve throughout the glittering and influential careers for which Oxford and Cambridge trained their élite youth.

The Cambridge group, based around an intellectual club named 'the Apostles', produced at least four important Soviet spies. They were Kim Philby, who was the official British liaison officer with US intelligence in Washington as the Cold War intensified, and rose to be deputy head of MI6, the British intelligence arm; Donald Maclean, who served in the Foreign Office, and photocopied top secret documents for Moscow from at least 1938, and was chief aide to the post-war British Ambassador in Washington, Lord Inverchapel; Guy Burgess, the flamboyant homosexual who escaped to Russia with Maclean in 1951; and Anthony Blunt, who served in MI6 in the war, and later became the curator of the royal art collection. The attractions of Oxford and Cambridge for young Americans in the 1930s brought an American connection to this network. Michael Straight, later editor of the *New Republic* magazine, finally confessed his participation in 1963, in the course of the FBI security check required when President Kennedy asked him to run a federal agency to encourage the arts. There was also a similar and parallel Oxford group, whose work has just begun to emerge from the Soviet archives.[25]

It is clear that Maclean and Philby helped Soviet intelligence in its efforts to penetrate US nuclear secrets, and the discovery of their work cast a long shadow over the intimacy and trust between the British and American intelligence operations which had been forged in the war against Hitler, and continued throughout the Cold War. But the use of Americans as Soviet agents, whether in the nuclear field or the more mundane spheres of the economy and general diplomacy, gave the American spy mania of the 1940s a hysterical and deeply politicised character.

On 3 August 1948, with the Berlin airlift under way and Chiang Kai-shek's armies reeling back to southern China, the House Committee on Un-American Activities called a *Time*-magazine editor, Whittaker Chambers, to testify under subpoena. Chambers said that he had been a Communist from 1924 until 1937, and in the course of his underground work had met a series of American officials. They had since risen to senior positions, and he could identify them as Communist agents or resources. Among others, Chambers named Harry Dexter White, who had become assistant secretary at the US Treasury, and Alger Hiss, a State Department official. Hiss had attended the Yalta conference as an aide, had helped organise the conferences at

Dumbarton Oaks, and been the secretary-general of the founding sessions of the United Nations at San Francisco.

'So strong is the hold which the insidious evil of Communism secures upon its disciples,' Chambers told the hushed Congressmen, as he described the moment he decided to leave the party, 'that I could still say to someone at that time "I know I am leaving the winning side for the losing side, but it is better to die on the losing side than to live under Communism." '[26]

The confrontation between these two Americans, Chambers from the Communist underground and *Time* magazine, and Alger Hiss of Harvard Law School and the State Department, dramatised the issues of the Cold War for the American public in an extraordinary way. The charges and countercharges went on for years, as Hiss denied the accusations but then acknowledged that he might have met Chambers, sued him for libel and lost the case. Hiss was then tried and imprisoned for perjury, still protesting his innocence of treason, while Chambers produced ancient papers typed on Hiss's typewriter from a hiding place in a pumpkin on his farm. The prolonged Hiss–Chambers affair popularised and Americanised the ideological issues behind the Cold War, and licensed unscrupulous politicians to launch Red witch-hunts throughout American society.

The Cold War entered the popular culture. Take Hollywood's classic movie of the Red Menace, *I was a Communist for the FBI*. It was made in 1951, based on the true story of Matt Cvetic, who had infiltrated the Communist Party in Pittsburgh. The film poster said it all, our hero pointing as his girlfriend is beaten up and kidnapped in an alley by his party comrades: 'I had to sell out my own girl – so would you.' It won an Oscar nomination for best documentary.[27]

Look magazine ran a cover story, 'Could the Reds Seize Detroit?' The Catechitical Guild Educational Society, a religious group based in Minnesota, printed and distributed four million copies of a comic titled *Is This Tomorrow? – America under Communism*. The Bowman Gum Company, famous for its baseball cards, brought out a new set of cards to go with its chewing-gum in 1951. Called 'Children's Crusade against Communism', its slogan was 'Fight the Red Menace'. Card 35 showed police bursting into an apartment. The text read:[28]

> Why is this Russian family being arrested? Perhaps the radio is a clue. These people may have been listening to the Voice of America. The Voice, you know, is a radio program in which our State Department tells the truth about the free world. The Red leaders do not want the Russian people to learn what real freedom is like. They might ask it for themselves. But who reported that this family tuned in on the

> Voice? Perhaps someone they thought was a friend. Who can tell who may be a spy for the secret police?

The politician whose name became most linked with the witch-hunts for Communists was Senator Joe McCarthy, who claimed to have lists of varying numbers of Communists in the State Department, in the Pentagon, in the army and other institutions of the state. His drinking habits, and the increasing wildness of his accusations, served to discredit him when leading figures who had too long been silent, like General Marshall and President Eisenhower, finally stood up to his bullying and slanderous tactics. But the Congressman who really began the process, cultivated Whittaker Chambers as a witness and led the prosecution of Alger Hiss, was the one leading politician in the West who can claim to have been in at the birth and death of the Cold War.

Richard Nixon had served in the US Navy during the war, and returned to his native state of California to run for Congress. 'The Hiss case brought me national fame,' Nixon later wrote.[29]

> I received considerable credit for spearheading the investigation which led to Hiss's conviction. Two years later I was elected to the US Senate and two years after that General Eisenhower introduced me as his running mate to the Republican national convention as 'a man who has a special talent and an ability to ferret out any kind of subversive influence wherever it may be found, and the strength and persistence to get rid of it'.

Nixon, and Senator Joe McCarthy after him, and with J. Edgar Hoover's FBI as their tool, unleashed a kind of intellectual and political civil war in the West. Some Republicans tried to make this a party matter. Congresswoman Clare Booth Luce charged that the Communist Party 'has gone underground, after the fashion of termites, into the Democratic Party'. But the Democrats were too cautious to permit this cleavage to take place along party lines. President Truman appointed the first commission to review the loyalty of civil servants. And it was the Democratic Attorney-General, Tom Clark, who told the Cathedral Club of Brooklyn on 15 January 1948: 'Those who do not believe in the ideology of the United States, shall not be allowed to stay in the United States.'[30]

By comparison with Stalin's Gulag, this was a soft repression, but it cannot have felt that way to Hollywood screenwriters and university academics and diplomats whose careers and livelihoods were deliberately disrupted. And the vicious effect of the febrile anti-Communism was publicly and resolutely challenged. The radical journalist I. F.

Stone was in the forefront of these American dissidents for civil liberties. 'In our milder fashion, we are continuing the practice of the "purge",' he observed. 'Though so far only Communists have gone to jail, thousands of others have been reduced to second-class citizenship, defamed, "exiled" internally (as in Russia), deprived of reputation and livelihood, held up to public contumely. This was Stalin's way with the opposition, and it is now ours.'[31]

Stone wrote those words in 1956, in the month that the ironic but effective charge of income-tax evasion was brought against the Communist Party, and the offices of the *Daily Worker* were padlocked. It was eight years after the denunciation of Alger Hiss. The anti-Communist hysteria was prolonged. The Hiss trial for perjury did not end until 1950, when the Red Spy scare revived with the arrest of Julius and Ethel Rosenberg, on charges of masterminding the Soviet espionage network into America's atom-bomb secrets.

The main evidence was the testimony of Ethel's brother, David Greenglass, a spy so amateur that he claimed to have stolen uranium from Los Alamos by putting it in his pocket. Their trial and appeals process was also long drawn-out, and they were finally executed in the electric chair on 19 June 1953. The American mood of the week in which Judge Irving Kaufman passed the first espionage death sentence upon American civilians in peacetime may be recaptured by the front-page headlines of the *New York Times* for 28 March 1951:[32]

ACHESON EXHORTS AMERICANS TO MEET SOVIET PERIL NOW

US POWER MUST 'FRIGHTEN' ENEMY, WILSON ASSERTS

DANGER OF ATOM BOMB ATTACK IS GREATEST IN PERIOD UP TO THIS FALL, EXPERT ASSERTS

RED CHINA REJECTS MACARTHUR'S OFFER

FERRER DENIES HE IS RED

The point that Stone missed, but which was central to Congressman Nixon's design (and he was Vice-President when the Rosenbergs were executed), was not simply to root out and crush the Communists. It was also to intimidate their potential sympathisers among the liberals. As Nixon concluded:[33]

> Hiss was clearly the symbol of a considerable number of perfectly loyal citizens whose theaters of operation are the nation's mass media and universities, its scholarly foundations, and its government bureaucracies. They are of a mind-set, as doctrinaire as those on the extreme right,

> which makes them singularly vulnerable to the Communist popular front appeal under the banner of social justice. In the time of the Hiss case they were 'patsies' for the Communist line.

These arguments carried more force with each year, from the defection of Igor Gouzenko of the Soviet Embassy in Canada in 1945, with the first evidence of atom bomb espionage, to Churchill's Iron Curtain speech the following year. In 1947, the Truman Doctrine and Marshall Plan were predicated on the existence of a death struggle between freedom and Communism, and in 1948, the Hiss case suggested that Nixon and Chambers were right, that Communist moles had indeed burrowed deep inside the American bureaucracy. In 1949 came the final collapse of Chiang Kai-shek and the Communist victory in China, and the detonation of the first Soviet atom bomb. And the following year, the divided land of Korea saw dramatic new evidence that the West's defences might not hold, that the bounds of containment could fall to armed invasion.

Nixon's sneer at 'patsies' had a particular target, the Secretary of State, Dean Acheson, who declared that whatever the House Un-American Activities Committee might say, he 'would not turn [his] back on Alger Hiss'. For Acheson, this was the code of a gentleman; for Nixon, the mark of the patsy, soft on Communism. Nixon could hardly have been more wrong. As Hiss was being convicted, the Policy Planning group at the State Department were preparing, on Acheson's orders, the blueprint for the rearming of America and the conduct of the Cold War. NSC-68, as it was known from its National Security Council classification, was the considered response of the Truman Administration to the new threat which followed the fall of China: 'Soviet efforts are now directed toward the domination of the Eurasian landmass.'[34]

NSC-68 began with the familiar theme: 'What makes the continuing crisis, is the polarisation which inescapably confronts the slave society with the free . . . the US must lead in building a successfully functioning political and economic system in the free world.' The novelty of the document lay in the cost estimates of this global effort, raising the US defence budget from its current level of $13.5 billion a year towards $50 billion. The first drafter, Paul Nitze, had consulted with Professor Leon Keyserling of the President's Board of Economic Advisers, to establish that on Keynesian principles of deficit spending, the US could afford it, and perhaps even benefit from the flood of state-directed investment. NSC-68 was clear: 'Foreign economic policy is a major instrument in the conduct of US foreign relations [and] . . . peculiarly appropriate to the Cold War.'[35]

The original plan was to publish the document in order to rally American and Western opinion. Acheson preferred to keep it top secret, and to use it 'to so bludgeon the mind of top government that not only could the President make a decision but that the decision could be carried out'. Kennan loathed the document, which he saw as crude and mechanistic, and taking the precise lineaments of his own 'containment' theory too far. But NSC-68 pointed out that the problem of containment was that it required superior military strength, and now that the Soviet Union had the atom bomb, the US could no longer afford to bluff its way through with the bomb alone. Massive conventional rearmament was required, since: 'The Republic and its citizens, in the ascendancy of their strength, stand in their deepest peril.'

NSC-68 was certainly aggressive, and in the spring and early summer, as it circulated around Washington it was seen as outlandishly expensive. In spite of the support of Pentagon, State Department, CIA and the White House staff, NSC-68 did not entirely convince President Truman. Indeed, on 1 June, he told a press conference that the world was 'closer to real peace than at any time in the last five years'.[36]

Thus three weeks later, the invasion of South Korea on 24 June came as a complete surprise to Washington, even though a CIA report of 10 March had predicted an invasion in June.[37] On 20 June, Dean Rusk, who ran the Far Eastern desk at the State Department, had told Congress that he saw 'no evidence of war brewing'. And had there been, all the public pronouncements of US officials agreed that they would not fight it in Korea. Most US and Soviet troops had been withdrawn, and spasmodic skirmishes between North and South Korean troops had become normal enough to be treated with equanimity. In March 1949, General MacArthur said that the line of US defence in the Pacific 'starts from the Philippines and continues through the Ryukyu archipelago, which includes its main bastion, Okinawa. Then it bends back through Japan.' On 12 January 1950, in a speech to the National Press Club in Washington, Acheson repeated this geographic formula, which carefully excluded the island of Formosa, the new base of Chiang Kai-shek's exiled government, as well as Korea.[38]

More to the point, at that press conference Acheson made a thoughtful and ultimately prophetic argument that Soviet designs on Manchuria and Sinkiang, and the virtual annexation of Mongolia, would eventually offend Chinese nationalism. 'Those who proclaim their loyalty to Moscow proclaim loyalty to an enemy of China,' he noted. Either suggestion, that Korea was not inside the American defence perimeter, or that the United States was waiting for an inevitable Sino-Soviet split, might have helped provoke the North Korean invasion. It may also have given Chiang Kai-shek and Syngman Rhee, the South Korean leader who had just suffered a severe setback in his country's election on 30 May, a motive to force the issue and demand US support. The American press noted that after the election, Rhee's regime, which had made repeated threats of invading the North, 'was left tottering by lack of confidence, both in Korea and abroad'.[39]

At a swiftly convened council of war, Truman and his advisers agreed (without consulting their allies) to use US air power against the invading North Korean tanks, and for the first time to give physical protection to Formosa by sending the Seventh Fleet to steam between the island and mainland China. This was not done without trepidation. A Chinese invasion by hordes of wooden junks was expected, and the Seventh Fleet discovered on their first exercise that junks were very hard to sink. 'We didn't have enough shells to fire a single round at each junk,' reported Dean Rusk. None the less, Rusk argued at the war council on 27 June that 'a South Korea absorbed by the Communists would be a dagger pointed at the heart of Japan'.[40]

Truman had one crucial and accidental asset. The Soviet delegates were boycotting the United Nations because the Chiang Kai-shek government still occupied the Chinese seat on the Security Council. Moscow insisted that the seat should go to Mao's government. In spite of Foreign Minister Gromyko's advice, Stalin refused to send back the Soviet delegation to veto any UN action and voice Gromyko's view that: 'The puppet government of South Korea was being egged on by the USA to start war on North Korea.'[41] In the absence of the Soviet veto, and with only Yugoslavia opposed, and Egypt and India abstaining, the UN voted to support South Korea against aggression. Even though there is no doubt that US troops would have fought anyway, they were able to do so under the UN flag. This was something between a fig-leaf and a fiction. General MacArthur later informed the US Senate: 'I had no direct connection with the UN whatsoever.'[42]

There was a grain of truth in Gromyko's argument, but the invasion, and thus the act of aggression, came from the North. Still, there was little sign that the South was prepared or willing to fight for Syngman Rhee's regime. The American troops were willing, but woefully under-equipped. The pace of demobilisation since 1945 had left MacArthur's infantry divisions lacking 62 per cent of their fire-power, and 80 per cent of their sixty-day supply of ammunition was found to be unusable.[43] Within weeks, the US and the remnant of the South Korean forces were driven back and besieged in a small perimeter around the port of Pusan. The demobilisation since 1945 meant that the US had only limited ground forces, and the Pentagon immediately warned against transferring troops from Europe, since the attack on Korea could be a deliberate diversion. But in September, in a daring and amphibious flank attack at Inchon, close to the old border on the 38th parallel, General MacArthur retrieved the situation. His attack used the US Marines, one of the few fully trained and equipped divisions immediately available. Their swift occupation of the capital Seoul, far to the rear of the North Koreans, sent the invaders fleeing back in rout. MacArthur chased them over the border, and all the way up through North Korea to the Chinese frontier on the Yalu River.

What happened next might have been expected. The Chinese had issued enough warnings. 'Crisis, like a volcano, is menacing American imperialism,' Mao had declared at the height of the civil war. 'This situation forced American imperialists to establish a plan for enslaving the world: to plunge like wild beasts into Europe, Asia and other places, muster the reactionary forces of various countries – those dregs spat out by the people – to organise the imperialist, anti-democratic front against all forces headed by the Soviet Union, and prepare war.'[44]

Cables from the Chinese leadership to Stalin in October 1950, recently released from Chinese archives, suggest that Mao's motive in entering the war was essentially defensive. On 2 October Mao cabled: 'If we allow the US to occupy all of Korea, Korean revolutionary power will suffer a fundamental defeat, and the American invaders will run more rampant, and have negative effects for the entire Far East . . . We must be prepared for the US to declare and enter a state of war with China. We must be prepared that the US may, at a minimum, use its Air Force to bomb major cities and use its Navy to assault the coastal regions.' Mao went on to argue that without a swift victory by the Chinese forces in Korea, leading to a diplomatic settlement, the fate of the Chinese revolution itself was at risk. Such a war, Mao told Stalin, 'would arouse dissatisfaction towards us among the national bourgeoisie and other segments of the people. They are very afraid of war.'

Mao's cable went on to make clear that the Chinese attack depended on the expectation of Soviet help. After the first attacks upon American and South Korean troops inside North Korea 'north of the 38th parallel, they will await the arrival of Soviet weapons'. Although the documentary evidence remains fragmentary, this almost certainly included Soviet air support. Mao's cable says that the attack was planned for 15 October, but Stalin's refusal to deliver the promised military support led Mao to delay the invasion. On 13 October, a second cable from Mao to prime minister Zhou Enlai, then in Moscow to press Stalin for support, said that the Chinese Politburo had unanimously agreed to go ahead with the invasion anyway, and again cited the domestic threat inside China: 'If we do not send troops, allowing the enemy to press to the Yalu border and the arrogance of the reactionaries at home and abroad to grow, this will be disadvantageous to all sides.'

Between those two cables, two US warplanes strafed the Soviet air base at Sukhaya Ryechka, near Vladivostok, sixty miles from the North Korean border, in a surprise attack on 8 October. Eleven days later, ironically the very day Chinese troops began to cross the Yalu into North Korea, the US offered an apology for a navigation error. One of the Soviets who took cover from that raid was General Georgi Lobov, commander of the 303rd air division, who had been transferred in August from the air defence of Moscow to the Siberian front. In 1992, General Lobov for the first time published his own recollection of the strictly limited air war which Stalin authorised him to fight after 1 November 1950. His initial force of 32 MiG-15 jets, later increased to 150, were painted in Chinese colours, the pilots issued with Chinese uniforms and identification papers, and based at the Chinese military airfield of Antung, on the Yalu River. They were not allowed to operate within sixty miles of the battlefront, nor to fly over the sea, and their main role was to defend the Yalu River crossings from American attack. The MiGs came as a sharp surprise to the US and allied aircraft, establishing local air superiority until the US F-86 Sabre jet evened the balance. Some 200 Soviet pilots died in this limited air war, which lasted into 1952, and Lobov claimed that his MiGs shot down at least 1,300 American planes.

Although known to the US Air Force and the US authorities in Washington, the limited Soviet intervention was deliberately kept from the public. Paul Nitze, at the State Department's Policy Planning Staff, prepared a memorandum entitled 'Removing the Fig Leaf from the Hard Core of Soviet Responsibility', but a decision was taken not to release it. 'The argument was that if we publicised the facts, the public would expect us to do something about it, and the last thing we wanted was for the war to spread to a more serious confrontation with the Soviets,' Nitze explained in 1992, when the historian Jon Halliday unearthed this intriguing sub-plot of the Cold War.

China sent diplomatic warnings through India that an invasion of North Korea, or a move to the Yalu, would provoke its intervention. The first Chinese prisoners were taken in October, a full month before the full weight of the Chinese Army intervened to throw the UN forces back far below the 38th parallel. The US troops, and their British and Australian allies (fighting as a Commonwealth division), the Turkish troops and various other national contingents who had rallied to the UN cause, were badly mauled in that terrible winter.

The situation was so desperate that President Truman incautiously suggested to a press conference that the atom bomb might have to be used. This sent Prime Minister Attlee flying across from Britain to seek assurance that the United States would not go nuclear without at least consulting its allies. Truman blithely agreed to do so, until Dean Acheson discreetly reminded him that this would be illegal under US law. An emollient form of words was found which implied, but did not promise, consultation. The military situation was not, in the event, quite so desperate. Finally the UN forces regrouped and with their air power clawed their way back to the original border on the 38th parallel, and established a long and costly stalemate that was to last for another two years, before a truce was signed and the division of the two Koreas became as fixed a symbol as the two Germanies of the world's Cold War partition.[45]

But the real balance of forces around the world had been transformed, far from the battlefield. 'Korea saved us,' Acheson later observed. Without the war, the costly plans of NSC-68 would have faced an arduous uphill campaign. The first defence budget presented by President Truman after the war began was for $50 billion, the precise figure Acheson had hoped for. The US Army doubled, to over three million men. The number of Air Groups doubled to ninety-five, and were deployed to new bases in Britain, Libya, Morocco and Saudi Arabia. Everything changed with Korea. American diplomacy, defence budgets and military reach exploded across the globe in the aftermath of the invasion, as US taxpayers and Congress alike gave the unstinted political support the strategic planners had hitherto sought with only limited success.

The new American activism unlocked a series of diplomatic doors. After months of patient cajoling of the French to accept German economic support in the new Nato, Acheson met the French and British foreign ministers at the Waldorf Hotel in New York and dropped his new bombshell. As the Marines stormed ashore at Inchon, Acheson announced that the US now wanted full-scale German rearmament within Nato, and was prepared to station permanently in Europe four US Army divisions.[46]

Even though a furious row ensued at the Waldorf, as Britain and France and the smaller European allies grasped the enormity of the transformation this implied for America's concept of Germany and for Germany's role in Europe, the French found it difficult to refuse. The month after the Korean War broke out, the Americans decided that the whole of Asia was at risk. Not only had the US sent the Seventh Fleet to guard Formosa, it also agreed for the first time to send a US military mission to support the French in Vietnam. Hitherto, there had been US aid for France, which was understood to be available for use in Vietnam. But now the US commitment to an essentially colonial war had become explicit, against a Vietnamese resistance whose founding document quoted the American Declaration of Independence.[47]

The good fortune of the Soviet walk-out from the UN could never be repeated, so Acheson pushed through a brisk procedural reform of that body which was designed to get around any future Soviet veto. Called 'Uniting for Peace', it gave the General Assembly the right to propose collective security measures, including the use of force, if a Security Council veto blocked urgent action: a cunning ploy when the US dominated the General Assembly, with loyal Latin American votes, but risky in the years after colonial independence during which the General Assembly was flooded with new and independent states.[48]

At the same time, the Korean War transformed the role, the status and the economy of Japan. The classic example is the extraordinary change in the fortunes of Shotaro Kamiya, president of the fledgeling Toyota company. He arrived in the USA on the day the Korean War broke out, desperate to reach a licensing deal with Ford and save his struggling company, then selling barely three hundred trucks a month. He failed; Ford were not interested. When he arrived disconsolately back in Japan, he found it already bustling as the base for the exploding American war effort. Kamiya was greeted by a flood of urgent orders from the Pentagon for 1,500 trucks a month. The profits from the trucks financed Toyota's expansion into passenger cars. After the Korean War, Toyota never looked back.[49]

The Japanese boom was financed by the United States, through a war-emergency system known as Special Procurements. Almost unnoticed at the time, this system pumped $3.5 billion into Japan, which with other US funds meant that Japan received as much as the Marshall

Plan had invested in the West German economy. The Special Procurements were a way for the armed forces to buy supplies locally, without going through the complex purchasing and tender system which the Pentagon was required to follow back in the USA. In 1950, for the first six months of the war, they amounted to $149 million. In 1951, Special Procurements in Japan grew to $592 million. They peaked in 1953 at $809 million, and were still $557 million as late as 1955.[50]

A modern army has a vast hunger for all kinds of supplies, from processed foods to clothing, from oils and lubricants to medical syringes and beer, from paints to disinfectants, bootlaces to matches. Japan supplied them all. The American money went to companies like Toyota for its trucks, to the textile trade for winter clothing, sleeping bags and hospital sheets, and to the health industries for everything from bandages to pharmaceuticals. The investment poured into the muscles of future growth like oil-refining facilities, and to revive the Japanese shipyards. Cargo ships were scarce, and so the United States, which had in 1946 planned to strip the Japanese shipbuilding industry for war reparations, reversed its policy and plunged its Aid Counterpart Funds into new shipbuilding facilities. By 1956, Japan had the most modern shipyards in the world, was launching 26 per cent of the world's shipping, and seizing a lead it was to maintain for a generation.[51]

This change in America's economic policy towards Japan was matched by political shifts. The civil liberties which MacArthur had been keen to introduce in 1945–6 were curtailed with the war. In the month of North Korea's invasion, MacArthur's office ordered the dismissal of seventy Communist Party 'members and sympathisers' from the pro-Communist newspaper *Akahata*. Shortly afterwards, with the US troops reeling back on Pusan, *Akahata* was banned indefinitely, and another 700 Communist sympathisers were purged from the Japanese press. The following year, all the 351 Japanese journalists who had been dismissed in 1945–6 as too sympathetic to the militarist regime of wartime Japan, were reinstated.[52]

Whatever resentments these measures may have inspired were eased by the flood of prosperity. Japan's manufacturing output leapt by almost 50 per cent between March 1950, before the war broke out, and March of the following year. By 1952, Japanese economists estimated that at last living standards had returned to their pre-war levels.[53] And the boom continued. By 1953, manufacturing output was more than twice the level of 1949, with the US war-related funds continuing to pour in to the point where the Japanese recovery became self-sustaining. This was not private investment. Between 1950 and 1966, a meagre total of some $300 million in foreign private investment came into Japan, less than 9 per cent of the sums that Special Procurements alone pumped into the Japanese economy between 1950 and 1955. And all thanks to the American taxpayer.[54]

Not only did the Pentagon, acting on the immediate strategic priorities of the Korean War, finance the boom which was to create America's most formidable trade competitor; the US military authorities re-created the management mechanisms which steered Japan to greater success. Once the Korean invasion began, there was no more talk of closing or breaking up the zaibatsu. These vast industrial trusts, institutionally committed to a religion of strategic investments for long-term growth, were positively encouraged. The beneficiaries were the three great pre-war zaibatsu: Mitsui (which includes Toyota and Toshiba and Mitsukoshi department stores); Mitsubishi (which includes Nikon, Kirin Beer, Meiji Life and NYK Shipping); and Sumitomo (which includes NEC electronics).[55]

Moreover, they flourished with the help of American management and production experts who were flown to Japan to teach the most advanced methods of assembly-line and productivity techniques.[56] The best-known of these American experts, W. Edwards Deming, the intellectual father of quality control, is revered in Japan to this day, where companies compete for the annual Deming Medal.[57] Since the commercial opportunities of the Korean crisis were obvious to the Japanese political leaders, they were from the beginning quite explicit about the relationship they perceived between their prosperity and their security status under the US occupation.

Prime Minister Shigeri Yoshida, writing in the late autumn of 1950, with the war under way but before the Chinese counter-attack, spelt out the bargain in *Foreign Affairs*, the house magazine of the American foreign-policy establishment:[58]

> The UN relief and rehabilitation program will eventually call for quantities of building materials, rolling stock and machinery, besides clothing and all manner of miscellaneous articles. And we are right on the spot to supply them. But in order that Japan may become a real workshop of East Asia and contribute abundantly to its progress and prosperity, she must have a peace treaty. It is essential that we be guaranteed an equitable and equal treatment in international commerce, the rights of travel and residence, and full freedom of trade and shipping in this and other quarters of the globe. Such conditions of commerce and navigation can be realised only after the conclusion of peace and Japan's restoration as a free and independent member of the society of nations.

Accordingly, the Japanese peace treaty was concluded in September 1951 by the Republican Senator (later to be Eisenhower's Secretary of State) John Foster Dulles. It returned full sovereignty to Japan's home islands, while granting the US control over the Ryukyu chain, and the main US base of Okinawa. The US also had the right to keep military bases in Japan. Since the country was now more a strategic asset than a defeated foe, the US evidently regretted Article IX, the non-belligerency clause in the Japanese constitution. In 1953, Vice-President Richard Nixon was to describe it as 'an honest mistake'.[59] The clause was popular in Japan, and released government revenues for more productive purposes, but the Japanese Self-Defence Force grew anyway, to 130,000 men by 1954, with a naval arm in 1952, and an air force in 1954.[60]

Japan's prosperity had itself become important to US security, as Dulles explained in discussion meetings of the Council of Foreign Relations while the treaty was being drafted. Since the United States did not want Japan to revive its traditional trading links with now-Communist China, Dulles explained, it was important that those parts of Asia which were not Communist, which included South Korea, South-East Asia, and the countries now known as the Pacific Rim, should remain so. Japan would need access to their raw materials, and their markets.[61] A parallel case was made by Joseph Dodge, the American banker brought to Japan by General MacArthur, in his report *US–Japan Economic Relations in the Post-Treaty Period*. This spoke of 'substantial reliance on Japan . . . for production of goods and services important to the security of the US and the economic stability of non-Communist Asia; cooperation with the US in the development of raw materials resources of Asia; development of Japan's appropriate military forces as a defensive shield and to permit the redeployment of US forces'.[62]

The irony of this was apparently lost upon Dodge and Dulles. America's war in the Pacific had been fought against Japan's 'Greater East Asian Co-Prosperity Sphere'. And now, just five years after winning that war, it had become US policy to help re-establish that sphere. The logic of the Cold War led the USA directly to the deliberate resurrection of Japanese economic power. Once again, the image of the Cold War as tennis match is compelling. America reacted to the 'loss' of China by beginning its reconstruction of Japan. That in turn may have helped inspire the North Korean invasion. And the rhythm of volley and counter-volley went grimly on; the Korean War not only intensified the American resolve to build up Japan, and South Korea and Formosa, as strategic assets, but also inspired the United States to build up West Germany on the far side of the world.

The perilous implications of the Cold War had reconciled France and Britain to the economic revival of West Germany. But they were aghast at Acheson's announcement at the Waldorf Hotel that the post-Korean threat now required German rearmament. France had spent five years under German occupation; Britain had been bombed, blitzed, and impoverished by the exertions of the war against Hitler. Now the Germans were to be not only re-industrialised, but to be restored as a military power. The reaction of the Soviet Union to German rearmament, after its monstrous losses in the Nazi invasion, was inevitably far more strident. It saw American troops and a resurgent Japan on its Siberian front, and once again was faced by German panzer divisions to the west, this time backed up by American industrial might.

The Korean War had not settled very much on the Asian mainland, although the US decision to go to France's support in Vietnam stored up a terrible new harvest for the future. The Korean border remained where it had been, on the 38th parallel. At least 600,000 Koreans died, and close to a million Chinese. Of the United Nations forces, 54,246 Americans died, along with 3,194 of America's allies.[63]

But the Korean War had dramatically sharpened the American purpose, even while giving that purpose a global focus. By going global, the Cold War brought a new intensity, a new Germany, and a new militarisation, back to the heart of Europe. That was not all. For the second time, the US and Soviet Union were learning how to manage the state of crisis between them. The blockade of Berlin had been countered in a way which avoided direct military confrontation. The Korean War, which saw major US casualties and direct clashes between US and Soviet warplanes, was also managed in a way that avoided a wider war. Stalin's limited objective of using the Soviet MiGs to defend the Yalu crossings and sustain the Chinese armies was in effect accepted by the US, and the Korean War ended in an uneasy draw. In Germany, with the Berlin air lift, and in Asia, with the blind eye turned to General Lobov's MiGs, Washington and Moscow alike were learning to operate in a new strategic environment in which the need to prevent a crisis from expanding into full-scale war was more important than any local victory. The Cold War, as a system of international control, was becoming an institution.

Chapter 4

New Leaders and Lost Opportunities

When the horror subsided the floodlights went out
we discovered that we were on a rubbish heap in very strange poses
some with outstretched necks
others with open mouths from which still trickled my native land
still others with fists pressed to eyes
cramped emphatically pathetically taut.

'The Awakening', Zbigniew Herbert

The Cold War had fallen under new management by the time the Korean War armistice was finally signed in July 1953. The three most important governments had been transformed. The first was in Britain, where Winston Churchill's Conservatives won a narrow election victory over Labour and returned to office in October 1951. Four months later, after being embarrassed in the New Hampshire primary election, President Truman decided not to run again for the White House, and General Dwight Eisenhower won the Presidency in November 1952. He did so on an aggressive foreign-policy platform, written by his future Secretary of State John Foster Dulles, which promised not to contain Communism but to confront and to defeat it.

A Republican victory, the party promised, would 'mark the end of the negative, futile and immoral policy of "containment" which abandons countless human beings to a despotism and Godless terrorism which in turn enables the rulers to forge the captives into a weapon for our destruction'. To the alarm of the European allies, Dulles promised a new policy 'to liberate the captive peoples', and to roll back the Soviet and Chinese advance. And while Eisenhower in his election campaign speeches stressed that this liberation would have to be by peaceful means, Dulles pointedly did not.[1]

Six weeks after Eisenhower was sworn in, Joseph Stalin died at his dacha outside Moscow on 5 March, and a period of political uncertainty followed at the Kremlin. The secret police chief Lavrenti Beria was arrested at a Praesidium meeting in June 1953, and Malenkov,

Bulganin, Molotov and Khrushchev organised a loose, collective leadership until Khrushchev used his control of the party machine to consolidate his own supremacy by 1957.

The period of collective leadership introduced a time of extraordinary if tremulous hope. Stalin's death marked an emotional historical moment which gave his successors the opportunity to think and act without his terrifying restraint. Inside the Soviet Union, the writer Ilya Ehrenburg called the period 'the Thaw', in a novel of the same name which condemned Stalin's vaunted 'New Soviet Man' as a self-serving toady.[2] By 1956, Khrushchev had begun opening the gates of Stalin's Gulag, and started a process of *détente* with Yugoslavia, and with the West. The bloody draw in Korea signified not an end to hopes of Soviet and Communist expansion, but an object lesson in the way that even serious conventional conflicts could be kept geographically limited, and prevented from spilling over into the nuclear war which terrified both sides.

The experience of the Korean War offered the possibility of stability, or what Soviet premier Malenkov called 'peaceful coexistence', in a speech to the Supreme Soviet in August 1953, just five months after Stalin's death. Beria had dropped a similar hint even earlier.[3] But this was to be a false stability, at the mercy of events elsewhere. Both sides had reason to believe that, in the long run, their cause must prevail. For the Soviet and the Chinese leaders, the struggle for national liberation from colonial rule in Asia and Africa implied the weakening of Britain and France, and the establishment of friendly new regimes and bridgeheads around a globe which the US Navy and Air Force effectively commanded.

The process of decolonisation, which the Kremlin saw undermining the West from the rear, offered relief from the besetting syndrome of military inferiority which gripped the Soviet leadership. 'I would even say that America was invincible, and the Americans flaunted this fact by sending their planes all over Europe, violating borders and even flying over the territory of the Soviet Union itself,' Khrushchev recalled. 'Right up to his death, Stalin used to tell us, "You'll see, when I'm gone the imperialist powers will wring your necks like chickens."'[4] But as decolonisation gathered pace, there were more and more chickens competing for the West's attentions.

In Iran, the Mossadeq government nationalised Britain's oil holdings in 1951. In Guatemala, the moderately socialist Arbenz government nationalised 400,000 acres of unfarmed banana plantations belonging to the American United Fruit Company in 1952. Arbenz also invited the Communists to join his coalition. In Egypt in the same year, King Farouk's corrupt old regime was shouldered aside in a military coup which eventually brought young Colonel Nasser to power, intent on nationalising the Suez Canal. In Vietnam, the French humiliation at the battle of Dien Bien Phu in 1954 signalled the coming of a new Communist nation.

If the Kremlin hoped that the process of decolonisation would bring them reinforcements and the promise of eventual global victory, the United States and its allies saw their own achievements consolidating healthily in Europe, the heartland of the Cold War. The economic success of the Marshall Plan became plain in Europe even while the Korean War was still being fought. In Western Europe as a whole, industrial production rose by 62 per cent in the two years after the desperately low point of 1947. Such a swift improvement on the previous year's economic figures was reassuring. But the important psycho-logical comparison was with Western Europe's memories of the last years of peace before World War Two. It took until 1951 for Western Europe's food production to increase over that of 1938 by a modest 10 per cent, and industrial production by a far more energetic 43 per cent.[5]

These raw figures of continental growth mask two important developments. The first was that as well as being re-industrialised, Europe was also being rearmed. The European Nato countries increased their spending on defence from $4.4 billion in 1949 to $8 billion in 1951. These were heroic efforts. Britain, for example, increased its defence budget to a straining 18 per cent of GNP in 1951. But they still served to point to the vast disparity in resources between Europe and a USA which had a defence budget of $50 billion in 1951 – six times greater than that of Nato Europe combined.[6]

The second striking feature of the Marshall Plan's contribution to European recovery is the disparity in its impact on various countries. Between 1949 and 1950, West Germany's foreign trade doubled: it rose another 75 per cent the following year. In 1946, the Western zones of Germany had produced 2.5 million tonnes of steel, which soared to 9 million tonnes in 1949, and to 14.5 million tonnes in 1953. The pace of industrial recovery was extraordinary in Germany, dramatic in France, and rather more modest in Britain and Italy.[7]

In France by 1954, industrial production was 50 per cent higher than it had been in the last year before World War Two. The number of tractors on French farms jumped from 25,000 in 1945 to over 100,000 by 1949, the year when France stopped issuing food-rationing coupons. But in Britain, there was far less sign of recovery until September 1949, when the pound was devalued, from $4 to

$2.80 to the pound.[8] The British dollar deficit then began to ease, and to disappear altogether within two years. American Marshall Aid assistance to Britain ended in late 1951, ahead of schedule. But Britain's traditional trading links with its colonies and Dominions had already been eroded by US pressure. At the General Agreement on Tariffs and Trade talks at Geneva, Britain agreed to freeze its system of colonial trading preferences, whose tariffs could henceforth only be reduced, and never raised.[9]

Britain, while by far the strongest military and economic force of the Western European powers, was still locked into the pretensions of not simply great-power status, but of global ambition. A painful decade was to ensue before the Suez débâcle made the country's reduced weight in the world brutally clear. But in the late 1940s and early 1950s, Britain tried to maintain a leadership in Western Europe while simultaneously clinging to the shreds of Empire overseas. Even after the withdrawal from Greece and Palestine and the independence of India, Britain maintained forces around the globe.

In July 1950, when forces had to be found for the Korean War, Britain maintained two infantry divisions and an airborne brigade in the United Kingdom; one infantry and one armoured division in West Germany, with seven more armoured regiments, an artillery regiment and two infantry battalions. There was another infantry brigade in Austria, and two infantry battalions and an anti-tank battalion in Trieste, on the disputed Yugoslav–Italian border. In the Middle East, stretched from Libya through Egypt to the Persian Gulf, there was an infantry division, and three artillery and two armoured regiments. In Malaya, there was a Gurkha division and one infantry and one Commando brigade. And in Hong Kong, there was another infantry division, and an artillery and an armoured regiment. The Royal Air Force maintained 120 squadrons around the globe, and the Royal Navy was still powerful enough to deploy a fleet in the Atlantic, another in the Mediterranean, another in the Indian Ocean, and still send an aircraft-carrier, two cruisers and four escorts to the Korean crisis from the China station.[10]

These were costly forces, betraying commitments beyond Britain's economic strength. And these imperial traditions and post-imperial ambitions inhibited the Labour government from taking the role in Europe which both France and the USA urged upon them. In 1949, as the Marshall Plan worked its magic on the economies and morale of Western Europe, the Americans laid out a vision for the future which was to prove both compelling and defining. The Organisation for European Economic Cooperation, the body which implemented the

Marshall Plan, held a council meeting on 31 October 1949. Paul Hoffman, the president of the Studebaker auto corporation who was the OEEC Administrator, delivered a plan for 'the integration of the European economy'. This was not just an idea, Hoffman insisted, but 'a practical necessity':[11]

> The substance of such integration would be the formation of a single large market within which quantitative restrictions on the movement of goods, monetary barriers to the flow of payments, and eventually all tariffs are permanently swept away. The fact that we have in the US a single market of 150 million consumers has been indispensable to the strength and efficiency of our economy. The creation of a permanent, freely trading area comprising 270 million consumers in Western Europe, would have a multitude of helpful consequences. It would accelerate the development of large-scale, low-cost production industries. It would make the effective use of all resources easier, the stifling of healthy competition more difficult.

Hoffman was spelling out not only the formation of the European Economic Community, but of the target which would not be reached for another four decades, until the EC's maturity in the late 1980s finally brought forth the strategic goal of the European 'single market' by 1992. The main obstacle to Hoffman's ideas was Britain. Knowing of the American support for the idea of an integrated Europe, Bevin wrote to Acheson just before the OEEC conference that while Britain would do everything possible to support the principle, in practice all concerned 'must have regard to the position of the United Kingdom as a power with world-wide responsibilities, as a leading member of the British Commonwealth and sterling area'.[12]

The irony was rich. A large part of the logic to the spread of the British Empire through the Mediterranean and the Suez Canal and the Persian Gulf, around the African shoreline to the Cape of Good Hope, into islands in the Atlantic and Indian Oceans, was to safeguard the sea routes to India, the jewel in the imperial crown. The need for coaling stations as the Royal Navy shifted to steam power reinforced this logic with logistics. Once India became independent in 1947, the strategic case for much of the rest of the Empire began to crumble, and the hard self-interest of commercial calculation came more strongly into play.

Britain's reoccupation of Hong Kong and its hopes of trade with China led her swiftly to recognise Mao's Communist government, even though the United States refused to do so. Britain's dependence on imported oil dictated an aggressive role to secure that oil in Iran and the Middle East, and a pro-Arab tilt to British policies in Palestine which infuriated the American allies. Britain's determination to cling to privileged access to the tin and rubber of Malaya involved its troops in a prolonged and unusually successful guerrilla war. The mineral wealth of South Africa and the copper of Northern Rhodesia reinforced the ties of sentiment, of military alliance and imperial nostalgia.

The British self-interest involved was draped in the concept of the Commonwealth, which had been given legal force by the Statute of Westminster of 1931. This brought together Canada, Australia, New Zealand, South Africa and Ireland as equal and sovereign nations in a free association 'united by a common allegiance to the Crown'. In 1932, under the impact of the Great Depression, this airy concept was given economic force by establishing a system of tariffs, the Commonwealth Preferences. As a way of maintaining the economic advantages of Empire without the political embarrassments, it proved effective and resilient enough to absorb the wave of decolonisation of the 1950s and 1960s. The system finally perished in the 1970s, after Britain joined the EEC.

But the global alternative, which the Commonwealth embodied, prevented Britain from joining wholeheartedly into the cause of European integration which Paul Hoffman had defined, and on which France was to seize. The seduction of the Commonwealth was enduring, lasting far beyond the humiliation of Suez 1956. The Labour Party leader Hugh Gaitskell, influenced by his brother Arthur – who had served in the Sudan civil service – and by socialist leaders in Commonwealth countries like Singapore's Lee Kuan Yew, fought bitterly against joining the EEC at the Labour conference of 1962. It would mean, said Gaitskell, 'selling the Commonwealth down the river . . . the end of a thousand years of history'.[13]

What Britain rejected, France embraced. France adopted the European idea even though her imperial ties and commitments were at the time just as strong as those of Britain, and with a colonial war raging in Indo-China and another about to erupt in North Africa, much more burdensome.[14] The Americans perceived this early, and Dean Acheson was to play off the French and British and also the Germans against one another with considerable skill. 'France and France alone could take the decisive leadership into integrating Western Germany into Western Europe,' Acheson cabled to his lieutenant, assistant Secretary of State, George Perkins, as the Americans prepared for the OEEC meeting.[15] The British may have temporarily prided themselves on a special relationship with the Americans leading to special treatment. The price Britain paid was to exclude themselves from the economic dynamism which European integration entailed, locking them into a pattern of relative economic decline which steadily reduced their value to their American partner.

Just before that OEEC conference at which Hoffman delivered his call for an integrated Europe, America's Ambassadors to the various European countries met in Paris on 21 October. They had to grapple with the emerging reality of alliance politics: that in Britain, France and Germany there were three distinct policies on the future of Europe and the American role within it. The US Ambassadors, including Averell Harriman as Marshall Plan administrator, Chuck Bohlen from the Paris Embassy and George Kennan who intervened by cable from Washington, had all been of similar mind in the simplest stage of the Cold War. It was easy to agree on containment of the Soviet Union; it was far more difficult to agree on the kind of Western Europe best suited to help contain it.[16]

Acheson, backed up by the Pentagon, which saw Britain as strategically indispensable, was prepared to appease Britain's desire to have the financial privileges of European integration without surrendering a scrap of sovereignty or its global role. Kennan blamed matters on the French 'neurosis' about Germany. Bohlen blamed Britain's 'fiction' that it could still act as both a good European and a global power. The Ambassador to Paris (and later to London) David Bruce, complained that Britain's assumption of a special relationship with America, and of an exclusive position in Europe, could upset the whole Europe-wide purpose of the Marshall Plan. Behind these American arguments about Europe lay a series of anguished political debates within the various European countries. The quixotic flavour of national pride and resentment of American power was illustrated by the vote of the French National Assembly, just before the American Ambassadors gathered, 'to prohibit the import, manufacture and sale of Coca-Cola in France, Algeria and the French Colonial Empire'.

The underlying debate was serious and compelling, and dominated the pages of the leading French newspaper of the day, *Le Monde*. The choice was no longer between joining either the Soviet or the American camp. Only French Communists, and not all of them, accepted the thought of a Soviet sphere of influence. The new options, as French recovery got under way, were more subtle. On the one hand lay the Atlantic Alliance with the rich, generous USA, which carried the disadvantages of being non-European and overly pro-British. On the other hand, there beckoned the prospect of a different course, towards a Europe that was culturally Atlanticist, but politically and strategically neutral between the US and Soviet Union. This would be a Europe well enough armed for its own security, and increasingly prosperous through the integration of the various European economies. The leading French historian of the day, Étienne Gilson, argued as follows:[17]

> That which America is disposed to buy from us with their dollars is our blood, once again, in a third invasion of Western Europe which will make the earlier two of 1914 and 1940 look like pleasure parties. It is too much to pay. We have a right to refuse to sacrifice ourselves for the USA. European neutrality is not inconceivable, so long as it is well-armed.

Gilson's arguments, and the support given them by *Le Monde*'s editor, Hubert Beuve-Méry, aroused furious protests, from the French foreign minister Robert Schuman, and from Beuve-Méry's fellow directors of *Le Monde*. René Courtin, the Resistance leader and law professor, and Christian Funck-Brentano, resigned from the board at the end of 1949, writing in farewell: 'If the USA, disheartened by the way in which we thank them for their aid, abandon Europe and France to misery, despair and Bolshevism, then *Le Monde*, Gilson and you will bear some of the responsibility.'[18]

In Britain, the debate was conducted on different terms. There were few voices supporting an embrace of Europe, but many who saw the Commonwealth not only as an alternative to the American alliance, but also, since that alliance looked economically inevitable, as a moderating influence upon it. Even among America's friends, there was a persistent arrogance about the British approach, embodied in one of Bevin's letters to his prime minister, Clement Attlee: 'Now is the time to build up the strength of the free world, morally, economically and militarily with the US, and at the same time to exert sufficient control over the policy of the well-intentioned but inexperienced colossus on whose co-operation our safety depends.'[19]

From left and right throughout the post-war period, the British tone was aggrieved, and sometimes openly resentful of the dependence upon America. From the Conservative Parliamentary benches, Robert Boothby complained at 'selling the British Empire for a packet of cigarettes'. (The US tobacco lobby had insisted that tobacco exports be included in the Marshall Plan, although they were not requested by the Europeans.) From the left, the later Labour leader Michael Foot complained that Britain had become 'a pensioner of America, a junior partner in an American security system'. And in his resignation speech from the cabinet, complaining at the cuts in the National Health

Service to pay for rearmament, Aneurin Bevan charged: 'We have allowed ourselves to fall too far behind the wheels of American diplomacy.'[20]

In Germany, the political debate assumed an acutely political and nationalist form, between the Christian Democrat leader Konrad Adenauer and Kurt Schumacher, the Social Democrat. For Adenauer, an aged Catholic Rhinelander, German unification was a secondary or even lower priority. Instinctively, he thought in terms of the traditional principalities of Bavaria, Prussia, Silesia and the Rhineland which Bismarck had welded into a single national empire just five years before Adenauer's birth. Germany was almost an upstart presence to Adenauer, who spoke repeatedly of the ancient Holy Roman Empire as if it could be reborn in his own day. His first objective for Germany was the restoration of national sovereignty within the western half of Germany. And as he told Dean Acheson at their first meeting in 1949, that sovereignty would probably have to follow his grander vision of Western European integration.

'His great concern was to integrate Germany completely into Western Europe,' Acheson recalled. 'Indeed, he gave this end priority over the reunification of unhappily divided Germany, and could see why her neighbours might look on it as almost a precondition to reunification.'[21]

By contrast, Schumacher wanted a united Germany, and believed that this could be made acceptable to the Soviets if all foreign troops were withdrawn and Germany became formally neutral. This was not an outlandish proposition; in 1954, just such an agreement was reached over Austria. And as early as November 1949, the Soviet Politburo's Georgi Malenkov had suggested in his formal speech on the anniversary of the 1917 Revolution that the Kremlin would support free elections in a unified Germany so long as it was demilitarised and neutral.[22] But for an avowed neutralist, who had lost an arm and a leg in twelve years in Nazi concentration camps, Schumacher spoke in disturbing tones of a traditional German nationalism. He denounced Adenauer as too pro-Western, 'not the Chancellor of Germany but the Chancellor of the Occupation, of the Allies'.[23]

Schumacher's arguments would have been stronger before the crisis of the Berlin airlift foreclosed any serious prospect of Soviet–Western agreement over Germany. 'Our fundamental attitude is to go ahead with the establishment of a Western government come hell or high water,' Acheson told the State Department press corps in May 1949 as the Berlin blockade ended. Against most expectations, Adenauer won the elections of August 1949, and proceeded with a steady pressure towards his goal of full German sovereignty. And just as Japan was to be transformed by America's new strategic priorities of the Korean War, so Adenauer found his way eased by the war on the far side of the globe.

The week before the invasion of South Korea, the American Proconsul in Germany, John McCloy, rejected Adenauer's appeal for a national police force of 25,000 men. The week after the invasion, McCloy accepted it. In the mood of intense panic in Western Germany, so fearful of imminent Soviet invasion that Adenauer's office appealed to McCloy for 200 pistols to defend themselves against Communist fifth columnists, McCloy cabled Washington a dramatic recommendation for German rearmament.

'If no means are held out for Germany to fight in an emergency, my view is that we should probably lose Germany politically as well as militarily without hope of regain. We should also lose, incidentally, a reserve of manpower which may become of great value in event of a real war,' McCloy wrote.[24]

The American decision to seek German rearmament, with Germany as a member of good standing in the Western alliance, was taken in the wake of the Korean invasion. It was not, and could not be, immediately fulfilled. The alarm of France and Britain saw to that. And as the European allies clambered out of that economic prostration which had left them so few options, Washington had to learn to manage the growing complexities of alliance politics. Three main strands of European policy began to emerge. The Germans were keen on the American alliance as the way to recover full sovereignty, and to make the change from occupied enemy to trusted ally. The British supported the United States with distinctive imperial reservations. And the French grudgingly paid lip-service to American tutelage, at least so long as it bought US support for France's colonial wars, while never abandoning the idea of a European third force between the two superpowers.

Ironically, it was the combination and interplay of these three separate policies which created the conditions that gave birth to the European Common Market in the early 1950s, and allowed that Community to prosper and to flourish under an American military umbrella. The EC began with the Treaty of Paris in 1951 as France, West Germany, Italy, Belgium, the Netherlands and Luxembourg formed the European Coal and Steel Community. This arrangement explicitly surrendered their national sovereignty over the production and use of the two key raw materials of industry. Britain refused to join. The Labour government's new foreign secretary, Herbert Morrison, defended this historic and strategic decision in the most parochial of terms, saying: 'It's no good. We can't do it. The Durham miners won't wear it.'[25] In fact, British thinking was far deeper than Morrison's comment would suggest, and was explained in some detail to the one Frenchman who was universally admired in Whitehall, Jean Monnet. The French architect of Europe, who had during the war worked for both the British and French governments, Monnet had drafted Winston Churchill's dramatic appeal for Franco-British union as Hitler's armies conquered Paris in 1940.[26] Monnet wrote after his London talks in 1950:

> Britain has no confidence that France and the other countries of Europe have the ability or even the will effectively to resist a possible Russian invasion. Britain believes that in this conflict continental Europe will be occupied but that she herself, with America, will be able to resist and finally conquer. She therefore does not wish to let her domestic life or the development of her resources be influenced by any views other than her own, and certainly not by continental views.[27]

By staying out, Britain gave France and Germany the room to create and to dominate what became, with the Treaty of Rome in 1957, the European Common Market. But by staying loyal to the American alliance, the Germans and British gave the Common Market the security and strategic breathing space which allowed it to grow. France wanted a policy independent of America; Britain wanted one independent of Europe; and only Germany squared the circle by cleaving steadfastly to the Atlantic Alliance in strategic affairs, while committing Germany's economic future to the emergent Europe. This German commitment in turn helped give the French the prosperity which later allowed de Gaulle to pursue his own vision of neutralist grandeur. In short, the emergence of the EEC was a compromise resulting from three separate national policies of the three leading European powers. It was, like the original decisions to rebuild the economies of the old German and Japanese enemies, an unplanned but fortuitous outcome.

Successive American governments became resigned to the bickerings among their European allies, and there was one very important reason why they had little choice but to do so. Until the 1960s, with the development of the land-based Minuteman and sea-based Polaris intercontinental ballistic missiles, the US nuclear deterrent was dependent on bombers. And until the B-52 intercontinental began to deploy in large numbers in the 1960s, those bombers were B-47s, with a combat range of 1,700 miles, and veteran B-36s, with a combat range of 3,000 miles. Neither bomber could reach the Soviet heartland from US bases. Even with in-flight refuelling, the Strategic Air Command reckoned in 1952 that it required eighty-two bases overseas to be sure of menacing the Soviet Union.[28] During the 1950s, the US nuclear status was uncomfortably dependent upon the airfields of its allies.

To this strategic dependence was added the messianic anti-Communism of the new Secretary of State, John Foster Dulles. Britain and France were encouraged to pursue their distinct national and colonial policies by the Republican Administration which took office in January 1953. The change was dramatic. In 1951, faced with the nationalisation of its only oil supply which did not have to be paid for in dollars, Britain's Labour government had tried and failed to get US support for some traditional gunboat diplomacy against Iran. Dean Acheson, the US Secretary of State, had warned of Soviet intervention, Communist coups in Tehran, disturbances throughout the Middle East, and virtually forced the British to continue fruitless negotiations with Iran.

As soon as Acheson was replaced by Dulles, Britain tried again, in the person of C. M. 'Monty' Woodhouse. A senior official in British intelligence, Woodhouse reckoned that the new Administration would be more amenable. 'The Americans were more likely to work with us if they saw the problem as one of containing Communism rather than restoring the position of the Anglo-Iranian Oil Company,' he explained.[29] So it proved. With the support of Dulles and the CIA, an Anglo-American covert operation succeeded in toppling Mossadeq, and restoring the Shah. The spoils were subsequently divided in accordance with the new realities: Britain's monopoly of Iranian oil concessions was cut to 40 per cent, American companies were given an equal amount, and Royal Dutch Shell and French interests shared the rest.

The Eisenhower Administration was also ready to be of help to its European allies in Indo-China, where the French were going down to defeat in Vietnam. The United States had already supplied the French with $1,200 million in military aid, with US military advisers and with transport aircraft, and in the spring of 1954, serious consideration was given to the use of nuclear weapons. The State Department and Pentagon discussed dropping three tactical nuclear weapons on the Vietminh troops surrounding Dien Bien Phu, and the French foreign minister Georges Bidault later claimed that Dulles had suggested offering US nuclear bombs to France.[30] The final decision not to go nuclear in Asia was taken by Eisenhower himself, after the British allies refused to accede to his plea for 'united action' to contain China.[31] Eisenhower later told his biographer that he had said to his nuclear-minded advisers: 'You must be crazy. We can't use those awful things against Asians for the second time in less than ten years. My God.'[32]

In the event, the Americans and French settled for a compromise on the Korean model, under which Vietnam was partitioned. The Communist Vietminh took the North, and a pro-Western and independent nationalist government took the South. The Vietnamese and their Chinese supporters were put under intense pressure to agree to this settlement at the Geneva peace conference. The French premier, Pierre Mendès-France, threatened to send a million conscripts to Vietnam unless some fig-leaf of an honourable solution was reached. And the American hints of readiness to use the nuclear weapon had not been lost in China.

The Eisenhower Administration had rattled the nuclear sabre before, with equal success, in forcing the Chinese to agree to an armistice in Korea. The US Embassy in Moscow and Pandit Nehru in India were both used to send firm messages to China that the United States was prepared to widen the war unless China and North Korea agreed to a truce. 'The US had already sent the means to the theatre for delivering atomic weapons. This became known to the Chinese through their good intelligence sources and in fact we were not unwilling that they should find out,' Dulles later explained.[33] The nuclear threat was the more credible because it had been made bluntly public in a dramatic foreign-policy statement by Dulles in January 1954, a year after the Eisenhower Administration took office. This Administration was a coalition, of Cold War warriors like Dulles who would go to almost any lengths to challenge the Soviet threat, and of Republican businessmen like Charles Wilson, the former General Motors director who became Secretary of Defense, who feared overstretching the US economy and wanted to curtail the defence budget. For Dulles, the solution was simple: massive retaliation with nuclear weapons would be cheaper than massive conventional forces.

'We need allies and collective security,' Dulles explained in his speech to the Council on Foreign Relations.[34]

> Our purpose is to make these relations more effective, less costly. This can be done by placing more reliance on deterrent power and less dependence on local defensive power . . . Local defence will always be important, but must be reinforced by the further deterrent of massive

> retaliatory power. The way to deter aggression is for the free community to be willing and able to respond vigorously at places and with means of its own choosing.

This was an alarming strategy not only in itself, but also because the Pentagon and the growing band of nuclear theorists at the Rand Corporation in Los Angeles knew it was thoroughly impracticable. It had taken the Soviet scientists four years to catch up by testing their first atom bomb. The United States was already working on the next generation of nuclear weaponry, the hydrogen bomb. The first American test, on 1 November 1952, delivered a twelve-megatonne blast which removed the tiny Pacific island of Elugelab from the face of the earth. This time, it took the Soviets just nine months to follow, with the first Soviet test of a hydrogen bomb, in August 1953. Now the US no longer enjoyed a thermonuclear monopoly. More alarmingly for the Pentagon, the US Air Force investigation of the radiation cloud from the Soviet test discovered the presence of lithium. This suggested that the Soviets had taken the technological lead. The American H-bomb required a heavy refrigeration plant, which took its weight to well over a tonne, too heavy for anything but a heavy bomber to carry. The lithium in the Soviet device suggested that no refrigeration was required. Already worried by the vulnerability of its bombers to Soviet nuclear attack, the US Air Force now had to fear that the Soviets would be able to mount their much lighter H-bomb on to an intercontinental ballistic missile.[35] The 'missile gap' theory was born and – suddenly confronted with the prospect of eventual nuclear inferiority – the United States plunged into development of the Atlas and Polaris missiles.

At the same time, the nuclear equation was complicated when Britain exploded her own first atom bomb in October 1952, and began developing British strategic bombers to deliver this independent deterrent. Partly insurance against being abandoned by the United States, partly a product of national pride, the British bomb came at a time of resurgent British confidence about the country's place in the world. The death of King George VI and the accession of Queen Elizabeth II provoked an extraordinary sentiment of optimism, touched by atavism. Harking back to the sixteenth-century days of Good Queen Bess, the new monarch was hailed as the harbinger of a new Elizabethan age. A series of events contributed to the patriotic mood. The most popular was the coronation of the new Queen, happily accompanied by the conquest of Mount Everest by one of her subjects, the New Zealander, Edmund Hillary. The Fairy

Delta 2 test plane briefly held the world air-speed record. The De Havilland Comet seemed (until it began to crash) to be seizing the potential world market for a jet passenger airliner. Four Oxford University students helped Roger Bannister, the one with the fastest finish, become the first man to run a mile in four minutes. The British economy was recovering quickly, with food rationing progressively abolished until the final item, sweets, was taken off the ration in 1955.

This sense of returning self-confidence was echoed across Europe, but for Britain there were some successes on the diplomatic scene which encouraged a sense of greater grandeur. In Iran, Mossadeq had been toppled and Britain's oil supply was once more secured. Britain was now part of two new regional security systems, modelled rather loosely on Nato: the Baghdad Pact for the Middle East; and the South-East Asia Treaty Organisation, which gave institutional force to Britain's global pretensions. An accommodation had been reached with the new Egyptian government, with agreement to withdraw British troops from the Canal Zone by 1956. The Geneva conference to settle the French war in Vietnam, chaired by Britain and the Soviet Union, suggested both a useful and an independent role in statesmanship. Britain had resisted the US calls for help in Vietnam, and had helped broker an acceptable settlement. Most important of all, the new foreign secretary, Anthony Eden, finally settled the most contentious issue of the Atlantic Alliance, the terms on which France would swallow German rearmament.

Acheson had thought he had resolved it, first in September 1950 in New York, and then again at the Lisbon conference in February 1952. The military price of reassuring the French, by stationing US troops in Europe permanently, had already been paid. But Acheson had been after rather greater game than just German rearmament and the Nato alliance. He had seen the combination of economic integration and a joint defence system leading towards European political integration. Acheson had been encouraged by Jean Monnet, by the Belgian social democrat Paul-Henri Spaak, and by the British. The new Conservative government was, characteristically, all in favour of European integration and a European army, so long as it did not have to include them. As Churchill put it, 'I meant it for them, not for us.'[36]

Acheson had fought a long and successful battle with a suspicious US Senate to authorise the Nato treaty, with its commitment to four US divisions to be based in Europe. He had fought another with the Europeans to gain agreement in principle to the idea of a European Defence Community. This was intended to lead to an integrated defence force that would bring German military manpower, without

German political authority, to the common defence. The vogue word for this process, much favoured by Monnet, was *engrenage*, or enmeshing. The French National Assembly, and the chronically unstable constitutional system of the Fourth Republic, stubbornly refused to mesh, and Acheson left office frustrated.[37]

The EDC had one implacable foe, who was to frustrate America's European policies for years to come, and was honourable enough about his intentions to say so. General Charles de Gaulle, in political exile at Colombey-les-deux-Églises after handing power back to the squabbling civilians, told an interviewer from the *New York Times* that the EDC was 'plain idiocy', and that the idea of integrating the French forces with a German army of up to 500,000 men would never pass the French National Assembly. 'I will do everything against it. I will work with the Communists to block it. I will make a revolution against it. I would rather go with the Russians to stop it.'[38]

With Dulles warning darkly of an 'agonizing reappraisal' of US commitments to Europe, Eden tried again at the London conference of 1954. This time he succeeded, by making the same military commitment that Acheson had already delivered for the Americans. Eden's proposal was that Germany should join Nato as a full member, but pledge never to acquire nuclear weapons. He then went further, and as the French Ambassador wept openly with gratified emotion, pledged to keep four British divisions and a tactical air force on European soil. It was a curious paradox, that to create a credible Nato to defend Europe against the Russians to the East, both Britain and the United States had to commit their forces to the North German plain to reassure the French that a rearmed Germany would not turn its guns once more against its neighbour to the West. The old saw that Nato was a conspiracy to keep the Russians out, the Americans in, and the Germans down was made wellnigh explicit at the London conference. It worked. Germany formally joined Nato in 1955.[39]

Perhaps all this success went to Britain's head. It certainly fed Eden's legendary vanity, and with Churchill's retirement in 1955 Eden finally succeeded to the prime ministership he had so long craved. And France, liberated from the costly war in Indo-China and turning to a similar war to keep its possessions in North Africa, felt confident enough to reassert its traditional position in the Mediterranean. Even with the US Sixth Fleet now the most potent force, that inland sea remained an Anglo-French lake. The British had Gibraltar, Malta and Cyprus as bases. France dominated the northern and southern shorelines. The two powers jointly owned the Suez Canal. And both Britain and France fretted at American tutelage.

A year before the Suez crisis erupted into war, in October 1955, Eden had told his cabinet:

> Our interests in the Middle East are greater than those of the US because of our dependence on Middle East oil, and our experience in the area [is] greater than theirs. We should not therefore allow ourselves to be restricted overmuch by reluctance to act without full American concurrence and support. We should frame our own policy in the light of our interests in the area and get the Americans to support it to the extent we [can] induce them to do so.[40]

The crisis was precipitated by Dulles, who decided in July 1956 to stop the planned American loan to help Egypt build the Aswan Dam on the River Nile. Dulles believed that Egypt's Colonel Nasser was getting uncomfortably close to the Soviet bloc, buying Czech weapons and seeking to undermine the Baghdad Pact. As in Iran, US and British intelligence had been preparing discreet contingency plans to bring down this troublesome Arab leader, and the decision to block financing for the dam was seen by Dulles as a moderate step to bring Nasser to heel. Nasser's response was to seek Soviet financial support and, a week after Dulles's announcement, to nationalise the Suez Canal on 26 July 1956. Assuming US support, or benign indifference, Eden prepared for military action to topple Nasser and maintain Western control of the canal.[41]

With an American Presidential election looming in the autumn, this was not a wise time to assume that the Americans would back what looked like a classic reprise of imperial gunboat policy. Perhaps encouraged by the absence of any reference to the crisis at the Republican or Democratic party conventions of that summer, Eden pressed ahead, calling up British reservists in August. Meanwhile the Egyptians proved just as capable of managing the pilot and control duties of the canal as the Anglo-French company had been.

Even though the US chiefs of staff proposed supporting Britain, on 2 October Dulles warned that Suez was not part of America's obligations to her Nato allies. Dulles went further, stressing that the United States was not 'identifying itself 100 per cent with the so-called colonial powers'. But if America was hesitant, Eden knew that the French were with him, and the French thought that there might be another local ally in Israel. On 16 October, Eden and Selwyn Lloyd, his foreign secretary, travelled to Paris for secret discussions with the French premier Guy Mollet, which were formally agreed in writing on 22 October at another secret meeting at the château of Sèvres, and again on the 24th.

It was a remarkably complex conspiracy. Israel was to invade Egypt through the Sinai, and move on the canal. Under the transparent excuse of protecting an international waterway, British and French troops were then to intervene and occupy the canal. Neither the British cabinet nor the US ally were told of the plot. In conditions of great secrecy, which delayed the arrival of the heavy British armoured forces by slow sea passage, the tripartite adventure began with the Israeli invasion on 29 October. The next day, London and Paris announced their ultimatum to both Egypt and Israel to withdraw from the canal within twelve hours. Israel agreed, in accordance with the plot, and Egypt refused. On 31 October, British warplanes began attacking Egyptian airfields.

Had the British and French ground forces followed hard on the heels of the airstrikes, the plot might have worked. But the slow troop and tank-landing ships were still at sea. The British and French paratroops did not land until 5 November, and by then there had been a hostile American resolution at the United Nations calling for a cease-fire, a Soviet invasion of Hungary, a run on the pound, and an extraordinary phone call to Downing Street from the White House. 'Is that you, Anthony?' it began. 'Well, this is President Eisenhower, and I can only presume you have gone out of your mind.' The call was taken by William Clark, Eden's press secretary.[42] But Eisenhower may have been right about Eden's mental condition. The British prime minister was out of his depth, under intense stress, and gobbling amphetamines.

When Britain and France vetoed the American resolution in the UN Security Council, Dulles reintroduced it in the General Assembly. It was the week of the presidential election, and Eisenhower's campaign speeches were stressing the point: 'We cannot subscribe to one law for the weak, another for the strong; one law for those opposing us, another for those allied with us. There can be only one law, or there shall be no peace.'[43] George Humphrey, the US Treasury Secretary, took the Suez invasion as a personal affront. 'You will not get a dime from the US government if I can stop it, until you have gotten out of Suez,' Humphrey shouted at the British Ambassador. The British Chancellor of the Exchequer, Harold Macmillan, later accused Humphrey of deliberately selling sterling to intensify the run on the pound, which lost 15 per cent of its reserves in November. Humphrey also blocked Britain's perfectly legal application for funds to the IMF.[44]

Worse still, the Soviet Union sent bellicose letters to London and Paris warning of Soviet intervention, and even threatening the use of missiles, unless Britain and France agreed to a cease-fire and to withdraw their troops. The Atlantic Alliance held up well enough for the CIA to pass on the information that this was an empty threat; the Soviets had no such missiles capable of delivering nuclear warheads on London and Paris. But the French took the menace seriously enough to launch their own bid to become a nuclear power.[45]

The logic of this French decision is not clear. Britain was a nuclear power, but this had neither deterred the Soviet threat nor induced the Americans to support its closest ally in an hour of strategic need which was also a deep national humiliation. At the United Nations, only Australia and New Zealand had stood by Britain. Canada had abstained. India had condemned the intervention. West Germany had been appalled: 'Britain and France will face a long, hard, bloody war, while suffering the icy hostility of nations who only yesterday were proud to think of them as friends,' ran the editorial in *Die Welt*.[46]

It was a brutal puncturing of Eden's grandiose dreams of a new Elizabethan age. Even when Eden agreed to the cease-fire and to the troop withdrawal on 6 November, and Eisenhower forgave him over the phone, and invited him to Washington to clear up 'the family spat', the personal links which had so long sustained the Anglo-American relationship suddenly sundered. Eisenhower's aides persuaded him to withdraw the invitation. Perhaps the most frustrating moment of all for the British came when Selwyn Lloyd finally visited Washington, and called on Dulles in hospital, to be greeted with the question, 'Why did you stop?' The answer, of course, was military incompetence. The British had simply not been able to get their troops to Suez fast enough to present the world, and their American ally, with a *fait accompli*.[47]

By cruel contrast, the Soviets had no such logistic difficulties in Hungary. The Soviet motive behind the nuclear threat was to take advantage of Western disarray to distract attention from their own invasion to crush the nationalist uprising in Budapest. This involved two curious ironies. While Britain and France suffered international humiliation from having too little power to enforce their colonial prerogatives at Suez, the Soviets acquired a different kind of international infamy for deploying too much power. And while the Franco-British embarrassment was the result of a thoroughly reactionary policy, the Soviet reassertion of power in Hungary was the result of a bold attempt at the liberalisation of Stalin's empire.

Throughout the Cold War, the purely diplomatic or strategic relations between East and West were always hostage to sudden changes or developments in the domestic politics of each side. Rarely were Soviet and US politics more out of step than in 1953. Stalin's death and Beria's execution had encouraged the new collective leadership to seek a form of *détente*, just as Dulles came into office with his policy of roll-back and massive retaliation. The first sign came within days of Stalin's death, as Zhou Enlai returned from being one of the pallbearers at Stalin's funeral to break the log-jam over a cease-fire in Korea. With Moscow's approval, and new promises of Soviet economic support, he reversed the Chinese insistence that all Chinese and North Korean prisoners be repatriated.[48]

In an attempt to comprehend what was now facing them, the Central Committee commissioned the private translation of the available American documentation. Georgi Arbatov, later director of Moscow's USA and Canada Institute, was assigned James Burnham's *Containment or Liberation* in 1953. The Russians were right to be baffled. Dulles was saying one thing, but on 16 April, a month after Stalin's death, President Eisenhower was saying another. In his speech to the American Association of Editors, Eisenhower held out the prospect of normalising relations now that Stalin had gone.

The Soviet bewilderment was plain. *Izvestiya*, the official journal of the Supreme Soviet, which was Malenkov's power base, reprinted the speech in full; *Pravda*, official journal of the Central Committee, and thus under Khrushchev's influence, published a critical commentary.[49] Then the author of the 'Iron Curtain' speech confused Moscow further. In May, Winston Churchill spoke of the possibility of a 'spontaneous and healthy evolution which may be taking place inside Russia', and proposed in the House of Commons a summit meeting between himself, Eisenhower, and Malenkov. Eisenhower rejected the idea.[50]

The confusion of the Moscow collective leadership became intense over Berlin. In May, the East German government announced that it had been over-hasty in collectivising agriculture and retail trade and promised relaxation. The Soviet contribution to this gentle thaw was to remove political authority from the Soviet military commander, and shift it to a civilian Commissioner. This commissioner in turn was charged with 'maintaining relations with the occupation authorities of the US, Britain and France in all questions of an all-German character'.[51] This sounded as if Moscow were trying to turn back the clock to the joint-control system in force before the Berlin airlift. But then in June, the East German government suddenly raised the factory production targets which were linked to wages. This effective cut in incomes provoked demonstrations, which turned into riots, that became a general strike, cheered on by the US radio stations in West Berlin. Soviet tanks were deployed in East Berlin, Leipzig, Dresden and Jena. There was shooting, and a still unknown number of deaths, and the CIA station chief in Berlin, Henry Heckscher, cabled back for permission to arm the Berlin workers with sub-machine-guns.[52] He was refused. Dulles's vaunted policy of 'roll-back' proved hollow when tested.

But a form of Soviet roll-back, a voluntary withdrawal of military forces from advanced strategic positions, had begun long before Dulles came to office. The Red Army had withdrawn from eastern Czechoslovakia in December 1945, in parallel with the US withdrawal from the western half of the country. In the spring of 1946, Soviet troops withdrew from northern Iran, and from the Danish island of Bornholm with its strategic position in the Baltic, and from Manchuria. The Soviet army was reduced to 2.8 million men under arms by the outbreak of the Korean War in 1950. The image in Dulles's mind of a relentless Communist advance looked very different from Moscow's perspective. But just as the Korean War had led the US to strengthen its alliances and rebuild its former adversaries in Europe and Asia, the Soviet system reacted in a broadly similar way. The Red Army grew back to 5.8 million men by 1955, even while Malenkov was making speeches about the need for 'peaceful coexistence', and the Soviet army was withdrawing from its zone in Austria and from the Finnish naval base of Porkkala.[53]

Both Moscow and Washington had reason to be confused by the difference between what the other superpower was doing and what it was saying. In each case, internal politics had much to do with this. The difference in the way *Izvestiya* and *Pravda* reacted to the Eisenhower speech of April 1953 reflected the emerging rivalry between Malenkov and Khrushchev. This was not only played out in the sphere of foreign policy, but in domestic planning, with Malenkov pressing for more investment in consumer goods, and Khrushchev wooing the armed forces by stressing the need for more heavy industry and modernised defence production. Khrushchev also won the support of Molotov by agreeing to tighten the security coordination with the Eastern European countries through what became the Warsaw Pact. Malenkov argued that nuclear weapons made peaceful coexistence 'both necessary and possible'. Khrushchev countered that the proletariat was not to be cowed by the nuclear threat, when the vastness of the Soviet Union and the smaller size of its cities left it less vulnerable than the US.[54]

When Malenkov was forced to resign in February 1955, the prevalent Western reaction was that Khrushchev, the hard-liner, had triumphed.[55] This proved to be unfounded. Khrushchev's priority was to repair the damage Stalin had done within the Soviet camp. In 1954, he made a formal visit to China for the ceremonial return of Port Arthur to Chinese control, and to announce closer economic links, agreeing to send Soviet technical experts to build 150 strategic industrial centres. Khrushchev then set about repairing the rifts Stalin had made on the western frontier, flying to see Tito in Belgrade. He delivered a formal apology, and withdrew Stalin's otiose definition of the Tito government as 'a military Fascist dictatorship'.

Stalin's death provided a perfect excuse for the new course at home and abroad. It was easy to blame everything on the old dictator. In May 1955, Khrushchev overrode Molotov's objections to the Treaty which guaranteed Austrian neutrality, withdrew Soviet troops, and them demanded in return a summit.[56] This was a considerable Soviet concession since in the same month West Germany was formally granted full sovereignty, Nato membership, and the right to rearm. Although inevitable, this represented a major defeat for Soviet German policies since 1945. Accordingly, the Warsaw Pact was formally signed as a military counterweight to Nato in the same month.

Dulles was deeply suspicious of Khrushchev, warning the American people in a radio broadcast that 'the new set of dangers comes from the fact that the wolf has put on a new set of sheep's clothing, and while it is better to have sheep's clothing on than a bear's clothing on, because sheep don't have claws, I think their policy remains the same'. But the Geneva summit took place, with Britain, France, the United States and the Soviet Union all attending. Although the Russians bizarrely suggested that if Nato was indeed dedicated to peace, then the Soviet Union might be permitted to join, very little was decided. After asking Gromyko whether he was indeed serious, Dulles agreed to consider the application, and nothing more was ever heard of the matter. 'They simply hushed it up,' Gromyko later complained. The main achievement of Geneva was the very fact that the session took place, the first summit since Potsdam, and the first serious sign of relaxed tension since the Berlin crisis. For months thereafter, *Pravda* referred to 'the spirit of Geneva', so at least it helped Khrushchev persuade his home audience that he had engineered a more hopeful international outlook than Stalin.[57]

The price of this relaxation was the quasi-permanent division of Germany, much to the horror of West German Social Democrats and conservatives alike. Axel Springer, the newspaper magnate, flew to Moscow to inquire whether it was still possible to have unification in return for neutrality. His flagship newspaper, *Die Welt*, stressed: 'Only one way is open, to co-exist with Russia by moving a non-aligned, independent state.'[58] But that option had been overtaken by events. Ever the pragmatist, Khrushchev accepted the new situation in Germany, opening formal diplomatic relations with the Adenauer government in September 1955, and granting East Germany sovereignty over its own foreign affairs at the same time.

The high point of Khrushchev's thaw came early in the following year, with the twentieth Congress of the Communist Party and the celebrated secret speech which for the first time condemned Stalin's crimes from the party's own inner sanctum. The purge of Beria had forced the first round of releases from the Gulag. Some ten thousand political prisoners were freed by 1955, and the great flood of millions of releases came after Khrushchev's speech in the following year.[59] The denunciations of Stalin's terror in the secret speech, deliberately leaked to a Western correspondent through the former KGB official Kostya Orlov, has overshadowed the rest of the proceedings of the twentieth Party Congress.[60] But Khrushchev's open remarks on foreign policy were almost equally significant.

Khrushchev simply ditched the classic thesis of Marxism–Leninism that capitalism and imperialism made war inevitable. That had been true before 'the world camp of socialism became a mighty force', he said. 'At the present time, however, the situation has changed radically . . . War is not fatalistically inevitable.' He went on to acknowledge that there were different forms of transition from capitalism to socialism, including the parliamentary route of free elections which 'may become an organ of genuine democracy'. The socialist camp would win eventually, he insisted, because 'the socialist mode of production possesses decisive advantages over the capitalist mode'. But this did not mean the Soviet Union was seeking to export revolution – 'it is ridiculous to think that revolutions are made to order'.[61]

The implications of Khrushchev's public and private speeches reinforced one another with devastating effect. On the one hand Stalin's authoritarian way was discredited, and on the other the methods of parliamentary democracy were hailed. For the authoritarian Chinese party, this was a shock; for the countries of Eastern Europe, it was something close to a promise of liberation. The dissolution in April 1956 of the Cominform, Stalin's chosen vehicle for the enforcement of orthodoxy, added to the rising expectations. So did the removal of Molotov from his post as foreign minister. And so did Khrushchev's new readiness to make Moscow far more open to the world, welcoming the new leaders of the newly independent states, and travelling himself to China and India, to Britain and France.

Khrushchev visibly enjoyed himself in this flurry of public diplomacy. And the rapturous reception he received in India, where he and Bulganin had to be rescued and lifted by their escorts above the heads of the enthusiastic crowds, became a propaganda victory in itself. This was clearly not the grim Stalinist style. Khrushchev was open to the world at a time when the world itself was opening, and Khrushchev's Moscow seemed far more in tune with the emerging Third World than did America and its Western allies, still fighting their rearguard battles for the remaining colonies.

The Bandung conference of Asian and African states in April 1955 represented the moment when this Third World tried to come of political age, and to define some room for independent manoeuvre between the two blocs. This was not easy, with pro-American Japan attending, alongside Communist China, while India's Pandit Nehru tried to define what national sovereignty and underdeveloped solidarity could mean in a Cold War world. China announced, and the Soviet Union later supported, the Five Principles of Co-Existence, which were offered as a code of conduct for world affairs. Originally presented to India by Zhou Enlai, they proved of little value when China and India went to war five years later over a territorial dispute in the Himalayas. The Five Principles pledged mutual respect for each other's territorial integrity and sovereignty, non-interference in each other's internal affairs, non-aggression, equal and mutual benefits in economic relations, and peaceful coexistence.[62]

The elevated language of the Five Principles contained one carefully placed booby trap for the West, or at least for its investors, banks and developers, whether public or private. Equal and mutual benefits in economic relations was something that capitalist economies, by definition, found difficult to manage. Unless given in the form of grants or soft loans with non-market interest rates, Western aid and investment sought a profit. This also applied to the World Bank and International Monetary Fund. The Soviet Union, by contrast, was able to point to the generosity of its economic support for China, for India, and subsequently for Egypt. Bandung was the moment when this implicit economic rivalry between West and East took on a strategic dimension, as the countries of the developing world ceased to be pawns and spectators in the global rivalry, but began to become players in their own right. Egypt's Colonel Nasser took advantage of the meeting with Zhou Enlai to ask him if China or the Soviet Union would supply the arms the United States had failed to deliver, and also whether the

Soviet Union might help finance the Aswan Dam. When Dulles tried to pressure Nasser by withdrawing the Aswan finance, Nasser already had his alternative, thanks to Bandung.[63]

Bandung and the Geneva summit of 1955 emphasised Khrushchev's success in convincing both First and Third Worlds that the Soviet Union was under new and rather more promising management. Khrushchev's speech at the twentieth Party Congress of 1956 convinced the Second, or socialist World too. And that, ironically, was to prove the trouble. As Mikhail Gorbachev was to learn a generation later, Soviet leaders may unleash change and stimulate expectations; the trick is to control them. And in Eastern Europe, they began to get out of control very fast. Within a month of Khrushchev's speech, the Polish party leader Bolesav Bierut died of what seems to have been natural causes. The Polish party wanted to replace him with Roman Zambrowski, quickly vetoed by Moscow apparently because of his Jewish origins.[64] Edward Ochab took over, presumed loyal by Moscow because of the venom with which he had denounced the purged Polish 'Tito-ist' Wadisaw Gomuka.

Gomuka had been one of those Eastern European Communists who had believed sincerely in the possibility of a different, national form of socialism in the wake of World War Two. General Secretary of the Polish party until the Cold War turned icy, Gomuka had said publicly in 1948 that Tito and the Yugoslav Communists should have been conciliated rather than condemned. When Stalin reasserted complete party control from Moscow, Gomuka was dismissed, expelled from the party, and finally imprisoned in 1951. Released after Stalin's death, as part of the wave of hesitant relaxation which freed an entire generation of Stalin's victims in Eastern Europe, Gomuka was a national symbol.

So when the new Polish government of Ochab began to liberalise in 1956, and came under instant pressure as the workers of Poznań began to strike for more, Gomuka represented a form of Communism that both Polish strikers and Moscow might be prepared to swallow. Ochab's government had little choice. The strikes were serious, and on what was to become known as Black Thursday, Ochab sent two divisions and 300 tanks of the Polish Army to suppress their own people. Most estimates reckon that at least a hundred Polish workers were killed, and another three hundred wounded. Gomuka summed up the result: 'The loss of the confidence of the working class means the loss of the moral basis of power.'[65]

Bulganin and Marshal Zhukov flew in from Moscow for the Polish party's emergency plenum of the Central Committee, insisting that the Poznań strikes and riots be blamed on 'imperialist agitators'. They also declared that Gomuka would not be an acceptable member of any reformed Polish government. Ochab stressed that there was little choice, and won Chinese support for the right of the Poles to resolve their own problem at the eighth Congress of the Chinese Party in Beijing in September.[66] Khrushchev was torn between his unwillingness to return to Stalin's ruthless domination of Eastern Europe, and the pressure from the hard-liners in Moscow to crush this threatening development. The Chinese reaction may have proved decisive.

Khrushchev flew unexpectedly to Poland for another emergency plenum in October, so unexpectedly that his aircraft was bounced by Polish fighters until belated clearance was received from Warsaw.[67] This may have explained Khrushchev's furious waving of his fist at the Polish party leaders who gathered to meet him, and the sudden deployment of the Soviet troops in Poland into positions from which they could attack the cities. But it may also have persuaded Khrushchev to take Gomuka seriously when he warned that if the Soviet troops attacked, the Polish Army would fight back, and he would rouse the Polish people against the invader.

Once he assessed the mood of the Polish party, and heard of the mushrooming of workers' councils, and the meetings of peasants declaring the end of their hated collective farms, Khrushchev grumpily accepted Gomuka as the new General Secretary. When he was assured that Poland would continue to be a firm ally of the Soviet Union and remain within the Warsaw Pact, Khrushchev also swallowed the removal of Marshal Konstantin Rokossovsky as head of the Polish armed forces. Khrushchev's options were limited. As Gomuka said in his address to the plenum, the events in Poland were a direct result of Khrushchev's own speech to the twentieth Party Congress in Moscow. In accordance with that speech, Gomuka went on, he now intended to pursue 'the Polish path to socialism'.

Khrushchev could accept that, and accept the immediate release of the Roman Catholic Cardinal Stepan Wyszynski, so long as Poland remained loyal in the strategic sense. And indeed, the cardinal swiftly reached a concordat with Gomuka which pledged that 'the State would find in the Church hierarchy and clergy full understanding'.[68] But already the wave had spread beyond Poland, and the day that Gomuka told a mass meeting of 500,000 people in Warsaw that the Soviet troops were returning to their bases, the students of Budapest began their own demonstrations. When the Hungarian police moved against the students, the Budapest workers joined them, and together they toppled the giant statue of Stalin in the Hungarian capital.

In panic, Moscow and the Hungarian party looked for Budapest's version of Gomuka, an acceptably nationalist Communist, preferably one who had served a prison term in Stalin's day. Imre Nagy, the former prime minister, who had been purged but not arrested, did not quite fit the bill. But in the sudden collapse of party and government authority in Budapest on the night of 23–4 October, the Hungarian Central Committee could come up with no one better. By the time he took office as prime minister the next day, Soviet T-34 tanks were already rumbling into Budapest. They were greeted with Molotov cocktails and barrels of liquid soap which made their tracks spin helplessly on street corners. The CIA broadcasting network, Radio Free Europe, reported it all breathlessly, and constantly declared the West's solidarity with the Hungarian freedom-fighters.[69] Thus encouraged, and with the support of elements of the Hungarian Army, the Budapest rebels began looting party buildings, and the Hungarian secret police were hunted down like rats in their own dungeons.

Nagy announced an amnesty for political prisoners, and invited non-Communists into his government. He assured Moscow of Hungary's loyalty, and in the hope of a Hungarian version of Gomuka's national-Communism, Khrushchev withdrew Soviet troops from Budapest on 28 October. They were still pulling out when the long-delayed Suez conspiracy was triggered, and Israel invaded the Sinai peninsula. American attention was torn between two crises, and their own imminent Presidential election. Radio Free Europe continued to give an encouragement which proved hollow, and Yuri Andropov, the Soviet Ambassador, looked desperately for someone more reliable than the weak and vacillating Nagy.

In Janos Kadar, who had served a prison term in Stalin's day for 'nationalist deviationism', Andropov found his man, and the basis for a deal. On 30 October, the terms were spelt out, with a formal Kremlin statement of principle on the future relations between socialist states.[70] In effect, it said that loyalty to the Warsaw Pact would guarantee non-interference by the Soviet Union in the internal affairs of allied countries. Perhaps encouraged by Radio Free Europe, certainly under pressure from the growing confidence of his own nationalist supporters, and doubtless carried away by the sheer pace of events, Nagy replied the same day. Hungary was leaving the Warsaw Pact, announced its neutrality, and appealed to the United Nations for support.

This was too much. Khrushchev began a round of consultations, with the Chinese deputy leader Liyu Shaoqi who was visiting Moscow, with Gomuka at Brest-Litovsk, with the Czech and Romanian leadership in Bucharest and even with Tito on the island of Brioni. They all agreed: Nagy had gone too far.[71] On 4 November, as the lumbering British troopships ploughed towards Suez and the British and French paratroops boarded their aircraft, 200,000 troops and 2,500 tanks of the Soviet Army stormed back into Budapest. First reports claimed that at least 20,000 Hungarians lost their lives. In fact, the final death toll was around 3,000.[72]

In Washington, President Eisenhower's staff were checking the last election-eve speeches, in order, as one of them put it, 'to tone down Dulles's references to "irresistible" forces of "liberation" unleashed in Eastern Europe'. In Eisenhower's own speech was a plaintive promise to Moscow 'to remove any false fears that we would look upon new governments as potential military allies'. Once the speech was delivered, and the die cast, the President turned to Emmett John Hughes and spoke of his fears of Moscow:[73]

> Those boys are both furious and scared. Just as with Hitler, that makes for the most dangerous possible state of mind. And we better be damn sure that every Intelligence point and every outpost of our armed forces is absolutely right on their toes. And if these fellows start something, we may have to hit 'em – and if necessary, with everything in the bucket.

The West did not stir. The last plaintive appeals of Radio Budapest for American help gave way to curses and accusations of betrayal before the airwaves fell hauntingly silent. Refugees mobbed the Austrian frontier as Janos Kadar began his national-Communist government. In Italy, the old socialist leader Pietro Nenni, who had in 1948 split his party rather than abandon his alliance with his wartime comrades in the partisans, finally broke with Communists in disgust. Nenni even sent back the money he had been awarded with his Stalin Peace Prize, and took his Italian socialists into a coalition government with the Christian Democrats he had spurned.[74]

The Communist parties of the West, already reeling under the revelations of the secret speech, plumbed the depths of shame. Far away in Ohio, the veteran American Communist John Steuben, a union man who had spent his life among the steelworkers of Cleveland, was dying. He had always been loyal to Moscow, through Stalin's Terror, through the purges, through the Nazi–Soviet Pact and the vilifications of Tito. He had endured, through the beatings by the anti-union goon squads of the 1930s and through McCarthy's witch-hunts, because it was part of his larger loyalty to the cause of the working class, and the ideals of Communism. But the bloody repression of Hungary proved too much, and with his last words, he spoke for many like him: 'I want to live the rest of my life in agony and silence.'[75]

Chapter 5

Spies in the Sky: Sputnik to U-2

The capitals are rocked with thunder
Of Orators in wordy feuds.
But in the depths of Russia yonder,
An age-old silence broods.

'Russia', Nikolai Nekrasov

'We accuse the Soviet Government of murder,' said the editorial in the *New York Times*, as the blood dried on the tank tracks in Budapest. 'We accuse it of the foulest treachery and basest deceit known to man. We accuse it of having committed so monstrous a crime against the Hungarian people yesterday that its infamy can never be forgiven or forgotten.'[1]

Within three years of that denunciation, Nikita Khrushchev was being honoured and fêted on the first visit to the United States by a Soviet leader. But by then, one of the more unexpected results of the bloody suppression of Budapest was starting to become apparent. In Gomuka's Poland, as in Tito's Yugoslavia and even in Kadar's Hungary, that national-Communism which had been hesitantly tried ten years earlier was given a deliberate chance to show that it might work. The curious result of the Soviet brutality in Hungary was that it produced rather more tolerable regimes in Poland and Hungary than those countries had suffered before the uprisings.

But first the whip was cracked, with trials and executions in Hungary. Promises of safe passage for negotiations were made to Imre Nagy and to the leaders of the Workers' Council who had called a general strike, only to be broken. They were arrested and Nagy was later shot. On 15 January 1957, the Kadar government enacted the death penalty for any workers who went on strike in key industries.[2]

Some strikingly independent new shoots flourished in this period, from Leszek Kolakowski's deeply moralistic attempt in Poland to define a liberal Marxism, to the Yugoslav party's defence of the rights to private property and its denunciation of 'every aspect of ideological monopoly'. Doubtless in some shame, and certainly in some fear of unrest spreading throughout Eastern Europe, Gomułka and later Kadar were given significant economic concessions. The equivalent of $500 million in Polish 'debt' to the USSR was cancelled, new trade credits were offered. Polish citizens living in the USSR since 1940 were allowed to return home. The need to buy off Eastern European unrest was to cost Moscow the rouble equivalent of $1 billion in 1957. This sharply reduced the aid available for China, with what were to prove momentous results.[3]

The Soviet Union of the 1950s could easily afford the sudden flood of aid to the Warsaw Pact nations. It was enjoying an economic boom. From 1950 to 1958, the Soviet Union claimed an annual 7.1 per cent growth in its gross national product, more than half as large again as the US rate.[4] The year after Stalin died, the state prices paid for agricultural products were raised, the collective farms were to be paid extra for any food they produced above their quotas, and the tax on the peasants' private plots was halved. In 1958, the taxes were scrapped altogether.

The results were remarkable. By the 1960s, these private plots, which amounted to less than three per cent of the arable land, were producing over thirty per cent of the country's fruit and vegetables. Old-age pensions were increased in 1956, the working week was cut. Industrial production rose that year, so the official statistics said, by 11 per cent. The Virgin Lands, the traditional pasture lands of northern Kazakhstan put under the plough for the first time, began to produce and that year saw a record harvest of 127 million tonnes. The Lenin stadium, the world's largest sports complex, was opened in Moscow, and the first nuclear-powered ship, the icebreaker *Lenin*, was launched the next year.

The symbols of relaxation, most haunting in the return of the 'Zeks' from Stalin's not entirely emptied Gulag, were everywhere. The Kremlin, closed to all but the party élite in Stalin's day, was opened to the public, and on New Year's Eve there was a party for the children of Moscow. There were visas for Western tourists, and an international youth festival which brought rock 'n' roll to Moscow, and left behind two subterranean youth cults, the *shtatniki* (America-lovers) and the *beatniki*. Such was the enthusiasm for Western popular music that a lively cottage industry grew up, and since there was no vinyl, depended on used X-ray film to make bootleg records. A new generation of young poets began declaiming unorthodox verse in Pushkin and Mayakovsky squares. And Alexander Solzhenitsyn, among millions of others freed from the camps, began to write.[5]

Barely noticed in the West, or dismissed as so much propaganda after the slaughter in Budapest, the changes within the Soviet Union suddenly thrust themselves upon the world's attention on 4 October 1957 as the first man-made satellite was launched into space. The Sputnik (the word means fellow-traveller), with its cheeky electronic beeps, was announced as a Soviet contribution to the UN's world geophysical year. The proven capacity to launch a 184lb payload in space orbit was not interpreted as a peaceful gesture by the West, which belatedly remembered Khrushchev's earlier and disregarded claim that the Soviet Union had developed the world's first intercontinental ballistic missile. The implicit threat was clear. The American homeland was now in pawn to superior Soviet technology.

'America has lost a battle more important and greater than Pearl Harbor,' Dr Edward Teller, the father of the American H-bomb, told the national TV audience. 'The Russians have left the earth and the race for control of the universe has started,' commented Senator Lyndon Johnson's adviser, George Reedy. The *New York Times* reported that, on its first day in space, the Sputnik had been 'tracked in four crossings over the US'. In the White House, the shock was visceral. James Killian, appointed by President Eisenhower to be his scientific adviser, later recalled, 'What I felt most keenly was the affront to my national pride.'[6]

The beeps of Sputnik, followed a month later by the launch of a larger satellite which contained a small dog called Laika, echoed in the ears of a top-secret US committee which was composing an alarming document known as the Gaither Report. They delivered its twenty-nine pages, officially entitled *Deterrence and Survival in the Nuclear Age*, to the President on 7 November. One month later, on the anniversary of Pearl Harbor, the United States tried to launch its counter, a tiny 4lb satellite aboard a Vanguard rocket. It rose just twenty-five inches from the Cape Canaveral launch pad, before falling back in full view of the world's waiting news cameras. The contrast could hardly have been more humiliating. London's *Daily Mirror* summed up the disaster with a front-page headline that paid a wry tribute to both Soviet achievement and American failure – 'Phutnik'.[7]

Worse was to come. Just five days before Christmas, the *Washington Post* published an account of the secret Gaither Report, and in sensational language rammed home the frightening implications as explained to the President by America's strategic experts:[8]

> The still top-secret Gaither Report portrays a United States in the gravest danger in its history.

> It pictures the nation moving in frightening course to the status of a second-class power.
>
> It shows an America exposed to an almost immediate threat from the missile-bristling Soviet Union.
>
> It finds America's long-term prospect one of cataclysmic peril in the face of rocketing Soviet military might and of a powerful, growing Soviet economy and technology which will bring new political, propaganda and psychological assaults on freedom all around the globe . . .
>
> Only through an all-out effort, the report says, can the US hope to close the current missile gap and to counter the world-wide Communist offensive in many fields and in many lands.

This was not quite the tone of the report, but the *Washington Post*'s spine-chilling version set the mood for the wave of something close to national panic which followed. The report proposed a crash investment on $20 billion in nuclear fallout shelters, and so school districts around the USA began staging air-raid warnings in response to the demands of local parents and politicians. Private enterprise rose to the challenge, with a family-size fibreglass-and-concrete shelter for $2,395, installation extra.[9]

The missile gap implied a technological gap, which in turn implied a research gap, and thus an education gap and so on. In the space of three months, the United States had passed from a blithe self-confidence in its security, its economy and its technology and plunged into a form of national inferiority complex. There were other roots of the insecurity; another Presidential illness, with Eisenhower's stroke in the month after Sputnik was launched, and also the first harbinger of what was to prove a debilitating and shaming confrontation with the unsettled tragedy of America's racial heritage. That summer, the governor of the southern state of Arkansas, Orval Faubus, had sent his National Guard into the city of Little Rock to prevent the racial desegregation of its schools. Eisenhower eventually, after deep hesitation, sent US paratroopers of the 101st Airborne into the city to enforce the desegregation law, and prevent the ugly mobs from intimidating black children. This was not in any sense an American Budapest, but like the Anglo-French invasion of Suez, it served to blur the moral lesson of Hungary. And Eisenhower's White House knew it.

'The crude practice of racism in the self-styled sanctuary of freedom,' sighed Eisenhower's speechwriter, Emmett John Hughes.[10]

> The tale carried faster than drum signals across black Africa. It summoned cold gleams of recognition to the eyes of Asians, quick to

> see the signs, in the heartland of America, of the racial enmities that had helped to make colonialism through the generations so odious to them . . . to all peoples, in all lands, the trained and instructed voice of Soviet propaganda could relay, in almost affectionately fastidious detail, the news of Little Rock.

One of the great merits of Eisenhower, stemming from an almost unparalleled experience of war and crisis, was that he very seldom panicked. He did not do so now. The Gaither Report warned that the Soviet economy was growing with dramatic speed; that their machine-tool industry was out-producing that of America; that the United States faced an increasing threat which might become critical in 1959 or early 1960; that they had produced the fissile material for 1,500 nuclear warheads, and that in missile technology 'they have probably surpassed us'. It recommended increasing the US defence budget by 50 per cent forthwith. Hard on Gaither's heels came the new mandarins of nuclear theory from the Rand Corporation, telling a stunned White House briefing that under the current alert and warning system, the bombers of Strategic Air Command could be destroyed in a Soviet surprise attack. The United States had no guaranteed retaliatory force; it thus had no credible deterrent.[11]

Eisenhower did not swallow it. He knew from intelligence reports that the Soviet missile production capacity for the new Semyorka ICBM was low, and that the Soviet long-range Bison bombers coming from the Fili production plants were misleadingly numbered to make the force appear much larger than it was.[12] He knew also that by 1960, the US atomic stockpile would have expanded to 1,000 weapons, and that the new Polaris submarines would be ready. Eisenhower accelerated plans for the deployment of Thor and Jupiter medium-range missiles in Europe, and pushed the production schedules of the American Atlas and Titan ICBMs.[13] But he refused to distort the US economy by further massive spending on defence, even though the Gaither Report had seductively suggested their recommendations would 'help sustain production and employment'.

Confident that national security was intact, Eisenhower's priorities were strategic in a rather different sense. First, he wanted to mend the breach with his bruised allies, Britain and France, and to sketch out the ground rules for the changing relationship with the increasingly confident Germany. And second, he understood that the shock of Sputnik had created a vast expectation among the American people for some form of reassuring response, and it had also pointed to a useful long-term remedy. The Soviet investments in education and science were impressive; the American education system could do with some improvement.

Perhaps the most enduring result of the Sputnik was America's National Defense Education Act of 1958, which began pumping $2 billion a year into what was frankly explained as a way to prevent the Russians from winning the brain race. After 1958, 25 per cent of construction costs on American campuses was financed by federal funds, and by 1960, the federal budget provided 20 per cent of university operating expenses (at Harvard, the figure was 25 per cent) and the taxpayer also paid for 70 per cent of university research.[14] By 1960, some 100,000 students were going to college with money borrowed from the government. This astonishing expansion of American university education was a direct result of a strategic decision by the national government. By 1960, there were 3.5 million students at America's institutions of higher learning. By 1970, there were 7 million, the result of 'a frenzied concern for national security'.[15]

The psychological shock of Sputnik hit Eisenhower all the harder because of the rift with his main European allies. The mood of estrangement after Suez was so intense that Dulles told the British Ambassador to Washington, Sir Harold Caccia, to call on him at home rather than invite comment by coming to the office.[16] But Eden had resigned, and the new British prime minister Harold Macmillan was an old wartime friend. He and Eisenhower had served together in North Africa after the Torch landings. After his appointment, as Macmillan went to the Turf Club to celebrate with oysters and champagne, he received a warm personal note from the White House: 'Remember the old adage, "Now abideth faith, hope and charity – and greater than these is a sense of humour." With warm regard, As ever, DE.'[17]

Inside the Foreign Office, a fundamental reassessment of Britain's position was under way, and its conclusions were formally submitted to the cabinet in January 1957. It acknowledged that the long pretence that Britain was still a great power was now demonstrably hollow. Even though Britain's own H-bomb was scheduled for its first test within three months, the weakness of the economy meant that the price of staying in the arms race would be bankruptcy. 'We should pool our resources with our European allies so that Western Europe as a whole might become a third nuclear power comparable with the US and the Soviet Union.'[18]

The British cabinet itself would not go quite so far. But as Macmillan embarked upon his premiership, he did so with a cabinet consensus that the old Atlantic relationship could no longer be trusted through thick and thin. It was time to consider the historic shift towards Europe, the cabinet minute recorded:[19]

> The Suez crisis had made it plain that there must be some change in the basis of Anglo-American relations. It was doubtful whether the US would now be willing to accord to us alone the special position which we had held as their principal ally during the war. We might therefore be better able to influence them if we were part of an association of Powers which had greater political, economic and military strength than we alone could command.

This was a half-hearted way to describe a strategic decision of such fundamental importance. More than a characteristic British compromise, the syntax of the cabinet decision reflected the deep reluctance with which it was made. Perhaps inevitably, compromise was what resulted. Macmillan, whose mother was American, counted a great deal on his personal ties with Eisenhower to restore the special relationship with America, while simultaneously exploring the new possibilities with Europe. In the same busy month of March 1957, Macmillan met Eisenhower at Bermuda and agreed to base sixty Thor missiles on British soil, and also met French premier Guy Mollet in Paris to discuss the Common Market.

At the same time, the young cabinet minister Reginald Maudling was instructed to carry out 'Plan G', the exploration of a European Free Trade Area, either as an alternative to, or including, the six members of the EEC. 'Be something of a St Paul, not merely the Jews but the Gentiles should be his care,' Macmillan wrote.[20] It was not so much that the British wanted to have it all ways – the American alliance, European free trade and Common Market too – but that in the wake of Suez, nothing seemed fixed, and all seemed fluid in a dangerously swirling world. As Macmillan recalled his first day in office, 'I had found our friendship with the United States destroyed, the European alliance almost shattered, and dismay and uncertainty in many parts of the Commonwealth.'[21]

By instinct, tradition and ancestry, and because Eisenhower's friendship was a lever which could redeem the problems in Europe and elsewhere, Macmillan resolved to mend his American fences first. And at Bermuda, the two elderly gentlemen relished their reunion, wandering in and out of each other's rooms in their pyjamas, chatting of old times and new challenges. Eisenhower was more than happy to make up, and later said the meeting had been 'by far the most successful international conference I had attended since the close of World War II'.[22]

Not only did they agree to base America's Thor missiles in Britain – for another four years the only US nuclear missiles that could reach the Soviet Union – but to equip them with a system of joint Anglo-American control. They were to be manned by British troops, but a dual key would be required to fire the weapons, one held by the Americans, the other by the British. Within the year, the Sputnik shock allowed Eisenhower to persuade Congress to erode the McMahon Act and share information with Britain on the design and manufacture of nuclear weapons, and also to share fissionable materials.[23] But nuclear weapons were not the only benefit of the special relationship which Macmillan had re-established; he needed American influence on a wider basis.

'The French have it in their power to wreck the European Free Trade Movement, and that in the long run must mean a further division of Europe, the probable end of Nato and most serious reorientation of British policy,' Macmillan wrote to Caccia, his Ambassador in Washington, asking him to arrange for the Americans to put pressure on the French. There was no certainty that the Common Market would actually develop. Philip de Zulueta, the Foreign Office liaison as Macmillan's private secretary, expressed the orthodox view: 'We really don't think the French and Germans will ever bury the hatchet to the extent of getting together to make the Common Market work.'[24]

Wrong-headed in retrospect, de Zulueta seemed right at the time. The French humiliation after Suez complicated the vicious war being fought in Algeria, which France insisted was no colony but a part of *la Patrie*. One of the French motives in attacking Egypt had been to stop Nasser's support for the Algerian independence movement, the FLN. After Suez, Nasser's support for the FLN intensified, and Soviet propaganda in the Middle East began, not unreasonably, to focus on Algeria as a symbol of Western imperialism. The war became increasingly controversial in France after *Le Monde* published the secret Béteille report, which acknowledged that the systematic use of torture was a central feature of the French campaign.[25]

In the two years after Suez, France gave every appearance of being ungovernable. Immediately after Macmillan's lunch with Guy Mollet, the French government fell, and there was no replacement for twenty-two days. Strikes and demonstrations against the Algerian war continued. *Le Monde*'s offices and the homes of its editors were fire-bombed. The dock-workers of Marseilles refused to unload the coffins of the conscripts. In May 1958, the French Army mounted a coup in Algeria, bringing on a political crisis in Paris, which was resolved only when General Charles de Gaulle was brought back to power. De Gaulle restored stability by killing off the Fourth Republic, and replacing it with a far more stable constitution which gave him as President sweeping powers to appoint and dismiss governments. In effect, he saved a kind of democracy in France by becoming a kind of dictator.

One of de Gaulle's first acts was to invite the US Commander of Nato forces, General Lauris Norstad, to give him and his military staff a full briefing on Nato deployments in France. Norstad did so, but spoke only of conventional weapons. De Gaulle then asked the American general to continue, spelling out the deployments of all the nuclear weapons in France, and their targets. De Gaulle's biographer recounts the momentous scene which ensued.

'Sir, I can answer only if we are alone,' Norstad said. 'So be it,' said de Gaulle. The two staffs withdrew. 'So then?' de Gaulle pressed. 'Then, Sir, I cannot reply to your questions, to my very great regret . . . ' And de Gaulle in conclusion: 'General, that is the last time, and make yourself understand it, that a responsible French leader will allow such a response to be made.'[26]

Technically under the terms of the Nato treaty, and under US law, General Norstad was right. But de Gaulle's country was in the front line of any Soviet attack. War would mean that those US nuclear bases on French soil would inevitably be targets for Soviet nuclear weapons. Nato prided itself on being an alliance of free states, in defence of the Free World, and not a Western version of the Warsaw Pact in which the Soviet Union dominated its satellites. The spirit of the Nato alliance entirely justified de Gaulle's cold fury. It was therefore an otiose and unnecessarily offensive non-reply which General Norstad gave to an allied head of state, when President Eisenhower was only a transatlantic phone call away.[27] Eisenhower had gone to great lengths to restore to the British that intimacy over nuclear affairs to which every British government had felt morally entitled since British physicists first persuaded President Roosevelt to launch the Manhattan Project, and helped to build the original atom bomb. Eisenhower could, and almost certainly would, have authorised Norstad to tell his old wartime comrade-in-arms whatever he needed to know. But that bizarre exchange between the American general, and the leader of an allied state he was sworn to help defend, foreshadowed the difficult decade which was to culminate in France's withdrawal from the military obligations of the Nato alliance, and the polite but firm request for all US troops to leave French soil, in 1966.

Behind de Gaulle's reaction lay a much deeper cause for concern, which was shared by the British. The technology of the ICBM transformed the strategic situation. It opened one possibility of a US–Soviet nuclear war, with the missiles passing over untouched European heads. It opened another, of the Soviets threatening a nuclear war with the United States in order to make gains in Europe. For de Gaulle, and indeed for all European leaders in private, there was a new nightmare, that the Kremlin might offer an American President the dreadful choice of surrendering Paris and Bonn without a fight, or risk losing Chicago. The ICBM imposed a monstrous burden of trust upon the Nato alliance and its nuclear deterrent. For the alliance to work, the Americans had to be able to convince the Europeans that they would be prepared to take nuclear hits on American cities, rather than abandon Western Europe.

In the aftermath of Suez, Western European leaders had good cause to ask themselves whether America would stick by them through thick and thin – particularly in the days before an American Presidential election. The question was acute for Adenauer's government in West Germany. For him, the immediate result of the Suez crisis was a visit to Bonn by Harold Macmillan to explain that the British air force in Germany was to be halved, and the army garrison reduced from 77,000 to 64,000 men.[28]

At the same time, George F. Kennan, America's intellectual father of the Cold War, was spending an academic year at Oxford, where he was invited to give the Reith Lectures for the BBC. Kennan suggested that it was time for both the United States and the Soviet Union to withdraw their troops from Germany, and leave it as a unified, demilitarised and neutral country. 'Until we stop pushing the Kremlin against a closed door, we shall never learn whether it will be prepared to go through an open one,' he suggested.[29] Back in the United States, James Burnham, that other Cold War intellectual who had opposed Kennan's containment policy as defeatist and had called for a policy of liberating Eastern Europe, startled conservative friends by agreeing with Kennan. Burnham too called for German neutrality, and a withdrawal of the troops.[30]

Such men were influential, which explains the stunning shock which greeted Adenauer in July 1958, when he received a personal letter from the American Secretary of State which began: 'My dear friend . . . ' Dulles went on to ask the West German Chancellor what he thought of a new idea to reduce the armaments of both sides in Germany 'through establishing significant zones of inspection which could greatly minimise the fear of massive surprise attack'. Dulles stopped some way short of suggesting unification, but this was the thin end of a wedge which led to demilitarisation of a freshly sovereign German state which had just won the right to rearm.[31]

Adenauer was appalled. Dulles, the man who had vowed 'to liberate the captive nations', was now conniving at their abandonment. The American commitment to Europe was suddenly, in these post-Suez and post-Sputnik days, far, far weaker than he had thought. The British were cutting back their forces. Adenauer's understandable reaction was to look to the only other support to hand, to France and de Gaulle, which meant to accept the French concept of Western Europe, and pay whatever economic price was required to the new Common Market in order to secure a French alliance.

Irony piled upon irony. The Western alliance had fallen into crisis because of the Anglo-French colonial adventure at Suez. Now both Britain and France were making amends. De Gaulle began taking the decisive step of abandoning French Algeria, and would face down another attempted military coup and a prolonged terrorist campaign in order to grant full independence in 1962. Under Harold Macmillan, Britain began quickly to divest itself of what had been the world's most extensive colonial empire. Ghana and Malaya were granted independence within the Commonwealth in 1957, Nigeria followed in 1960, and Kenya in 1963. More symbolically for Britain, and for that Western vulnerability to Soviet anti-colonial propaganda which so chafed American opinion, Macmillan made the divestiture with some generosity, considerable grace, and a ringing statement of decent principle. On his visit to South Africa, Macmillan addressed the parliament which had passed the racist legislation of apartheid, and announced:[32]

> The wind of change is blowing through this continent . . . As a fellow member of the Commonwealth it is our earnest desire to give South Africa our support and encouragement. But there are some aspects of your policies which make it impossible for us to do this without being false to our own deep conviction about the political destinies of free men, to which in our own territories we are trying to give effect.

And yet, having recognised with Suez that the game was up for colonial powers, Macmillan was simultaneously embarking on an unprecedented burst of gunboat diplomacy and troop deployments. The difference was that he was doing it in conjunction with the Americans, and doing so in the Middle East, to shore up some of those Western strategic and petroleum interests which had been imperilled after Suez. On 14 July 1958, General Abdel Karim Kassim led a military coup against the pro-British government of Iraq, and announced friendly relations with Nasser's latest diplomatic coup, the United Arab Republic. This was a loose federation of Egypt, Syria and Yemen, held together by little more than Nasser's Arab nationalist convictions. But the implications were momentous throughout the Middle East, not least in Lebanon, where pro-Nasser Muslims had begun a civil war against the Christians.

Eisenhower and Macmillan moved fast. British paratroops landed in Jordan, to shore up the nervous regime, and 14,000 US Marines waded ashore on the Lebanese beaches. They landed far enough from the fighting to be cheered by sunbathing women in bikinis. Dulles explained to the US Congress that 'recent Soviet political activities . . . [meant] . . . it was time to bring a halt to the deterioration in our position in the Middle East'.[33] Nasser flew to Moscow seeking support, and was refused. The new Iraqi government hastily announced that all oil contracts with Western companies remained in force.

Two years later, Iraq moved again, threatening to take over its '19th Province', the newly independent sheikhdom of Kuwait, just released from the British colonial yoke. The sheikh asked for the yoke to return in protective mode, and British troops flew back again. And at the southern end of the Persian Gulf, where the UAR member state of Yemen was supporting a nationalist movement in British-occupied Aden and in the colony of Muscat and Oman, British troops were reinforced yet again. The war in Oman was to sputter on well into the 1970s. And at the far end of the Indian Ocean, the British were about to deploy the largest military force they had sent overseas since 1945 to help defend the former colony of Malaysia against an aggressive Indonesia.[34]

Just as France was to deploy troops repeatedly in Africa in the 1960s and 1970s, so Britain was to find itself deploying troops to the Middle and Far East (and to Central America in the 1970s, during the Belize crisis with Guatemala) rather more frequently and into rather more danger after granting independence, than when trying to enforce its colonial grip. Just as Britain and France found themselves being forced to turn inwards to a strategic future in Europe, they were dispatching troops all across the old empires. But this was not bringing Britain and France any closer together. Macmillan's success at restoring his nuclear and strategic relationship with Eisenhower intensified de Gaulle's suspicion of the Anglo-Saxons. The closer Britain cleaved to America, the more de Gaulle leaned to Adenauer.

And Adenauer's alarm at the American fashion for theories of German neutralisation inclined him towards France.

'De Gaulle is bidding high for the hegemony of Europe,' Macmillan recorded in his diary, as de Gaulle invited Adenauer for a personal visit to his home at Colombey.[35] Perhaps. But de Gaulle was clearly seeking to build a Europe that could be independent of the arrogant Americans and their British Trojan Horse. The British were not prepared to make the European commitment, he told Adenauer. They should be excluded from the Common Market, and the Common Market should also stay out of that British plot for a European Free Trade Area. Under Macmillan's grandiose vision, this would include the Common Market and all the other nations, Austria, Denmark, Portugal, Switzerland, Norway and Sweden.

For de Gaulle, this was all a British ploy to weaken the Common Market into nothing more than a customs zone, and make Western Europe all the more vulnerable to the penetration of American capital. At Colombey, and during a return visit to Adenauer at Bad Kreuznach, de Gaulle engineered German support for the veto on British entry he finally announced on 14 November 1958. It was just six weeks before the Treaty of Rome came into force, to establish the European Economic Community and to seal Britain's exclusion. More tellingly, for the British and American assumption that the Soviet threat would eventually force de Gaulle back into line, his veto was announced four days after Khrushchev launched a new Berlin crisis, with the demand that Britain, France and the United States remove their 30,000 troops from West Berlin and make it into a free city.[36]

Something new was under way. In the Cold War's first decade, Western Europe had huddled together under American protection, and suspended most of the traditional jealousies for the greater imperative of survival. But the combination of strategic stability with prosperity in Europe brought back all of the old continent's pretensions, and its nationalist rivalries. The Suez adventure had been one symbol of this revival of European confidence. Another was that formal date of European economic recovery in 1958, the open convertibility of all their currencies against the dollar. The intra-European squabbles which followed Suez were yet another sign of maturity, albeit of an unhappy kind. It was a period of jostling for position between Britain, France and Germany, a revival of the culturally familiar nineteenth-century game of the European powers.

Suez and Sputnik, Dulles and de Gaulle, had combined to put the Western alliance under intense pressure in the late 1950s. But Nato and the West looked wholly cohesive by contrast with the disrepair in the Communist bloc. Indeed, the word bloc could hardly be applied to the region from Berlin to Beijing, after the twin blows of Khrushchev's de-Stalinisation and the Hungarian uprising. Khrushchev himself was almost toppled, the old guard in the Kremlin taking advantage of his visit to Finland in June 1957 to mount a palace coup within the Praesidium. It failed, in part because Marshal Zhukov was on Khrushchev's side, and made military aircraft available to fly back to Moscow the far-flung members of the Communist Party Central Committee. But the real significance of Khrushchev's victory was that it depended upon a form of party democracy. Khrushchev simply refused to accept that the Praesidium had the right to sack him. He had been elected General Secretary by the Central Committee; only they could dismiss him. He insisted that a full plenum of the committee be assembled, and vowed to abide by the result. Khrushchev won overwhelmingly.

This was one striking illustration of how matters had changed since the de-Stalinisation speech. The second was the fate of Khrushchev's enemies. They were not shot or dispatched to the Gulag. Molotov was demoted to Ambassador to Mongolia, Malenkov was appointed manager of an electric-power plant, and Kaganovich was made director of a cement factory. Kaganovich even telephoned Khrushchev, tearfully begging him 'not to allow them to deal with me as they dealt with people under Stalin'. Khrushchev replied: 'You will be given a job. You will be able to work and live in peace if you work honestly like all Soviet people.'[37] That at least was the version Khrushchev gave to the twenty-second Party Congress. And certainly, all the conspirators of what was called the Anti-Party Group lived, even if not permitted to tell their tale.

China had been appalled by the attacks upon Stalin, disappointed by the modesty of Soviet economic help, and increasingly worried at Khrushchev's attempts at *détente* ever since the Geneva summit of 1955. There were two distinct themes to Chinese policy after 1956. The first was self-reliance. 'China must rely upon her own resources as much as possible,' declared Li Fu-chun, chairman of the State Planning Commission, in May 1957. His colleague, Po Yi-po, chairman of the State Economic Commission, took the sentiment further, announcing that China must 'reduce reliance on foreign countries'.[38]

The second theme was that the newly evident Soviet technological superiority meant, in Mao's words to the Moscow conference on the anniversary of the October Revolution: 'The international situation has now reached a turning point. There are two winds in the world today, the East wind and the West wind . . . I think the characteristic of the situation today is the East wind prevailing over the West wind.'[39] And from there, it was but a short step to the new image of the West that became a cliché of the Chinese press, that the imperialists were paper tigers.[40]

Mao's blithe readiness to accept the inevitability of a nuclear war, and its possible utility as a way to bring about the final defeat of capitalism, stunned his comrades from other countries. According to China's later denunciations of Moscow, it was during this conference that the Soviet leadership agreed in principle to give China uranium-enrichment facilities and a demonstration model of the atom bomb. It was never delivered: Mao's immediate reaction may have given them pause for thought.[41] Shmuel Mikunis, the leader of the Israeli Communist Party, recorded a conversation in the Kremlin between Mao and Palmiro Togliatti, the Italian party leader:[42]

> Togliatti then asked him: 'But what would become of Italy as a result of such a war?' Mao Tse-tung looked at him in a thoughtful way and replied, quite coolly, 'But who told you that Italy must survive? Three hundred million Chinese will be left, and that will be enough for the human race to continue.'

Throughout 1957, as the Chinese party operated under Mao's permissive slogan 'Let a hundred flowers bloom', it was assumed in Moscow as in the West that China was undergoing its own version of de-Stalinisation and relaxation. But within months, in the words of one young Central Committee official in Moscow, 'having allowed the hundred flowers to bloom, the Chinese leadership began mercilessly to mow them down, and the new policy began to look like a provocation'.[43] Just as Khrushchev was hoping to assert the unity of the Communist world, and contrast it with the disarray of the West, China then put intense pressure on Khrushchev to condemn Yugoslavia for 'revisionism'. Khrushchev acceded, as the price of maintaining his ties with China. But then these too began to fray, as China plunged into a double crisis, at home and on its nervous coastline.

The Chinese economy had never recovered from the civil war, and the attempts to impose collective farms on a vast country with poor communications proved disastrously inefficient. The Chinese leadership, after an angry internal debate, decided on the massive gamble of the Great Leap Forward. The goal was to concentrate twenty years of Soviet-style development into a single year. The method was draconian, to militarise the land, reducing 700,000 collective farms into 26,000 communes. Each unit of 20,000 peasants became the farming equivalent of an army division, and disciplined in military fashion. In the cities, the disappointing industrial production was to be doubled by exploiting backyard industry, asking blacksmiths to do the work of miniature steel mills.

While this giant and ultimately abortive upheaval was under way, China began shelling the offshore islands of Quemoy and Matsu, occupied by the forces of Taiwan. The American Seventh Fleet shipped Taiwanese reinforcements to the islands, and provided extra artillery capable, at least in theory, of firing atomic shells. Mao appealed for Soviet nuclear weapons; Khrushchev responded only with assurances, that the Soviet Union would come to China's support if the Americans actually attacked.[44]

For China, this was betrayal. For Khrushchev: 'We didn't want to give them the idea we were their obedient slaves, who would give them whatever they wanted, no matter how much they insulted us.'[45] Fundamental differences between Beijing and Moscow also developed over the levels of Soviet aid, and above all over the way to respond to the US–British show of force in the Middle East in 1958. China, which seemed to have an overblown view of the strategic superiority the Sputnik implied, was adamant. China's official *People's Daily* declared: 'There cannot be the slightest indulgence towards American imperialism's act of aggression.' Khrushchev, who knew that the Soviet armed forces at that time had in fact a very modest nuclear arsenal of about one hundred warheads, and fewer than thirty missiles to deliver them, appealed for a summit with Eisenhower.[46]

'Our country and the United States are the two most mighty powers in the world. If other countries fight among themselves, they can be separated. But if war breaks out between American and our country, no one will be able to stop it. It will be a catastrophe on a colossal scale,' Khrushchev told a party rally in Dnepropetrovsk, shortly before his trip to the United States finally took place in 1959.[47] He had made a similar point to a visiting group of American state governors shortly before that. He seems to have been entirely genuine in his realisation of how dreadful a nuclear war would be, and firmly opposed to granting such weapons to the less restrained Chairman Mao. So how are we to explain Khrushchev's occasional forays into the kind of brinkmanship which appeared to risk nuclear war? His threat to Britain and France at the time of Suez may have been empty. But it could have provoked that American nuclear response which we know Eisenhower was steeling himself to make, if missiles actually landed on London and Paris. Khrushchev's spasmodic provocations over Berlin may seem a lesser kind of crisis. But he kept jabbing at that nerve, with his demand for a withdrawal of Western troops in 1958, the building of the Berlin Wall, and the sudden stand-off between US and Soviet tanks in 1961. Any such confrontation always carried the risk of unexpected escalation, of junior commanders panicking and shooting, of a process getting under way which might easily escape the control of the cooler heads in Washington and Moscow.

Khrushchev's Berlin campaign was seen by one of the key Americans who had to face it, President Kennedy's national security adviser McGeorge Bundy, as a logical result of the Sputnik event. For the White House, the Berlin crisis was: 'A Soviet exercise in atomic diplomacy . . . an effort to use a new appearance of Soviet nuclear strength to force changes in the center of Europe.'[48] It was the first deliberate nuclear challenge by the Kremlin, a foray into the world of risk and what Dulles had labelled brinkmanship. A complexity of motives were at work here: the pride of the Soviet military; the Kremlin's determination to be seen to command American respect; the temptation to test the depth of American resolve, and the cohesion of the Nato alliance, by some nuclear pressure. A final factor may have been Khrushchev's own internal jostling with political rivals and constituencies, in the Soviet Union and perhaps in China.

But the Americans too played at brinkmanship. The United States under Truman had rattled the nuclear sabre when it first sent B-29 bombers to Britain at the time of the Berlin blockade. President Eisenhower made another nuclear flourish to bring about an armistice in Korea. He and Dulles had done so again, perhaps more discreetly, when Britain refused to join them in support of the French in Vietnam at the time of Dien Bien Phu, to force the Vietminh and the Chinese to the Geneva negotiating table. Rather less discreet was the dispatch of nuclear-capable artillery to Quemoy and Matsu in 1958. To the Kremlin, these were clear messages, whether explicit threats through diplomatic channels, or mobilisations and deployments of nuclear-capable forces. Both sides were gaining experience in this delicate game of 'exercises in nuclear diplomacy'.

The same complexity of motives that can be ascribed to Khrushchev came into play in the White House. Eisenhower had allies to reassure, and military and political constituencies in Congress and the Pentagon, to appease. He too came under occasionally intense military pressure, particularly at the time of Dien Bien Phu, to use nuclear weapons. The US Air Force chief of staff, General Nathan Twining, was all for it: 'I don't think that three small A-bombs placed properly would have caused too much trouble or set a precedent, but it would have taught those Chinese a good lesson, we would have saved the French and perhaps our present difficulties in Southeast Asia could have been avoided,' the general recalled for the Dulles oral history project. 'I still think it would have been a good idea.'[49]

In spite of all these motives that impelled them into the risky arena of nuclear diplomacy, there is no sign that Eisenhower or Khrushchev was ever seriously prepared to initiate the final step towards war. But each man was also, for reasons of personal and national prestige, reluctant to be seen to back down at any point. The stakes involved in nuclear diplomacy were so great that each leader during a crisis was poised on an uneasy see-saw, having to keep a tenuous balance between sinking into war on the one side, or into a perceived kind of surrender on the other. A subtle gamesmanship came into play as each side began to invent entirely new rules of etiquette in this nuclear world. While it was tempting to see the other side lose balance and fall into a retreat which signalled humiliation, it was also dangerous. Too hasty an attempt to restore equilibrium after tilting towards surrender could send the see-saw plunging fast the other way. It became almost as important to save the other side's face in a crisis as to save one's own. The basic rule of this new game was that it had to be kept going; to end it could mean the end of the world.

The difficulty in maintaining this nuclear balance was that so many unpredictable weights would suddenly land on one end or the other of each side's see-saw. The allies, for wholly internal reasons that had nothing to do with the US–Soviet balance, could suddenly send their leaders teetering on the brink of losing control. The Anglo-French invasion of Suez was but the first and most dramatic of these sudden shocks to stability. China was just as unpredictable for Moscow. Just as Khrushchev began angling for a summit meeting with Eisenhower in 1958, the Quemoy–Matsu crisis blew up off the Chinese coastline, and the Iraqi officer corps decided to mount their military coup.

The nuclear balance was constantly at risk from the unexpected. On the first day of the new year of 1959, Fidel Castro's guerrillas seized power in Cuba after four years of fighting. At least the Cuban crisis took some months to build, time for both Khrushchev and the United States to start making some assessments of the dangers and opportunities that a pro-Soviet Cuba might present. Oddly enough, these slow-building but constant crises proved far more dangerous than the sudden storms in the Middle or Far East that came without warning. The two most dangerous moments in the nuclear relationship came over Berlin and over Cuba, two flashpoints in which the superpowers had the luxury of time to establish their priorities and their policies.

In the case of Berlin, they even had the benefit of a rehearsal. The Soviet government had every reason to try to settle the still unresolved question of a peace treaty that would formally end World War Two and establish the frontiers of Eastern Europe. Khrushchev's proposal contained a good deal of sense. He suggested that the USA, UK, France and Soviet Union all sign with the two Germanies a peace treaty which recognised the de facto frontiers. This would open the way for the Polish and Czech frontiers to be ratified too. Recognising that Berlin was a problem, with the island of West Berlin still surrounded by what Khrushchev called the German Democratic Republic, he proposed making Berlin a free city. It would be demilitarised and self-governing, its integrity and access to the outside world guaranteed by the four powers and both Germanies.

For the West, this entailed an insurmountable legal problem. It would mean that the land access to Berlin would pass from the control of the Soviet Union, a fellow signatory of the four-power occupation agreement of 1945, to the sovereign government of a newly recognised East Germany. The implications of such a move also worried the West. It would signal a retreat from an outpost that had been so staunchly defended during the Berlin airlift. It would set a precedent of Western withdrawal from West German interests, and from the principle of eventual German unification. It would also remove from the heart of the Soviet Empire a Western outpost, glittering in prosperity and beaming out radio waves and TV transmissions of the capitalist promise. It would close an extremely useful intelligence listening post, and it would dismay the West German allies, who were at the heart of both Nato and the new EEC.

These were not considerations the West chose to over-publicise, so they stuck by the legal argument, even when Khrushchev in his impatience set a six-month deadline for the West to agree. The alternative, he declared, was that he would sign his own independent peace treaty with East Germany, and let the West worry about negotiating their own access past East German border guards. All this was put with characteristic bluntness, and in his meeting with Chancellor Adenauer, the Soviet Ambassador was deliberately offensive, as Soviet officials usually were when dealing with West Germans. Adenauer could never forget his first meeting with Khrushchev, in Moscow in 1955. Adenauer was seeking the return of the estimated 130,000 German POWs still in the Soviet Union. In response to Adenauer's request Khrushchev snapped that there were only 10,000, all of them Nazi war criminals. When Adenauer persisted, Khrushchev shouted at him to remember the Italians who had come on the German side to invade Russia. They had gone home too – all in coffins.[50]

So on 11 March, President Eisenhower found himself at a White House press conference being asked if the United States was prepared to conduct a nuclear war if necessary to defend free Berlin. Eisenhower picked his words with care: 'I didn't say that nuclear war is a complete impossibility. I said it couldn't, as I see it, free anything . . . We have got to stand right ready and say, We will do what is necessary to protect ourselves, but we are never going to back up on our rights and responsibilities.'[51]

It was a neat encapsulation of the nuclear dilemma. The weapons were, in themselves, so destructive that they were militarily useless. They could not free anything, only eradicate it. But the issues on which they stood guard went to the very core of a state's identity and interest. They could neither be rationally used, nor rationally forsworn. The trick was to identify one's own core interests, and those of the nuclear adversary, and be careful not to trespass upon them. Years later, in retirement, Eisenhower told his biographer, 'There is nothing in the world that the Communists want badly enough to risk losing the Kremlin.'[52] This was true, but missed half the point. The trick of nuclear diplomacy was to define what, whether territory or allies or that elusive oriental concept of face, the Soviet leadership would so dread losing that they might indeed prefer to risk losing the Kremlin.

That first Berlin crisis was settled when Khrushchev dropped his deadline once Eisenhower agreed to negotiate, and to invite Khrushchev to the United States. The very fact that he had done so suggested that Soviet nuclear diplomacy was working, that West Berlin was a nerve that the Soviets could irritate as and when they chose. But the problem of losing face now began to afflict the American side. Sputnik was in the sky, and was now joined by a new satellite weighing 1.5 tonnes, which made the military potential of a Soviet ICBM brutally clear. America was still discussing the Gaither Report, and doing so on the basis of that best-seller of 1959, *The Uncertain Trumpet*, the explosive book by the former US Army chief of staff, General Maxwell Taylor.

General Taylor argued that the doctrine of 'massive retaliation' had run its course, and 'could offer our leaders only two choices, the initiation of general nuclear war, or compromise and retreat'. The book was a passionate argument for a more flexible and much larger military force, capable of fighting effectively various levels of war, regional or global, without having to resort to nuclear weapons. And it concluded with a warning from one familiar with the Gaither Report: 'It must be made clear to our citizens that the nation will face a serious crisis beginning about 1961. For a period of years thereafter, the balance of military strength will tip dangerously in favour of the Communist bloc unless we take drastic action now.'[53]

Taylor's call, with all the authority of one of the country's leading generals, became one of the texts of the 1960 Presidential election campaign. Each of the three Democratic candidates, Senator Lyndon Johnson of Texas, Senator Stuart Symington of Missouri, and Senator John F. Kennedy of Massachusetts, campaigned hard on the missile gap. Kennedy, who won the Democratic nomination, was by far the most hawkish on the size of the gap, on its strategic implications, and on the evil nature of the enemy. 'The enemy is the Communist system itself – implacable, insatiable, unceasing in its drive for world domination,' ran the speech with which he opened the autumn campaign, at the Mormon Tabernacle in Salt Lake City. 'This is not a struggle for supremacy of arms alone. It is also a struggle for supremacy between two conflicting ideologies; freedom under God versus ruthless, godless tyranny.'[54]

In his stump speech of the campaign, the core message which he repeated at every stop along the campaign trail, Kennedy promised a programme of rearmament that would ensure that the United States would not lose that struggle. 'We will mould our strength and become first again. Not first if. Not first but. Not first when. But first period. I want the world to wonder not what Mr Khrushchev is doing. I want them to wonder what the United States is doing.'[55]

There was no missile gap, and Kennedy knew it. Eisenhower had arranged for the Democratic candidate to be briefed by CIA Director Allen Dulles, by Strategic Air Command, and by the joint chiefs at the Pentagon. They all told Kennedy the same thing. Khrushchev might claim that his factories were turning out missiles like so many sausages. He was not. The main Soviet nuclear strength lay in medium-range missiles that threatened the whole of Nato Europe, and in long-range manned bombers that were a threat, but not a crippling one. Of ICBMs that could reach the United States, there were but a handful, and they were being produced very slowly. In fact, US intelligence later established that only four examples of the first model of Soviet ICBM had been built.[56] By contrast, the first Polaris missile-armed submarine, the *George Washington*, became operational in 1960. Within two years, there were eight more at sea, carrying a total of 144 nuclear-tipped missiles which were invulnerable to Soviet retaliation.

Much of Khrushchev's nuclear diplomacy was based on bluff, and the credibility given to that bluff by Sputnik. For the world public, Soviet pre-eminence in missiles was further established in September 1959 when Khrushchev marked his arrival in the United States with the impact of the Lunik, a Soviet research missile, upon the surface of the Moon. When they met, he thoughtfully presented President Eisenhower with a replica of the Soviet pennant the Lunik had carried.[57] Although little was decided in their meetings, Khrushchev returned to Moscow waxing lyrical about 'the spirit of Camp David', the President's country retreat, where they had at least agreed to meet again in a four-power summit the following year.

The Soviet missile bluff could not be long sustained after 1956, when the US Air Force bought forty-eight single-seater models of Lockheed's U-2 spy-plane, and five two-seater models. Flying too high for Soviet anti-aircraft missiles or fighters, they roamed the skies above the Soviet Union with impunity after 1957.[58] From bases in Japan, Turkey and Britain, they stayed in the air for twelve hours, mapping and photographing the vast land mass, its air and missile bases and factories. Eisenhower's scepticism of the missile gap was based on hard evidence. He had been charmed and convinced of the powers of the U-2 when the CIA gave him a photograph of himself playing golf at Augusta, taken from 70,000ft. He could even discern the golfball.[59] But the evidence was never quite complete, and in 1960, as Eisenhower prepared for a new summit with Khrushchev in Paris, the CIA pressed for one last mission, to establish whether there might be a missile plant or base near the Urals, in an area which had only been sketchily surveyed. It was a mission too many; the latest version of anti-aircraft missiles finally caught up with the American technology.

On 5 May, as the summit was about to begin, Khrushchev announced that a U-2 had been shot down over Soviet territory. The immediate American reaction was to deny that it had been on a spy mission, but had merely lost its way. This thin tale Khrushchev triumphantly refuted by producing the pilot, Gary Powers, his suicide needle, cameras, and irrefutable evidence that this had been an espionage mission. Eisenhower accepted responsibility, and declared in Paris that the spy flights had taken place with his full knowledge. Khrushchev was evidently determined to take maximum advantage of the event, even if the summit collapsed. He insisted on an American apology, a promise not to do it again, and that 'the criminals be punished'. Eisenhower refused. De Gaulle pointed out that modern technology was making sovereignty over a state's higher airspace a more and more elusive concept; a Soviet satellite, he pointed out, was orbiting over France. Macmillan tried to reach a compromise, but then sank into gloom and the pages of his comforting Jane Austen novel.[60] The Paris summit never took place.

The thaw was over, and the spirit of Camp David had expired. A month later, the Soviet delegation walked out of the Geneva disarmament talks, where Macmillan had been pushing hard for a nuclear-test control agreement. Macmillan, de Gaulle and Eisenhower were all baffled by the vigour of the Soviet reaction. But then the Commonwealth proved its worth. Tunku Abdul Rahman of Malaysia wrote to Macmillan to suggest that the Soviet hard line was less to do with East–West relations than with the growing crisis in Sino-Soviet affairs.[61] Macmillan had never thought of that. Two weeks after the Tunku's letter, Khrushchev delivered his first open attack upon the Chinese with an eighty-page letter of denunciation at the Bucharest conference of the Romanian party.[62] The Sino-Soviet split was public.

The split had been coming for at least two years, but Khrushchev had tried to paper it over. He had kept silent when Chinese troops crossed the Indian frontier, and scattered the Indian forces, in August. Immediately after the Camp David meeting with Eisenhower, Khrushchev had flown to Beijing for a disastrous visit. The Chinese denounced his casual statement that Eisenhower evidently enjoyed the support of the American public. This was dangerous ground. Khrushchev was not so secure in Moscow that he could afford a split with China, at least on the grounds that he was being too conciliatory to the West. There were enough among the Soviet generals and the party who might agree, or find that argument a useful lever to pry him from office. Khrushchev's retort that his policy of *détente* would yield useful results was unproven. There was no sign of any settlement on the German question, and the provocative American spy flights continued. With the U-2 scalp hanging from the belts of his proud generals, Khrushchev found it politically expedient to take their side.

He had tested his generals' loyalty far enough. In the four years after the de-Stalinisation speech, the Soviet armed forces had been reduced from 5.8 million to 3.6 million men. Shortly after Marshal Zhukov had saved Khrushchev's political life during the attempted palace coup of June 1957, Khrushchev had sacked Zhukov, who was dangerously powerful, and replaced him with Marshal Malinovsky. At the same time, he accelerated the military cuts, retired over 14,000 officers, and imposed a new degree of party control by establishing a main Political Directorate for Army and Navy as a department of the party's Central Committee apparatus. In January 1960, at the Supreme Soviet session, he announced a further deep cut of 1.2 million men, reducing the Soviet armed forces to 2.4 million in total, their lowest level since 1938.[63] Khrushchev argued that missiles and nuclear weapons meant that the nature of Soviet security no longer relied on mass armies, but the social effects of this cut were highly disruptive. Almost 100,000 officers and even more veteran NCOs were dismissed, and many of them were left homeless and unemployed for a prolonged period. The morale of the conventional armed forces sank, even as the party's political control over them tightened, and the promotions and the remaining budgets were lavished on the new arm of the Strategic Rocket Forces. In this context, it is evident why Khrushchev held off the Sino-Soviet split as long as he could, and tried to maintain something of that spirit of Camp David with which he justified his defence cuts.

Equally, it is clear why Khrushchev gave up on the lame-duck President Eisenhower, when he knew he would face a vigorous new generation in the White House within six months. The choice was already becoming evident, between Vice-President Richard Nixon, who had led the persecution of Alger Hiss and the American left, or Senator Kennedy, who was campaigning on the need to close the missile gap. Neither one was promising. But if Khrushchev was beset by the schism with the Chinese, the Americans had new difficulties in their own back yard. Nixon had been mobbed by anti-American demonstrators in Venezuela, and the Americans had a new enemy. In July 1960, alarmed at the course of the new government of Fidel Castro in Cuba, they cut Cuba's sugar quota from the US market. The Soviet Union signed a trade pact to buy Cuban sugar in exchange for petrol and technical help. For Khrushchev, the American alarm was a Soviet opportunity: 'They feared, as much as we hoped, that a socialist Cuba might become a magnet that would attract other Latin American countries to socialism.'[64] Exactly: the pattern of the new confrontation with the new American President was set.

Chapter 6
The Torch Has Been Passed

> You above all who have come to the far end, victims
> Of a run-down machine, who can bear it no longer;
> Whether in easy chairs chafing at impotence
> Or against hunger, bullies and spies perserving
> The nerve for action, the spark of indignation –
> Need fight in the dark no more, you know your enemies.
> You shall be leaders when zero hour is signalled,
> Wielders of power and welders of a new world.
>
> *'The Magnetic Mountain'*, C. Day Lewis

The central importance of the Cold War to politicians, generals and state officials was not always apparent to the taxpayers who sustained them. By most standards of statesmanship, the British Conservative governments which had been in office throughout most of the decade of the 1950s had performed miserably. They had exposed the nation to an unprecedented international humiliation at Suez. The old colonial empire, source of so much pride that the wall maps in the state schools were still dominated by great swathes of imperial crimson, was being divested apace. Britain's former command of the oil resources of Iran and Iraq had been sharply curtailed.

The government had failed in its attempt to persuade the whole of Western Europe to join a free-trade area, and its belated scratching at the door of the European Economic Community had been rebuffed. The alternative of the Atlantic Alliance was still clutched, and American nuclear bases on British soil, where a token Royal Air Force officer was nominal camp commander but where British laws no longer ran, were now a permanent feature. But Suez had revealed the limits of American forbearance and support. In the great game of nations, the Conservative governments had played a series of losing hands. And yet they were triumphantly re-elected to office in October 1959, increasing their majority over all other parties in the House of Commons from 67 to 107 seats.

The explanation lay in economics, and the growth of prosperity, astutely exploited by the advertising firm of Coleman, Prentice & Varley. Hired for the unprecedented fee of £500,000 to sell the Conservative cause to the public, they pasted on billboards across the country the slogan: 'Life's Better Under the Conservatives – Don't Let Labour Ruin It'. Macmillan's own throwaway remark, 'You've never had it so good', may have enjoyed more popular resonance. The growth rate of the 1950s averaged slightly less than 3 per cent a year. This was good by British standards, and sufficient to win the 1959 election. But by comparison with the Western European economies, this growth rate was feeble, and it spelled relative decline. The British growth rate of the 1950s averaged something between one-third and one-half of the growth rates enjoyed by Italy (5.9 per cent annually) or Germany (7.6 per cent) during the same period. Prime Minister Harold Macmillan's reaction to this was both resigned and rather weary: 'Of course, if we succeeded in losing two world wars, wrote off all our debts – instead of having nearly £30,000 million in debts – got rid of all our foreign obligations, and kept no force overseas, then we might be as rich as the Germans.'[1]

When writing his first letter, of congratulation and amicable advice, to the newly elected President Kennedy, Macmillan made clear his conviction that economics lay at the very heart of the confrontation with Communism. It was not simply that wealth was essential to buy weapons and military research, but that the Cold War itself was a form of economic competition. He began by suggesting to Kennedy that the Atlantic Alliance was 'not properly adjusted to the realities of the 1960s', and went on to warn that this was a race the West could yet lose. Macmillan did not say so, but the Soviet economy in the 1950s had been growing more than twice as fast as the British.

The main question, Macmillan suggested to the President-elect, was:[2]*

> what is going to happen to us unless we can show that our modern free society – the new form of capitalism – can make the fullest use of our resources and results in a steady expansion of our economic strength . . . If we fail in this, Communism will triumph, not by war, or even subversion, but by seeming to be a better way of bringing

* This letter to Kennedy was deemed important enough for Professor J. K. Galbraith to be summoned to the Oval Office to discuss its implications. When Galbraith arrived, the letter could not be found. The White House was turned upside down, until the document was finally located in the nursery of Caroline, the President's three-year-old daughter.

> people material comforts. In other words, if we were to fall back into anything like the recession or crisis that we had between the wars, with large-scale unemployment of men and machines, I think we would have lost the hand.

Macmillan's 'new form of capitalism' was the mixed economy, which depended on a blend of private enterprise and strategic intervention by the state. The state was able to direct national resources to provide a welfare safety net for its citizens, to support chosen industries, and to manipulate the money supply and interest rate to speed or slow the economy. It was based very largely on the theoretical work of Keynes, and on the practical lessons of the Great Depression of the 1930s. Governments took the big decisions, as Eisenhower had done to build the Interstate road network, or to pass the post-Sputnik Education Acts, or to spend their way out of recessions.

With an economy as dominant as that of the USA, the state could also deploy its investments into building up the economies of whole continents. Europe was thriving after the Marshall Plan, Japan was booming after the Korean War 'Special Procurements'. To have been an official in the US State Department or in the Treasury in the 1950s was to have felt, quite literally, like a master of the universe. The global economy lay there, waiting to be kissed into glowing life by an astute deployment of the US dollar. There were recessions and bumps along the road, to be sure. But the self-assurance of governments that their economies could be steered into self-sustaining growth was remarkable, a modern equivalent of that sublime Victorian faith in 'progress'. It seemed, as Macmillan had written to Kennedy, that governments had at last found the golden key to endless economic growth.

But other words were ringing simultaneously in the new President's ears. As John Kennedy came into office in that cold January of 1961, Eisenhower had delivered a farewell address that was uncharacteristically thoughtful, and sobering. He warned that the Cold War had produced something 'new in American experience . . . the conjunction of an immense military establishment and a large arms industry . . . [its] influence is felt in every city, every state house, every office in the federal government . . . In the councils of government, we must guard against the acquisition of unwarranted influence, whether sought or unsought, by the military–industrial complex.'[3]

The awesome weight of the defence budget in the American economy had weighed heavily on Eisenhower. In 1960, defence expenditure took 52.2 per cent of federal spending,[4] or just over 10 per cent of

GDP. It had been even higher, peaking at 12.7 per cent of GDP in 1954, and the Eisenhower Administration's reliance on the doctrine of 'massive retaliation' had been justified as a cheaper way of deterring the Communists. It was still expensive, and as Eisenhower warned, budgets of that size created powerful political and institutional constituencies. They were to be found in trade unions as in the Pentagon; among real-estate developers around the booming new defence plants of Texas and Georgia and California; and among the politicians whose electors worked in them. They all sought to ensure that the money continued to flow. Wall Street too enjoyed the Cold War. Aerospace stocks rose in value, three times higher than the stock-market average, between 1947 and 1956.[5]

Sums of this size – and the US defence budget was for the first two decades of the Cold War about half the size of the entire British economy – not only generate their own supporters. The ability to control and direct a defence budget worth 10 per cent of American GDP also gave governments a powerful lever to stimulate the rest of the economy. Keynes's theory of government intervention in the economy, and Eisenhower's military–industrial complex, combined in a marriage made in that heaven of Harold Macmillan's 'New Capitalism'. The Gaither Report had already made this explicit, talking of the beneficial impact upon the economy of the massive civil-defence project it recommended.

Even without such a programme, the Cold War was transforming the industrial geography of the United States, and shifting the new manufacturing base to the Sunbelt. The southern and western states had right-to-work laws, which weakened the role of trade unions. The South also enjoyed stable state politics, which meant that sheer longevity had won them the chairmanship of the key Congressional committees where the Pentagon's spending decisions were made. Lyndon Johnson of Texas was the Senate Majority leader, and Georgia's Richard Russell and Carl Vinson ran the Senate and House armed services committees between them. The resulting symbiosis brought the Houston space centre to Texas, where Bell helicopters and the Vought division of LTV Industries also boomed. Georgia's boom came with military bases, and the Lockheed plants at Marietta.

Since World War Two, the aerospace industry had been building new industrial bases away from the traditional industrial heartland of the north-east and the Great Lakes. The long military spending boom and the McDonnell–Douglas, North American and Hughes Aircraft plants helped explode the Californian population sixfold in the five decades after 1940, while Boeing expanded in the north-west. General

Dynamics and McDonnell–Douglas helped create another regional military–industrial complex in St Louis. And in the name of national security, and justified in terms of the need to evacuate the cities in a nuclear alert, all of these new industrial centres were linked into a continent-wide grid through the Interstate highway network.

A similar process, far more intensively planned and ruthlessly directed, was under way in the Soviet Union. Like the growth of California, it had begun during World War Two, but in more urgent circumstances. In one of the most remarkable transmigrations in industrial history, the Soviet system dismantled and evacuated a total of 1,523 strategic factories from the path of the advancing Germans in the winter of 1941–2, and shipped them to the new industrial areas beyond the Urals, out of bombing range. Just over 700 of them were rebuilt in a vast new industrial zone around Sverdlovsk and Chelyabinsk, which was to become a nuclear weapons development complex in the 1950s. Another 350 factories were shipped across the Caspian Sea to Kazakhstan, where a new coal and steel zone was humming at Karaganda. And another 200 of these arms and machine-tool plants were transported over the Trans-Siberian railway to the Soviet Far East.[6]

The cataracts of defence spending and investment in the three most heavily armed states, the USA, Britain and the Soviet Union, produced oddly contradictory economic effects. The investments in armaments plants spurred the raw statistics of 'growth', but only in the way that those deceptive statistics would record a car accident as 'growth' because of the economic activity generated by the towing firms, the hospitals and the insurance companies. There were some hugely important exceptions, where military technology transferred directly into the civilian economy. The benefits were evident in electronics, satellites and the Boeing 707 jet airliner, which began life as a military refuelling tanker for Strategic Air Command.

But much of the military spending was economically hollow. The defence-industry payrolls may have enriched California and Texas and Sverdlovsk, yet the output of those plants did not generate more growth in the civilian economy. The products of the defence economy found their justification mainly in the protection they provided the civilian economy which financed it. The tanks and aircraft and submarines went to training camps and airfields, were crashed or destroyed, mothballed and finally broken up for scrap. They gave the appearance of power, but over the years the diversion of research and manpower investment resources into the defence industries eroded that power's financial base. The fastest-growing economy of the period, Japan, never spent more than 1 per cent of GDP on defence. West Germany's defence budget peaked at 5 per cent of GDP in 1965, but fell below 4 per cent in 1975 and remained there. The economy which invested the most in defence spending, the Soviet Union, proved over the long term to be the most damaged by this distorted allocation of resources.[7]

The burden of superpower status was already becoming apparent in the United States as John Kennedy took the oath of inauguration as President in January 1961. The steady leakage of gold from Fort Knox had become so worrisome that he told one visitor that the two things that troubled him most were nuclear war and the payments deficit. It was, if not money well spent, then money with a strategic purpose behind it; what one historian called 'the expenses of running a Pax Americana'.[8]

In 1946, at the end of World War Two, the US held 60 per cent of the world's gold reserves. By 1949, the US share had risen to 72 per cent, in part because of the onerous repayment terms imposed on the British for post-war loans. To this degree, the Marshall Plan's effusion of dollars into Europe was forced by the way US economic dominance drained Europe of gold and dollars in the immediate post-war years. The Marshall Plan, and the later foreign-exchange costs of keeping US troops overseas, reversed the situation. The United States ran a constant balance-of-payments deficit throughout this period, and financed those deficits not with gold, but in paper dollars. Those paper dollars were, however, backed by gold. If the Europeans suspected that the dollars might not be sound, they were legally entitled to demand gold from the vaults at Fort Knox.[9]

The cautious Europeans, and in particular France, suspected that this paper financing might eventually end in a dollar devaluation. As a result, between 1949 and 1959, they used the US dollars piling up in their banks and their treasuries to purchase $5.7 billion of gold from the US. The US financial authorities had brought this upon themselves, with the post-war economic system that was devised at the Bretton Woods conference. As the world's reserve currency, the US dollar had to finance the emerging global economy. Robert Solomon, of the Federal Reserve Board, noted in retrospect: 'Of the $8.5 billions increase in world reserves in the years 1949–59, the US provided $7 billions through the increase in its liabilities to foreign monetary authorities.'[10]

As Kennedy took office, the balance-of-payments deficit was $2 billion, and gold was leaving Fort Knox at a rate of $1.5 billion a year and rising. This was a significant fraction of the $22 billion in gold and international monetary reserves which President Kennedy discovered to be held by the US government in January 1961. Eisenhower's Treasury Secretary had already visited the European central bankers to ask for their restraint, with little success, and it was his deputy, the Republican Douglas Dillon, whom the worried Kennedy appointed to be his own Treasury Secretary. Dillon, whose European credentials and tastes were reflected in his purchase of France's Haut-Brion vineyard, found his efforts frustrated by Kennedy's own economic policies.[11]

Eisenhower had tried, and failed, to balance his budgets, and suffered a $12 billion budget deficit in 1958. Kennedy was a more enthusiastic Keynesian, and in 1961 began a series of fiscal deficits in the federal budget that were to last until 1969. The budget deficit averaged $6 billion a year in the 1960s, until the Vietnam War took it to $25.2 billion in 1968. And America's balance-of-payments deficit on official settlements went from $3.4 billion in 1960 to $10.7 billion in 1970.[12] At Bretton Woods in 1945, the United States had sown the seeds of its own economic crisis by rigging the rules of international currencies to suit itself, and match its economic dominance. But that dominance could not be indefinitely sustained, and by force-feeding the growth of the Japanese and Western European economies, the United States brought the day of reckoning closer. The US economy was so vast and resilient that the harvest was only to be reaped in the 1970s, but throughout the 1960s it was growing and ripening. The Democratic Administrations of 1961–9 financed – all on deficits and on credit – their rearmament boom, their domestic welfare reforms and 'Great Society' programmes, as well as the Vietnam War and their growing private investments in Japan and in Western Europe. It was too much.

Had the US economy kept pace with those whose growth it had financed, the dominance of the post-war years could have been maintained. But during the 1950s, industrial productivity in Germany increased by 6 per cent a year, and in France by 4 per cent. US productivity, by contrast, was growing at 2.4 per cent annually over the decade. This not only implied a relative decline of US economic efficiency, it also became a self-sustaining trend, as US corporations realised they could make better returns on their investment in Europe than at home, and began to export more capital overseas to take advantage of it. In 1950, the book value of US holdings in Europe was $1.7 billion, and by 1969 it had increased more than tenfold to $21.5 billion.[13]

Most of the profits of these American-owned enterprises remained in Europe, to be reinvested, and help swell that astonishing new international currency, the Eurodollar. The Eurodollar was homeless money, the American money which had left the United States and stayed in European banks to become a new financial instrument. By 1966, there were some $15 billion in Eurodollars being traded in the European markets, an uncontrolled currency whose size and volatility helped force the devaluations of the original dollar in the 1970s.[14]

From the traditional US point of view, this was a progression towards national impoverishment. But tradition was a poor guide to the extraordinary transformation which the Cold War was inducing in the American economy. Until 1940, when conscription was first introduced in peacetime, America had always had a tiny standing army. In 1939, it numbered only 174,000 men, and although the US Navy represented a substantial investment, the defence budget took only 3.4 per cent of the GDP. The Cold War changed all that. The Army grew with the special demands of the Korean and Vietnam wars, but even in nominal peacetime, the US Army was maintained at a complement of around one million men, and the share of the overall US economy devoted to defence remained between two and three times the levels of 1939.

The US economy was not only to this degree militarised by the Cold War, it was also internationalised. American patterns of trade and investment were transformed, and what had been a virtually self-sufficient economy before the Second World War became locked ever more deeply into the global trading system that was emerging. The trend is plain. From the depth of the Great Depression in 1933, when total US exports amounted to $1.65 billion, America's trading relationships with the rest of the world simply exploded. A snapshot of US exports at the start of each new decade shows the following (in billion dollars):

1950	1960	1970	1980	1990
$10.2	$20.4	$42.6	$216.7	$421.6

Exports tell but part of the story. The investment by American companies in the Western European economy, and increasingly in Japan too, intensified this trend of the deepening interdependence of the Western world. From a total of $1.7 billion in 1950, to a total of $21.5 billion in 1969, by 1989 this flood of private investment was running at the extraordinary level of $150 billion a year. This was the global economy with a vengeance. And these investments were not made by government strategists or bureaucrats or statesmen as the

Marshall Plan had been, but by wealth-seeking managers and entrepreneurs. Just as the Cold War had forced the USA to internationalise its military commitments and spread its bases across the globe, so trade followed the flag and internationalised the US economy too. The process also transformed the nature of industrial organisation.

If the classic managerial structure of the first phase of the industrial revolution in Britain had been the joint stock company, and the next phase of industrial expansion was led by the cartels of individual nations, the characteristic formation of the Cold War's global economy was the multinational corporation. By 1968, for example, a mere twenty US-based corporations accounted for more than two-thirds of all US investment in Western Europe, and some 40 per cent of US investments in France, Britain and Germany were held by three multinationals, Ford, General Motors and Standard Oil of New Jersey, better known as Exxon.

Seen from Western Europe, two interpretations of this process were possible. An economic nationalist like President de Gaulle, or his austere financial adviser Jacques Rueff, could see this as an American economic invasion, financed on the sly by paper money and an inflating dollar. Taking the longer view, we can see this as an essential stage in the building of a global economy. The American balance-of-payments syndrome became the mechanism by which the wealth the United States had accumulated during and after World War Two was redistributed in productive investments elsewhere. The United States might have hoped to maintain for ever that 50 per cent of global GDP which it enjoyed in 1946, but the 25 per cent share it was to enjoy by the 1980s was a smaller share of a vastly larger global economy. Americans might not have kept pace with the economic growth rates of Europe and Japan, but they had got very much richer anyway.[15]

This steady shifting of economic weight from the United States to the European allies it had rescued and financed makes American strategic policy in the 1960s look like altruism comparable to the generosity of the Marshall Plan. It was also, of course, done in the longer-term American national interest. National security, not to say the verdict of the next US Presidential election, was deemed to hinge on maintaining the countries of Western Europe as American allies and trading partners and the areas as a US sphere of influence. But this national security was not cheaply bought. The United States continued to devote a far greater share of its wealth than the Europeans to its defence budget, at least a third of which could be ascribed to Nato.

The US sold cheaply to Britain the technology and equipment necessary to maintain British nuclear pretensions, and later secretly donated nuclear skills to France.[16]

The United States was so lavish with its nuclear weapons that in 1960, while the world and particularly the Soviet Union were constantly assured that West Germany would never become a nuclear power, the Joint Committee on Atomic Energy of the US Congress discovered that this was not so. By accident, in the course of a visit to a Nato airbase in Germany, they discovered German-manned fighter-bombers sitting on alert on the edge of the runway, and equipped with nuclear weapons. The only evidence of the much-vaunted 'American control of warheads' was the presence of a US Air Force officer, equipped with a revolver, 'somewhere in the vicinity'.[17] As a result of this incident, PALs, or Permissive Action Links, to give real control over the warheads, were developed and deployed. Such was the US generosity, and good sense in a hair-trigger nuclear world, that the PAL technology was later made freely available to the Soviet Union by US Defense Secretary Robert McNamara.[18]

This incident on the German airfield took place as the United States was facing the very real possibility of nuclear war with the Soviet Union over Berlin. It was for the West a heroic and beleaguered outpost, and for the Warsaw Pact it was an open sore, through which spies and radio and TV propaganda leaked one way, and East Germany's own best-educated citizens leaked out in the other direction. The tension of the time is caught by Khrushchev's offhand remark to the US Ambassador Llewellyn Thompson at a Kremlin New Year's Eve party at the end of 1960. Talking blithely of the need to avoid nuclear suicide, Khrushchev said that fifty nuclear bombs were assigned to France, 'more than enough to destroy that country'. Another thirty each were allocated to Britain and West Germany. Mrs Thompson asked how many were devoted to the USA. 'That is a secret,' Khrushchev replied.[19]

He may have been joking. One suspects not. The prospect of war was extraordinarily close at the start of the 1960s, and even without nuclear war, the Soviet leader was convinced that the eventual defeat of the West was inevitable. Indeed, two days before President Kennedy was inaugurated, Khrushchev published a truncated version of a speech he had given to party propagandists on 6 January. Nuclear war would destroy civilisation, he said, but the 'sacred struggle of national liberation . . . [was now] . . . the only way of bringing imperialism to heel'. Kennedy had copies of the speech circulated to his top advisers, with the comment 'Read, learn and inwardly digest'.[20] Kennedy's own rhetoric proved even more fiery, and the combination of his inaugural address and his first formal statement to Congress was bluntly bellicose towards Moscow, and deliberately alarmist for his own people and allies.

'We shall pay any price, bear any burden, meet any hardship, support any friend, oppose any foe to ensure the survival and success of liberty,' he declared in the address. The later phrase, 'My fellow Americans, ask not what your country can do for you; ask what you can do for your country', certainly caught the imagination of his fellow countrymen.

In Moscow, the trick was to comprehend which message was being sent to them. Was it the call to talks – 'Let us never negotiate out of fear, but let us never fear to negotiate'? Or was it the following, even more ambiguous clarion call?[21]

> Since this country was founded, each generation of Americans has been summoned to give testimony to its national loyalty. The graves of young Americans who answered the call to service surround the globe. Now the trumpet summons us again – not as a call to bear arms, though arms we need; not as a call to battle, though embattled we are; but a call to bear the burden of a long twilight struggle, year in and year out, rejoicing in hope, patient in tribulation, a struggle against the common enemies of man; tyranny, poverty, disease and war itself.

These were stirring words, high-flown and deliberate oratory which retain a certain magic today. But what do the words actually say? Moscow's bafflement in the face of these balanced but contradictory phrases commands sympathy. The plight of the Central Committee's translators was acute. Doubtless they in the Kremlin were the 'tyranny', identified as the first of the common enemies of man. That was clear. But were they being invited to an international coalition to give foreign aid to the poor, or to a nuclear war? Were the Americans called to arms or not? Were these already embattled Americans being called to a new battlefront, and if so where, and against whom?

Matters were somewhat clarified ten days later, in the second Kennedy address, to the Joint Houses of Congress, although again the penchant of the Presidential speechwriters for the balanced cadences imbued the entire statement with a studied ambiguity. But there was no mistaking the thrust of the message. Now that the new President had looked at the international situation, and at the means he had inherited to cope with it, one conclusion was compelling. The West was losing the Cold War.[22]

> No man entering upon this office, regardless of his party, regardless of his previous service in Washington, could fail to be staggered upon learning – even in this brief ten-day period – the harsh enormity of the trials through which we must pass in the next four years. Each day the crises multiply. Each day their solution grows more difficult. Each day we grow nearer the hour of maximum danger, as weapons spread and hostile forces grow stronger. I feel I must inform the Congress that our analyses over the last ten days make it clear that – in each of the principal areas of crisis – the tide of events has been running out, and time has not been our friend.

Kennedy announced a crash programme to bring the new Polaris and Minuteman strategic missiles into operation. Two months later, after a brisk defence review, he announced that the Polaris building programme would be doubled that year, and the increased total of twenty-nine boats, each armed with sixteen nuclear missiles, would start coming from the shipyards at the rate of one a month. The Minuteman production capacity was also doubled, and the B-52 and B-47 nuclear bomber force was to be placed on a crisis footing. Half of the entire force was to be on fifteen-minute alert at any given time.

While this capacity for massive retaliation was being assembled, the doctrine of massive retaliation was itself to be modified: 'Our objective is to increase our capacity to confine our response to non-nuclear weapons.' Accordingly, conventional forces of men and ships and warplanes were to be increased, along with the airlift capacity to deploy them. They would be trained for new battlefields with new quasi-guerrilla tactics and equipment. 'Non-nuclear wars, and sub-limited or guerrilla warfare, have since 1945 constituted the most active and constant threat to free world security.'[23]

Between the announcement of 'the hour of maximum danger' and the military responses to it, the crises had brewed. On 13 February, the Soviet Union threatened to intervene in the newly independent Congo, after the assassination of its first leader Patrice Lumumba. The CIA was involved in this, even if the final killing was carried out by Congolese troops. The local CIA station chief, Lawrence Devlin, had in fact been ordered to arrange Lumumba's death, and given a suitable kit of toxins and hypodermic needles.[24] The pro-Communist Pathet Lao were so close to taking control of Laos that 'detailed plans for the introduction of American forces were presented to the President' on 9 March.[25] On 18 March, a nationalist uprising broke out in Angola against the Portuguese colonial regime, a Nato ally. The uprising was, in the words of Kennedy's special counsel Ted Sorensen, 'supported by America's African friends'. On 21 March, at the Geneva talks on a nuclear testing ban, the Soviet negotiators called for a veto over the special inspections being envisaged to verify compliance with the treaty, which the United States saw as ditching the prospects for a test ban.

While the new defence-spending speech was being written, two further crises were gestating. At Baikonur, the Soviet space station, Lieutenant Valentin Bondarenko died in an accidental oxygen fire on 23 March while preparing to become the first man to be launched into space.[26] And in their secret CIA training camps in Guatemala, the 1,400 men of Cuban exile Brigade 2506 were preparing to invade Cuba. The stage was set for another symbolic confrontation, a new Soviet success in space to set against a new American disaster. On 12 April, Yuri Gagarin, who was Lieutenant Bondarenko's first reserve and had stood over his deathbed, more than repeated the triumph and the shock of the Sputnik launch four years earlier. Soviet man had once again paraded his technological prowess, winning the race to orbit the earth, and was quick to trumpet the implications. Said *Pravda*:[27]

> You wish to know what Communism is, gentlemen? Then open your eyes to the heavens and you will see that Labour has become master of a considerable part of the world, and behold what it produces. A Soviet man has left the confines of the earth. This sentence alone, like a mathematical formula, sums up the preceding history of human society, the harnessing of the mighty forces of nature and the growth of man himself.

On the day this *Pravda* editorial appeared, the Cuban exiles landed on Zapata Beach at Cuba's Bay of Pigs. The surprise air-strike by B-26 bombers, provided by the CIA and masquerading as Cuban Air Force defectors, failed to destroy the Cuban fighters on their airfields. The obsolete B-26 bombers were then shot from the sky by the Cuban jet trainer aircraft, who also sank the ammunition supply ship on which the invaders depended. Fidel Castro's army and militia reacted with impressive speed and military skill, and within three days, had killed, captured or thrown off the entire landing force. They had seen themselves as liberators, but the expected popular rising against Castro did not occur. Indeed, the defeat of the US-backed invasion testified to the strength of Castro's popular support.

This was not Kennedy's operation, but an inheritance from Eisenhower. It had been planned since March of the previous year by the

CIA's highly confident covert operations branch under Richard Bissell. Kennedy was personally assured by the CIA chief Allen Dulles that the invasion would succeed in toppling Castro.[28] Kennedy insisted that no US forces be directly involved, although US aircraft were to fly an ill-coordinated air-cover mission, and to help retrieve some of the attackers from the beach.[29] It was a humiliating disaster, fraught with ominous implications for Kennedy's policy towards that developing and newly independent world he had addressed in his inaugural speech. 'We pledge our word that one form of colonial control shall not have passed away merely to be replaced by a far more iron tyranny,' he had said then. And while his meaning is clear, the Bay of Pigs was an unhappy way to go about it. The concern the defeat aroused among America's allies about the future US role in the developing world was regretfully expressed by *Le Monde*: 'Soviet propaganda will find it easy to convince world opinion, starting with the peoples of Latin America, Africa and Asia, that the vaunted anti-colonialism of the USA is no more than a façade which shelters a hypocritical idealism.'[30]

The Soviet Union was, in fact, drawing a rather different lesson. Still flushed with Gagarin's space triumph, *Pravda* noted: 'The time has passed forever when the US could brandish its stick in the belief that it was the biggest and longest, because the other side now has equally long and heavy, and no less powerful sticks.'[31]

The reaction of the world's press to the Bay of Pigs is instructive, in part because this was an audience in which Kennedy took great interest, believing that the Cold War was ultimately a struggle for the hearts and minds of people across the globe. The massed editorials, and the role of the US press in particular, also reveal the degree to which the media felt it was part of the struggle. The *New York Times* and the *Washington Post* both knew of the invasion in advance, as they had known of the U-2 spy flights over the Soviet Union, and held back their stories in the national interest. At the request of the CIA, the *New York Times* withdrew its reporter from Guatemala, which at least saved him the embarrassment of being on the scene of a story which would not be run. Phil Graham, publisher of the *Post* and a friend of Kennedy, even 'killed' a critical editorial on the eve of the invasion.[32]

There was no doubt whose side the newspapers were on. 'The struggle now going on for Cuba is like a battle in a long, complicated and spread-out war . . . The US is engaged in an all-out struggle to save the Western Hemisphere for democracy and freedom,' ran the *New York Times* editorial. But this was already more than a regional or hemispheric issue. Khrushchev in Moscow had warned: 'We shall render the Cuban people all necessary assistance in beating back the armed aggression against them.' The *Washington Post* was supportive of the White House, but depressed by the implications of failure: 'If now the invasion should fail, it would appear to the world as if the Soviet Union had saved [its] Cuban stooges by intimidating the United States. That is the unlovely prospect that may confront this country unless the effort to deliver Cuba from the Communists quickly catches hold.'[33]

Equally interesting is the degree to which the leading papers of the European allies echoed this reflex support of the American position. West Germany's conservative *Die Welt* strained to see the entire affair as a Western victory: 'The unmistakable "Halt" which the young President has conveyed to Khrushchev leaves no more doubt about American policy towards the USSR and its lust to expand. The USSR is fully answered, in the proper form, in an unshakeable manner.' And Italy's *Corriere della sera* openly mourned: 'This failure is a tragedy. A tragedy for that courageous band of men who went to fight against a bloody tyranny and who are now, in part, its prisoners.'[34]

This media support was in sharp contrast to the wave of anti-American demonstrations across Latin America, and the stoning of the US Embassies in Tokyo, New Delhi and Cairo. The goodwill which Kennedy had sought to build in the developing world with his promises of more aid programmes and the Peace Corps was seriously jeopardised. The reaction was particularly severe in Latin America, which Kennedy liked to call 'our sister republics south of our border', and which had the previous month been promised an Alliance for Progress: a commitment to $20 billion in US aid over the next ten years. Generous in view of the balance-of-payments pressure on Kennedy's Treasury, this was strategically an indispensable investment if it could buy off the seductions of Cuba, the first socialist outpost in the western hemisphere.

'The great battleground for the defence and expansion of freedom today is Asia, Africa and the Middle East, the lands of the rising peoples,' the President told Congress just a month after the invasion's defeat.

> The adversaries of freedom did not create the revolution, but they are seeking to ride the crest of its wave, to capture it for themselves. Yet their aggression is more often concealed than open. They have fired no missiles, and their troops are seldom seen. They send arms, agitators, aid, technicians and propaganda to every troubled area. But where fighting is required, it is usually done by others, by guerillas striking at

> night, by assassins striking alone – assassins who have taken the lives of 4,000 civil officers in the last twelve months in Vietnam alone – by subversives and saboteurs and insurrectionists, who in some cases control whole areas inside independent nations. With these formidable weapons, the adversaries of freedom plan to consolidate their territory, to exploit, to control and finally to destroy the world's newest nations; and they have the ambition to do so before the end of this decade. It is a contest of will and purpose as well as force and violence – a battle for minds and souls as well as lives and territory. And in that contest, we cannot stand aside.

This was more than rhetoric; it was a summons to war and engagement and intervention on a global scale. Announcing his 'Freedom Doctrine', Kennedy asked for $2.65 billion in civilian aid to developing countries, for another $1.9 billion in military aid, and for more money for the US Marine Corps, for new helicopters, and to increase the size of the Army reserve. He also announced a new programme of civil defence to designate and prepare public buildings as nuclear fallout shelters to 'protect millions of people against the hazards of radioactive fallout in the event of large-scale nuclear attack'. And he gave his response to the successful space flight of Yuri Gagarin, announcing 'the goal, before the decade is out, of landing a man on the moon and returning him safely to earth'.[35]

This was an extraordinary and grandiose shopping list. Far more than a rearmament programme, the President was summoning the nation to an unprecedented global ambition. Kennedy cast his Freedom Doctrine around the world, beneath it for the nuclear fallout shelters, and far above it with his space programme. His appeal went beyond America. That combative speech behind him, Kennedy flew to Europe for his first summit with Khrushchev in Vienna. On the way, he stopped in Paris to see de Gaulle, and also to address the Nato council, to rally them behind his far-flung crusade.

'It is a matter of vital strategic significance to the future of your countries and mine that we concern ourselves with the whole southern half of the globe where we are now in danger, and where freedom is now in danger, and where those who place themselves on the opposite side of the table from us seek to make their great advances,' Kennedy told Nato.[36]

Nato did not know what to make of it. Theirs was a defensive and essentially European alliance, whose treaty committed each of them to come to one another's aid if attacked. Suddenly, they were being summoned to a far grander vision. Their reactions were not supportive. Germany's constitution prohibited sending its military forces outside the Nato area. The Netherlands, France and Britain discreetly reminded the American officials travelling with Kennedy that this new global mission was a bit late. Where had this American perspective been when they were chivvying the Dutch out of Indonesia, letting the French down at Dien Bien Phu, and lecturing their French and British allies at Suez? If the Western alliance was going to become aggressive and global and start proselytising for the cause of freedom in areas which the Soviets and Chinese saw as their sphere of influence, what did this imply for Europe? What would be the reaction of the United States, under its new Freedom Doctrine, to another Hungary-style uprising?

Kennedy had raised the point himself, stressing in his speech to Nato that 'Even the experience of those countries behind the Iron Curtain show a strong desire to be free and independent'. For a Western Europe that was settling down to peace and prosperity under the stabilising structure of the Cold War, Kennedy's activism was alarming. It also came from a young and untested President who had just been through the serious reverse of Cuba, and who had yet to confront the Soviets. In Paris, de Gaulle warned him against involvement in Laos, and implicitly against the whole logic of the Freedom Doctrine. In the Freedom Doctrine, the European allies like de Gaulle and Macmillan – who knew a thing or two about colonial entanglements and battles that did not go exactly as the military men promised they would – saw the ominous outlines of what was to become the Vietnam War. They argued against the Laos operation, and Macmillan in March and de Gaulle in June were able to talk him out of it.

'The more you become involved out there against Communism, the more the Communists will appear the champions of national independence, and the more support they will receive, if only from despair . . . You will sink step by step into a bottomless military and political quagmire,' de Gaulle forecast.[37] Macmillan had warned Kennedy against the Laos intervention plan in much the same terms at their first, daylong meeting at Key West in March. Kennedy had invited Macmillan to sit through a military briefing on the plan; when Kennedy asked his opinion he replied: 'Not much. It's not on.' There were three choices, Macmillan went on: a pro-American puppet government that would be corrupt, unpopular and require eventual US support; or US financial and military support straight away, which would mean 'armies that will get bigger and bigger'; or stay out altogether.[38]

On this occasion, Kennedy took the advice, and was able to reach a temporary accommodation with Khrushchev for an unstable form of neutralisation of Laos. It was an unsatisfactory and short-lived arrangement, but it was to be the nearest to an achievement that was reached at the disastrous Vienna summit. Kennedy was not well. His bad back had been weakened by the earlier visit to Paris, which combined a gruelling social round with some intensive talks with de Gaulle. Prescribed a daily shot of cortisone for his Addison's disease, an adrenal deficiency, Kennedy sometimes before or after a gruelling day demanded a double dose. He also took procaine injections regularly for his back pain. Moreover, he frequently used the services of the fashionable Dr Max Jacobson. This 'Dr Feelgood' of social Manhattan dispensed hypodermic cocktails which blended vitamins, hormones, enzymes, amphetamines and steroids, with sometimes alarming results. Dr Jacobson claimed to have treated Kennedy in Paris, and to have flown to Vienna with him to continue the treatment during the stress of the summit.[39]

We know more about the Kennedy–Khrushchev summit than we do of almost any top-level gathering of comparable importance. Thanks to the American historian, Dr Michael Beschloss, and the US Freedom of Information Act which he used in a four-year private campaign, the official memorandum of the meetings taken by Kennedy's translator has now been made public. It makes depressing reading, as the two men simply fail to make anything that could be described as human contact. In the transcript, Khrushchev reads as if he was the one taking amphetamines, as he bullies and blusters, doubtless testing out the young adversary whom he already reckoned to have shown some weakness over Cuba. Kennedy kept trying to get the discussions back on track, to find some common ground, but became steadily steelier in the final session which closed on a deeply ominous note.[40]

They began with a long argument about the Third World, Kennedy complaining at Communist subversion, Khrushchev asserting with evident sincerity that Communism was bound to win the battle of ideas. Kennedy suggested they should try to manage their differences, that the struggle of ideas should be kept at arm's length from the vital interests of the two countries. When Kennedy then warned about the dangers of 'miscalculation', Khrushchev exploded angrily, 'We don't make mistakes. We will not make war by mistake.' After lunch, they walked privately in the gardens, and argued over Berlin, Khrushchev wagging his finger at the President.

At the next formal session, Khrushchev was enormously gratified when Kennedy suggested that he saw the 'Sino-Soviet forces and the forces of the United States and Western Europe as being more or less in balance'. This helped produce the half-agreement for neither side to push too hard in Laos. But this session too was filled with bickering. Khrushchev accused the US of seeing the Kremlin's hand in every liberation struggle, when it was really the US support of 'tyrannical regimes' which provoked revolutions. There was enough truth in this Soviet assertion, in South Korea and Central America and in the Persian Gulf, to irritate Kennedy to retort with a pointed question about the possibility of having a free government in Poland. Khrushchev countered that if the USA could intervene in smaller countries, why not the USSR? 'If the US believes that it is free to act, then what should the USSR do? The US has set a precedent for intervention in the internal affairs of other countries. The USSR is stronger than Iran or Turkey, just as the US is stronger than Cuba,' reads the transcript of Khrushchev's transparently threatening reply.

At the final day's sessions, mainly over Berlin, the two men snapped at each other like schoolboys. It was now three years since Khrushchev had first raised the need for a new Berlin settlement with an American President. He had been stonewalled or fobbed-off, he complained, and had paid a stiff price both in the restiveness of his generals and with the sneers of the Chinese at his patience. It may have been Khrushchev's sensitivities over the Chinese factor which got the day off to a bad start, as the two men tried and failed to break the impasse over the negotiations on verifying a nuclear test ban. Kennedy quoted a Chinese proverb, that a journey of a thousand miles starts with a single step. That step could now be taken. The transcript suggests that Khrushchev's mood changed from that point on, as if he suspected Kennedy of hinting that he understood the dangerous strategic implications of a Sino-Soviet split. The dialogue degenerated fast as they turned to Khrushchev's demand for a peace treaty to settle the borders of Eastern Europe and recognise East Germany's sovereignty.

'If the US refuses to sign a peace treaty, the USSR will have no other way out than to sign such a treaty alone . . . History would judge their actions . . . If the US wants to start a war over Germany, let it be so. Perhaps the USSR should sign a peace treaty right away and get it over with. That's what the Pentagon has been wanting,' reads the Khrushchev transcript.

Kennedy said US prestige was involved, along with US good faith to its allies. 'It is an important strategic matter that the world believe the US is a serious country.'

Each man then backed away a little, discussing whether the matter could be delayed some months, and agreed to a final, unscheduled session. It proved to be the worst of all. Khrushchev said an interim agreement would guarantee the Western allies' right of access to West Berlin for six months, 'then it would have to go'. They may have been speaking at cross-purposes here, Kennedy assuming this meant an attempt to evict or bar the Western troops from the city, while Khrushchev was still thinking of his earlier suggestion that the Western forces would have to renegotiate their access to West Berlin with a new and sovereign East German government.

If Khrushchev was going to take this drastic action, he could not believe that the West was serious, said Kennedy. This would be a mistake. He was about to leave Vienna to see Macmillan in London, and would have to tell his British ally that Khrushchev had offered a bleak choice between 'accepting the Soviet action on Berlin or having a face-to-face confrontation'.

Khrushchev then spoke of permitting token troop contingents, including Soviet troops, to be stationed in West Berlin, perhaps under an agreement registered at the UN. But East German sovereignty would have to be recognised. This was a sticking point for Kennedy, an agreement to a permanent division of Germany. It meant letting down his West German allies, and changing a US position which had been firm for fifteen years. It would involve a major loss of personal prestige to do so.

'I want peace, but if you want war, that is your problem,' Khrushchev snapped, banging his hand on to the table.

'It is you, and not I, who wants to force a change,' Kennedy replied after a grim silence.

Khrushchev then declared solemnly that the USSR had 'no choice other than to accept the challenge. It must respond and will respond. The calamities of war will be shared equally. War will take place only if the USA imposes it on the USSR. It is up to the USA to decide.' His decision to sign a peace treaty with Eastern Europe was irrevocable, Khrushchev added, and it would be signed in December. That gave a six-month deadline.

'If that's true, it's going to be a cold winter,' said Kennedy, and his only summit with a Soviet leader came to a deeply ominous end. As he left Vienna, he confided to the *New York Times* reporter James Reston, 'He just beat the hell out of me.'

Kennedy flew to London to see Macmillan, and described the dreadful encounter. Macmillan thought him 'rather stunned, baffled would perhaps be fairer, impressed and shocked'. Macmillan's note of their conversation spoke of the 'brutal frankness of the Soviet leader. The Russians are (or affect to be) on top of the world. They are no longer frightened of aggression. They have at least as powerful nuclear forces as the West. They have interior lines. They have a buoyant economy and will soon outmatch capitalist society in the race for material wealth. It follows they will make no concessions.'[41]

That extraordinary comment, that the Soviet Union 'will soon outmatch capitalist society in the race for material wealth', reflects Macmillan's own penchant for gloom. It illustrates his almost fatalistic sense that while the British could be the wise and experienced Greeks to the new Roman Empire of the brash Americans, that Empire was already beset by the new barbarians. Kennedy in January had spoken darkly of 'the hour of maximum danger . . . time has not been our friend'. And now in June, Macmillan's notes of his talk with Kennedy echoed this foreboding of Western defeat. Even though Kennedy and Macmillan each knew that there was no missile gap, and that the Soviet nuclear arsenal was only a partial deterrent, the psychological battering of the West by Sputnik and Yuri Gagarin was having a potent effect.

The following week, on 10 June, Khrushchev made his six-month deadline for Berlin public. There were US press reports of American mobilisation. On 8 July, Khrushchev announced that the planned Soviet defence cuts, to reduce the armed forces by 1.2 million men, had been cancelled 'as a forced measure'. The Soviet defence budget was increased by 30 per cent. East Germans began to flood into West Berlin at the rate of more than a thousand a day.

It took until the end of July, after long consultations with his allies and generals, for Kennedy to reply. He could not have been less compromising. In a solemn television and radio address to the US people, and pointing at a map to show beleaguered Berlin, the President doubled and tripled the draft calls to bring in new conscripts, increased the armed forces by 15 per cent, and doubled the active reserve. He called for another $3 billion for defence costs, and announced other measures that would swell the US forces by twelve new Air Force wings, and seventy new warships.

Again, Kennedy increased the funds for civil defence, and spoke more frankly than any national leader had yet done about the likelihood of nuclear war. He demanded funds to stock fallout shelters with food, water and medicines. 'We owe that kind of insurance to our families, and to our country,' he said.

> I have heard it said that West Berlin is militarily untenable. And so was Bastogne. And so in fact was Stalingrad. Any dangerous spot is tenable if men – brave men – will make it so. We do not want to fight –

> but we have fought before . . . We cannot and will not permit the Communists to drive us out of Berlin, either gradually or by force . . . There is peace in Berlin today. The source of world trouble and tension is Moscow, not Berlin.

This ranks with Kennedy's speech on the Cuban missile crisis as a moment when nuclear war seriously threatened. But Kennedy also used in that speech a curious phrase which turned out to be prophetic, and may even have been deliberate: 'The endangered frontier of freedom runs through divided Berlin.' So it was to prove.[42]

Khrushchev did not back off, warning the visiting American diplomat John McCloy that if the Western troops tried to force their way through to Berlin: 'We will oppose you by force. War is bound to be thermonuclear, and though you and we may survive, all your European allies will be completely destroyed.' He had summoned McCloy to his Black Sea dacha for the meeting, and while describing the force of the 100-megatonne H-bomb the Soviet Union was about to test, Khrushchev made McCloy's small daughter burst into tears.[43]

Diplomacy could do better than this, and so could politicians. Senator Michael Mansfield had in June mused about the possibility of making Berlin a 'free city'. On 30 July, on a TV talk-show, the influential Senator William Fulbright of the Foreign Relations Committee suggested that the immediate crisis of the fleeing East German refugees might be eased by closing access to West Berlin. 'If they [the East Germans] chose to close their borders, they could, without violating any treaty.'[44] Kennedy's aide Sorensen may or may not have been sarcastic when he described this to the President as 'helpful'. Fulbright's proposal was cited by the East German leader Walter Ulbricht when he flew to Moscow to see Khrushchev on 6 August. Arguing that the Americans had already signalled their acceptance, Ulbricht sought and won Soviet agreement to seal off East Germany, rather than seal off West Berlin, with a barbed-wire fence.

Four days later, Kennedy was asked about the Fulbright proposal at a press conference, and replied blandly that the US neither 'attempted to encourage or discourage the movement of refugees, and I know of no plans to do so'. This was something between a green and an amber light. None the less, Kennedy that weekend was given a briefing on the procedures for reaching the special nuclear bomb shelter that had been built for him on Nantucket Island, near his holiday home. Khrushchev warned that if the West went to war over Berlin, Soviet H-bombs would destroy Europe – 'the orange groves of Italy, the people who created them . . . the Nato bases in Greece, and of course, they will not have mercy on the olive orchards or on the Acropolis'.[45] Khrushchev knew that this was so much bluster, and that the immediate crisis was about to be eased. The Wall went up on the night of 12 August, just after a last day's record of some 2,000 East Germans crossed into the West. Kennedy kept public silence for eight days, while West Berliners demonstrated, and the Mayor Willy Brandt bombarded the White House with angry teletypes. The West tested the access routes to the city from West Germany with a US battle group of 1,500 men. The Soviet and East German border troops let them pass. There was no interference with Western air traffic.

The situation stabilised, in a form which amounted to a sharp propaganda reverse for the Soviet Union, which was now visibly reduced to walling its people in to prevent them fleeing to the West. As if to punctuate the affair with a final defiant bluster, Khrushchev unilaterally ended the three-year moratorium on nuclear tests on 28 August. A series of massive explosions culminated in a fifty-eight-megatonne monster, which sounded vastly impressive, but which could hardly do any more damage to a city such as New York than a single-megatonne weapon, which was already some sixty times more powerful than the Hiroshima bomb. The real purpose of these mammoth bombs was for use against military targets, whether entire missile bases, or as monstrous depth charges in those Persian Gulf, North Sea and Barents Sea areas from which the relatively short-range Polaris missiles would be launched.

There was one further moment of tension, when to enforce the intermittently disrupted access rights of US and British military personnel to and from East Berlin, the US commander General Clay sent ten US tanks to Checkpoint Charlie. He had already rehearsed secret wall-demolition exercises in the West Berlin woods, which had been photographed by Soviet military intelligence. The tanks which suddenly deployed at Checkpoint Charlie were equipped with bulldozer blades. The Soviets had reason to suspect that the US Army was about to break down the Wall, and sent a force of their own tanks to the junction.

A prolonged and much-photographed stand-off took place with the tanks literally a stone's throw apart, the most publicly direct confrontation of the Cold War. It was all done on General Clay's initiative, and took some tricky back-door diplomacy to resolve. President Kennedy's brother Robert met on a regular but discreet basis a senior KGB official, Georgi Bolshakov, nominally the press attaché at the Soviet Embassy in Washington. Through this link, President Kennedy privately requested Khrushchev to withdraw the Soviet tanks, and undertook that the US tanks would quickly follow suit. So they did, and so ended what Secretary of State Dean Rusk later described as 'the silly tank confrontation at Checkpoint Charlie brought on by the macho inclinations of General Clay'.[46]

The Berlin crisis has been a dreadful moment, but it was followed in Europe by a prolonged period of stability, if not calm. The Soviet Union was not unhappy with the outcome. The foreign minister Andrei Gromyko noted that the Wall had done its job: 'This step was so effective that, within two years, Adenauer, the spiritual father of West Germany's militarist ambitions, went into retirement.'[47] The bald effrontery of this remark accompanied a sense of Soviet satisfaction. A problem had been solved. For the 190 people who were to die in the attempt to escape across the Wall, it was solved with grim finality. For the seventeen millions left in the German Democratic Republic, as East Germany called itself, their citizenship was now uncomfortably close to imprisonment.

The continent's political permafrost settled deeper, creeping over that open wound which West Berlin had represented. The hole in the Iron Curtain had now been ringed with steel and concrete. Europe settled down into its two armed camps, into its year-in and year-out readiness for the greatest tank battle in military history, and for what would almost certainly have become a tactical nuclear war. Conscripts were called up on both sides to train for the war that never came, were demobilised and saw their sons and in some cases even their grandsons called up for the same stagnant watch on the frontier. By the time the Berlin Wall finally came down, twenty-eight years after it was built, and in the fifth decade of Churchill's Iron Curtain, it had become an institution and a standing art gallery. The grassy zones between barbed wire and concrete wall had become an unintended nature reserve, undisturbed and filled with rabbits.

Chapter 7
The Cuban Missile Crisis

While we were fearing it, it came,
But came with less of fear;
Because that fearing it so long
Had almost made it fair.

'While we were fearing it', Emily Dickinson

The building of the Berlin Wall was a shaming event, an admission of Soviet inadequacy and nastiness which heartened and vindicated those in the West who saw the Cold War in austerely moral terms. But as Khrushchev had tried to argue at the Vienna summit, the Soviets also had some moral arguments on their side. The Bay of Pigs invasion had been a blunder unredeemed by success, and the State Department White Paper which sought to justify it, written by Arthur Schlesinger, compounded the discomfort of the US position. 'The Inter-American system [was] incompatible with any form of totalitarianism,' the White Paper said.[1]

This principle was not easy to reconcile with the authoritarian regimes of the Duvalier family in Haiti, the Somoza family in Nicaragua, and the dictator Rafael Trujillo in the Dominican Republic. Once Trujillo became an irritant for the US, the CIA helped provide the guns for his assassination in May, six weeks after the Bay of Pigs. Totalitarian, or at least crudely and cruelly authoritarian, regimes were happily tolerated throughout Latin America, so long as they were reliably anti-Communist. And if not, American principles did not shrink from murder. 'The maintenance of Communism in the Americas is not negotiable,' Adlai Stevenson, the US Ambassador to the UN, declared in October 1962.[2] And on the principle that global wars, and revolutionary wars, are not won by the squeamish, America developed de facto alliances around the globe with little regard for the democratic principles it claimed to be defending. 'We must work with some countries lacking in freedom in order to strengthen the cause of freedom,' President Kennedy acknowledged frankly in a speech to

Washington University during the Berlin crisis. 'As the most powerful defender of freedom on earth, we find ourselves unable to escape the responsibilities of freedom, and yet unable to exercise it without restraints imposed by the very freedoms we seek to protect.'[3]

In 1963, just over one million US servicemen were stationed in 203 bases, and another 1,040 'installations' overseas. And as President Kennedy noted in a speech to the Protestant Council of New York in the month of his death, the backing of US foreign assistance programmes 'makes possible the stationing of 3.5 million troops [non-American but allies] along the Communist periphery at a price one-tenth the cost of maintaining a comparable number of American soldiers'.[4] There were US air bases in Fascist Spain, and Dr Salazar's quasi-Fascist Portugal was a member of the Nato alliance. The unpleasant South Asian regimes of Ayub Khan in Pakistan and the Shah in Iran were less openly pro-American, but depended on US armaments and provided intelligence listening posts and occasional basing facilities for the US Air Force. There was an American electronic monitoring station in Ethiopia, and the two partitioned Asian states of South Vietnam and South Korea were both authoritarian and vicious to their internal dissidents.

Great powers have always defended their empires and their influence in terrible and overbearing ways. They have traditionally done so without being accused of hypocrisy, and without being much concerned if they were. But the great-power tussles of the Cold War were waged in a very new kind of arena, in which the rhetoric and political rationalisations of the great powers could be tested and judged by an increasingly informed and concerned audience. First, there was the presence of the ever-expanding United Nations, a court of world opinion which both US and Soviet Union took seriously enough to invest heavy diplomatic and financial resources. Second, there was television.

The Berlin Wall and the stand-off between US and Soviet tanks were the first international crises to be screened widely on both sides of the Iron Curtain. The televised Kennedy–Nixon debates made the 1960 Presidential election into the first in which TV played a decisive role, and broadcast the features and the personalities of the two antagonists across the globe. The youthful, vigorous President Kennedy and his attractive wife Jackie were the first political stars of the TV age. His assassination in Dallas in November 1963 was a uniquely public and international shock, watching the death of a man millions of non-Americans felt that in some way they knew.

There was a vibrant tension between the inspiring image and democratic rhetoric that Kennedy was able to convey through television, and the methods by which that democracy was defended. Kennedy carried conviction when he declared, as he did throughout the 1960 campaign, that: 'The cause of all mankind, is the cause of America . . . We are responsible for the maintenance of freedom all around the world.'[5] But simultaneously, the freedom marches of the Civil Rights movement in the segregated cities of the South, the unleashing of police attack dogs and fire hoses upon black protesters, brought a televised contradiction to Kennedy's claims in his own country, just as so many of America's allies betrayed those ideals of freedom abroad.

'America is today the leader of a world-wide anti-revolutionary movement in defence of vested interests,' the British historian Arnold Toynbee declared in a well-publicised and controversial lecture tour of the United States in the first year of the Kennedy Administration.[6]

> She now stands for what Rome stood for. Rome consistently supported the rich against the poor in all foreign communities that fell under her sway; and since the poor, so far, have always and everywhere been far more numerous than the rich, Rome's policy made for inequality, for injustice, and for the least happiness of the greatest number. America's decision to emulate Rome has been deliberate, if I have gauged it right.

What Toynbee did not foresee was the effect of the 'new capitalism' of which Harold Macmillan had spoken. This meant that increasingly in the USA, and in its most affluent allies in Western Europe and Japan, the poor were ceasing to be 'far more numerous than the rich'. Poverty was still widespread in all these countries, but growing material comfort, job security and unemployment benefit, home ownership and pensions, were slowly transforming the age-old paradigm which Toynbee had cited. The process was fastest and most visible in the United States. To take one crude symbol of the spreading personal affluence: in 1947, there had been just over 30 million registered passenger cars in the country. By 1960 the figure had doubled to 60.1 million. By 1970, it had risen yet again to 92 million, and by 1980 had leapt to 127 million.[7]

Rather more slowly and painfully, this prosperity was by the 1960s beginning to spread into Eastern Europe and the Soviet Union too. By the 1970s, it was a commonplace of the developing world's rhetoric to say that the real distinction was no longer between East and West, Communist and Capitalist, but between North and South, between the rich white world of the northern hemisphere, and the poor brown, yellow and black world of the southern lands. This was not a welcome concept to the rich white North. By a verbal sleight of hand, American politicians used the concept the Free World to juxtapose against the Communist countries. In fact, there were at least three worlds: the prosperous 'new capitalist' states of the northern hemisphere; the Communist lands; and the third, developing world.

Each of these worlds could be subdivided almost infinitely. The Communist bloc had become divided between the Soviet Union and those Eastern European countries where Communism had come with the Red Army, and the three countries of Yugoslavia, China and Cuba where Communism had succeeded as the result of genuine and local revolutions. The developing world had its own geographical distinctions between Asia, Africa and Latin America. There were massive economic and social differences between those once-prosperous Latin American states of Argentina and Uruguay which had gone into decline, and the abandoned raw colonies like the former Belgian Congo which had known nothing but the crudest exploitation of its human and mineral wealth. There were military regimes and civilian oligarchies, oil-rich sheikhdoms and resource-poor states trying to make some sense of the quasi-European parliaments and assemblies they had been bequeathed.

For the newly enfranchised peoples and leaders in those countries, whose independence was constrained by the corset of Cold War rivalries, the choice between East and West was by no means obvious. The West was richer, but historically much of that wealth had been earned through a hated colonial system from which these new countries were emerging. The West might have more aid available, but as Egypt's Colonel Nasser had learned with the Aswan Dam, that aid could be withdrawn for the West's own strategic purposes. And the Soviets, who shared an anti-colonial rhetoric and who seemed from their space triumphs to be building a society of tomorrow, could then step in. To choose the Western side was not only to foreclose an option, it was also to choose a Western economic model, of the World Bank and International Monetary Fund, of subordinating a new country's own economic policies to decision-makers in Washington, London and Paris. It meant opening one's markets to foreign investors and Coca-Cola, and locking in one's exports to a Western market where the terms of trade appeared frankly rigged to ensure the rich got richer.

To choose the Soviet side was equally worrying. It meant a large Soviet Embassy, and a flourishing Communist Party, and a growing

Communist influence in what were meant to be the national armed forces. Soviet investment funds were limited, their capacity to pay for imports with anything but arms and steel mills were constrained. The US economic blockade around Cuba was a grim warning of the price to be paid for supporting Moscow. The obvious solution for most independent nations was to keep the foreign-policy options open, to stay on good terms with both sides of the distant civil war between the rich white folks of the northern hemisphere. Unfortunately, this was not an option which the United States and its allies, or the Soviet Union, were happy to extend.

President Kennedy and Chairman Khrushchev had each declared that with the classic battlefields of Europe strategically frozen, this Third World was to be the new arena of confrontation. Under Kennedy, special military units and new forms of tactics and equipment were developed at the new jungle-warfare training schools at Fort Bragg, in North Carolina, and in the Panama Canal zone. Kennedy took a personal interest in the development of the Green Berets, the special forces. He increased their numbers sixfold, overseeing their uniforms, their special boots and light weapons, to fit them for the new kinds of essentially political and guerrilla warfare he envisaged.[8]

For Kennedy,[9] this was

> a struggle in many ways more difficult than war . . . taking place every day, without fanfare, in thousands of villages and markets and in classrooms all over the globe. Armies and modern armaments serve primarily as the shield behind which subversion, infiltration and a host of other tactics steadily advance . . . exploiting the legitimate discontent of yearning peoples and the legitimate trappings of self-determination.

This is best understood as a post-nuclear, or instead-of-nuclear strategy, a way to continue the struggle against Communism without risking full-scale war or nuclear attack in the northern hemisphere. It was the nuclear age's version of that Great Game which the British and Russian empires had played in Central Asia in the nineteenth century. And just as that Great Game produced the fictional archetype of secret agents in Rudyard Kipling's *Kim*, so the new Great Game produced its own fictional genre in the vogue for spy stories in both East and West. Kennedy was an early fan of James Bond, and Leonid Brezhnev, Yuri Andropov and Mikhail Gorbachev were all readers of Yulian Simyonov, the Soviet equivalent of Ian Fleming. Western cinema audiences flocked to the James Bond films; Aeroflot flights never took off when the serial of Simyonov's *Seven Days in May* was being screened on Soviet television.[10]

But the great irony of Kennedy's attempt to wage a different kind of war on a non-nuclear battlefield is that it was in the South-East Asian theatre he had chosen, and for which his Green Berets had trained most intensively, where America was to suffer its worst reverse of the Cold War. And it was in the nuclear confrontation, which he had sought to avoid, that Kennedy scored his own most dramatic success. There are few more glaring examples of the grand designs of statesmen not going according to plan, of the play of the contingent and the unforeseen.

Kennedy, however, was playing with a stacked deck. The U-2 flights and the first of the new spy satellites had made it clear by late 1961 that the United States had overwhelming superiority in the ability to deliver nuclear weapons against the other side, even if not in warheads. The blurred early photographs were not altogether convincing, until confirmed by three microfilms delivered to the CIA by Colonel Oleg Penkovsky, the Soviet military intelligence official who had been recruited and run by British intelligence. By September 1961, General Lyman Lemnitzer of the joint Chiefs of Staff was able to assure Kennedy that the Soviet Union had between ten and twenty-five ICBMs, none in hardened silos, and all slow and difficult to fuel before launch.[11]

The Berlin crisis persuaded Kennedy that Khrushchev was not only making international political capital out of his claim to Soviet strategic superiority, but that he was in danger of becoming a prisoner of his own delusions. Accordingly, the deputy Defense Secretary, Roswell Gilpatric, was directed to make a policy statement of the US confidence in its own superiority, not only in delivery systems, but in such an abundance of strength that the United States could withstand a Soviet sneak attack and then destroy the enemy with a retaliatory strike.

Daniel Ellsberg, one of the new breed of nuclear theorists from the Rand Corporation, and now working in the Pentagon, drafted the speech. With that flair for unorthodox simplicity which later won him fame for publishing the Pentagon Papers on Vietnam, Ellsberg suggested that it would be simpler to send Khrushchev the precise geographical coordinates of the Soviet ICBM bases at Plesetsk, or even copies of the photographs taken by US satellites.[12] Since part of the intended audience for the Gilpatric speech was the President's American critics, this interesting suggestion was not adopted.

Ellsberg's suggestion was the more pointed, since he had recently completed a study which showed that the Pentagon's nuclear war-fighting manual and procedures were so rigid that the targeting plan could not be amended in the event of war. The White House might order those US bombers based in Guam and Okinawa not to bomb China, but to strike Soviet Siberian targets instead. But the plan could not be changed. Even with no declaration of war, the lack of changeable codes and the strict system of pre-planned orders meant that China would be hit anyway.[13]

'Our forces are so deployed and protected that a sneak attack could not effectively disarm them,' Gilpatric began. 'We have a second-strike capability which is at least as extensive as what the Soviets can deliver by striking first. Therefore, we are confident that the Soviets will not provoke a major nuclear conflict.'[14] The message was reinforced in further statements by Defense Secretary McNamara, and in diplomatic briefings. It was delivered during the twenty-second Party Congress in Moscow, a difficult time for Khrushchev, who was facing intense criticism from the Chinese. Khrushchev, who knew the real state of the nuclear balance, was constantly nervous at Kennedy's vulnerability to the advice of his Pentagon advisers that the United States could fight and win a nuclear war. The Soviet leader was to stress this fear in his private correspondence to Kennedy during the Cuba missile crisis, when he informed the US President: 'My role was simpler than yours because there were no people around me who wanted to unleash war.'[15]

Nuclear-war theory had percolated far down into the mainstream American political debate in 1960, with the sale of 30,000 copies of Herman Kahn's magisterial study *On Thermonuclear War*, which brought concepts like 'counter-force' and 'second-strike' into the general vocabulary. By thinking aloud, Kahn made the idea of such a war thinkable, and argued that such a war would be survivable. There would be much more human tragedy, he acknowledged, but 'the increase would not preclude normal and happy lives for the majority of survivors and their descendants'. The appalled review of Kahn's book in *Scientific American* commented: 'This is a moral tract on mass murder: how to plan it, how to commit it, how to get away with it, how to justify it.'[16]

These attitudes were not restricted to the ivory towers. The head of Strategic Air Command, General Tommy Powers, was famous for laughing off the effects of nuclear radiation on genetic mutations with the quip: 'Nobody has yet proved to me that two heads aren't better than one.' General Powers had little time for the civilian nuclear theorists who talked of counter-force strategies, deliberately avoiding Soviet cities and attacking only their missile bases. 'Restraint? Why are you so concerned with saving their lives. The whole idea is to kill the bastards,' he shouted at Rand's William Kaufmann during one briefing. 'At the end of the war, if there are two Americans and one Russian, we win.'

Kaufman retorted: 'Then you had better make sure that they are a man and a woman.'[17]

Doubtless similar sentiments might have been heard from the Soviet Strategic Rocket Forces. But in March 1962, the idea that the United States might be prepared to mount a first strike against the Soviet Union was made publicly by President Kennedy himself. The veteran correspondent Stewart Alsop, known to be a personal friend of Kennedy, wrote an article on 'Kennedy's Grand Strategy' for the *Saturday Evening Post* on the basis of a long interview with the President. The text and quotations were cleared by the President before publication. The key phrase was: 'Khrushchev must not be certain that, where its vital interests are threatened, the US will never strike first. As Kennedy says, "In some circumstances we might have to take the initiative." '[18]

Kennedy's statement, coming on top of his rearmament programme, hit Moscow like a thunderbolt. The Kremlin's immediate reaction was to order a special military alert. *Pravda* condemned the President's 'incomprehensible upside-down logic'. Defence minister Marshal Malinovsky demanded 'an even greater reinforcement' of the rocket forces, and in a special article for *Kommunist*, warned that this was no accidental outburst from the White House: 'Subsequently, the President confirmed this statement and stressed that it represented the traditional position of the US.' The Soviet public was left in no doubt what this shift in Soviet priorities from consumer to defence spending meant for them: guns not butter. Meat and butter prices were raised by 20 per cent on 1 June 1962. And the Soviet authorities were equally left in little doubt of the political price this involved. In the Ukrainian city of Novocherkassk, the price rises coincided with a cut in the piece-rate pay scale for the workers at the Budyenny locomotive works. The demonstrations grew into riots serious enough to require the intervention of KGB troops.[19]

The Kremlin's reaction was the more acute in that the Soviet political and military high command were still wrestling with the budgetary implications of planning for a nuclear war. Did this automatically render obsolete the Soviet traditional reliance on numerical and tank superiority, if they were simply to be fatter nuclear targets? Did it mean recasting Soviet military strategy along the American lines of a 'bigger bang for the buck', of heavy investment in nuclear weapons and fewer conventional forces? Or should they copy Kennedy's expansion of both conventional and nuclear forces? For Soviet theorists, the Kennedy Administration's doctrine of 'flexible response' suggested a way to fight a nuclear war, rather than avoid one.

The two sides, once again, were talking past one another. McNamara's new nuclear theorists believed that the Dulles doctrine of 'massive retaliation' was inherently dangerous, and not believable. No sane Soviet could think that an American President would really risk incinerating Chicago if the Soviets took West Berlin. But all the evidence suggests that the Soviets did believe that, or at least were not prepared to take the risk entailed in disbelieving it. McNamara's theorists accordingly pushed the idea of flexible response, Nato's ability to fight at various levels, according to the degree of the threat. Under flexible response, the United States was prepared to fight a conventional war, and resort to increasing use of tactical nuclear weapons as the conventional forces came under increasing pressure. The idea was to convince the Kremlin that the United States was ready for anything.

'The US has developed its plans in order to permit a variety of strategic choices,' McNamara explained in his speech to the Nato alliance in Athens that year. 'We have also instituted a number of programmes to engage in a controlled and flexible nuclear response in the event that deterrence should fail.'[20]

From the Kremlin's point of view, it looked simply as if the Americans were arming at every level at once. Under the Kennedy rearmament programme, not only were conventional and strategic nuclear forces strengthened, but preparation was made for a whole new level of tactical warfare. Between 1962 and 1964, the United States began deploying six new types of tactical nuclear weapon. There were the two short-range nuclear rockets, Pershing and Sergeant; there were two new types of self-propelled nuclear artillery, the Davy Crocket rocket, and nuclear mines.[21]

Seen through the eyes of a Soviet marshal, Nato was preparing the weaponry to destroy the one area in which the Soviet military had an advantage, its vast tank armies. At a time when Khrushchev's defence cuts were reducing the size of the Soviet conventional forces, this could theoretically give Nato the capacity to launch its own attack upon Eastern Europe with a blitzkrieg tactical nuclear strike upon its tank parks. A subsequent Nato 'liberation' of Prague, East Berlin and Warsaw would then invite the Kremlin into the dreadful choice between giving up its European allies or risking the annihilation of Moscow and Kiev. This may have been unreal, but it was such a contingency as the marshals and generals of any army are paid to consider, and to plan against.

Kennedy's initiative thus came at an important stage in the development of Soviet military doctrine. The 1959 formulations that a future war would be primarily nuclear helped Khrushchev's plans for reducing conventional military forces. The 1959 doctrine had accepted that Soviet security would rely increasingly on the Strategic Rocket Forces, which were established in that year. Marshal Malinovsky's restatement of doctrine in 1961, that a future war would require coordination of all arms, nuclear and conventional, was in a sense the Soviet response to McNamara's 'flexible response'. But it also reflected growing military influence in the Kremlin, and was a direct response to Kennedy's rearmament programme. Malinovsky's counter-programme effectively ended Khrushchev's defence cuts.[22]

This was the alarming context in which the Kremlin decided to take the great strategic gamble to install nuclear missiles in Cuba. Khrushchev had two clear motives. The first was to defend Cuba against the constant possibility of either an American-inspired or openly American invasion. There was a degree of honour involved here. Dean Rusk recorded Anastas Mikoyan saying: 'You Americans must understand what Cuba means to us old Bolsheviks. We have been waiting all our lives for a country to go Communist without the Red Army, and it happened in Cuba. It makes us feel like boys again.'[23]

Khrushchev's second motive was to create a nuclear balance. The Soviets were very much more advanced at intermediate-range nuclear missiles than in the more complex field of ICBMs. It would take almost a decade to establish parity in ICBMs; but parity could be achieved overnight through the back door, by installing medium-range missiles in Cuba. If Kennedy was seriously considering the possibility of a first strike, then parity through Cuba might be the way to save the Soviet Union. It would also, if Kennedy's 'initiative' statement were taken at face value, be a way to save the world from its first nuclear war. On the public evidence available to Khrushchev, this was an understandable position.

Khrushchev devised the plan while visiting Bulgaria, between 14 and 20 May 1962. His memoirs tell only part of the story: 'The Americans had surrounded our country with military bases and threatened us with nuclear weapons and now they would learn just what it feels like to have enemy missiles pointing at you.'[24] But he gave a much fuller account in a still classified letter to Fidel Castro. The letter was edited by the Central Committee aide and Khrushchev speechwriter, Fyodor Burlatsky, who described how and when the idea of deploying the missiles was born:[25]

> Khrushchev described a visit to Bulgaria, where he was walking along the beach at Varna on the Black Sea with USSR Defence Minister Rodion Malinovskiy, who pointed out to him that American military bases with nuclear warheads capable of wiping out the cities of Kiev, Minsk and Moscow in a matter of minutes were located on the opposite shore [in Turkey]. Khrushchev then relates to Castro that he asked Malinovskiy, 'And why then can we not have bases close to America. What's the reason for such imparity?' And right then and there Khrushchev told Castro that he began to question Malinovskiy about whether or not it would be possible to deploy missiles secretly in Cuba and whether or not Castro would agree. Malinovskiy assured him that the missiles could be deployed without detection [this of course turned out to be incorrect]. Khrushchev notes in his letter that Castro reacted negatively to the plan at the beginning of the negotiations, but he subsequently gave it his full support.

The CIA was accustomed to alarmist reports from Cuban exiles of Soviet missiles being installed in Cuba, and the large size of Soviet anti-aircraft missiles made the confusion understandable. But by late July, the CIA knew of sixty-five Soviet ships heading for Cuba, ten of them known to be carrying military equipment. The new CIA Director, John McCone, who had replaced Allen Dulles after the Bay of Pigs disaster, sent the White House a memorandum in mid-August, warning that missiles were a probable cargo. The impact of this was reduced by his decision to depart immediately on honeymoon. An Oval Office meeting of the President, his brother Robert, who was both Attorney-General and alter ego, Dean Rusk and McNamara all concluded Khrushchev would not be so rash.

A U-2 flight on 29 August found a series of anti-aircraft missile sites on the island. This was enough, in the heated political atmosphere before the mid-term Congressional elections in November, to provoke a flurry of rumours and allegations by conservative Republican Senators that Cuba was about to become a Soviet nuclear base. On 4 September, the political fuss inspired Kennedy to announce that there was no evidence that offensive missiles had been installed, but, 'Were it to be otherwise, the gravest issues would arise.'[26]

On 8 September, the Soviet cargo ship *Omsk* docked in Havana, and at night, to defeat spy planes, unloaded its cargo of medium-range missiles (MRBMs). A second shipment of these SS-4 missiles arrived one week later on the *Poltava*. These shorter missiles had a range of some 600–1,000 miles, and from their Cuban bases could reach Washington DC, and about 40 per cent of the bomber bases of Strategic Air Command, with a flying time of less than twenty minutes. Since the US radar early-warning system was designed to detect incoming missiles from the Soviet Union, there would have been little warning if they were fired. The Soviets prepared six bases for the MRBMs, and three for the longer-range SS-5 IRBM missiles. These intermediate-range missiles, which could reach 2,200 miles, would be able to hit most of the continental United States, and all its SAC bases. The planned deployment of forty launchers with eighty warheads would have increased the Soviet first-strike capability by about 80 per cent, according to a study written at the time by the State Department analyst Ray Garthoff. Once fully deployed and operational, only 15 per cent of the US strategic forces could be assured of surviving a Soviet first strike.[27]

Because of poor weather, and a stand-down of the U-2 spy flights after a Chinese anti-aircraft missile shot down a Taiwanese U-2 in September, the Soviet preparations were not discovered until a U-2 flight over western Cuba on the early Sunday morning of 14 October. Analysed the following day, the photographs showed near San Cristóbal the characteristic shape of an SS-4 site under construction. The information was passed to the CIA Director, and from there to top intelligence staff at the State and Defense Departments. They in turn informed McGeorge Bundy, at the National Security staff office in the White House later on the Monday evening, who decided to permit the President to get a good night's sleep after a strenuous weekend of campaigning.[28]

The next thirteen days were the most dangerous period of the Cold War. A nuclear exchange was so close that both White House and Kremlin officials frankly expected the bombs to fall. At a retrospective discussion of the crisis in the Novosti building in Moscow in March 1988, the then US Defense Secretary McNamara spoke of coming up for air from the White House situation room on the Saturday, 27 October. Robert Kennedy would later call it 'Black Saturday'. 'It was a beautiful fall evening, the height of the crisis, and I went up into the open air to look and to smell it, because I thought it was the last Saturday I would ever see,' McNamara said. Fyodor Burlatsky, who had been one of Khrushchev's advisers in the crisis, went pale. 'That was when I went and telephoned my wife and told her to drop everything and get out of Moscow. I thought your bombers were on the way,' he said.[29]

For the first six of the thirteen days, the news of the American discovery was kept from all but a small group of some fourteen senior US officials known as Ex-Comm, the executive committee. Pierre Salinger, the official press spokesman, was not among them. When he was instructed to deny a report in the *Miami Herald* of 19 October that Soviet offensive missiles were deployed in Cuba, he was able to deny it with conviction. Britain, the closest ally, was not informed until Sunday evening, 21 October, just twenty-four hours before Kennedy made his television address. And by then, the main decisions had effectively been taken.[30]

Ex-Comm explored the various options. The first, to bomb the missile bases and destroy them in a *fait accompli*, was ruled out by Robert Kennedy, who noted at one point that he knew how General Tojo must have felt when planning Pearl Harbor. The USA had gone 175 years without engaging in sneak attacks, and this was no time to start, he maintained.

The second option, to appeal to the United Nations and the international community, was dismissed as taking too much time. As fresh film from the now constant U-2 flights showed the missile bases being established with remarkable speed, this course was deemed inadequate. On Friday, 19 October, the CIA reported that four of the MRBM sites were operational, and some missiles appeared ready to fire. Two IRBM sites were declared to be operational within six to eight weeks. There is little evidence of this on the transcripts of the White House tape recordings of the crucial meetings which have since been published, but the thought of the domestic political criticisms of a simple appeal to the international community cannot have been far from the politicians' minds.

The third option was full-scale invasion, and plans were put in hand for this, should it prove necessary. The final option, a naval blockade of the island, and a firm ultimatum for the missiles to be withdrawn, was the course eventually adopted.

In retrospect, once the decision was taken to apply the naval blockade, four other issues were important during the Ex-Comm discussions. The first was McNamara's response to the President's question whether this affected the strategic balance. 'Not at all,' McNamara said. 'I don't think there is a military problem.' In Moscow, twenty-six years later, McNamara expanded on this theme.

> At the time, we had 5,100 nuclear weapons that we could deliver onto the Soviet Union and they had only 300 they could deliver onto the US. We knew that, and we knew our knowledge was reliable. And that

> was strategic parity. We were prevented from using our 5,100 nuclear weapons because we knew that whatever damage we did to you, you would have enough left to inflict unacceptable damage on the United States. So that was parity.[31]

This was a highly contentious statement, challenged by General Maxwell Taylor, chairman of the Joint Chiefs of Staff, and by Assistant Defense Secretary Paul Nitze. Nitze's biographer, Strobe Talbott, quotes Under-Secretary of State George Ball recalling that 'Paul Nitze was leading the charge of the hawks. I didn't believe the President would consent to an air strike on the missile bases in Cuba, but I was scared to death that Nitze, [Treasury Secretary Douglas] Dillon and Taylor would wear the President down.' This is a significant echo by a American participant of Khrushchev's statement that Kennedy was surrounded by some advisers who indeed wanted a war. Nitze did not want a war, but he was certainly prepared to take some breathtaking risks.

The second important issue to emerge was the legality of the situation. As Fidel Castro was to assert, there was nothing illegal in international law about a sovereign country like Cuba inviting its allies to install nuclear weapons and missiles on its soil. This complicated the option of any appeal to the international community. The missiles were an affront to US security, and a breach of the venerable Monroe Doctrine, but they were in no sense illegal. The Soviet Union was surrounded by US nuclear bases on Allied territory in Britain, France, Germany, Italy, Turkey, South Korea and Japan. Medium-range missiles equivalent to those in Cuba were based in Britain, Italy and Turkey. An American acceptance of this point was to prove one of the two keys to a resolution of the crisis.

The third important issue was raised in an extraordinary intervention by that grand old man of Cold War strategy, Dean Acheson, who had been invited to take part in some of the Ex-Comm sessions. On Black Saturday, when it was not clear whether the Soviet Union would accept the naval quarantine and McNamara believed that a US invasion of Cuba was now virtually inevitable, Acheson declared that the missiles would have to be knocked out. He was asked, according to Theodore Sorensen's account in the Kennedy Library's oral history programme, what the Soviets would do then.

> 'I know the Soviets well. I know what they are required to do in the light of their history and their posture around the world. I think they will knock out our missiles in Turkey,' Acheson said.
>
> 'What do we do then?' he was asked.

> 'I believe under our Nato treaty, with which I was associated, we would be required to respond by knocking out a missile base inside the Soviet Union,' Acheson went on.
>
> 'Then what do they do?'
>
> 'That is when we hope,' Acheson replied, 'that cooler heads will prevail, and they will stop and talk.'

This was a splendid illustration of the essential absurdities of nuclear theory. It was predicated on the maintenance of rationality in the most irrational of circumstances. It relied upon the maintenance of clear chains of political command over the military in circumstances of national survival when the military would feel it their duty to assume the responsibility for the national defence. It represented, in the most lofty councils of a superpower, the mathematics of the school playground; that in exchange for a base in Cuba, a base in Turkey should be destroyed, and then a base in Russia, in an escalating pattern of retaliation that offered no obvious relief.

In the event, and mercifully, the cooler heads did prevail before any bases were attacked. On Monday evening, 22 October, President Kennedy announced the presence of the missiles in a TV address, declared the naval quarantine (the word preferred to blockade) and warned: 'I have directed the Armed Forces to prepare for any eventualities.' He announced the reinforcement of the US base at Guantánamo Bay in Cuba, condemned the Soviet Union's 'secrecy and deception' in installing the missiles and repeatedly lying to the United States about them. Any missile launched from Cuba against any nation in the western hemisphere would bring 'a full retaliatory response upon the Soviet Union'. When he finished, and the camera lights winked off, Kennedy said, 'Well, that's it, unless the son of a bitch fouls it up.'

The reaction of America's allies, when Acheson was dispatched to London, Paris and Bonn to alert them, was automatic support. The international community also rallied around the United States, rather to American surprise. The Organisation of American States was unanimous in support, and African nations swiftly declared a suspension of landing rights for Soviet aircraft bound for Cuba.

The consultations with the British brought two useful results. Sir David Ormsby-Gore, an old friend of the President, had been appointed British Ambassador to Washington at Kennedy's personal request. Kennedy was later to comment that he had come to 'trust David as I would my own Cabinet'.[32] Ormsby-Gore suggested that time could be bought and little security lost if the initial quarantine zone of 800 miles from the Cuban coast be brought back to 500 miles. He also suggested that the clearest satellite photographs of the missile sites be published, and their unveiling at the United Nations by US Ambassador Adlai Stevenson had the useful effect of turning that assembly into an impromptu world court. President de Gaulle had waved the photographs away when Acheson offered them, saying he felt no need to verify the word of the White House. Harold Macmillan, by contrast, had said, 'We must publish these right away – no one will believe this unless they see these.'[33]

The crisis came on the Saturday, 27 October, when the Soviet ships had slowed and paused as they approached the US quarantine line. The CIA reported that one vessel, the *Grozny*, had suddenly begun steaming directly towards the line. The FBI reported that the Soviet diplomats in New York had begun destroying sensitive documents. The Strategic Air Command was dispersed and on full alert. The White House was in confusion, having received two separate and apparently incompatible messages from the Soviet Union.

The first, a secret message sent through diplomatic channels from Moscow on Friday evening 26 October, was conciliatory. It suggested a deal. 'You would declare that the US will not invade Cuba with its forces, and will not support any sort of forces which might intend to carry out an invasion of Cuba. Then the necessity for the presence of our military specialists in Cuba would disappear.'

The second was a rather tougher message, broadcast over Moscow Radio on 27 October. It offered a rather different kind of deal, an American undertaking not to invade or permit the invasion of Cuba, but with an extra demand: 'We agree to remove those weapons from Cuba which you regard as offensive weapons. We agree to do this and to state this commitment in the United Nations. Your representatives will make a statement to the effect that the US, on its part, bearing in mind the anxiety and concern of the Soviet state, will evacuate its analogous weapons from Turkey.'

According to Soviet officials recalling the events nearly thirty years later, Khrushchev's first message, which did not mention Turkey, was drafted with civilian advisers under the fear that nuclear war was imminent. The second, on the Saturday, was drafted in the presence of his generals.

Every straw was clutched. A Walter Lippmann column in the *Washington Post* on the morning of 26 October was seized on by Khrushchev's advisers as an inspired hint from the White House that the missiles in Turkey and Cuba might be traded away. 'The Soviet military base in Cuba is defenceless, and the base in Turkey is all but obsolete. The two bases could be dismantled without altering the world balance of power,' Lippmann suggested.

The tension was acute. Khrushchev was sleeping in his clothes on a couch in his office in the Council of Ministers building of the Kremlin, and there was another unexpected shock to consider. Colonel Oleg Penkovsky, the West's best-placed spy, had been arrested in Moscow on 22 October, the day Kennedy announced the presence of the missiles on American television. Clearly he had given the Americans considerable information on the real weakness of the Soviet nuclear arsenal. But how much? And how far had America believed him? How far was it possible to bluff with a weak nuclear hand?

The first message from Khrushchev was given to the US Embassy in Moscow at 16.43 hours on Friday, 26 October, which was 08.43 hours Washington time. Through extraordinary delays in translation and transmission, the final text was not received in Washington until twelve hours later. It arrived in four sections between 18.00 and 21.00 hours Washington time on the Friday evening. It was formally considered by Ex-Comm on the Saturday morning, 'with high hopes'. Khrushchev's offer to withdraw the missiles in return for an American promise not to invade Cuba had also been raised through other channels. One was the Soviet Ambassador to the UN, and the other was a bizarre back channel between ABC-TV's diplomatic correspondent John Scali and the Soviet Embassy press counsellor Aleksandr Fomin (in reality, a KGB official named Aleksandr Feoktisov).

But then came a second Khrushchev message, broadcast on the radio at 17.00 hours Moscow time, on Saturday, 27 October, and received in Washington shortly after 09.00 hours, as Ex-Comm was meeting. At the same time, Ex-Comm learned that one of the U-2s had been shot down over Cuba. Ironically, it was being flown by Major Rudolph Anderson, who had piloted the U-2 which brought back the first evidence of the missile installations thirteen days earlier.

Kennedy ordered fighter cover for future U-2 flights, and a retaliatory strike against the SAM anti-aircraft sites in Cuba was prepared. He also ordered State and Defense Departments to 'prepare for the worst' in Berlin, Turkey and Iran, where Soviet retaliation was expected. At the same time, he learned that another U-2 had 'strayed off course' deep inside Soviet territory, that fighters had been scrambled against it, but failed to make contact before the U-2 escaped. US forces around the world were on full alert, and more ready for a fight than the White House may have understood. Unknown to McGeorge Bundy, the National Security adviser, the US Air Force commanders had 'taken it upon themselves to give their alert orders in unencrypted language so that their message would more certainly reach Moscow . . . the naval campaign of surveillance over Soviet submarines may have been prosecuted well beyond the immediate requirements of the quarantine . . . the Army's plan for invasion probably included the movement of tactical nuclear weapons to Cuba'.[34]

Over one thousand demonstrators were massed outside the White House, some demanding peace, others shouting for war. Kennedy called up twenty-four reserve troop-carrier squadrons of the US Air Force, ready to fly reinforcements to the Nato front line in Europe. The biggest amphibious invasion force assembled since World War Two was massing in Florida ports, awaiting the order to attack Cuba. Had they sailed, they would have met a terrible response. The Soviet garrison on the island comprised 42,000 men, twice as many as US intelligence had reported, and they were equipped with tactical nuclear weapons. This was not known to the Americans. Authority to use them, in the kind of emergency which left no time to contact Moscow, lay with the local commanders. An American invasion, still being urged by the Joint Chiefs of Staff, would almost certainly have provoked a nuclear attack upon the beachhead and the naval force.

Neither leader was in any doubt about the stakes. On 18 October, before the missile bases were made public, Ex-Comm asked the President where would they all be if the Soviets invaded West Berlin. 'In World War Three,' he replied. On the Friday evening of the next week, as the Soviet ships reached the quarantine line, Kennedy drew aside his press counsellor Pierre Salinger to say of his Ex-Comm, 'Do you think the people in that room realise that if we make a mistake there may be two hundred million dead?'

On the Saturday morning in Moscow, during a military briefing by Marshal Malinovsky on the likely targets of the US nuclear bombers, Khrushchev asked his generals if they could guarantee him that

> holding fast would not result in the death of five hundred million human beings.
>
> They looked at me as though I was out of my mind or, what was worse, a traitor. The biggest tragedy, as they saw it, was not that our country might be devastated and everything lost, but that the Chinese or Albanians would accuse us of appeasement or weakness . . . What good would it have done me in the last hour of my life to know that though our great nation and the US were in complete ruin, the national honour of the Soviet Union was intact?

At McGeorge Bundy's suggestion, Kennedy decided to respond to the first Khrushchev message, not the second. Or at least, that was for years the official American version, presenting the Kennedy claim to a diplomatic triumph which was embodied in Dean Rusk's pungent phrase: 'We were eyeball to eyeball, and the other fellow just blinked.' But as well as accepting Khrushchev's first deal in public, Kennedy dispatched his brother Robert to the Soviet Embassy in Washington to accept the second part of the deal in private. There was a public promise not to invade Cuba, and a private undertaking that the fifteen obsolescent Jupiter missiles in Turkey would be later discreetly removed.

'It was like the aftermath of a wedding, when there is nothing to do but drink the champagne and go to sleep,' Harold Macmillan concluded. The crisis rumbled on for some weeks, with bitter exchanges about Soviet medium-range and nuclear-capable bombers in Cuba, but in effect the great confrontation was over. There were still moments of the blackest human comedy to follow. Khrushchev was at his country dacha at Uspenskoye on the Sunday, when he received Kennedy's message that the deal was acceptable. But Khrushchev understood from the Robert Kennedy back channel to the Soviet Ambassador in Washington, Anatoly Dobrynin, that there was a tight deadline for his reply to agree to dismantle the Soviet missiles or have them bombed by 17.00 hours Moscow time.

'Tell them if we don't get a reply by Monday, we'll start a military action against Cuba,' had been the President's parting words to his brother, before Robert Kennedy left to deliver the official reply to Dobrynin. In the presence of Rusk, Bundy, McNamara and Sorensen, the President added that Dobrynin should also be told that the missiles in Turkey could be discreetly removed.

For Khrushchev, the message was good; he had won both his negotiating points. But the deadline was dreadful. He decided that once again, because of the slowness of the US diplomatic channel, he would broadcast the text of his acceptance of the deal over Moscow Radio, where it could be instantly monitored in Washington. The courier, Leonid Ilyichev, got stuck in Moscow traffic on the way to the radio building, and barely made it to the studio in time.

The outcome of the crisis was two tactical victories for Khrushchev: the public guarantee against a US invasion of Cuba, and the private promise to withdraw the Jupiter missiles from Turkey. But in return, he had suffered a major strategic reverse. The plan to achieve swift strategic parity with the United States had been publicly and humiliatingly thwarted. The world had seen the Soviet ships turn back, which is to say backing down. Khrushchev had dismayed his senior military men, and in the arcane rituals of the Kremlin, hints of demotion followed. The town of Khrushchev changed its name to Kremges. *Pravda*'s reports of official banquets were no longer headed 'luncheon given by N. S. Khrushchev', but were 'on behalf of the Central Committee'. These were straws in the wind, avidly collected by the West's Kremlinologists and played back to the Soviet audience. More cutting was the Chinese attack, that Khrushchev's policy had moved 'from adventurism to capitulationism'.[35]

Khrushchev's fall was not to come for another two years, but the movements against him gathered pace with the Cuban reverse. He responded by shifting to the right. The economic reform programme known as Libermanism, a modest move to the profit incentive urged by Professor Liberman, was dropped in the month after the crisis. Three weeks later, Khrushchev's angry outburst of 'Dogshit' during a modern art exhibition at Moscow's Manezh hall launched what Khrushchev was to call in *Pravda* 'a declaration of war' on abstract art. At the same time, Khrushchev manoeuvred carefully to avoid giving too much ground to his Stalinist critics, personally forcing through the publication of Alexander Solzhenitsyn's seminal novel of the Gulag, *One Day in the Life of Ivan Denisovich*.[36]

The American military men were no happier with their leader. At a meeting with the Joint Chiefs of Staff on the Sunday immediately after the crisis was reached, Kennedy was left speechless by their anger. 'We have been had,' complained Admiral George Anderson. The Air Force chief, General Curtis LeMay, who was later to advocate bombing North Vietnam 'back to the Stone Age', was so wrought up that he banged his fist on the table, and insisted, 'It's the greatest defeat in our history, Mr President . . . We should invade today.'

Perhaps they knew what was coming. In his 28 October reply to Khrushchev's promise to dismantle and remove the missiles, Kennedy had concluded: 'We must devote urgent attention to the problem of disarmament . . . I think we should give priority to questions relating to the proliferation of nuclear weapons, on earth and in outer space, and to the great effort for a nuclear test ban.' When deputy premier Anastas Mikoyan visited Kennedy in Washington the following month, he suggested a detailed series of negotiations 'on all outstanding questions'. Khrushchev followed up with a letter in December, dealing with Berlin and Cuba, but suggesting that the way was open for a nuclear-test-ban agreement. The diplomats found it hard going, with the usual arguments over on-site inspections and verifications. Finally, they agreed to settle for second-best, a treaty to ban testing above ground, which could be monitored in the atmosphere.

The new pattern of the Cold War fell into shape with remarkable speed in the months after the Cuban crisis. The intensity of the stand-off between the Soviet Union and the US had reinforced the plain fact that this was now a bipolar world. The European allies were to be defended, but when it came to America's vital interests, they were to be informed rather than consulted. For most of Kennedy's strategic advisers, British and French nuclear weapons were a needless complication. McNamara called these 'limited nuclear capacities operating independently . . . dangerous, expensive, prone to obsolescence and lacking in credibility as a deterrent'.[37]

Various devices like the Multilateral Force, a spatchcock scheme for a nuclear-armed naval force crewed by polyglot Nato crews from all countries, were offered to dilute the British deterrent, and to deter the Germans from seeking to acquire their own. Convinced that they still had Eisenhower's promise of a Skybolt delivery system for their nuclear weapons, the British politely stalled the MLF and ignored McNamara's hints. Macmillan felt secure in his own relations with Kennedy, which had been strengthened by regular consultations during the second, public week of the Cuban crisis. But British self-esteem was wounded by Dean Acheson's caustic comment on 5 December that Britain 'had lost an Empire, but not yet found a role'. Nerves were still raw when McNamara arrived in London the following week to declare on his arrival at the airport that Skybolt's five tests had all failed. He offered no alternative.

It was a desperately difficult time for Macmillan. On 16 December, he visited de Gaulle at Rambouillet, who proved a traditional French host, organising a pheasant shoot at which Macmillan got seventy-seven birds. (He was surprised to find he was then charged £5 8s. for the 170 cartridges he used.) After a year of detailed negotiations, de Gaulle chose this occasion to cast considerable doubt on Britain's application to join the Common Market. 'France could say No against the Germans . . . Once British and all the rest joined the organisation, things would be different,' Macmillan's secretary, who took notes of the conversation, recorded.[38]

Macmillan flew on to Nassau in the Bahamas for a meeting with Kennedy, summoning all his tired old charm and skill to save the British nuclear deterrent. He had to work against the entrenched opposition of Kennedy's advisers. His only help was the State Department, which had prepared for Kennedy a written brief which warned, 'the special Anglo-American relationship is as threatened as it has been since Suez by the cancellation of Skybolt . . . The Prime Minister needs a successful meeting for political survival.'[39] By seriously misrepresenting what de Gaulle had said about the prospects for British entry into the Common Market, and with dark threats about the kind of neutralist Labour government that could follow him into office if the Americans inflicted this shameful humiliation upon America's most faithful ally, Macmillan got his way. Kennedy offered Britain the Polaris submarine missile system instead of Skybolt.

Within the month, and informing his ministers that this privileged nuclear deal (which had not been offered to France) made Britain the American Trojan Horse inside Europe, de Gaulle staged a grand press conference at the Élysée Palace to cast his veto against British entry into the Common Market. 'The end would be a colossal Atlantic Community dependent on America and directed by America, which would soon swallow up this European Community,' de Gaulle declared.[40] De Gaulle went on the next week to sign the Franco-German Treaty of Friendship, and Macmillan recorded in his journal that 'all our policies at home and abroad are in ruins'.[41]

So they were. But this was to be the pattern of the 1960s. Britain was dependent upon the United States for its nuclear technology and dwindling prestige. The Western European Community was to prosper and grow distinctly apart from the Anglo-Americans, dominated by the Franco-German alliance. And the USA believed the new ground rules of the confrontation with Moscow had been settled by the Cuban crisis in America's favour. The US was thus free to embark upon a policy of arms control on the strategic front, accompanied by an aggressive pursuit of anti-Communism in the developing world.

In one of the speeches by which Kennedy most deserves to be remembered, he put forward this new American attitude towards the prospect for a more positive relationship with the Soviet Union, which suggested: 'Not a Pax Americana enforced on the world . . . but a peace based not on a sudden revolution in human nature but on a gradual evolution in human institutions . . . We must conduct our affairs in such a way that it becomes in the Communists' interest to agree on a genuine peace . . . If we cannot now end our differences, we can at least help make the world safe for diversity,' Kennedy went on, in his speech to the American University.[42] It was an invitation to explore a regime of arms control, beginning with a nuclear-test ban, and Kennedy announced a unilateral US moratorium on above-ground tests to get the process moving.

The reaction in Moscow was extraordinary. The speech was reprinted in the Soviet press, and the jamming of Western radio stations was stopped. The Soviets immediately agreed to inspections of their nuclear power stations at the International Atomic Energy Agency in Vienna, and the Atmospheric Test Ban Treaty was signed within six weeks. What was to prove an enduring feature of the rest of the Cold War, virtually uninterrupted negotiations over nuclear-arms control, was finally under way. The following month, another enduring feature of the post-Cuba Cold War began. The Soviet Union made its first approach to buy US grain, 65 million bushels, paying the world market price, and agreeing that it be ferried in American ships.[43]

Amid this surging confidence in the White House in that summer of 1963, the next phase of the Cold War was simultaneously taking shape in South-East Asia. Ngo Dinh Nhu, brother of the South Vietnamese President, warned his country's generals that the US was going soft on Communism. The Test Ban Treaty was a symbol of 'appeasement', and South Vietnam must be prepared to maintain the anti-Communist crusade alone. Kennedy was indeed hoping to begin some limited troop withdrawals, of fewer than 1,000 of the 16,000 American military 'advisers' already there.[44]

Within three months, Kennedy was dead. His image glittered with triumph after the Cuban crisis, and with hope after the Test Ban Treaty. But one of his last decisions had been to authorise the US Ambassador to South Vietnam, Henry Cabot Lodge, to assure the country's generals of US support for a coup to overthrow Ngo Dinh Diem. Hitherto America's chosen strong man in the region, Diem was losing both the war and what little public support he could claim after a brutal campaign of repression against the Buddhists. The coup was successful, but followed by the murder of Diem and that brother who had feared American appeasement. The legacy of that decision, and America's doomed war in South Vietnam, was slowly to tarnish the laurels Kennedy had won. The war, and the deepening American commitment, emerged as a symbol of the overweening American self-confidence which the Cuban crisis had encouraged.

When Dean Rusk went to Moscow in August to sign the Test-Ban Treaty, Khrushchev invited him to his Black Sea dacha at Pitsunda, and in the course of their conversations, the Soviet leader made a prophetic remark. 'If you want to, go ahead and fight in the jungles of Vietnam. The French fought there for seven years and still had to quit in the end. Perhaps the Americans will be able to stick it out for a little longer, but eventually they will have to quit too.'[45]

Chapter 8
The Weary Titan

The weary Titan with deaf
Ears and labour-dimmed eyes,
Regarding neither to right
Nor left, goes passively by,
Staggering on to her goal,
Bearing on shoulders immense,
Atlantean, the load
Well-nigh not to be borne
Of the too-vast orb of her fate.

'Titan', Matthew Arnold

President Kennedy's last European trip, in June 1963, saw his last public triumph. The highlight was an appearance before massed crowds at the Rudolph Wilde Platz in the shadow of the Berlin Wall, to inform them that he was a doughnut. This was the literal translation of his ringing and defiant phrase, 'Ich bin ein Berliner.' This defined him as a local delicacy, a pastry which had taken the city's name.[1]* Kennedy had meant to convey that he and all other free men shared the citizenship of the Berlin enclave. The phrase he used helps to explain the moment of stunned silence before the crowd swallowed their grins and burst into the anticipated cheers. It was to be the last such truly popular appearance of an American statesman in Berlin for another generation, until President Reagan twenty-four years later appealed to 'Mr Gorbachev, tear down this wall.'[2] In the intervening years, that same Berlin square saw angry protests against the US war in Vietnam and against its nuclear weapons in Europe, and demonstrations of solidarity with American students and with American black activists. The automatic sense of loyalty to their main protectors

* A 'Berliner' is the local German slang for a sweet doughnut. While technically correct, 'Ich bin ein Berliner' could have been more happily and more clearly expressed as a statement of civic solidarity with the inhabitants of West Berlin had Kennedy said 'Ich bin Berliner' or 'Ich bin auch ein Berliner'.

which had made Berliners so enthusiastic for Kennedy did not last long. Indeed, while the thronging Berliners were still cheering the young American President, a sombre new mood was injected into the relationship by the veteran West German Chancellor, Konrad Adenauer.

'What did you think of this today?' Dean Rusk asked Adenauer, as Kennedy waved at the joyous Berlin crowds.

'I am worried. Does this mean that Germany could have another Hitler?' replied Adenauer, who recalled seeing his countrymen from Prussia and Berlin respond with another kind of passion to another charismatic leader a generation before. Adenauer was not alone in questioning the mood the American President had provoked. 'Kennedy himself wondered if he had gone too far in stirring up the emotions of the people of Berlin; the response was overpowering,' Dean Rusk recalled.[3]

'There are some who say that Communism is the wave of the future. Let them come to Berlin. There are some who say in Europe and elsewhere we can work with the Communists. Let them come to Berlin,' Kennedy had told the Berliners.[4]

Just sixteen days earlier, in his speech at the American University, Kennedy had insisted that the West not only could, but must work with the Communists. As so often when Kennedy let his policies become overdressed in the rhetoric he loved, it was difficult to know what he really thought, even on the topic that was to dominate his remaining weeks of life – America's deepening entanglement in Vietnam. Kennedy's aides and successors wrangle still about whether he would have plunged on with the full military commitment, or withdrawn from Vietnam before it was too late. The documentary evidence is ambiguous. As with Kennedy's plans for negotiations on arms control, and whether or not he could 'work with the Communists', either conclusion can be drawn.

But if President Kennedy had expected a new era of superpower *détente* and global calm to follow the haunting experience of the Cuban missile crisis, he would have been disappointed. His assassination in Dallas in November 1963 meant that he did not live to see the anger and frustration which followed his brief Presidency. But Kennedy's cabinet and White House staff, who stayed on to serve in the entourage of President Lyndon Johnson, inherited what Kennedy had sown. At home, the demands for racial equality in the civil-rights movement escalated into riots in the cities, and abroad Kennedy's aggressive anti-Communism was followed by a war of attrition and bombing in Vietnam. The aftermath of the Kennedy Administration soured and turned upside-down the idealism and romantic self-confidence he had brought to American policy.

With the explosion of the first Chinese nuclear weapon on 14 October 1964, the nuclear balance became suddenly less predictable. Having expected a period of stability in a bipolar world run by two powers who had learned the need for predictability in their behaviour, the 1960s became instead a decade of internal revolution in each of the emergent power blocs. Indeed, by the start of the 1970s, the only international institution which had remained essentially untouched by the tumults of the 1960s was the US–Soviet relationship. By 1971, when the costs of the Vietnam War forced the effective devaluation of the dollar and the surrender of the privileged status the US currency had enjoyed since the 1945 Bretton Woods agreement, the world had become a very different place from the old Cold War stand-off scene Kennedy had known. The United States after Vietnam was weakened, and its allies, from Israel in the Middle East to the Common Market in Europe, to Japan in Asia, very much strengthened.

After Kennedy's death, the remaining years of the 1960s saw a remarkably global convulsion, as if the entire planet was undergoing the domestic and international readjustments that usually accompany a major war. Simply to list the places of barricade and riot and revolution is to understand the process of televised internationalisation that was now under way. In West Berlin, Paris and London, students and an increasingly rootless European Left that no longer felt itself loyal to Soviet Communism, joined the passionate demonstrations against America's Vietnam War. It disrupted American and Japanese universities too. Many of these international waves of marchers watched one another on TV waving a little red book, the political homilies of Chairman Mao Tse-tung. It was wielded also by the Red Guards of Beijing in their own riots against a Chinese political élite whom Mao no longer commanded.

'Political power comes out of the barrel of a gun,' was the most famous of the truisms in Mao's book. But political influence was beginning to flow through the lenses of TV cameras, whose images could cross linguistic frontiers with far greater impact and immediacy than press reports. Having taken political advantage of TV-as-propaganda in publicising the aerial photographs of the Cuban missile sites in 1962, the USA subsequently paid the price of that same medium portraying both Vietnam War and Detroit riots in unprecedented intimacy. Those countries most committed to the freedoms which allowed the media easy access were disproportionately affected. The world saw more of the bombing of South-East Asia than of the purges in Prague, more of the students on the Paris barricades than the depredations of China's Red Guards.

The Red Guards, in retrospect, appear to have been the dangerous weapon Mao unleashed against his own colleagues in the Chinese party leadership, a weapon in an internal ideological war. The dismal failure of Beijing's attempts at swift growth through the Great Leap Forward required scapegoats. Setting the Red Guards upon the 'capitalist roaders' in the party, in the name of the new Cultural Revolution, was Mao's strategy to avert blame from himself. A similar attempt at counter-revolution from above took place inside the Kremlin in October 1964, when a palace coup toppled Nikita Khrushchev and began to haul back the cultural, political and economic reforms he had launched. This renewed conservatism in Moscow helped provoke a different kind of rupture when the still-loyal Communists of Czechoslovakia tried to develop a less rigid and more pluralist form of rule. The Czechoslovak offence against Soviet authority was far less provocative than that of the reformers of Hungary in 1956, and their fate was less bloody. But the Soviet methods of reasserting control, with tank columns and purges, were unchanged. Just as the Anglo-French invasion of Suez had vitiated the moral impact of the crushing of Budapest in 1956, so the bombing of North Vietnam and the black riots in American cities blurred the impact of Prague in 1968.

America was at war in South-East Asia, and skirmishing in its own inner cities and campuses, while the Soviet tanks were reasserting their power in Czechoslovakia. The two main political systems and power structures had rarely looked more alike, or less savoury. Distaste for the two superpowers led to the odd fashion among Western students and intellectuals for a distant Maoism, which had the advantage of being much less understood, and far less televised. A similar romantic cult of interest in Fidel Castro's Cuba, and in the doomed guerrilla adventures of Che Guevara in the jungles of Bolivia, inspired a blizzard of admiring posters in student dormitories throughout the West. The Cuban example electrified radicals throughout South America, where the revolutionary decade of the sixties did not really end until the bloody coup which crushed Chile's socialist experiment in 1973.

The stormy decade had begun with a wave of what were to be many anti-American riots in the booming ally of Japan, whose economy was growing at an astonishing 13 per cent a year in 1959, 1960 and 1961. By this time, the American special investments which were made in the years of post-war deprivation and in the military desperation of the Korean War had ended, to be replaced by the far more modest sums coming from the permanent presence of some 65,000 US troops after 1957. The cuts in US forces implied little reduction in the weight of US authority over Japan. As part of the Khrushchev thaw, the Soviet Union had in 1956 signed an agreement with Japan under which two of the Kurile Islands, seized by the Soviets as spoils of war in 1945, would be returned to Japan. Appalled by this prospect, John Foster Dulles summoned the Japanese foreign minister Mamoru Shigemitsu to London, to warn him bluntly that this would mean granting the Soviets permanent rights to the two northern Kurile Islands and this was unacceptable to the USA. If the Japanese went ahead, then the US would insist on sovereignty over the Ryukyu Islands, home to the vast US air and naval base at Okinawa. The Japanese government backed down, and faced a wave of protests.[5]

The US military presence in Japan was unpopular among the neutralist and pro-Soviet left, and hated by the nationalist right. For the majority in the centre, the implications of that presence had been established by the tragic incident in 1957 when US Army Specialist Third Class William Girard had fired a blank from a grenade launcher on an Army range, and hit and killed an elderly Japanese woman who was scavenging the range for scrap. Under the legal terms of the US presence in Japan, this act of manslaughter came under US military jurisdiction, and an angry controversy ensued as the Japanese press and politicians inveighed against a US military who were immune under Japanese law. A compromise was reached under which the unfortunate soldier was given a three-year suspended sentence in a Japanese court, and then swiftly assigned overseas by the US Army.

This incident remained a lively memory as the two countries renegotiated their alliance. The new treaty ensured a slightly greater Japanese contribution to their self-defence force, and guaranteed America's defence of Japan while giving the Japanese the right to be consulted about the deployment of US troops. The United States felt that they had been more than generous in the negotiations, and had expected the Treaty of Mutual Cooperation and Security to be sealed by a formal visit of friendship by President Eisenhower in 1960. Because of a wave of anti-American riots, the trip was cancelled, but not the treaty. Once the treaty was signed, the Soviet government withdrew its offer of a compromise deal over the Kurile Islands.

Significantly, while the negotiations were under way, Eisenhower's Treasury Secretary George Humphrey publicly fretted at what he called 'critical unemployment in the Pittsburgh area because of Japanese competition in the electrical instrument industry.' Eisenhower, who liked to echo the John Foster Dulles warning that, without Japan, the Pacific would be 'a Communist lake', asked Humphrey if American businessmen might not make some sacrifices in the interests of world peace. 'No,' replied Humphrey. 'The American businessman believes in getting as much as he can while the getting is good.'[6] In fact, the Japanese were at this stage still running a balance-of-payments deficit in their trade with the United States, a deficit which was not balanced until 1965, and then became an almost unbroken series of trade surpluses.[7]

The Japanese trading surpluses came as the anti-American riots started again in Japan, and both demonstrations and the trade shifts had a single cause – the Vietnam War. The Japanese bases were being used by US aircraft to ferry American troops and *matériel* to be deployed against Asians. Japanese students rioted in protest. Although the spirit of the 1960 treaty dissuaded the United States from sending warplanes to bomb Vietnam direct from Japanese bases, the B-52s used the US base at Okinawa, which the Japanese anti-war students, but not the Treaty, regarded as Japanese territory. (Okinawa was formally returned to Japanese sovereignty in 1972, as the United States was winding down its war in Vietnam.) After stormy debates in the Diet and even stormier battles on the streets, foreign minister Shiima acknowledged: 'Japan is not neutral in the Vietnam War.'[8]

In that year of 1965 when Japan recorded its first post-war trade surplus with the United States, the Tokyo daily *Mainichi* held an opinion poll which showed 40 per cent of its readers favouring an immediate US withdrawal from Vietnam, while only 4 per cent approved the US bombing effort.[9] But the US military effort was pumping more money into the entire Pacific rim. This encouraged Japanese businessmen even more than it offended the students. The fastest five-year period of growth in Japan's GNP came in the fiscal years 1966–70, the peak years of the US war in Vietnam. Growth averaged 14.6 per cent a year. Japan became an industrial base for the US war in Vietnam, just as it had been during the Korean War after 1950. The shipyards went on to triple shifts to meet the new demand for cargo ships and tankers to sustain the vast US war machine in South-East Asia. The low-cost PX stores at the American bases in Vietnam were filled with duty-free Japanese electronics and cameras. The impact of the Vietnam boom period upon Japan's relative standing in the world economy was dramatic. In 1964, Japan's share of world GNP, at 5.7 per cent, was behind that of West Germany, France and Britain. By 1973, as the US role in the Vietnam War was winding down, Japan's share of global GNP had risen to 12.9 per cent, the same as Britain and France combined.[10]

The degree of British decline was apparent in two telling figures from 1967, the year when the British pound was devalued from $2.80 against the US dollar to $2.40, after three miserable years of sterling crises. The final rescue package put together by the world's central banks to tide the pound through its devaluation, the crucial moment in the British currency's fight for its life, was worth $3 billion. This was more than the British government's reserves at the time. But it represented only six weeks of US spending in the war on Vietnam, then running at some $25 billion a year.[11]

Harold Wilson's Labour government had come into office with the election of 15 October 1964, a momentous day for reasons little to do with British politics. It was the day the world learned of the twin surprises of the fall of Nikita Khrushchev and the first Chinese nuclear test. Within the month, Lyndon Johnson was to win his own crushing election victory over the deeply conservative Republican, Senator Barry Goldwater from Arizona. Goldwater's election slogan had been 'Extremism in the defence of liberty is no vice; moderation in the pursuit of freedom is no virtue', one of those balanced phrases which could have come from Kennedy's speechwriters. But in Goldwater's case, there was implacable resolve behind the rhetoric, a readiness to accept the use of nuclear weapons which inspired the Johnson campaign to run the most haunting of all television campaign advertisements. It showed a little girl counting flower petals, counterposed against the countdown to a nuclear explosion. It was crude, but in the light of Goldwater's flippant comments on the use of nuclear weapons – 'I want to lob one into the men's room at the Kremlin and make sure I hit it' – not unjustifiable.[12]

Goldwater's challenge on foreign policy, campaigning on the need to prosecute the war in Vietnam to victory, was the more gruelling for Johnson in that Vietnam had not been his war, but his inheritance from President Kennedy. A veteran New Dealer who had learned his politics as a young teacher in a small Mexican-American school at Cotulla, Texas, in the 1930s, Johnson had focused on domestic affairs throughout his political career. His passion was that other war he launched, the War on Poverty. Many of the economic and social trials that the United States underwent in the 1960s can be attributed to Johnson's determination to fight that domestic war even while sinking deeper, and at a mounting cost, into the quagmire of Vietnam. Johnson told the Congress in 1966: 'We are a rich Nation, and can afford to make progress at home while meeting obligations abroad.'

In private, he put it more bluntly, declaring his refusal to abandon 'the woman I really loved – the Great Society – in order to get involved with that bitch of a war on the other side of the world'.[13]

After the 1964 Kremlin coup, Lyndon Johnson faced a new Soviet leadership which shared his domestic preoccupations. Khrushchev had been replaced by a triumvirate, and each of the three embodied some of Johnson's characteristics. Leonid Brezhnev was a machine politician, a glad-handing bully with large and self-indulgent appetites, who also shared Johnson's passion for driving large American cars very fast. Aleksei Kosygin, the technocrat from Leningrad, shared Johnson's domestic focus, pushing within the constraints of a congealing system for economic reforms and efficiency. Nikolai Podgorny, the oldest and least remembered of the three, had emerged from the Ukraine party machine with all of Johnson's toughness. Elevated to the formal post of head of state in 1965, Podgorny was a hard-liner in the decision to crush the Prague Spring of 1968.

By the mid-1960s, the United States, the Soviet Union and the UK were all governed by similar types of men; pragmatists who knew how to manipulate party organisations. Johnson, Brezhnev and Harold Wilson might not have liked one another, but they understood one another, each far removed from the essentially intuitive and flamboyant styles of a Kennedy or a Khrushchev. The sixties have come down to us in memory as a Dionysian decade, of fervour and ferment, of politics as passion. While the dominant politicians of the early sixties – Macmillan, de Gaulle, Kennedy and Khrushchev – were men of undoubted style and distinction, by 1964 the men in the White House, Kremlin and Number Ten were of a very different character.

Lyndon Johnson and Harold Wilson, who disliked one another almost on sight, had one great thing in common. Each man reckoned himself uniquely fitted, by conviction, experience and timing, to take advantage of the new stability – after the Cuban missile crisis – in East–West relations and to confront the great challenges of domestic reform. For Johnson, it was the final defeat of poverty and the fulfilment of Kennedy's promise of civil rights and a true equal opportunity for all Americans. For Wilson, it was to revive a stagnant British economy in order to end poverty and transform the traditional class system in order to create an equality of opportunity for all the Queen's subjects. The domestic agendas of the British and American leaders as they won their 1964 elections had seldom been more in tune. Each was to be blown off course by foreign disasters, and the economic embarrassments which ensued.

Wilson shared Johnson's passion for the welfare state, and constantly sought to justify his resignation from the last Labour government of 1951. He had complained at the diversion of resources from the National Health Service to the rearmament programme of the Korean War, and as prime minister sixteen years later, defended his Johnsonian priorities by referring back to 1951. In his address to the Labour Party conference at Scarborough in 1967, he proclaimed:[14]

> For every £100 allocated for defence [in 1951], £122 were being spent on social services. Today, for every £100 we are spending on defence we are spending £340 on the social services . . . I doubt if there is a delegate here who in 1964 – even though the gravity of the economic position was at the time deliberately concealed from us – would have expected that three years later we would be able to report an increase of £2,300 million, or nearly a half, in our provision for the social services.

But like Johnson, Wilson was committed to a series of expensive foreign and military ventures. In 1964, there were more British troops stationed east of Suez than on Nato's front line in Germany. The defence of newly independent Malaysia against Indonesia involved the deployment of 30,000 British troops, out of a total of 54,000 deployed throughout South-East Asia, including Hong Kong and the Indian Ocean fleet.[15] This was a larger force than the United States had stationed in Vietnam in 1964. British forces were also deployed in Aden, Bahrein, and later off the Mozambique coast to enforce the sanctions against white-ruled Rhodesia's unilateral declaration of independence. This was exactly what Britain's US ally wanted. After his first visit to Washington as defence secretary, Denis Healey reported back to the British cabinet that the Johnson Administration wanted the UK to 'keep a foothold in Hong Kong, Malaya, the Persian Gulf, to enable us to do things for the alliance which they can't do. They think our forces are much more useful to the alliance outside Europe than in Germany.'[16]

Britain and the United States shared in the 1960s an unhappy contradiction. Each wanted Britain to join the European Common Market. But each was bent on maintaining Britain's role as a surrogate of American interests in the Middle East and Asia. This involved a commitment away from Europe which confirmed President de Gaulle in his belief that Britain was not at heart a European nation. British foreign policy in the 1960s was torn between the conflicting objectives of the relationship with the United States and the aspiration to join Europe. But for the exigencies of the Vietnam War, these two policies might not have been incompatible. But Wilson was under constant pressure from President Johnson to send at least a token British force to Vietnam. The Secretary of State Dean Rusk asked a British correspondent in Washington at one point why London could not send 'just one battalion of the Black Watch'. Louis Heren of *The Times* tried to explain British policy. 'When the Russians invade Sussex, don't expect us to come and help you,' Rusk snapped.[17]

British dithering could not be long sustained. The state of the economy, steered by Wilson towards the welfare state and expansion of the new universities, would not permit it. Ironically, given the long and costly commitment to east of Suez which helped imperil the pound, devaluation was finally forced by the Suez Canal itself. The Six-Day War between Israel and the Arabs in June 1967, as the Jewish state refought the war of 1956 and this time showed it had no need of British and French support, had the side effect of closing the Suez Canal. It was now an armed ditch between Egyptians on the one side and the triumphant Israelis, who had conquered the Sinai peninsula, on the other. The war led to a global shipbuilding boom as vast new tankers were built to take enormous oil cargoes the long way around Africa. But it imposed what Wilson called 'a £200 million a year penalty' on the British economy.[18]

The 1967 devaluation of the pound was accompanied by defence cuts which required Britain's withdrawal by 1971 from all its bases east of Suez except for Hong Kong. Much of the job had been done. The confrontation with Indonesia had ended with a quiet victory. Singapore had declared an amicable independence from Malaysia. The unpleasant little war in Aden had ended with the city becoming the capital of independent South Yemen. Australia and New Zealand, who did send their small forces to fight alongside the Americans in Vietnam, had transferred their strategic relationship from the old imperial power of London to the new superpower of Washington in the ANZUS pact. British troops were to remain on guard in Oman for over a decade, along with British military advisers up and down the sheikhdoms of the Persian Gulf. An imperial era was almost, however, at an end. Some odd relics lingered. Among the forgotten booty was the shrunken head of a Japanese soldier from 1945, solemnly presented to the wife of Britain's departing defence minister by the headman of a Borneo tribe in his long-house. It was left behind a sofa in London's Admiralty House, to be discovered by a cleaning woman. She fainted.[19]

On occasion, the Anglo-American imperial watch had little idea what it was doing. In April 1965, the miserably poor Caribbean state of the Dominican Republic was undergoing one of its regular coups d'état. On the basis of amateurish intelligence and some wishful thinking, the Johnson White House assumed that a Cuban-inspired Communist revolution was under way. Observing that this was 'just like the Alamo', President Johnson sent in the US Marines, and an eventual total of 28,000 troops. The White House claimed that the revolt was led by Communists trained in Moscow and Havana, that Cuban intelligence was providing the weapons, and that 1,500 of the rebels came from local Communist parties.

Johnson's claim was based on a CIA report, finally delivered on 7 May, which 'identified' three Communist strongholds, each the home of one of the leaders of the squabbling Communist factions. The CIA later acknowledged that they could find no trace of Cuban involvement, and that one Cuban-trained Dominican had been specifically ordered to take no part in guerrilla activity. The CIA's list of, variously, fifty-seven, eighty-three and eighty-nine Communist rebel leaders included people who had long left the country, and a former Ambassador of the deposed anti-Communist dictator Trujillo. National Security Adviser McGeorge Bundy spent ten days trying to mediate on the island, before reporting back apologetically that the US had become embroiled in 'an interrupted civil war'.[20]

Britain sent troops, and a rather more suitable contingent of unarmed British policemen, to its own Caribbean comic opera in the island of Anguilla in 1969. After the break-up of the ill-fated Caribbean Federation of Britain's former West Indian possessions, the 6,000 Anguillan islanders were unwilling to become part of a smaller federation with the islands of Nevis and St Kitts. A British official who tried to tell them better was bundled off the island. Faulty intelligence convinced London that the island was about to be taken over by the American Mafia as a tropical gambling den. Her Majesty's forces were dispatched. Mostly Royal Engineers, they found no *mafiosi*, but stayed on to do useful work building bridges and roads, and, like the police, became very popular.[21]

Such was the imperial twilight, bumbling if well-intentioned. There was nothing bumbling about the American mission in Vietnam, conducted in the bright sunshine of power. It was well-intentioned in its ideological way, determined to stop a perceived Communist advance. But which Communism had to be stopped was never quite established. The logistic and economic support given by both the Soviet Union and China to North Vietnam throughout the war helped persuade the Americans that the old Communist-bloc loyalties still held good. In fact, these were the years of the most public vituperation between Moscow and Beijing. The prospect that North Vietnam's Ho Chi Minh might have been an Asian Tito, an independent nationalist as much as Leninist ideologue, was never seriously explored. Centuries of rivalry and confrontation between Vietnam and China, and the Sino-Soviet split, meant that there were three prickly Communisms to contend with, all wrapped up in a war of national liberation which the Vietnamese had conducted with unbroken vigour and fortitude against Japanese, French and now Americans.

Kennedy's concern about expansionist China was a constant theme. On the eve of his inauguration, he talked with George F. Kennan, the sage of anti-Communist containment, of the new Communism that might have to be contained with nuclear arms. 'I wonder if we could expect to check the sweep south of the Chinese with their endless armies with conventional forces,' Kennedy suggested.[22] After the Berlin Wall and the Cuban missile crisis imposed a stability in the US–Soviet relationship, Kennedy was deeply concerned about China, and the prospect that it too would become a nuclear power.

In a conversation with the French cultural minister André Malraux, who had written a powerful and sympathetic novel of the earlier Chinese Communist rising of 1929, Kennedy sought to pass on to de Gaulle the need for the West to coordinate its new containment of Chinese Communism. 'This was the great menace in the future to humanity, the free world and freedom on earth,' recalled the State Department's William Tyler, who sat in on the meeting with Malraux:[23]

> Relations with the Soviet Union could be contained within the framework of mutual awareness of the impossibility of achieving any gains through war. But in the case of China, this restraint would not be effective because the Chinese would be perfectly prepared, because of the lower value they attach to human life, to sacrifice hundreds of millions of their own lives, if this were necessary in order to carry out their militant and aggressive policies.

But there was equivocation in America's Vietnam policy from the beginning. On 1 November 1961, while pondering the report of General Maxwell Taylor which called for the dispatch of US military advisers, Secretary of State Dean Rusk was doubtful. He cabled to Kennedy: 'While attaching the greatest possible importance to security of South East Asia, I would be reluctant to see the US make major additional commitments of American prestige to a losing horse.'[24]

That was clear enough. But then days later, Rusk sent President Kennedy another memorandum, this time jointly signed by Defense Secretary McNamara. It was very different:[25]

> The loss of South Vietnam to Communism would not only destroy SEATO [the South-East Asia Treaty Organisation] but would undermine the credibility of American commitments elsewhere. Further, loss of South Vietnam would stimulate bitter domestic controversies in the US and would be seized upon by extreme elements to divide the country and harass the Administration . . . The US should commit itself to the clear objective of preventing the fall of South Vietnam to Communists . . . We should be prepared to introduce US combat forces if that should become necessary for success. Dependent upon the circumstances, it may also be necessary for US forces to strike at the source of the aggression in North Vietnam.

Rusk's two memoranda neatly encapsulate the ambivalence of US policy in Vietnam, reluctant to risk American prestige by losing, but equally reluctant to risk American prestige by being seen to let down an ally. With the policy-makers thus torn, the clear advice of the military men, with their promises of speedy achievement through the deployment of US combat troops, assumed a decisive influence. And as Dean Rusk never tired of pointing out, there was another firm influence upon the Kennedy–Johnson Administrations: the terms of the SEATO treaty, which had been negotiated by the Eisenhower Administration in 1955, and ratified by the US Senate. Article IV committed each country joining SEATO to recognise that 'aggression by means of armed attack in the treaty area would endanger its own peace and safety, and [to agree] that it will in that event act to meet the common danger in accordance with its constitutional processes'. In testimony on behalf of the treaty before the Senate, Secretary of State Dulles explicitly said that Article IV would cover an attack on South Vietnam 'by the regime of Ho Chi Minh'.[26] In this sense, Vietnam was Dulles's war, too.

The United States crept slowly into the war, beginning with 685 military advisers in 1961, 18,000 by 1963, and 25,000 at the time Lyndon Johnson won his election in 1964. But by then, another legal die had been cast. Both Houses of the US Congress, by a majority of 416–0 in the House of Representatives and 88–2 in the Senate, passed a resolution to come to the assistance of those protected by the SEATO Treaty, including the use of armed force 'as the President shall determine'. It was an open-ended commitment which tied the hands of Congressional opposition for the rest of the decade.

This was the result of the Gulf of Tonkin incident, when the US Navy destroyer *Maddox* claimed to have been attacked by North Vietnamese gunboats in international waters on 2 August 1964. One was left dead in the water and two more were damaged after the *Maddox* called in air strikes from the carrier USS *Ticonderoga*. Although Defense Secretary McNamara denied it at the time, the *Maddox* was on what amounted to a spying mission, monitoring from ten miles offshore the prearranged raids of South Vietnamese commandos on the North Vietnamese coast. The ship was trailing America's coat along Vietnamese waters, an act of some provocation. The US then mounted the first air strikes against North Vietnam, attacking the naval bases of the patrol boats. Johnson informed Nikita Khrushchev over the hot line, to reassure the Soviet Union that this was a limited action and not the prelude to an attack which would shift the balance of power in the region.[27] But in his subsequent televised address to the nation, President Johnson declared it to be another round in twenty-five years of the Cold War.

'The challenge that we face in South-East Asia today is the same challenge that we have faced with courage and that we have met with strength in Greece and Turkey, in Berlin and Korea, in Lebanon and in Cuba,' he said.[28] What had worked in those crises, Johnson assumed, would work again. A sufficient input of American arms and money and resolve would make it clear to Moscow and Beijing that the US was committing its prestige, and they would encourage their Vietnamese clients, already intimidated by American strength, to back down. The problem was that Vietnam was different, with a proud and confident political and military leadership that had fought the Japanese and defeated the French, and were by no means subservient clients of Moscow and Beijing. They were not even entirely dependent on China and the Soviet Union to sustain the war, as North Korea had been. In drawing parallels with those other Cold War crises, Johnson revealed how thoroughly the US was misreading the political dynamics in South-East Asia.

North Vietnam responded to the Gulf of Tonkin incident by sending regiments of their regular army to reinforce the Vietcong, the South Vietnamese guerrillas of the National Liberation Front, who were coming under serious pressure from the growing numbers of US reinforcements. Each side began to raise the stakes, in a self-perpetuating rhythm of escalation. The North Vietnamese were responding to the new mobility given the ARVN (Army of the Republic of Vietnam) by the swarms of US helicopters. The US increased its 'advisers' and logistic and air-support troops until, by July 1965, they numbered 75,000. This was not enough.

As President Johnson and his top advisers gathered in the White House on 1 July, they were faced with a report which said that with North Vietnamese reinforcements in the central highlands South Vietnam was about to be cut in two. In spite of passionate arguments by Under-Secretary of State George Ball, who warned that the United States was heading for the kind of defeat the French had suffered a decade earlier, President Johnson chose to Americanise the war. US forces were increased immediately to 125,000, with an open authorisation for more. Within six months, the troop levels had increased to 184,000, and Johnson flew to Honolulu in February 1966 for a long meeting with his generals. One of Johnson's motives was to distract attention, and keep some key witnesses away from the scheduled televised hearings into the war by Senator William Fulbright, chairman of the foreign relations committee. These hearings represented the moment when opposition to the war became respectable within the American Establishment. But the advice which the US commander in Vietnam, General William Westmoreland, presented to the President at Honolulu was to increase that opposition dramatically by extending the requirements of the draft.

Westmoreland said that the US reinforcements so far had turned the tide and staved off defeat. To seize the military initiative and win the war, he now needed massive new forces. The immediate target, Westmoreland went on, was to reach 'the cross-over point', at which the Vietcong and NVA (North Vietnamese Army) were taking more casualties than they could replace. He said this point could be reached by the end of the year, if his troop requests were met. They were. President Johnson authorised an increase of US forces from 184,000 to 429,000 in the next six months, and wishing Westmoreland happy hunting, asked him to 'nail the coonskin to the wall'.[29]

At the beginning of 1965, there had been one serious attempt to interrupt this implacable spiral of reinforcements from both sides, organised by U Thant, the secretary-general of the United Nations. The official American version, as described by Dean Rusk in his memoirs, is that U Thant was engaged in wishful thinking that came close to outright invention about the North Vietnamese offer to engage in talks in the neutral capital of Burma. 'I thought U Thant lied like a sailor,' Rusk recalled.[30] U Thant, the North Vietnamese and later American scholars believed there was a serious possibility of negotiations. The Soviet foreign minister, Gromyko, whose recollections are as partisan as those of Rusk, commented: 'Despite the many meetings I and other Soviet officials had with our US counterparts over the question of Vietnam, we faced an impenetrable, unhearing wall.'[31]

The Soviets felt themselves to have been placed by the Americans in a deliberately difficult situation, with the United States seeking to exploit the Sino-Soviet split and to expose Moscow either to another open confrontation with the United States, or to see its Communist ally of North Vietnam humiliated or defeated. Soviet ideology, and policy speeches from both Khrushchev and his successor Leonid Brezhnev, had maintained that the future victory of socialism lay through national liberation struggles in the Third World. This Soviet sense of being America's real victim was sharpened when the US bombing of North Vietnam began as premier Alexei Kosygin was visiting Hanoi in February 1965. Moscow offered economic aid, and military equipment including anti-aircraft missiles. Ironically, Kosygin was urging the North Vietnamese to open talks, and accept a compromise solution like that in Laos: a neutral and coalition interim government in South Vietnam which could eventually become Communist-dominated.[32]

President Johnson finally accepted the persistent recommendation of his generals for US bombing raids after Vietcong attacks on US army bases at Pleiku and Qui Nonh. The bombing was spasmodic at first, and occasionally interrupted by 'pauses' which the Americans saw as invitations to negotiations. The raids were to continue for over three years, and unload more explosives than were used in Europe throughout World War Two. But North Vietnam was not the kind of industrialised economy which could easily be disrupted by aerial bombing. The Ho Chi Minh trail which took supplies into the South was not a highway, but a network of dirt roads and trails through Laos and Cambodia as well as Vietnam. Just as the trenches of the First World War had frustrated the generals of the day, the Vietcong and NVA learned to dig deep underground shelters and military command bunkers, barracks and hospitals in their tunnels.

When the First Air Cavalry used mobility and air power to win the first set-piece battle against North Vietnamese regiments in the Ia Drang valley in November 1965, the NVA learned from their mistake, and stopped fighting on American terms. The Americans wanted to fight a war of attrition by fire-power. The North Vietnamese soon understood that they would have to fight a war of political attrition, and developed a strategy of endurance. They steeled themselves to outlast the Americans' political will to prosecute a draining, costly war against an enemy which seldom made itself conveniently available to be killed. McNamara understood this strategy, and informed

President Johnson the following month that there was 'no sure victory . . . we have been too optimistic'.[33]

The continuity in the Johnson cabinet is important. Most of President Kennedy's key men, Dean Rusk at the State Department, McNamara at the Pentagon, McGeorge Bundy at the National Security Council and a host of lesser figures, remained in place, with their reputations still shining from the Cuban missile crisis. The phrase 'the Best and Brightest' later took on a mocking tone, but as Johnson plunged wholeheartedly into the Vietnam War, Johnson believed he was acting on the finest available advice from these eminent policy-makers and thinkers, aides and courtiers of the Kennedy–Johnson Administrations.

Overconfident they might have been, and over-trustful of the confident figures of Vietcong 'body-counts' and 'pacified villages' which the Pentagon constantly provided to McNamara's intensely numerate mind. But these aides were quick enough to see that the current policy was not working. Short of sending ever more US troops and ever more US bombing raids, however, they were unable to devise a strategy that might have worked. The original scheme that had seemed so promising in Kennedy's day, of the dashing Green Berets, élite American guerrilla fighters able to confront the Vietcong on their own terms, had not succeeded. Air power had proved inadequate. The South Vietnamese army sucked in men, equipment, funds and US military advisers, but never proved more than spasmodically effective. The idea behind the deployment of hundreds of thousands of US troops was to buy time for the South Vietnamese army to train, and for its political establishment to sink roots of loyalty and commitment among the populace. But the American troops stayed and died in ever larger numbers, while neither the forces nor the political institutions of South Vietnam ever came close to being able to take the strain alone.

Hanoi understood sooner than the US government the importance of international opinion and of American domestic politics in an extended war. For all the criticisms of the American military establishment and its stubborn argument that more bombs and more troops would finally succeed, the Pentagon understood this too. As McNamara's doubts deepened in 1966, Chairman of the Joint Chiefs of Staff Earle Wheeler wrote a paper which said the US would have to prepare, militarily and politically, for a prolonged effort. 'We cannot predict with confidence that the war can be brought to an end in two years . . . the communist leaders in both North and South Vietnam expect to win this war in Washington, just as they won the war with France in Paris.'[34]

American strategy was frustrated at every turn. They found it impossible to discover any convincing civilian government in South Vietnam, and finally had to settle for the military regime of General Thieu and Air Marshal Ky. Washington was able to rally Australian, New Zealand, Philippine and South Korean troops for the war, but none of its major European allies. American diplomacy was unable to persuade the Soviets to bring the Vietnamese to the negotiating table, particularly as Moscow perceived the extent of America's entanglement and the prospect of a major humiliation for the West. On the battlefield, the ill-trained American conscripts were not impressive, and US air power proved too crude a weapon to break the will of the Vietnamese. The image of a baffled giant, flailing with impotent anger at the taunting Vietcong as his feet sank deeper into the mud of the paddy-fields, became compelling.

This was simply not a conflict where America's strengths could be brought into play. Even bribes did not work. The offer of 'at least one billion dollars' for a South-East Asian reconstruction programme – part of the American fourteen-point peace overture which accompanied the Christmas bombing pause in 1965 – had no effect. 'We have put everything into the basket of peace except the surrender of South Vietnam,' Rusk declared. Not exactly. Various Polish and British and even Soviet attempts to establish some terms for talks or a cease-fire or even a pause in the bombing always broke down in such a way that Hanoi had grounds to question America's good faith. At one point in February 1967, as Harold Wilson and Alexei Kosygin in London were trying to put a new peace effort together, Washington dithered over whether or not to say it would stop the bombing when Hanoi promised the infiltration of troops from North Vietnam 'will stop', or when it 'has stopped'.[35]

President Johnson's pride and American prestige were both wrapped up in a war which the Pentagon did not know how to win, and which Johnson did not know how to end. This was psychologically important. Johnson led the United States into Vietnam at the high point of American self-confidence after the Cuban missile crisis. But that confidence was not rooted deeply enough to withstand the double blows of frustration in Vietnam and riots at home. The war effort in Vietnam expanded towards its peak, as the black ghetto of Watts in Los Angeles exploded in 1965 in the first of what became a series of urban riots. The Vietnam War became an American trauma with the Tet offensive of 1968, when the television image of Vietcong guerrillas fighting inside the US Embassy grounds in Saigon made it clear that any prospect of American 'victory' was far, far distant. Three months later, in awful counterpoint to disasters abroad, the civil-rights leader Dr Martin Luther King was assassinated in Memphis. Two months after that, Bobby Kennedy's victory in the California primary and what seemed to be an unstoppable bid for the Presidential nomination was cut short by another assassin.

These dreadful twins, the war in Vietnam and something which looked through a TV screen like a kind of war at home, gestated together throughout the 1960s. And they did so at an unusual demographic moment, when the children of the post-war baby boom in Europe and North America had grown into teenagers and young adults, an unprecedented youthful bulge in the population. They were not only the largest youth cohort these countries had known, but also the tallest, the best-educated and the most affluent of generations. In his speeches to the anti-war protests at American universities, Dr Benjamin Spock used to address the students as 'My children', and indeed many of them had been raised in accordance with his best-selling advice to post-war mothers of breast-feeding on demand. Perhaps they had been pampered by their parents, but they were most certainly courted as a generation by the entertainment industry, with TV programmes and rock music and films which helped define their generation as somehow culturally distinct from the societies which had nurtured them.

This was not only an American phenomenon. Britain was one of the liveliest sources of the youth culture, with its Liverpool sound playing back to the 1960s a tamed and white version of black American rhythm and blues, rather as Elvis Presley had purveyed a similar half-assimilated form of black music in the 1950s. In France and West Germany, the youth cult adopted a more rigorously political form, rooted in fast-expanding universities. The German Social Democrat leader Willy Brandt experienced what was dubbed the generation gap in acutely personal form, when his two sons were detained in demonstrations against his own decision to join the Christian Democrats in a 'grand coalition' of government.

In the Soviet Union too, where a new generation of poets like Yevtushenko and Voznesensky had come to symbolise Khrushchev's Thaw, a similar political and cultural movement was emerging from this demographic bulge, whatever the political character of the parent society. In the Soviet Union, some of this generational energy was deliberately tapped to voice its opposition to the Vietnam War. In Western Europe and in the United States, freedoms of speech, press and assembly facilitated the spontaneous expression of opposition to the war. In the sudden wave of protest songs, the international idioms of rock music and student demonstrations, these currents swirled ominously together. These were the underlying symptoms of what was becoming a moral crisis for the Western alliance, raising the disturbing question of the legitimacy of American leadership and of American purpose. There were several forces at work here. For the United States, and for the Soviet Union, the dependent states of the immediate post-war era had matured, stabilised, and were beginning to grow away. The reformist movement of the Prague Spring in Czechoslovakia was one part of this trend, with a different political objective from China, but with a very similar root in the growing urge to independence from Moscow. A similar movement was under way in the West. In France, where President de Gaulle's restiveness at US leadership was becoming something uncomfortably close to an economic war against the primacy of the US dollar, there was government licence for anti-Americanism. It was deepened by de Gaulle's decision to remove France from the military commitments of the Nato alliance, although not from the alliance itself. But de Gaulle's blunt eviction of Nato headquarters from Paris was a dramatic symbol of the changing form of the Atlantic Alliance.

The nature of the US war effort in Vietnam made the shifting alliances crystal clear. Not one of America's European allies, in whose defence and security the United States had invested a constant garrison of some 300,000 troops for a generation, came to fight alongside the US forces in Vietnam. America's allies in the field during that miserable war were the Asian and Pacific countries of Australia, New Zealand, South Korea and the Philippines. President Johnson's argument that the war in Vietnam was simply another front in the endless global confrontation against Communism was simply not accepted by the Nato allies. They had other, more local concerns, thrust upon them by the new stability given to the old continent by the Berlin Wall and the Cuban missile crisis.

The first clear sign of the new European concern came in July, 1963, when the German Social Democrat Egon Bahr began the course of thinking that would move him and Willy Brandt to *Ostpolitik*, a strategy of *détente* with East Germany and Eastern Europe as a whole. Under the title 'Wandel durch Annäherung' (Change through Contact), Bahr committed the SDP to a policy of opening diplomatic and economic links with the East.[36] This was not solely a Social Democratic initiative. Adenauer's replacement as German Chancellor, Ludwig Erhard, presided over the opening of German trade missions in Romania, Bulgaria, Poland and Hungary. Their welcome suggested the degree to which Eastern European states were ready to explore ways in which relations might be rendered more normal. In Yugoslavia, the tradition of a highly independent and nationalist Communism had flowered into a serious exploration of the mixed economy, with the beginnings of a stock market.

In spite of their preoccupation with Vietnam, the Americans were receptive to an easing of tensions in Europe, but found the experience of dealing with increasingly prosperous and wilful Europeans to be frustrating. The Americans genuinely tried to please everybody, with predictable results. In order to accommodate the desire of the West German right wing, notably Franz-Josef Strauss of Bavaria, for nuclear weapons, the Kennedy and Johnson Administrations explored the idea of a Multilateral Force. This was the kind of compromise that could only have been devised by a politician. It called for nuclear-armed Nato ships with multinational and multilingual crews. The British mocked it, the Pentagon thought it a technical nightmare, and the Germans knew it to be a sop rather than serious access to nuclear weapons. In order to accommodate British nuclear pretensions, the US provided Polaris, infuriated the French, and undermined that broader US policy of integrating Britain into the European Common Market.

'We must improve the East–West environment in order to achieve the unification of Germany in the context of a larger, peaceful and prosperous Europe,' President Johnson declared on 7 October 1966. This speech, which foreshadowed the policy of *détente* by calling for a 'peaceful engagement' with Eastern Europe, had been drafted for him by Zbigniew Brzezinski, later to become President Carter's National Security Adviser.[37] It was followed within the year by President Johnson's first summit, a meeting with Premier Kosygin at Glassboro, New Jersey. The summit was an outlandish, fruitless but highly significant occasion. Kosygin's North Vietnamese ally was being pounded by American bombs as they met. On the floor of the US Senate, the Mansfield Resolution for a withdrawal of the majority of US troops in Western Europe had failed by 49 votes. But for the heroic lobbying efforts of Dean Acheson and other grand old men of US foreign policy, it might well have passed. In order to maintain the US military commitment to Europe, the Johnson Administration had to promise to seek to reduce it, by negotiating mutual and balanced force reductions with the Soviet Union. In order to keep the Nato alliance together after the French withdrawal and the German turn to the East, the US had to agree to make Nato into an oddly schizoid organisation, both militant and pacific at the same time. The contradiction is caught neatly in the phrasing of the Harmel Report, which Nato adopted as the basis of its new doctrine in 1967: 'Military security and a policy of *détente* are not contradictory but complementary.'[38]

So Kosygin and Johnson met, to discuss Vietnam and make the first exploration of what was to become the arms-control process, acutely conscious of their loneliness as superpowers. The European allies in Nato and Warsaw Pact alike were drifting away from their familiar tutelage. Both the Soviet Union and USA were deeply embroiled in Asia, the one in the Vietnam War and the other in a hostile border confrontation with China. Each superpower found the cost of maintaining that status daunting. It was distorting and slowly undermining the domestic economy on which superpower grandeur was based. In short, as one fought against the creeping threat of Communism in Asia, and the other dispatched its tanks to crush the creeping threat of liberal reform within the Soviet Empire, the awareness of a curious empathy began to steal over them. A symbiosis crept into the relationship with what proved to be an enduring sale of surplus US grain to a Soviet Union which could not feed itself. They had more in common with one another than with their fractious and unruly allies. At the same time, the negotiations which led to the long minuet of arms control suggested to both Moscow and Washington that they had something rather unique in common. As the Soviet Union hastened to establish nuclear parity in the aftermath of the Cuban missile crisis, the strategic relationship between the two superpowers began to assume a life of its own. Even as Soviet aid and arms rolled into Vietnam, to be met by American bombardments, the diplomats were negotiating what came to be the keystone of arms control, the Anti-Ballistic Missile Treaty.

This was important not only in itself, as the first mutually restraining treaty, but also as the first formal recognition that each superpower had an interest in protecting the strategic arsenal of the other. By limiting development and deployment of missiles designed to nullify each other's deterrent by shooting them down in flight, the ABM Treaty enshrined and legitimised a strange and almost poetic stillness at the heart of the Cold War. The stability of their nuclear relationship had become more important than the ideologies and ambitions which divided them. The contrast between that frozen equipoise and the tumult in the world beyond the nuclear duet was dramatic. But there was a common theme. Both the USA and the Soviet Union were facing challenges of self-determination which were testing the familiar Cold War constraints. Self-determination for

Vietnam, for China, for France and West Germany and Czechoslovakia, emerged as the common force disrupting alliances. And challenges of a different form of self-determination were disrupting the home front, from the black ghettoes of American cities, to the first serious stirrings of the dissident movement in Moscow. And there was an ugly symmetry to the response.

The unleashing of the tanks upon Prague was a moment of political catalysis inside the Soviet Union. What had been a restive and intermittently bullied literary intelligentsia, and a strong anti-Stalinist sentiment that reached far up into the party hierarchy, started to become a more general disaffection for the foreign policy and the character of the Brezhnev regime. The KGB was trained and large parts of its organisation dedicated to internal surveillance and control. By the standards of Stalin's day, the KGB of the Brezhnev period conducted a soft repression, using psychiatric prisons and deportation and sackings rather than the wholesale slaughter. Life was hideous enough for those brave souls who defied the Soviet system, with banners of protest in Red Square after the invasion of Prague, and the far larger numbers who followed to produce the dissident underground journal *Chronicle of Human Events*.[39]

In the police state of the Soviet Union, whose laws and customs frankly authorised the use of such state measures against its subjects, this was to be expected. In the USA, where the laws and customs and the democratic rhetoric of politicians and officials abjured such misuse of authority, the rigour with which the state would act in the name of national security came as much more of a surprise. And as the extent of this illegality by the organs of state security became known, so public scandal followed. In the USA, the COINTELPRO project of the Federal Bureau of Investigation to infiltrate and destabilise the militant Black Panthers and the anti-Vietnam War movement, ran roughshod over US laws and civil liberties in the name of national security. In defiance of its own charter, which banned operations in the United States, the Central Intelligence Agency began covert work at home. The illegal Chaos operation, seeking (and failing to find) foreign roots of the anti-war movement, opened files on 7,200 US citizens.[40]

Great empires defend their interests in terrible ways. The point is not that the Soviet Union and USA were becoming different sides of the same authoritarian coin, but that they were vast and complex economies and political organisms, feeling beset by enemies within and without, distrustful of their allies and deeply frightened by the implications of defeat. To see this in terms of moral equivalence between the flawed freedoms of the American democracy under intense pressure, and the flawed authoritarianism of a Soviet state which was consciously trying not to revert to full-blooded Stalinist type, is to miss the essence of the situation. If the USA and Soviet Union looked uncannily and unpleasantly akin at the end of the 1960s, their similarity was not only to one another but to that older archetype of imperial Rome, nearly two thousand years before. The modern echoes of that earlier imperial paranoia, as defined by one perceptive historian, are as illuminating as they are poignant:[41]

> There was no corner of the known world where some interest was not alleged to be in danger or under actual attack. If the interests were not Roman, they were those of Rome's allies; and if Rome had no allies, then allies would be invented. When it was utterly impossible to contrive such an interest – why, then it was the national honour that had been insulted. Rome was always being attacked by evil-minded neighbours, always fighting for a breathing-space. The whole world was pervaded by a host of enemies, and it was manifestly Rome's duty to guard against their indubitably aggressive designs.

Chapter 9

Defeat in Asia: Hope in Europe

> Civilisation is hooped together, brought
> Under a rule, under the semblance of peace
> By manifold illusion; but man's life is thought,
> And he, despite his terror, cannot cease
> Ravening through century after century,
> Ravening, raging and uprooting that he may come
> Into the desolation of reality.
>
> *'Meru', W. B. Yeats*

The bloodiest and most costly battle of the Cold War began to draw to its unhappy conclusion on the day that Lyndon Johnson called back to service the old men who had first rallied the Western alliance in the years after 1945. On 1 November 1967, the group of Wise Old Men, who inevitably became known as the WOMs, gathered at the State Department for an optimistic briefing on the Vietnam War by General Earle Wheeler, chairman of the Joint Chiefs of Staff. Dean Acheson, Clark Clifford and Averell Harriman were joined by Douglas Dillon, who had served in the cabinets of both Eisenhower and Kennedy. General Omar Bradley, who had commanded the US troops who stormed ashore on D-Day in 1944, and Kennedy's favourite General Maxwell Taylor, and the former Saigon Ambassador Henry Cabot Lodge also attended. The WOMs were convinced. Just as Johnson had intended, the foreign-policy establishment was loyal to his policy on the war.

'This is a matter we can and will win,' Acheson told the President as they met him in the White House on the following day. 'We must understand that we are not going to have negotiations. When these fellows decide that they can't defeat the South, then they will give up. This is the way it was in Korea. This is the way the Communists operate.'[1]

Acheson spoke for most of this older generation of Best and Brightest. But not for all. Paul Nitze had been doubtful of a land war in Asia from the beginning, and so had George Ball, who had resigned as Under-Secretary of State the previous year. Harriman remained almost completely silent, but later went to see Acheson at his home. Harriman found that the old Secretary of State was far less confident than he had sounded. Acheson had been even more frank in a letter he wrote to another old friend, the former British prime minister, Anthony Eden:[2]

> For the first time, I begin to think that LBJ may be in trouble. It is not Vietnam alone. The country would probably stay with him on that. But Vietnam plus the riots is very bad. It spells frustration and a sense of feebleness at home and abroad. Everyone pushes the USA around. Yellow men in Asia, black men at home, de Gaulle a ridiculous type in Europe, and Nasser threatens to have the Arab states seize what is regarded as 'our' oil properties. Americans aren't used to this, and LBJ is not a lovable type. He is the one to blame.

These were the closing years of the third Cold War decade. And just as it had seemed after the 'loss' of China and Czechoslovakia in the 1940s, and after the humiliation of Sputnik and the fear of the missile gap in the 1950s, there was once more the grim foreboding of Western defeat. The mood was to get much, much worse with the Tet offensive, and the siege of the US Marines in Khe Sanh, another misbegotten outpost dependent on air support which began to look ominously like that graveyard of the French military mission, Dien Bien Phu.

Two months after that first gathering of the WOMs, Acheson went to see President Johnson, and told him in the bluntest terms that he feared the information coming from the Pentagon was being sanitised. Acheson asked to see the raw data. This was granted, and George Carver of the CIA, Philip Habib of the State Department, and General William DuPuy began visiting Acheson's Georgetown home to educate the grandest of the WOMs in the realities of Vietnam. Robert McNamara, who had slipped into a nervous breakdown and had taken to sobbing quietly into the curtains of his Pentagon office, resigned as defence secretary, to be replaced on 1 March by Clark Clifford. Clifford had been the author of one of the first great policy statements of the Cold War. One of the first meetings Clifford arranged after moving into the Pentagon was with Paul Nitze, who for Dean Acheson had written NSC-68, that other prime text of America's post-war policy. Nitze told Clifford that Vietnam was a disastrous sideshow which was obsessing the White House to the point at which they were in danger of losing their European allies. Clifford then asked Acheson for his views on Vietnam, and after his special briefings Acheson was by now convinced that the war was, if not a lost cause, then one not worth the political and international costs.

The mood of crisis was intense, and deepening. On 10 March, the *New York Times* reported that General Westmoreland was requesting another 206,000 troops. On 12 March, Lyndon Johnson barely won the New Hampshire primary election over the quixotic campaign of the anti-war Senator Eugene McCarthy, whose election canvassers were made up of hosts of student volunteers. They included the young Wellesley student Hillary Rodham, later to become better known as the wife of President Bill Clinton. On 14 March, Townsend Hoopes, one of Clifford's under-secretaries, presented him with a long and formal memorandum which said bluntly: 'We are progressively tearing the country apart in order to win the hearts and minds of its people. Unfortunately, the end and the means are mutually exclusive.'[3]

On 17 March, a political rebellion erupted against Johnson. Senator Robert Kennedy announced that he would run for the Democratic Presidential nomination, against his own party's incumbent. Clifford began orchestrating establishment opinion, in particular the WOMs, for a formal reassessment of the war. On 23 March, General Westmoreland was withdrawn from Vietnam, and kicked upstairs to be Army chief of staff. On 25 March, the WOMs gathered again at the State Department for more briefings, this time from Acheson's own sources, Carver, Habib and DuPuy. The next day, the WOMs informed President Johnson that he must find a way to disengage. In Acheson's words:[4]

> Neither the effort of the Government of Vietnam nor the effort of the US government can succeed in the time we have left. Time is limited by reactions in this country. We cannot build an independent South Vietnam. Therefore, we should do something by no later than late summer to establish something different. The issue is can we by military means keep the North Vietnamese off the South Vietnamese. I do not think we can.

Five days later, on 31 March, President Johnson announced a bombing pause, said that he would not stand again for the Presidency, and designated Averell Harriman as his representative at peace talks with North Vietnam.[5] In retrospect, Lyndon Johnson had been partly persuaded, but also partly panicked into this decision. Had the Army and the CIA retained more credibility, after so many years of false hopes, their oddly optimistic assessment of the Tet offensive might have made Johnson think again. Tet was a stunning political victory, but a military disaster, for the Vietcong. In almost sacrificial attacks, these guerrilla forces of the South-based National Liberation Front hurled themselves upon the American fire-power. They scored some dramatic propaganda successes, most notably in the assault on the US Embassy compound, but took devastating losses. The NLF was never the same again. Not only the guerrillas, but whole cadres of the political leadership were killed or arrested. Perhaps as Hanoi had intended all along, the remainder of the war was now very firmly in the control of North Vietnam's regular forces. The CIA reported that the Vietcong losses during the Tet offensive had been around 80,000 dead. By contrast, the CIA and US Army count of North Vietnamese regular troops had risen, from some 70,000 in November of 1967 to over 100,000 in February, immediately after the Tet offensive.[6]

One final and possibly crucial factor was the crisis in the US budget. Johnson had refused to deepen American opposition to the war by raising taxes to pay for it. The mounting costs of the war therefore led to a Federal budget deficit of $24.2 billion in 1968, more than the total deficits of the previous five years.[7] The calculations of Air Force Under-Secretary Townsend Hoopes, as forwarded to Clark Clifford on 14 March, estimated the current 1968 costs of the war at $25 billion a year – which meant that it alone accounted for the budget deficit. General Westmoreland's planned increase of another 200,000 US troops would take the cost to $35 billion a year.[8]

The youngest of the WOMs, McGeorge Bundy, stressed the implications of this in a private letter to the President. It said:[9]

> The really tough problem you have is the interlock between the bad turn in the war, the critical need for a tax increase, and the crisis in public confidence at home. If I understand the immediate needs correctly, the most important of all may be the tax increase, simply because without it, both the dollar and the economy could come apart – and with them everything else.

President de Gaulle, deeply opposed to the war and to the US way of financing it by printing dollars which then washed across to Europe, declared a form of economic war. The United States was able to take advantage of the Bretton Woods system, which made it the world's reserve currency, and force the rest of the world to accept its unilateral expansion of the global money supply, unrestrained by any pressure on its exchange rate. By returning dollars to the USA, and insisting that the Americans redeem them in gold from the Fort Knox vaults, de Gaulle found a way of bringing just such a pressure.

The US and its allies, in order to fend off this kind of sudden demand for gold, had formed a consortium called the Gold Pool, which unloaded gold on to the market in order to stop its price rising above the fixed rate of $35 to the ounce. In the single month of November 1967, when the devaluation of the British pound further destabilised the system, the Gold Pool had to sell $700 million to hold the price. Two days later, de Gaulle announced that France would no longer participate in the Gold Pool, and Johnson was forced to stop selling gold into the free market. Only central banks were now permitted to buy the metal. The system, however, was still intensely vulnerable to political storms. Four months later, on 14 March 1968, in the month of crisis at the White House, $400 million of gold had to be sold in a single day.[10]

The battle to persuade a reluctant Congress to increase taxes, in an election year and when inflation was approaching the then-high figure of 5 per cent, occupied as much of Johnson's time in the spring and summer of 1968 as the Vietnam War. There was little doubt about the depth of the crisis. The final argument had been made by Art Okun, chairman of the Council of Economic Advisers, who warned the cabinet on 14 May: 'The international consequences of a tax bill failure would be very great indeed. It could be a calamity. We could have a sharp rise in speculation in the American dollar and another gold run. It could force us to the bitter choice of suspending gold payments or – even worse – increasing the price of gold . . . We could get a real explosion in the world financial community.'[11] In June 1968, the Johnson Administration and Congress finally bowed to the inevitable and increased taxes. A 10 per cent surcharge was placed on all existing taxes. The result was that, in the following year, the Federal government recorded its only budget surplus between 1961 and the present day: a modest $3.2 billion.[12]

The United States was still by far the biggest and strongest and most productive economic system on earth, poised in 1971 to become the first trillion-dollar economy. But the implications of the financial crisis of 1967–8 were twofold. First, even an economy as rich as that of the USA could not afford guns, butter and a welfare state all at the same time. From the crisis of 1968 onward, a very clear shift takes place in American policy, and questions of finance and American economic health start to overshadow purely strategic considerations. Second, European economies were becoming serious commercial and financial rivals, with the leverage to embarrass US policy when they and the currency-market speculators chose.

American policies, both public and private, had brought this about. The United States had with the Marshall Plan stood both economic and security guarantor to its European allies. With that degree of security beckoning them on, American corporations and investors needed little more urging into Europe, even though Europe's increasingly self-confident citizens were questioning the degree to which they had become an American protectorate. This went far beyond economic issues. Europe's intellectual life was seriously penetrated by American strategic policy, with the CIA discreetly funding a series of centrist or social democratic journals and academic conferences. In February 1971, the American radical magazine *Ramparts* revealed that the CIA had inspired and financed, among other magazines, the British intellectual journal *Encounter*, and with exquisite irony, *Encounter* in April of that year ran an article exploring the extent of America's commercial success. It asked whether a consumer who shaved with a Gillette razor, breakfasted on Heinz beans, drove to work in a Ford car using Esso petrol, and used Remington typewriters and IBM computers in the office while his wife Hoovered at home and shopped at Woolworth's knew whether these were all US-owned.[13]

Until de Gaulle's economic nationalism became an obsession in the mid-1960s, American capital was welcomed throughout Europe, while firmly excluded from Japan. Between 1950 and 1970, the total US direct private investment into Japan was some $320 million, compared to $2 billion into Britain, and $3 billion into Germany in the same period. Japan forced US companies to license their technologies to Japanese companies. Rare exceptions such as Coca-Cola and IBM arose only when Japanese partners of these intruders themselves lobbied the relevant ministries and politicians.[14] Europe, by contrast, offered an open door to American capital, and the implications increasingly alarmed figures like Harold Wilson, who wondered whether the British were doomed to become 'woodcutters and water-carriers of industrial society'. Six per cent of the British workforce were employed by US firms in 1967; significantly, they produced 10 per cent of all British goods. One 1968 study found that US firms 'control three-quarters of the European computer market, produce one-half of France's telecommunications equipment, own one-third of Germany's oil-refining capacity'.[15]

Europe's concern was not altogether rational, harking back to the mercantilist days when trade was seen as a zero-sum game: each export a national gain, each import a national loss. But in the context of an emerging global economy and the dramatic growth of global trade, almost everybody could benefit from this process. However, there were distinct disadvantages for the US economy in the readiness of its multinational corporations to invest and expand overseas. They did so for the obvious reason that they believed they could get a better return on their capital abroad than at home. This may have begun as exploitation of cheap labour, but it quickly became the export of the most modern technology and management skills, often more modern than the plant the parent company was using back in the USA. In effect, US companies helped European exports. They accounted for some 17 per cent of British manufacturing exports in 1967.[16] But the relationship was not purely commercial, as the Johnson Administration made clear when it forced West Germany to cancel an export contract for steel pipe to the Soviet Union in 1964, and to cancel a $150 million order from China for a steel plant.[17] Strains also emerged in the Anglo-American relationship, with US objections to British bus exports to Cuba, and alarm in Britain that its merchant ships trading with North Vietnam were at risk from American bombing. But it was the nationalist perception that American capital was a threat which helped impel Britain to resume its efforts to join the Common Market in 1967. Addressing the Council of Europe in Strasbourg in January of that year, Harold Wilson said:

> Let no one here doubt Britain's loyalty to Nato and the Atlantic Alliance. Loyalty must never mean subservience. Still less must it mean an industrial helotry under which we in Europe produce only the conventional apparatus of a modern economy while becoming increasingly dependent on American business for the sophisticated apparatus which will call the industrial tune in the 70s and 80s.[18]

The contradictions here are bemusing. It was US policy to push Britain gently into Europe, and yet the British prime minister was justifying his application as a means of defending the British economy from the USA. The power of American capital was cited as a threat, and yet the evidence of American fiscal and industrial vulnerability was becoming clear at this time. In 1966, West Germany for the first time overtook the United States in its share of world trade, 19.7 per cent to America's 19.5 per cent. By contrast, in 1950, the US share had been 27.3 per cent, and the West German little more than a quarter of the US share with only 7.3 per cent.[19]

It was in this economic context of a schizophrenic Europe, enjoying its economic boom but fretting at its dependence on an America which could no longer afford its foreign-policy ambitions, that the policy of *détente* took root. For the Soviet Union, *détente* stemmed from the conviction that their strategic inferiority was over. Through

Numbers of US and Soviet nuclear launchers and warheads, 1962–80

	USA		USSR	
Year	*Launchers*	*Warheads*	*Launchers*	*Warheads*
1962	1,653	3,267	235	481
1963	1,812	1,612	302	589
1964	2,021	4,180	425	771
1965	1,888	4,251	463	829
1966	2,139	4,607	570	954
1967	2,268	4,892	947	1,349
1968	2,191	4,839	1,206	1,605
1969	2,109	4,736	1,431	1,815
1970	2,100	4,960	1,835	2,216
1971	2,087	6,064	2,075	2,441
1972	2,167	7,601	2,207	2,573
1973	2,133	8,885	2,339	2,711
1974	2,106	9,324	2,423	2,795
1975	2,106	9,828	2,515	3,217
1976	2,092	10,436	2,545	3,477
1977	2,092	10,580	2,562	4,242
1978	2,086	10,832	2,557	5,516
1979	2,086	10,800	2,548	6,571
1980	2,022	10,608	2,545	7,480

heroic and vastly expensive efforts, the Soviet military had by 1971 caught up with the United States in the number of launchers for nuclear weapons, although not in warheads. By 1973, the Soviet Union had a 10 per cent superiority in launcher numbers, and, by 1976, 25 per cent superiority (see table).[20] In war-fighting terms, or even in the scales of nuclear diplomacy, this small Soviet superiority was quite meaningless. Each power had enough megatonnage to guarantee the destruction of the other several times over. The US had felt deterred by a far smaller Soviet arsenal in 1962. Although a steady increase in defence spending had begun under Khrushchev, with a particular surge in naval budgets after 1963, it was the Brezhnev regime which followed that began the ruinous twenty-year surge in defence expenditure. In real terms, the budget began to grow by an average 4–5 per cent annually after 1964.[21]

The precise level of defence spending is not easy to determine, even after the partial opening of the Defence Ministry and Gosplan (state planning board) statistics after Gorbachev's reforms gave Supreme

Soviet committees the right to question budgetary officials in 1989. Defence procurement was spread among a host of ministries and throughout the budgets of the USSR and of the individual republics. In the period from the 1960s to the 1980s, Western governments relied heavily on CIA estimates of Soviet defence spending, and they in turn relied on their own arcane methods. One such ploy estimated the output of a particular defence plant from satellite photographs by calculating the available floor space. The CIA tried to put a dollar equivalent on the Soviet defence budget, which was distorted by the fact that the Soviet defence industries (and civilian industries too) enjoyed subsidised buildings, electricity and infrastructure. Real costs were almost impossible to ascertain. The CIA's suggestions of an average 12–16 per cent of Soviet GDP being spent on defence were dismissed after 1992 as sharp underestimates by Russian officials, whose own estimates ranged as high as 25 per cent of total Soviet output.[22]

The end of Soviet strategic inferiority was both reassuring and alarming. Soviet military doctrine moved away from the view that nuclear war was inevitable once hostilities had broken out.[23] But the new Soviet self-confidence began to prove alarming to the West in the 1970s, as Soviet political and military influence expanded in Africa, the Middle East, and ultimately in Afghanistan. The global opportunity inherent in *détente* had been clear in Soviet policy from Khrushchev's day, and Leonid Brezhnev's first formal speech as the new Soviet leader, on the forty-seventh anniversary of the 1917 October Revolution, was explicit.

'A situation of peaceful coexistence will enable the success of the liberation struggle and the achievement of the revolutionary tasks of peoples,' Brezhnev declared.[24] But the Soviets drew a clear distinction between the opportunities that *détente* presented in the developing world and the stability it offered in the traditional cockpit of the Cold War: Europe. The 1972 ABM (anti-ballistic-missile) Treaty established them as an equal partner in a nuclear relationship which was becoming both codified and stable. They could welcome Willy Brandt's *Ostpolitik* as a way to a final treaty that would set the seal on the European frontiers established by World War Two, legitimising their empire in Eastern Europe by winning international recognition for its most loyal client state, the German Democratic Republic.

In Brezhnev's view, *détente* was a way to stabilise its relations with an America chastened by Vietnam, and to normalise its relations with Western Europe. With that Western front stabilised, there came an opportunity for the Soviet Union, newly equipped with a great navy and confident in its new post-OPEC wealth from the vast Siberian oil- and gas-fields, to spread its influence further in a developing world whose suspicions of America and the West had been reinforced by the Vietnam War. It also offered a way for the Soviet Union to shift forces to the troubled frontier with China. For the United States, *détente* was a way of adjusting to a world which had grown uncomfortably hostile with the Vietnam War. The European allies were becoming introspective, turning their attention to the developing European Economic Community whose linchpin was a system of agricultural protection designed to keep out cheap American food. *Détente* was also a way to begin easing the economic burden of leading the free world. The Vietnam War had damaged the US economy almost as much as it had tarnished America's image. One original motive for arms control was to save money on the defence budget. The US rested on their strategic laurels in the building of new launch systems, whether missile submarines, ICBMs or manned bombers. But the production of nuclear warheads increased steadily, many of them tactical weapons for battlefield use, designed to save money by permitting a lower level of conventional battlefield forces.

Détente between the United States and the Soviet Union began as a form of conspiracy between the KGB and Henry Kissinger (the new national security adviser to the new President Richard Nixon, who took office in January 1969). Kissinger had been in touch with a KGB contact in the Soviet Embassy, Boris Sedov. In his memoirs, Kissinger revealed that Sedov had warned that Moscow was worried by the return of Nixon, the anti-Communist Vice-President of the 1950s. Sedov appealed for some public hint from the new President that the lines of communication to Moscow would remain open. The Soviet objective was to resume the plan for a new summit in Leningrad which had been arranged between President Johnson and the Soviet leaders for the summer of 1968. It was cancelled after the Soviet invasion of Prague. Accordingly, in his inaugural address, President Nixon declared: 'After a period of confrontation, we are entering an era of negotiation. Let all nations know that during this Administration our lines of communication are open . . . With those who are willing to join, let us cooperate to reduce the burden of arms, to strengthen the structure of peace.'[25]

Nixon had been thinking in these terms since March 1968, when, during the Vietnam crisis, he had prepared a speech which he never delivered because it was overtaken by President Johnson's decision not to seek re-election. Nixon had planned to speak of 'a new era in our relations with the Soviets, a new round of summit meetings and other negotiations'. It was predicated on American withdrawal from Vietnam with Soviet diplomatic assistance. The Soviet Union could be persuaded to help, Nixon reasoned, because they and the United States shared a common alarm over China and the way a North Vietnamese victory was assumed to serve the Chinese cause.[26]

Nixon's instincts were correct. The major military buildup of the Soviet forces during the 1960s had been along the Chinese border. In 1961, just before the Sino-Soviet split went public, the border was manned by twelve Soviet 'shadow' divisions, some at two-thirds strength, some at one-third strength with a divisional HQ which could be reinforced within about ten days. By 1969, there were twenty-five full-strength divisions, and forty-five divisions by 1973. Tactical aircraft numbers grew from 200 to 1,200 warplanes in the same period, along with 120 medium-range SS-11 ballistic missiles.[27]

In August 1969, *Pravda* dropped veiled hints on the possible use of nuclear weapons, and Viktor Louis, a Soviet journalist who wrote occasionally for less-scrupulous Western newspapers, ran a sensational story in September in the London *Evening News*, suggesting that Soviet missiles were poised to destroy the Chinese nuclear-test site at Lop Nor.[28] Henry Kissinger's memoirs relate that one discreet Soviet diplomatic initiative asked what the US reaction would be to a Soviet strike on the Chinese nuclear base. This was taken seriously enough for Under-Secretary Elliot Richardson to issue a public statement that: 'We could not fail to be deeply concerned, however, with an escalation of this quarrel into a massive breach of international peace and security.' Later US intelligence reports found that Soviet nuclear bombers had been transferred to the Chinese border, and had practised attacks on sites built to echo the layout at Lop Nor.[29]

This cumulative evidence of Soviet sensitivity over China virtually invited Nixon and Kissinger to 'play the China card', as the strategy became known. For Kissinger, a student of the European balance-of-power diplomacy in the first half of the nineteenth century, and an admirer of its master exponent, the Austrian Empire's foreign minister Prince Metternich, Soviet strategic parity suggested that the world was becoming once again a fertile field for such exquisite balancing of the new forces. The prime task of US foreign policy, he suggested was 'to manage the emergence of Soviet power', to educate their Soviet equals into civilised and stabilising behaviour.[30] With the stability of *détente* in Europe, the Soviets could best be deterred from over-adventurous policies elsewhere by means of Chinese pressure on their eastern frontier. After a round of secret negotiations, including clandestine visits by Kissinger to Beijing in 1971, Nixon paid his historic visit to China in the February of his re-election year, 1972.

For Kissinger, the interaction between European and Asian affairs was plain; the Sino-Soviet border clashes had followed the Soviet invasion of Czechoslovakia. China had been alarmed that the Brezhnev Doctrine, or the Soviet 'right' to maintain the Kremlin's orthodoxy in its satellites by force, might apply elsewhere. Zhou Enlai pointedly began giving public support to other countries in Eastern Europe that were exploring the bounds of independent action, wooing Romania and Yugoslavia. In a speech celebrating Romanian National Day on 23 August, he denounced the invasion of Prague as 'collusion' with the Americans, part of a US–Soviet plan to carve up the world between them.[31]

Moscow's difficulties with its allies over China began to acquire an uncanny resemblance to America's failure to persuade its European allies to join the war against Vietnam. At the Warsaw Pact conference of March 1969 the Soviet Union tried to persuade its Eastern European allies to send some symbolic military forces to join the Soviet watch on the Chinese frontier. Romania's Nicolae Ceauşescu publicly refused. The other Warsaw Pact allies were deeply reluctant. Moscow dropped the idea, but the connection between the Soviet Union's troubles on both eastern and western frontiers was not lost on Kissinger, and played directly into his and Nixon's deeper strategy of playing the China card.[32]

The policy had been well signalled. The year before his election, Nixon had published an article in *Foreign Affairs* which spoke of 'pulling China back into the world community'. In 1970, in his second year in office, when negotiations were already under way through Pakistan and Romania, he told *Time* magazine: 'If there is anything I want to do before I die, it is to go to China.'[33] The foreign-policy initiative for which he is most remembered, Nixon's decision to recognise Communist China, and accept its replacement of Taiwan in the United Nations Security Council, became a keystone of the American concept of *détente*. But it is through the China policy that the essential instability of the Kissinger–Nixon concept of *détente* becomes plain.

'*Détente* does not mean the end of danger . . . *Détente* is not the same as lasting peace,' Nixon emphasised.[34] Far from it. *Détente* for Kissinger and Nixon was a highly dynamic process, just as it was for Brezhnev and for Soviet policy. In Moscow, *détente* was intended to stabilise Europe, while the great game against America and the West continued elsewhere. In Washington, the strategy was much the same: to ratify the stability in Europe, but to nullify the global implications of Soviet strategic parity by opening a new and dangerous front in the East. If this could be exploited to widen the already apparent rifts between the Soviet Union and its Eastern European allies, so much the better. In that case, the stability of normalised relations between Eastern and Western Europe could develop into trade links and something more dynamic. In the long run, such a penetration of the Iron Curtain could undermine the Soviet Empire.

The public perception of *détente* as a method of easing tensions was thus an almost deliberate fraud. To paraphrase Clausewitz's observation that war is the continuation of politics by other means, *détente* was the continuation of the Cold War in other places, and by more subtle means that the mutual glowering of missiles.

For the Europeans of both East and West, *détente* also had a very particular agenda, which involved a degree of self-liberation from the tutelage of the dominant superpowers. It was a means through which they could recover responsibility for their own affairs, and find some space for independent manoeuvre in the new openings that *détente* was carving in the structures of the Cold War. This had been explicit in the policies of de Gaulle throughout the 1960s; it became an ever stronger motif of West German policy. *Ostpolitik*, the attempt to improve relations with East Germany, began in the Social Democratic Party, but drew significant support from the dominant Bavarian political figure Franz-Josef Strauss.

Strauss was the leader of the Christian Social Union, a conservative party with a Catholic and anti-Communist base, the Bavarian wing of Adenauer's Christian Democrats. A butcher's son, a man of coarseness and yet great perception, he once shouted at a left-wing heckler, 'I'd rather have Eisenhower's arse than Stalin's face!' As defence minister he rode roughshod over the constitution. He arranged the arrest (by the police of Franco's Fascist Spain) of the editor of *Der Spiegel* magazine, for printing embarrassing details of defence policy which Strauss claimed were secrets. Critically friendly of the United States, he argued, 'We want to be a partner of America, not a nuclear protectorate.' He had drawn the lesson from the failure of the Multilateral Force negotiations that the United States would not help West Germany become a nuclear power.

For Strauss, Europe was the vehicle that would control yet also embrace German energies. 'It is not natural for 300 million Europeans to be dependent on 190 million Americans or 200 hundred million Russians,' he told one British interviewer. Some saw him as a German

Gaullist, which was the right idea, but the wrong period. He was far more of a German prototype of Mrs Margaret Thatcher. Indeed, her own ambivalent attitude towards Europe could be summed up in Strauss's dictum on the continent's future: 'Not a melting pot, but a continent on which differences of character and temperament in the individual are preserved in a community which raises their standard of living without standardising their lives, and guarantees their security. In order to remain German, or British, or French or Italian, we must become Europeans.'[35]

As minister of finance in the Grand Coalition government of the Christian Democrats and Social Democrats, Strauss was a key figure in exploiting, rather than in creating, the power of the Deutschmark. Its financial strength had been achieved by Ludwig Erhard's *Wirtschaftswunder*, or economic miracle, during the 1950s and 1960s. But Strauss was the first to dig in his heels and support the Bundesbank in its refusal to revalue the Deutschmark in the massive speculative assault on the pound, and later on the French franc, in the winter of 1968–9.[36]

Strauss was anti-Communist, and sensitive to the deep animosity towards the Soviet Union felt by most of the fourteen million Germans who had come or been driven to the West in the years between 1945 and the erection of the Berlin Wall.[37] This massive transmigration of peoples, the social and political implications of which were rarely comprehended by West Germany's allies, helped build the economy. But those voters had politically powerful memories of the lost lands beyond the River Elbe, which had led to the policy known as the Hallstein Doctrine. Named after Walter Hallstein, the politician who formalised the West German policy of non-recognition and implacable hostility to the German Democratic Republic to the East, this doctrine was a powerful obstacle to *Ostpolitik*.

The Social Democrat leader Willy Brandt was foreign minister in the Great Coalition, but needed the approval of his coalition partners in the CDU–CSU to pursue the first, hesitant signs of his *Ostpolitik*. He was able to win the backing of a suspicious Strauss partly because he played to Strauss's grand if rather vague concept of a greater Europe, but also because this was a policy that Strauss could see infuriating the Soviet Union, and also alerting the Americans to the realisation that there was a distinctive German foreign policy once again. Even though Strauss was to condemn Brandt's *Ostpolitik* in the heat of the 1969 election campaign, Brandt's own definition of his modernisation of West Germany's foreign relations was calculated to appeal to Strauss. Brandt's policy was for Bonn to act on its own behalf 'instead of relying solely on others to speak for us. This meant that while remaining in touch with our allies and retaining their confidence, we became the advocates of our own interests vis-à-vis the governments of Eastern Europe.'[38]

Brandt's first success was to establish mutual diplomatic recognition between Romania and West Germany in 1967. The Soviet Union quickly pressured the other Warsaw Pact nations into a pledge that they would not recognise West Germany until Bonn in turn recognised the DDR. But Brandt had also made progress in establishing humanitarian links across the Wall. In 1968, 1.5 million East Germans, almost all elderly, had been given permission to travel to the West to see their relatives, and 1.2 million West Germans made the trip in the opposite direction.

The contrast is striking between these German family visits, and in the same year, the crushing of the Prague Spring by Soviet armed forces. The contrast between European and American responses to the Czech repression was just as sharp. The United States cancelled a planned summit; President de Gaulle's foreign minister referred to it blithely as 'a traffic accident on the road to *détente*'. Britain's prime minister Harold Wilson, while condemning the invasion as an outrageous act of blatant aggression, sought to use the crisis as a further spur to *détente*. In his speech to the House of Commons when Parliament was recalled to debate the Prague invasion, he had stressed: 'The lesson for us is that not only must our posture in Nato be flexible in its defensive postures; it must be flexible equally in its readiness to respond to the opportunities for *détente*.'[39]

The three main Western European powers were thus each committed to their own regional *détente* with the East, even as the Czech tragedy was under way. Europe's growing sense of financial strength and independence, and a perception of American weakness and distraction, underlay their approach. But the Czech experiment with 'socialism with a human face' was a sign that the Soviet grip on Eastern Europe was itself on the defensive, that the Eastern Europeans themselves were becoming actors in their own drama. Romania's independent foreign policy was one sign; the first strikes in Gdańsk, in Poland, in 1970, were another.

For Western Europe, the years 1969–70 were a crucial period. They saw the retirement of Charles de Gaulle after his defeat in a referendum, and the first victory of Willy Brandt's Social Democrats. They also saw the full flood of his *Ostpolitik* with the signature of a non-aggression treaty with the USSR, in August. This was followed by his historic visit to Poland to sign a formal 'normalisation' treaty in

December, where he fell to his knees in contrition at the site of the Auschwitz death camp. In 1970, Harold Wilson's Labour government was defeated by the Conservatives, led by Edward Heath, who immediately relaunched Britain's application to join the Common Market. This time, with de Gaulle gone, President Pompidou in his place, and Britain's membership enthusiastically supported by West Germany, the venture succeeded.

It was a historic shift, marking a transformation of a Cold War world which had for twenty years looked very much as it had in the 1940s. Britain's entry into Europe, the coming of *détente*, and above all the new financial crisis which dramatised American economic vulnerability, were like the deep tectonic movements which precede an earthquake. The crisis was thrust upon America by its closest ally, in August 1971, when the British Ambassador, Lord Cromer, called upon the US Treasury to request that $3 billion be converted into gold, or their equivalent in exchange-rate guarantees. The significance of Britain's new thrust into Europe became, suddenly, acutely plain. Britain's European commitment was one thing; an apparent conversion to de Gaulle's policies of economic war against the dollar was quite another. The fact that Lord Cromer had been the Governor of the Bank of England at a previous time when Britain had appealed for American support for the pound, added to the piquancy of the occasion.

'We knew that we would very soon have to confront a major crisis concerning the international economic position of the United States,' President Nixon recalled in his memoirs. He convened a session of his senior economic advisers at Camp David over the weekend of Friday, 13 August, until the Sunday night, when he announced 'the new economic policy'. Significantly, Dr Kissinger was not invited to attend – perhaps the last time that an American financial crisis would not be seen at once to have strategic and diplomatic considerations requiring the presence of the national security adviser.

Nixon unveiled a stunning package, a dramatic extension of state powers over the economy which – after a decade of dominant free-market theories – seem all the more sweeping in retrospect. He imposed a freeze on wages, on prices, and a tax on all imports, and effectively took the United States off the gold standard and the world off the dollar standard by finally closing the gold window. The USA would no longer make gold available for dollars to other countries' central banks. The motive of Nixon, and his Treasury Secretary, the Texan Democrat John Connally, was largely political: to free the US economy from balance-of-payments restraints and open the way for reflation to ensure the economy was growing comfortably in time for Nixon's re-election campaign the following year.[40]

The one dissenting voice at Camp David was Arthur Burns, chairman of the Federal Reserve Board, the US central bank, but he was outnumbered. Had Dr Kissinger been at Camp David, he might have warned that this dismantling of the Bretton Woods financial system, which had helped the Western world to an unprecedented period of growth and trade expansion, could have monstrous consequences. But perhaps not. Kissinger's ignorance of economic affairs was legendary; on one occasion he asked the British Ambassador Lord Cromer for some private tutorials.

The immediate reaction of American economists was enthusiastic. 'I applaud ending the fiction that the dollar is convertible into gold,' Professor Milton Friedman, yet to become famous as the father of the new monetarism, told the *Wall Street Journal*. Paul Samuelson, author of the standard textbook of the day, wrote in the *New York Times*: 'At last, Devaluation . . . if the dollar depreciates 7 to 15 per cent relative to the currencies of the surplus countries, there will be a movement from disequilibrium to equilibrium.' This was correct, as far as it went, and Wall Street rallied with a rise of thirty points.[41]

Wall Street's enthusiasm is explained by the statistics. In 1971, for the first time since the Second World War, the US recorded a deficit in the trade of manufactured goods.[42] The 1971 Federal budget deficit was $23 billion – back up to that figure which had forced President Johnson into a tax increase in 1968. The balance-of-payments deficit on official settlements had reached a record $10.7 billion in 1970. Europe was once more awash with dollars, which meant that the United States was exporting inflation, to the anguish of the West Germans, who found themselves with dollars worth over $13.5 billion in their reserves. The Bundesbank was also convinced that America would be forced to devalue, which would mean heavy losses for its own account. In the first hour of trading on 5 May 1971 another $1 billion had sloshed into the Bundesbank, effectively forcing the Deutschmark to float. The flood of dollars provoked the disruption in European currency markets which had led Lord Cromer to make his request for $3 billion of the Bank of England's dollars to be converted into gold.

'To be perfectly frank,' Treasury Secretary Connally informed a restive audience of bankers in Munich, 'no longer will the American people permit their government to engage in international actions in which the true long-run interests of the US are not just as clearly recognised as those of the nations with which we deal.'[43]

The least-noticed result of Nixon's decisions on 15 August may have been the most portentous. On 22 September, an extraordinary meeting of the Organisation of Petroleum Exporting Countries gathered in Beirut to adopt Resolution XXV.140:

> Noting that these developments have resulted in a de facto devaluation of the US dollar, the currency in which posted prices are established, vis-à-vis the currencies of the major industrialised countries . . . the conference resolves that Member countries shall take necessary action and/or shall establish negotiations, individually or in groups, with the oil companies with a view to adopting ways and means to offset any adverse effects on the per barrel real income of Member countries resulting from the international monetary developments as of August 15.

In that same year of 1971, and for the first time, the Saudi Arabian oil minister Sheikh Zaki Yamani had mentioned the possibility of an oil embargo as his ultimate bargaining weapon, during his negotiations with BP and Exxon. In February, the Gulf producers had demanded and won a 30 cents a barrel price increase, and the right to more than half of the oil-production profits. In April, the Mediterranean producers, led by Libya, had secured a 90 cents a barrel increase. Two years before the Yom Kippur war, OPEC was already feeling its muscles, and had formally determined to impose price rises if a dollar devaluation reduced their real income from oil.[44]

This was sombre news for the United States, which had just seen its peak domestic oil production of 11.3 barrels per day, and which could no longer count on any surplus from its own wells. The United States was increasingly dependent on oil imports, and thus on OPEC. US oil imports rose from 2 million barrels a day in 1967, or 19 per cent of total consumption, to over 6 million barrels a day by 1973, or 36 per cent of consumption. The US was becoming more vulnerable to OPEC pressure just as its dollar was becoming less acceptable to OPEC as payment.[45]

Beyond OPEC, the impact of Nixon's 15 August economic package was cruel. The Japanese government was given ten minutes' notice before the public announcement, which the Tokyo press noted sourly was seven minutes' less notice than Tokyo had been given of the announcement of Dr Kissinger's historic trip to Beijing.[46] In Britain, Prime Minister Ted Heath hit the roof. After reminding his advisers that US Treasury Secretary Connally had hitherto been best known for having ridden in Kennedy's car and being wounded in the assassination, Heath grunted, 'I knew they killed the wrong man in Dallas.'[47]

Finally, on 17 December, the major industrial nations met at Washington's Smithsonian Institution and agreed a wholesale revaluation of currencies. The yen was increased in value by 16.9 per cent, the Deutschmark by 5 per cent, and the dollar was devalued some 8 per cent against gold, the price rising from $35 to $38 an ounce. This was a purely notional price, since it was no longer to be sold by the United States, even to other central banks. On the commercial market, its price immediately rose to $44 an ounce.

President Nixon called this 'the most significant monetary agreement in the history of the world'. It lasted just eighteen months. By 1973, the world had entered the roller-coaster era of floating exchange rates. The removal of the traditional gold–dollar discipline led directly to an explosion in global money supply. The growth of global money had begun in the 1960s, when the US profligately printed dollars to finance its deficits (which is to say its Vietnam War) without increasing taxes. The enforced US devaluation of 1971 made matters worse. With the Smithsonian Agreement, the great inflation of the 1970s got under way. Between 1 January 1970 and 30 September 1974 international monetary reserves increased by 168 per cent. 'In this short span of three years, world monetary reserves increased by more than in all the previous years and centuries since Adam and Eve,' commented Professor Robert Triffin.[48]

In 1973, as the inflation rate was beginning to climb sharply to 8.8 per cent, a new record for the post-war era, the Nixon Administration began to dismantle the wage-and-price control system which had been imposed in 1971. Adding to the OPEC effect, this gave inflation another impetus, and in 1974, US inflation rates rose above 12 per cent as the economy sank into serious recession. Industrial production declined by almost 15 per cent, and unemployment rose to a peak of over 9 per cent. Even after this recession – which saw a cumulative GDP decline of 6 per cent – inflation still remained at the historically high base level of over 5 per cent. A new word – 'Stagflation' – had to be coined to describe this theoretically improbable combination of inflation and economic stagnation.[49]

Nixon had surrendered the dollar's grip on the gold standard, and dismantled the Bretton Woods financial system which had institutionalised America's economic predominance since the 1940s. In retrospect, it was doubtless the most important measure of his Presidency. It eased an immediate crisis, but stored up far more trouble for the future. Aside from the inflationary implications, and the way it provoked the OPEC oil-price rise, it also deeply soured America's relations with its allies. The Europeans and Japanese felt that their own hard-won prosperity was now being put at risk to sustain an American foreign policy in Vietnam with which they did not agree. Treasury Secretary Connally's attempt to argue that they were helping finance their own security, since the annual sum of the US balance-of-payments deficit tended to match the dollar costs of maintaining the US garrison in Nato, did not mollify them. After a dramatic export drive, the German central bank saw the dollars received for these exports collapse in value by almost half between 1970 and 1974 because of the steady decline of the US currency.[50]

Wealth is power, as the Americans had learned and enjoyed in the golden years after 1945. After 1971, the Europeans were learning the same lesson, and using that wealth to explore a greater freedom of action, even while fretting at the new American policy of paying their way through both domestic devaluation and exporting inflation. The clearest sign of this European independence came with the awful warning of a new nuclear confrontation, which helped convince both Moscow and Washington that superpower *détente* was not only desirable, but essential.

The Yom Kippur War of 1973, between America's closest ally in the Middle East and the Soviet-equipped armies of Egypt and Syria, suddenly exploded into a new crisis between the superpowers. The Israeli military superiority which had been so dramatic in the 1956 and 1967 wars had since been eroded. Soviet anti-tank missiles blunted the Israeli counter-attacks as the Egyptian tanks thrust across the Suez Canal. Faced with defeat and dwindling stocks of planes, anti-aircraft missiles and artillery ammunition, Israel appealed desperately to the United States for re-supply. The European allies, with the exception of Portugal, bluntly refused to let the US supply planes use their airfields. For the first time since 1945, America was not able to persuade its allies to acquiesce.

This was a more dramatic example of Europe's strategic independence than the refusal to send troops to America's support in Vietnam. This time, the Europeans refused to allow even the use of the American air bases on their soil. Their fear of an Arab oil embargo outweighed their loyalty to American policy. At the last minute, thanks to Portugal's permission for the Azores bases to be used, the American munitions arrived in Israel. The Israeli counter-attacks managed to encircle an Egyptian army in Sinai, threatening to cut it off. The Soviet Union insisted on a cease-fire and suggested that US and Soviet troops be deployed to enforce it. But Kissinger was determined to keep Soviet forces out of the region.

To warn Moscow that US vital interests were at stake, Richard Nixon declared the first nuclear alert since the Cuba missile crisis. At least, that is what was said at the time. This was DefCon 3, the highest state of alert short of war. It involved pre-launch checks of nuclear tipped missiles, and B-52 bombers leaving their runways to fly in holding patterns to be refuelled by air tankers, awaiting the final order to invade Soviet airspace. This move to the very brink of war was ordered by Dr Kissinger alone, without consulting the President, who was distraught by the latest turn in the Watergate scandal which was to topple him.[51]

On 19 October 1973, President Nixon had ordered his Attorney-General Elliot Richardson to dismiss the Watergate special prosecutor, Archibald Cox, who had issued subpoenas for the tape recordings of the President's Oval Office conversations. Richardson refused, and was fired on the following day. Richardson's deputy also refused when given a similar order. Resolutions calling for the President's impeachment were immediately introduced in Congress. Nixon suffered something close to a nervous breakdown, telling Kissinger that he was being attacked 'because of their desire to kill the President. And they may succeed. I may physically die.'[52]

The symbolism of this moment is acute. The Presidency was empty, and the National Security Adviser took over. Kissinger declared a nuclear alert as a diplomatic weapon in a regional crisis which was perceived purely in terms of diplomacy, strategy and the balance of power. But in fact, the real importance of the Yom Kippur War was its economic impact, which seems not have occupied Kissinger at all, at a time when the most serious long-term threat to American interests and strategy was its cumulative economic enfeeblement. Kissinger had no peers in the media promotion of the glamour of this Great Game of superpower diplomacy and his own masterly role within it. But in his obsession with power politics, Kissinger missed the far more serious shift in the economic balance of forces which was under way.

The Yom Kippur War meant that the Middle East had a far more important new role to play in global affairs. It represented the financial empowerment of the Arab world, even as it suffered another military defeat at Israel's hands. The month before the war began, OPEC was getting just over $3 a barrel for its oil, and the Arab states were pumping 20.8 million barrels a day (MBD). On 16 October, OPEC forced the price up to $5.40 a barrel. The 'embargo' (in fact, a cut-back) peaked in December with the Arabs still pumping 15.8 MBD. World oil output fell only 9 per cent, but internationally traded oil fell by 14 per cent. The surging growth of world oil consumption, running at over 7 per cent a year, helped explain the immediate panic. By November, Nigerian oil was being sold at $16 a barrel, and one Japanese buyer made a wild bid of $22.60 a barrel in a deal which was never completed.[53]

But the newspaper headlines of the day spread panic around the world. 'The Western industrialized world is up against a quasi-monopoly possessing unprecedented ability to halt most areas of economic life in Western Europe and Japan . . . For the long run, Arab oil blackmail is intolerable and ways to break that grip on the throats of Europe and Japan must be found,' said the *New York Times*. France preened itself on the security afforded by its nuclear-power programme, with a famous *Le Figaro* headline which gloated 'L'Europe à pied; La France à 50 kph' (Europe on foot, France motoring at 50 kilometres per hour).

The economic implications of the OPEC price rise were evident to all; the political results took longer to sink in. Egypt's *Al-Ahram* put the Arab viewpoint: 'Oil is a source of wealth which the Arabs put at the service of progress and the prosperity of the peoples of the world. It is their right that the world which benefits from this wealth should support their legitimate rights.' *Pravda* understood the new political alignments that OPEC's strength could imply – 'The genuine prospect of the use of oil as a political weapon by the Arabs compels Western European governments to disassociate themselves from the pro-Israeli policy of the USA.' But the clearest analysis of the transformed geopolitics of the Middle East came from the Italian daily *Corriere della Sera*, editorialising from the point of view of a moderately conservative newspaper which had traditionally been loyal to the Atlantic Alliance: 'The Europeans now find themselves confronted by a dilemma, between the necessity of supplies of Middle Eastern oil, and the convenience of supporting American global strategy. It will not be easy to decide between the dependence of their economies on oil and their dependence on the security of American protection.'[54]

OPEC's oil-price rise savaged the West's economies, while the Watergate scandal in Washington sapped America's influence, adding to the sense of American retreat and malaise which the collapse in Vietnam had made manifest. The attempts by Nixon and Kissinger 'to manage Soviet power' became hostage to the President's own predicament. The new round of US–Soviet arms control talks which led to the SALT Treaty looked like American acquiescence in a diminished role in the world, while the Helsinki Treaties of 1975 gave legal form to the once-challenged Soviet dominance of Eastern and Central Europe. If *détente* suggested that the Cold War was ending in a draw, to rising politicians like Margaret Thatcher and Ronald Reagan it looked more like a defeat for the ambitious Western strategy which Kennan had defined nearly thirty years earlier. Reagan even found an ominous new title for the Helsinki Treaties – another Yalta. 'At Kissinger's insistence, President Ford flew halfway round the world to sign an agreement at Helsinki which placed the American seal of approval on the Soviet Empire in Eastern Europe,' Reagan charged, as he challenged President Ford for the Republican nomination in 1976.[55]

Chapter 10

The Death of *Détente* and the Change of the Western System

> The last word on how we may live or die
> Rests today with such quiet
> Men, working too hard in rooms that are too big,
> Reducing to figures
> What is the matter, what is to be done.
>
> *'The Managers', W. H. Auden*

The Helsinki Treaties and the successful meeting in space of the American Apollo and Soviet Soyuz spacecraft took place in 1975, the high point of *détente*. But *détente*'s political nemesis in the West had already begun, with the election of Margaret Thatcher as the first woman leader of Britain's Conservative Party. This was followed in the USA by the Presidential challenge of Ronald Reagan in 1976. Even though the later 1970s were marked in Britain and the United States and in Canada (the largely Anglo-Saxon core of the Atlantic alliance) by a period of Labour, Democratic and Liberal leadership, a fundamental political shift was taking place. Exhausted, and increasingly discredited, the broadly social democratic ideology which had sustained the West throughout the Cold War was in retreat.

With hindsight, we may say that the historic tasks of that ideology had been accomplished. From the original post-war alliance of Harry Truman's Democrats and Clement Attlee's Labour government, the West had constructed a very different form of capitalism from that which had been discredited by the Great Depression of the 1930s. Inspired by Roosevelt's New Deal, the West's post-war consensus was based on the mixed economy, with state controls over trade and currency flows, and at times over wages and prices, and on some form of welfare state. In the United States, Britain and the other countries of Western Europe, governments saw it as their duty to command the strategic direction of large proportions of investment resources. Public money was poured into schools, the dramatic expansion of university education, and into the infrastructure of roads and airports.

Public ownership never went so far in the United States as in Western Europe, where strategic industries like coal and steel and the rail system and airlines and much of the defence industry, such as Britain's Royal Ordnance, were usually nationalised. But even in the United States, public ownership of port authorities, urban transit systems and parts of the power grid – the Tennessee Valley Authority was the best-known example – had been commonplace since the days of Roosevelt's New Deal in the 1930s. And progressive state governments in the USA were happy to push their own public investment into those areas which the Federal government left untouched. Mayor Hubert Humphrey of Minneapolis built a national reputation with his civic version of social democracy, and helped to found the liberal pressure group, Americans for Democratic Action. Humphrey's classic statement of that ideological space which social democracy could carve out between Communism and the political centre came in 1947: 'You can be a liberal without being a Communist, and you can be a progressive without being a Communist sympathizer, and we are a liberal progressive party out here.' That remained his political philosophy in the US Senate, as Lyndon Johnson's Vice-President, and as the Democratic candidate for the Presidency in 1968.[1]

The booming state of California was perhaps America's classic example of social democracy at work. Its power came from the federally funded dams along the Colorado River. Its thriving aerospace industry prospered under government research and manufacturing contracts, during World War Two and Cold War alike. In the period 1967–9, for example, California received 34.6 per cent of all Federal expenditure on research and development (R&D), and 36.3 per cent of Pentagon spending on R&D. In 1960, the state began a mammoth public-works project to ensure water supplies, and embarked on a dramatic expansion of the state university system. It grew to nineteen campuses with over 300,000 students by the late 1970s. Until the end of California's great period of public investment with the taxpayer revolt of Proposition 13 in 1978, the state spent on average 25 per cent more per head on education than the national norm. Jesse Unruh, the Democrat who led the opposition to Governor Ronald Reagan in the legislature, used to boast of the state's 'unmatched educational system, especially higher education, and especially the seventy community colleges, or junior colleges, which offer two-year courses of mainly vocational training, at very low tuition fees, and open to almost any high-school graduate'.[2]

This kind of social investment by individual states was accompanied in the 1960s by President Lyndon Johnson's development of something close to a European form of welfare state with his Great Society programmes. Better pensions for the aged, welfare payments for the poor, and publicly funded health care for both these groups through Medicare and Medicaid meant that Johnson could claim to have fulfilled the New Deal principles which had brought him into public life. They were not only sustained, but saw an honest attempt at improvement by the Republican President Richard Nixon.

There can be no more clarifying contrast between the Republicanism of Richard Nixon and that of Ronald Reagan than Nixon's extraordinary state interventionist measures of 15 August 1971. Nixon's wage controls, price controls, currency controls and import surcharges were the reverse of Reagan's free-market insistence that the role of government in the economy be curtailed. Nixon also recruited the former Kennedy and Johnson aide, and later Democratic Senator for New York, Daniel Moynihan, as his domestic policy adviser to develop a family assistance programme. While the scheme was defeated in Congress, Nixon was able to enact a revenue-sharing plan which spread Federal funds among the states, and contributed heavily to what the 1978 Advisory Commission on Intergovernmental Relations called 'an unparalleled expansion of government'.

'State and local governments in particular have grown rapidly, as demonstrated by the nearly threefold increase in their workforces from about 4.1 million to 12.2 million between 1953 and 1976, and the nearly tenfold increase in their own revenues during the same period,' the Commission reported.[3]

Poverty was not eradicated. Indeed, the statist measures introduced by the post-war and Great Society wave of social democracy probably institutionalised it for the least fortunate. But the great achievement of social democracy in the West was to create at least a basic welfare state and an efficient ladder of social mobility, which hugely expanded the middle classes. They could expect subsidies to buy their homes, to send their children to university, to sustain their sickness and their old age. And the social democracy had another component. In the Britain of the 1960s, the Wilson government improved a social welfare system which had been in place since the Labour government of 1945–51. But while the role of the state as social engineer was widened in the British social democracy of the 1960s, the traditional grip of the state as moral arbiter of cultural and personal life was deliberately relaxed. Divorce was made far easier, homosexuality was no longer a criminal offence, abortion was made available virtually on demand, and the rigorous old forms of censorship were dismantled. A similar wave of what advocates called civilising reforms, and critics dubbed permissiveness, took place in the United States and in Western Europe.

Having achieved all this, what remained for social democracy to do? The attempt by the Wilson government after 1974 to proceed further left towards a system of state planning and state corporatism could not command an enthusiastic majority within the party. Unable to recognise that its historic task of civilising the old capitalism had been achieved, the British Labour Party simply floundered without an agenda. The election victory of President Jimmy Carter in 1976 revealed a Democratic Party in a similar state, bereft of ideas beyond vapid slogans like 'a government as good as its people'. In his election campaign, Mr Carter spelt out his concept of the purpose of government in an interview on the public broadcasting system which revealed the emptiness of the Democratic project.

The purpose of government, Carter said, was:[4]

> To provide legitimate services to our people; to help preserve peace; to provide a mechanism by which the people's character can be expressed in international affairs. I think the purpose of government is to alleviate inequities, to provide for things that we can't provide ourselves . . . I would like to have a chance to change things that I don't like, and to correct the inequities as I discern them, and to be a strong spokesman for those that are not strong.

Even for a country yearning for calm after the defeat in Vietnam, the storms on its campuses and the great constitutional trauma of Watergate, this was an extraordinarily quiescent agenda. In Britain and in the United States, the intellectual and doctrinal condition of that social democracy which had rallied and administered the Western world since 1945 echoed the verdict of Benjamin Disraeli, when after the most reforming six years in British governance he regarded Prime Minister William Gladstone's front bench in 1874, and mocked them as 'a range of exhausted volcanoes'.

Not only were Western politics ready for a change, the social democratic record of economic stewardship was miserable in the mid-1970s. The proud post-war record of high unemployment, low inflation and steady growth foundered with the Great Inflation and the international economic crisis after the OPEC price rise (see table, page 234).[5] This dismaying record contrasted sharply with the rather more impressive performance of the Soviet economy, at least in the way the West then measured it. There were two striking features to Soviet growth, the oil boom after the discovery and exploitation of the Tyumen fields in the late 1960s (just in time to benefit from the OPEC

Unemployment, inflation and GDP in France, Great Britain, Italy, the USA and West Germany, 1970, 1975 and 1979

	France	*Great Britain*	*Italy*	*United States*	*West Germany*
			Unemployment rates (per cent)		
1970	1.7	2.2	3.2	4.7	0.6
1975	3.9	3.7	5.3	8.5	4.2
1979	6.0	5.3	7.5	6.0	3.9
			Inflation over previous year (per cent)		
1970	5.2	6.4	5.0	5.9	3.4
1975	11.8	24.2	17.0	9.1	6.0
1979	9.1	13.4	14.8	11.3	4.1
			Gross domestic product (percentage growth/decline over previous year)		
1970	+5.7	+2.3	+5.3	−0.3	+5.1
1975	+0.2	−0.6	−3.6	−0.1	−1.6
1979	+3.3	+2.4	+2.7	+2.4	+4.2

price rises), and the fulfilment of Khrushchev's target of overtaking the US economy by the early 1980s. In the terms in which Khrushchev defined the challenge, the Soviet economy succeeded. In 1961, at the twenty-second Party Congress, Khrushchev launched the Third Economic Programme, which promised the Soviet people that, within two decades, they would be producing more industrial goods than the USA. So they did.

By 1984, the Soviet Union produced 80 per cent more steel, 78 per cent more cement, 42 per cent more oil, 55 per cent more fertiliser, more than twice as much pig-iron and six times as much iron ore as the USA. Soviet factories produced five times as many tractors and almost twice as many metal-cutting lathes as their US counterparts.[6]

In 1961, these products embodied the sinews of industrial power. Had the world and its technologies stood still, the Soviet Union would have been its economic giant. The success of Khrushchev's plan represented the strength and the weakness of the centrally planned economy. A target was set by the politicians and planners: the country's resources in transport, raw materials, labour force and investment were deployed to meet it. The problem was that by the time these figures of raw Soviet output overtook those of the United States, the West was living in an entirely different economic system, a post-industrial world in which the new sinews of wealth were microchips rather than pig-iron, plastic rather than steel, and where conservation in the use of raw materials was becoming more important and more profitable than crude production.

The West was forced to jump-start its transformation into this post-industrial economy by the OPEC price rise, which not only raised the price of energy, but served to accelerate a general inflation that increased the price of most other raw materials too. A significant proportion of the industrial world's growth in the three decades after 1945 had come from a historic shift in the terms of trade, the ratio between the prices of food and raw materials (which fell steadily over this period), and the prices of industrial goods. This meant that the industrial nations were paying less for their essential imports, and could therefore devote more resources to consumption and to investment. To this degree, the developing world which exported raw materials helped subsidise the growth of richer industrial countries.[7]

This trend stopped sharply with the OPEC price rise. For the next ten years, while energy prices stayed high, the terms of trade shifted back to benefit some of the developing countries. The new combination of high energy prices and lower prices for the grain it imported was particularly helpful to the Soviet economy. It was able to extend a subsidy in energy and other prices to its Eastern European allies of some $8 billion a year (in 1980 prices) throughout the 1970s.[8]

In effect, the OPEC price rise forced the West to adjust, while encouraging the Soviet Union to continue with an economic system which seemed to be working. This was a delusion: it had begun in 1965, the year after Khrushchev fell, when Soviet geologists discovered the two trillion cubic metres (TCM) Zapolyanoe natural-gas field in Tyumen province of western Siberia. The following year, they found the Medvezhe field of 1.5 TCM and the largest of all, the four-TCM Urengoy field.[9] By 1985, natural gas provided one-third of all Soviet energy needs, and was flowing at a rate of 600 billion cubic metres a year. The growth in crude-oil supplies was equally dramatic. As the Caspian Sea fields began to decline in the 1970s, the western Siberian oilfields more than compensated. From 150 million tonnes of crude oil in 1960, production doubled each decade, to 350 million tonnes in 1970, and 600 million tonnes in 1980. The OPEC price rise, and the growth of Soviet energy exports, meant that the Soviet Union was earning large amounts of Western currency, sufficient to import $50 billion of Western machinery in the seven years after 1975.[10]

The political implications of this bonanza were heartening for Soviet leaders, who saw this growing wealth bringing an economic balance to match the strategic parity in the East–West relationship. On the thirtieth anniversary of the defeat of Nazi Germany, Leonid Brezhnev gave what was probably the finest speech of his career to a gathering of war veterans in the Kremlin.[11] It summed up not only the sense of Soviet achievement, but also towards its close carried the clear strategic challenge which came with the new confidence:

> The victory over Fascism enabled our people not only to heal the wounds of war, but also to increase the country's economic potential many times over, and to raise our economic output [Brezhnev began]. Today, we may confidently declare that our country's industry and agriculture are based on a sound foundation and are developing successfully. And along with this, our people have begun to live much better. That is how things are today, comrades, and how they will continue to be. The raising of the people's living standard and further improvement of the Soviet people's life is the unswerving line of our Party's policy.

'It has been a hard struggle,' Brezhnev went on, in a speech marked by the pride and emotion which still shine through the turgid Soviet prose.

> Hardly had the smoke lifted from the battlefield than we had to face the Cold War started by the most aggressive imperialist circles. Torrents of slander and provocations against the socialist countries, atomic blackmail, attempts at economic blockade, whipped up by hopes of our economy being temporarily weakened by the war – all these were used by the leaders of imperialism in the hope of preventing socialism from being strengthened and hampering the growth of influence in the world. But the forces of reaction which unleashed the Cold War miscalculated. They did not succeed in either suppressing or weakening socialism.
>
> In the new situation, the leaders of the bourgeois world have also come to realise that the Cold War has outlived itself and that there is need for a new, more sensible and realistic policy. Our calls for peaceful coexistence have begun to evoke serious responses in many capitalist countries . . . It is high time that those whom this concerns realised the simple truth: in our time, attempts to suppress the people's liberation movement are doomed to failure. And the best evidence of this comes from the fine victory scored by the Vietnamese people in the struggle

> against foreign interventionists and their henchmen. This victory is a triumph of the effective and militant solidarity of the socialist countries. It is also an indication of the great moral and political importance of the sympathy and support coming from the progressive forces of the whole world.

When Brezhnev gave that speech, so redolent of the new Soviet confidence after the American military defeat in Vietnam and the West's post-OPEC economic recession, the background to it was a leap of US–Soviet trade from $200 million in 1974 to just over $1,000 billion in 1975. With *détente*, America seemed to be adjusting to the new realities of what Brezhnev liked to call the 'businesslike' US–Soviet relationship, transformed from the crises of Khrushchev's day.[12] It was in this mood that Brezhnev happily signed the Helsinki Treaties, in which the thirty-five countries of Europe, and the United States and Canada, codified the European borders of 1945. They also established the broad principles of what was expected to be a stabilised relationship of *détente*, a cautious control of armaments, and a steady growth in trade and cultural links. In his speech to the Helsinki conference Brezhnev added: 'The main conclusion, which is reflected in the Final Act, is this: no one should try, from foreign policy considerations of one kind of another, to dictate to other peoples how they should manage their internal affairs.'[13]

In retrospect, the Helsinki Treaties of 1975 appear as the West's secret weapon, a time-bomb planted in the heart of the Soviet Empire. Throughout Eastern Europe and in the Soviet Union itself, a handful of brave and determined campaigners used the human-rights provisions of the Helsinki 'Final Basket' to insist that their governments live up to the commitments they had signed. The Charter 77 group in Prague, the Solidarity movement in Poland, and Helsinki Watch groups in East Germany and in Leningrad and Moscow never really combined, and still less were they able to coordinate their campaigns with the Soviet Jewish refuseniks and their devoted supporters in the influential Jewish communities of the West. But the human-rights movement, slowly but surely, reversed the moral defeat the West had suffered in Vietnam, and helped transform the Soviet Union into the pariah state, the new Gulag, the Evil Empire of Reagan's rhetoric.

Evil or improving – and the Soviet repression of the 1970s was incomparably less ruthless (and less effective) than in Stalin's merciless tradition – it remained an empire on the march. The fall of the Portuguese Empire in Africa saw an unprecedented expansion of Soviet influence there, where revolutionary governments in Angola and Mozambique were armed and supported by the Soviet Union, and black Africa was assured that Moscow was ready to join the liberation struggle against the apartheid regime of South Africa. In the Horn of Africa, with Machiavellian ruthlessness, the Soviets switched their backing from Somalia to the revolutionaries who had toppled Haile Selassie in Ethiopia, establishing what Dr Henry Kissinger defined as 'a new strategic bridgehead' at the gateway to the Suez Canal. The fall of Saigon offered the Soviet navy a new port in the Pacific, the Cam Ranh Bay facility which the United States had built to supply its troops in Vietnam.

The irony of the new industrial revolution of the 1970s was that the three rich countries of the northern hemisphere that proved least able to respond to the challenge were the three best supplied in energy resources: the USA, the UK and the Soviet Union. On the face of it, the increased value of their own oil, and the far lesser burden of paying higher prices for imported oil, should have helped their economies. In the very short term, it did help. In the medium term, it reduced their incentives to conserve energy use and to retool their manufacturing industries to cope with expensive energy. In sum, it slowed their response to the opportunity that lay beneath the OPEC challenge, and allowed more adaptive economies to surge ahead.

The most adaptive economy of all was Japan, the country which was by far the most dependent on imported energy. Partly because of the shock to the internal economy, and partly because Japan's customary export markets were also hit by the OPEC effect and not able to maintain their rate of increase in imports, Japan's growth rates slowed sharply and permanently (see table, page 239).[14] The pattern is plain: in the first half of the 1970s, the Japanese economy ran into a kind of wall, which cut their growth rates by some 10 per cent a year. The world's other economies were far less dramatically affected by the great inflation and the OPEC effect. The French growth rates halved, and like German rates, fell to British levels. The US economy slowed, recovered, and slowed again, but maintained the rough average growth rate it had enjoyed since 1947. The far more modest Japanese lead in growth which followed the OPEC shock was sustained by a far greater readiness to divert resources to investment. Japan's savings ratio, as a proportion of GDP, actually rose from 17.9 per cent in 1970 to 22.8 in 1975, and was still at 17.9 per cent in 1980, sharply higher than its industrial competitors'. In the United States, the savings ratio went from 9.8 per cent in 1970 to 11 per cent in 1975, and to 8.9 per cent in 1980.[15]

Average annual GDP growth rates in France, Great Britain, Japan, the United States and West Germany, 1947–50 to 1986/7 (per cent, in constant prices)

Years	*Japan*	*United States*	*Great Britain*	*France*	*West Germany*
1947–50	9.7	2.4	1.5	10.4	–
1951–5	10.9	4.8	3.4	4.5	11.4
1956–60	10.1	2.3	2.6	5.6	7.4
1961–5	11.3	5.1	3.4	6.5	5.3
1966–70	14.6	3.1	2.6	6.0	4.5
1971–5	4.7	2.3	2.3	3.7	5.2
1976–80	5.5	3.7	1.8	3.3	3.6
1981–5	4.2	2.7	1.9	1.5	1.2
1986/7	3.4	3.2	3.5	2.2	2.2

Japan's readiness to defer consumption today in order to invest to produce wealth tomorrow was matched by the speed of its transition to energy conservation. Between 1973 and 1983, Japan's use of energy per unit of chemical and steel production had dropped by 38 and 16 per cent respectively, more than double the US rate. By 1982, the Japanese private-car fleet of 39 million vehicles had achieved an average energy use of 31 miles per gallon, compared to an average 16 mpg in the US fleet of 125.4 million cars, and 22 mpg in the German fleet of 23.2 million cars.[16] The result was that American consumers increasingly turned to Japanese cars. Having sold only 3,000 cars in the USA in 1965, Toyota overtook Volkswagen as the leading imported car in 1975, selling 800,000 to American buyers. When the second OPEC price shock came in 1979, Toyota sold 1.8 million cars and Japanese imports had 20 per cent of a US market which wanted fuel economy, even if Detroit proved reluctant to provide it.[17]

In spite of Jimmy Carter's insistence that the energy crisis was 'the moral equivalent of war', the United States tended to emulate the Soviet Union, and not take the results of the OPEC price rise too seriously. In the five years after 1974, the United States increased its dependence on imported oil by 32 per cent, while the EEC countries reduced theirs by 4 per cent, a sharp distinction even allowing for the start of the flow of Britain's North Sea oil.[18]

There were difficulties and painful restructuring, and serious and wasteful setbacks, like the initial rush to build nuclear power stations, which stalled in the face of public opposition after an accident and mass evacuation at Pennsylvania's Three-Mile Island in 1979. But the West as a whole adapted to the new economic conditions. Fuel-efficient cars, the spread of computerisation and the Japanese system of just-in-time deliveries of components to assembly lines reduced manufacturing costs. Above all, in its finance and insurance companies, its design and marketing and communications systems, the West was able to signal its new economic concerns to manufacturers and consumers alike. The designers responsible for the tailfins and chrome which contributed to the profligacy of Western industry were able to adapt to safer and cheaper construction with lightweight materials. The marketing and communications systems were able to sell them, and the financial networks were able to redirect the investment and credit flows.

While the Soviet Union was laboriously building up the industrial hardware of the 1960s, the West suddenly found that it had developed the software which enabled it to transform the nature of its economic life. The OPEC shock was quickly turned to its advantage. The West's oil companies, whose combined profits had been stagnant at less than $7 billion a year from 1967 to 1972, suddenly saw their profits leap $11.7 billion in 1973, and $16.4 billion in 1974. This was because they found as much profit in the 'downstream' processes of refining and marketing the oil as they had in pumping it from the ground.[19]

The floods of money that were suddenly available to the OPEC countries did not simply disappear. The money was recycled through Western banks, invested in Western stocks and shares, circulated into arms purchases and new airports and cities and better living standards in Gulf states. The West usually provided the arms and construction firms and the teachers at the new universities and many of the goods at the supermarkets which became the local symbols of OPEC wealth. There was still money left over for French wines and casinos, English country houses and racehorses, American private jets and investment consultants, and Japanese TV studio systems. The sudden flash of primarily, but not exclusively, Arab wealth acted as a catalyst which stimulated the integration and the growth of the global economy.

The wealthy industrialised countries were not the only beneficiaries. The money deposited back into Western banks had itself to be recycled into new investments, and the Third World debt crisis of the 1980s was the result of the incautious loans made with the funds available from the OPEC deposits of the 1970s. In 1973, the total debt of the developing countries which were not fortunate enough to produce oil was $130 billion. By 1982, it had grown nearly fivefold, to $612.4 billion.[20] This was more than they could repay, and the result was the world debt crisis. Inevitably, this was also a crisis for the banks of the West, but particularly for the acutely exposed banks of the USA. In 1970, 15 of the world's largest commercial banks were American, 16 were European and 11 were Japanese. By 1990, only two of the world's top 50 commercial banks were American. Japan had 22, and Europe had 20. Within less than two decades, the world's commercial banking leadership had simply disappeared from American shores.[21]

The 1970s, the decade of defeat in Vietnam and of *détente* and the OPEC shocks, were revolutionary for their impact upon the USA's economic position in the world. The US share of global output slumped from 38 per cent in 1970 to 25 per cent just ten years later, while the European Community share overtook the USA's, rising from 26 to 30 per cent. Japan's share rose more modestly, from 8 to 10 per cent of world output.[22] This was the scale of shift which normally comes as the result of a major war. In 1970, the US economy had been bigger than those of Europe and Japan combined. Ten years later, those combined economies of Europe and Japan were 60 per cent bigger than that of the military ally on whom their security depended.

These underlying economic changes had their strategic implications, which were plain to Soviet as well as Western strategists. But those surface changes, which inspired the Soviet Union to shed some of the restraint it had shown in international behaviour since the Cuban missile crisis, concealed two deeper truths. The first was that if the United States had weakened, then it had done so as the economic strength of the West as a whole had increased. And second, that relative decline of the USA against its European and Japanese allies was the price being paid for a deep structural shift. In the ten years after the 1974 OPEC price rise, the USA went through the perestroika on which the Soviet Union did not embark until a decade later, and did so with political and social institutions far more resilient and capable of accommodating the social costs of that change. But this was not how it seemed at the time.

'Soviet officials have indicated that what they call the "correlation of forces" is moving in their favour, and that even though we may today believe that their proposals are one-sided and inequitable, eventually realism will bring us to accept at least the substance of them,' warned the veteran American Strategist Paul Nitze.[23] The occasion was his address to the House Armed Services Committee in

Congress in July 1974, when the combination of Watergate scandal and OPEC shock had reached its most demoralising pitch. Nitze had just resigned from the US delegation to the Strategic Arms Limitation Talks (SALT). And while Nixon conducted his last, desperate summit in Moscow on the very eve of his resignation, Nitze warned from Washington that the West was in danger of losing strategic parity. This was slowly but steadily to become a common view. Eighteen months later, while trying and failing to win Congressional support for major covert and overt operations to challenge Soviet influence in southern Africa, Kissinger echoed it.

'Angola represents the first time that the Soviets have moved militarily at long distance to impose a regime of their choice. It is the first time that the United States has failed to respond,' Kissinger warned Congress. 'An ominous precedent has been set. If the pattern is not broken now, we will face harder choices and harder costs in the future.'[24]

The mood in Washington in the mid-1970s was extraordinary, increasingly akin to Britain during the great debates over the appeasement of Hitler in the late 1930s. Indeed, this parallel was often cited by a coalition of Cold Warriors, both Republicans and Democrats, who began to campaign with increasing stridency for an end to *détente* and a new robustness. The coalition was the more effective in that it crossed party lines, with the Democratic Senator Scoop Jackson from Washington State making common cause with Republican hawks. Jackson's most devoted aide on arms control and national-security affairs, Richard Perle, was later to become Assistant Secretary of Defense in the Reagan Administration. Once installed there, Perle revelled in the nickname of 'the Prince of Darkness', a tribute to his devout anti-Communism and implacable suspicions of all Soviet actions.

Here again we see the collapse of that social democratic tradition which had guided the West in the first three decades of the Cold War on a policy of reform at home and anti-Communist vigilance abroad. The Democratic Party itself had been split, by the Vietnam War, into two wings known as hawks and doves. The split continued for a generation, once the doves captured control of the party's procedures to impose their Presidential candidate with the nomination of George McGovern in 1972. Similar divisions appeared in the social democratic parties of Britain and West Germany at the same time, although alleviated to a degree by Willy Brandt's *Ostpolitik*.

In the USA, the symbiosis between relaxed strategic tensions and normalised commercial links, which had been at the heart of the

Nixon–Kissinger approach to *détente*, proved to be a weak link. This hard-headed equation of trade and raw power made considerable sense, but did not allow for the current of idealism which had run through America's foreign-policy tradition at least since the days of Woodrow Wilson. Several important groups on the conservative wing of the Democratic Party took to heart different parts of what became jumbled together as 'human rights'.

The American trade unions, in particular the AFL–CIO, had been a loyal member of the Cold War coalition because of their support for the principle of free trade unions for Eastern Europe. They had frequently joined forces with the CIA in the name of that principle, and the first strike actions in Poland in 1970 had revived that tradition. Jewish groups in the Democratic Party, and those neo-conservatives around *Commentary* magazine who had shifted their allegiance to the Republicans because of their anti-Communism, developed a powerful campaign around the cause of Soviet Jews and their right to emigrate. Human rights was a cause everyone in the Democratic Party could agree upon, and which it would be churlish to oppose. To any politician, human rights in the Soviet Union offered an irresistible opportunity to challenge the *détente* policies of a Nixon, to condemn President Ford for refusing to honour the exiled writer Alexander Solzhenitsyn in the White House, and to snipe at the cold *realpolitik* of a Kissinger.

'Where the age-old antagonism between freedom and tyranny is concerned, we are not neutral,' Kissinger pleaded before the Senate Foreign Relations Committee in 1974. 'But other imperatives impose limits on our ability to produce internal changes in foreign countries. Consciousness of our limits is a recognition of the necessity of peace – not moral callousness.'[25]

Kissinger was then at the peak of his influence and his international celebrity. More the master manipulator of an uncritical media than the new Metternich, he had been awarded a Nobel peace prize for the Vietnam War he did not end. His star shining the brighter against the disgrace of Nixon and the clumsiness of President Ford, Kissinger was credited with almost magical skills. In retrospect, it is not quite clear why, except that he managed to create the perception of American influence and power even where it was palpably waning. The Kissinger cult grew to strange proportions. His staff were so in awe of the man that at one inter-agency working group on covert operations in Angola (run by the CIA), the men supposedly running African policy were reduced to discussing whether a Kissinger grunt should be interpreted as approval or rejection of their plan. They even tried to imitate the precise sounds Kissinger had made to see whether they could agree whether its tone had been positive or negative.[26]

At least one man was not intimidated by the legend, Senator Scoop Jackson of Washington. Nicknamed the Senator from Boeing, after the dominant industry of his home state of Washington, Jackson believed in buoyant defence spending, partly because so much of it went to his constituents at Boeing. Jackson's initial doubts about the Nixon–Kissinger arms-control policy were based on strategic considerations. But persuaded by Richard Perle, his aide who subsequently served in President Reagan's Pentagon, Jackson found that the issue of Jewish emigration gave extraordinary leverage over the whole *détente* process. In addition to arms control, Kissinger had sought to enmesh the Soviet system into other lasting and stabilising relationships with the West. Trade was the carrot, but the vehicle to achieve this, Most Favoured Nation status, was then legally linked to the pace of Jewish emigration from the Soviet Union by Senator Jackson's legislative masterpiece, the Jackson–Vanik amendment. This gave both the Soviet Union, and its opponents in the United States, a lasting grievance to exploit. Successive Soviet governments could complain that the USA did not live up to its commercial promises; anti-Communists could belabour the Soviet record on human rights.

An unsavoury trade developed, which at least had the merit of allowing some Soviet Jews to live where they chose. But human migration became hostage to the wider East–West relationship. From 35,000 in 1973, Jewish emigration fell to 14,000 in 1975 and 1976, rose again to 51,000 after Carter's wheat deal and the SALT II negotiations in 1979, and collapsed again after the invasion of Afghanistan.[27] The Helsinki Treaties of 1975, and President Carter's new stress on 'human rights' as a cardinal principle of his foreign policy, reinforced one another. The more that brave figures in Eastern Europe tried to make those rights real, like the signatories of the Czechoslovak Charter 77, the more the Communist regimes reacted in a way which justified the Western critics of *détente*.

There was no single Soviet action which turned the scale, more an accumulation of worries which widened the suspicion of *détente* to many other than the predictable hawks. The speed with which the Soviets MIRV-ed their missiles, putting up to ten miniaturised warheads where a single one had been, startled the Pentagon, which saw the number of US strategic warheads outnumbered after 1970. Brezhnev's increase in defence spending bore fruit with the introduction of four new models of strategic missiles in 1974, and then the Europeans had their own cause for alarm with the deployment of the SS-20 missiles in 1977. Each carrying three warheads (and far more accurate than any previous Soviet missile), the SS-20 was an intermediate-range system which had originally been developed with Chinese targets in mind, but was perfectly adapted to Europe. Previous Soviet missiles aimed at Europe had been terrifying but crude and relatively inaccurate, threatening cities rather than specific targets. The SS-20s raised the serious fear that the Soviet Union now had the equipment to wage a premeditated nuclear war in Europe alone, destroying the Nato airfields and ports and thus preventing the arrival of US reinforcements on which Nato depended.

This was taken the more seriously because the key Nato governments were under new management as the SS-20s were deployed. After eight years of Republican rule, Jimmy Carter had been inaugurated as President in January 1977, while James Callaghan had succeeded Harold Wilson in London. In West Germany, the discovery of a Soviet spy inside Willy Brandt's office led to his resignation. The new German Chancellor Helmut Schmidt was still a Social Democrat, but also a defence expert, and he deliberately chose to sound the new nuclear alarm in a speech to the International Institute of Strategic Studies in London. Warning of the threat of new Soviet weapons, Schmidt also argued that the link between Western Europe and the United States was at risk while the Americans engaged in a purely bilateral arms-control process with Moscow. 'Strategic arms limitation confined to the United States and the Soviet Union will inevitably impair the security of the Western European members of the alliance vis-à-vis Soviet military superiority in Europe,' Schmidt said.[28]

The military and European élites were worried. In April 1977, although he had campaigned on the promise to cut the defence budget by $5–7 billion, Carter pressed the European Nato governments to agree to increase defence spending by 3 per cent a year. For the Western public, there was geographic evidence of the spread of Soviet influence. As the West 'lost' Vietnam, the Soviets seemed to be 'gaining' Angola and Mozambique and Ethiopia. The Carter Administration dithered, even when warned by its allies in Africa and the Middle East of what the Sudanese President called 'a sinister grand strategy' by Moscow. After Cuban troops, already installed in Angola, began deploying in Ethiopia at the start of 1978, the National Security Adviser Zbigniew Brzezinski reported to President Carter: 'Soviet leaders may be acting merely in response to an apparent opportunity, or the Soviet action may be part of a wide strategic design. In either case, the Soviets probably calculate, as previously in

Angola, they can later adopt a more conciliatory attitude and that the US will simply again adjust to the consolidation of Soviet presence in yet another African country.'[29]

This was not the view of Secretary of State Cyrus Vance. Although by no means a member of the left-liberal or even the pacifist wing of the Democratic Party, Vance was a firm believer in *détente*, and an experienced diplomat who had seen the clumsy attempts of the Soviet Union in the Third World flounder before. He took a relaxed perspective:[30]

> We in the State Department saw the Horn [of Africa] as a textbook case of Soviet exploitation of a local conflict. In the long run, however, we believed the Ethiopians would oust the Soviets from their country as had happened in Egypt and the Sudan. Meanwhile we should continue to work with our European allies and the African nations to bring about a negotiated solution of the broader regional issues. We believed that in the long run, Soviet–Ethiopian relations undoubtedly would sour and Ethiopia would again turn to the West.

Vance may have been too optimistic in his view of the ability of the Ethiopians to change their government or its policies. As conservative commentators later noted, the Mengistu regime in Ethiopia was to outlast the Communist regimes of Eastern Europe.[31] In the broader perception of history, Vance's 'in the long run' may have been nearer the truth. But democracies moving into an election year in an atmosphere of crisis, amid talk of national humiliation, are seldom receptive to talk of the long run. The short run was looking far too alarming.

US interests appeared to be coming under threat throughout the world, with Soviet arms sales to Iraq and Syria, Soviet support for the PLO, the advance of the Soviet Union's Vietnamese allies throughout South-East Asia, and the new challenges to the pro-American regimes in Central America. The Kremlin's Cuban allies had established military control in Angola. On the maps of the world which American news magazines began to publish, with countries coloured in red for Soviet influence, the West's retreat was made to look graphically clear. Few of these countries were strategically significant, but in 1978, the linchpin of US policy in the highly sensitive region of the Persian Gulf began to fall apart.

The crisis in Iran had little to do with the Soviet Union. Indeed, members of the Tudeh, the Iranian Communist Party, were to be hunted down like rats by the Republican Guard once the Ayatollah Khomeini took over from the Shah. The Shah of Iran brought about his own downfall, through a combination of vicious repression by the

Savak secret police, and far-sighted reforms which threatened the entrenched interests of the Iranian gentry, its merchant classes and the Shi'ite Islamic church. The Shah's 'white revolution' had redistributed land from the traditional nobility, improved the status of women, and sought to exclude the Islamic religious leaders from secular affairs. But the oil wealth flooding into Iran after 1974 had transformed the country in more destabilising ways, provoking mass migration from the land to the cities. Combined with the land reforms and the effects of inflation, this meant that by 1978, Iran was importing over half of its food. The oil wealth did not spread far down into the population. There were heavy expenditures on a military establishment to sustain the Shah's plan to become a regional superpower, replacing the British presence in the Gulf. Most of this was spent on American arms, which brought over 10,000 US technicians into the country. Their presence provided a target for the Shah's domestic opponents, with terrorist bombings of American facilities and homes, and regular denunciations of this infidel presence from the mosques.

The activities of the Shah's secret police appalled Western opinion, and embarrassed defenders of the human-rights policy of President Carter. In 1977, on the Shah's state visit to Washington, the Shah and the President stood for their commemorative photograph, wiping their eyes from the tear gas being used to keep the anti-Shah demonstrators at bay. The more the Shah heeded American urgings to restrain his secret police, the feebler his grip on the country became. A wave of riots throughout 1978 convulsed Iran, and in the first month of 1979, the Shah fled the country, never to return. Unstable caretaker governments were swiftly succeeded by the theocratic and deeply anti-American regime of the Ayatollah Khomeini. And if the Shah's fall had not been perceived as a setback for the American interests, the subsequent seizure of the US Embassy in Tehran, and the taking hostage of its diplomats, most certainly was.[32]

The Iran hostage crisis was a humiliation which overshadowed the last year of the Carter presidency. The failure of a bold rescue attempt in April 1980, when US helicopters crashed in the Iranian desert, reinforced the sense of American military impotence, while another dramatic rise in the oil price led to gasoline shortages in the United States. In Iran, the USA not only lost an ally, but suddenly found that an entire strategic region, source of much of the West's energy supply, was at risk. Even if the Soviet Union were not visibly profiting from the Shah's fall, the new threat of Islamic fundamentalism spreading from Iran into Iraq and the Persian Gulf countries was as alarming.

Soviet expansion, Arab terrorism, Islamic fundamentalism and domestic stagflation all served to galvanise the West's conservatives and its hawks into a new militancy. In Britain Mrs Thatcher demanded a new Western firmness which won her the Soviet nickname of the Iron Lady, and in the United States, the Committee on the Present Danger warned that the Cold War was being lost. The committee had first been formed in 1950, to promote the massive rearmament plans which Paul Nitze and Dean Acheson had drafted in NSC-68, and 'to prevent a Korea in Western Europe'. It had been founded by the Under-Secretary of the Army, Tracy Vorhees, who had resigned over proposed Pentagon cuts. The committee had fallen into abeyance, until revived in 1976 and relaunched two days after the election of Jimmy Carter, with Paul Nitze as the chairman of policy studies. The committee was to form the core of President Reagan's Administration after 1980. Reagan himself was a member, along with his CIA director William Casey, his National Security Adviser Richard Allen, his Ambassador to the United Nations Jeane Kirkpatrick, his Navy Secretary John Lehman, his future Secretary of State George Shultz, and his Assistant Defense Secretary Richard Perle. The committee provided a remarkable total of thirty-two Reagan Administration officials. Nitze, Perle and Kirkpatrick had been Democrats, and the leading American trade unionist, the AFL–CIO president Lane Kirkland, was also a member. This was the anti-Communist establishment, the hawks all flocking together to argue for more defence spending and against the SALT II agreement.[33]

A rather more imaginative warning was sounded in Europe by the distinguished former soldier and military intellectual, General Sir John Hackett. Having parachuted into the battle of Arnhem in 1944 with his hunting-horn, General Hackett was sometimes dismissed as a Blimp by those unfamiliar with his silky mind. A literate and cultured man, he had been impressed by the success of a work of alarmist fiction in stimulating British public opinion in the 1850s to rearm against the threat of the France of Emperor Napoleon III. *The Battle of Dorking*, a best-seller in Victorian days, told the story of a successful French invasion across the Channel, and their victory at the last line of British defences before London. General Hackett collected a glittering assembly of Nato officials and European military men to help him write *The Third World War*, a thrilling account of a Soviet invasion of Western Europe.

In Hackett's version, the Soviet invasion was finally defeated, after the destruction of Birmingham and Minsk in a token nuclear exchange. The last, almost-despairing counter-attack of the Nato reinforcements helped push the ramshackle Soviet Empire into collapse as saboteurs in Poland blocked roads and bridges, and food riots in Moscow led to mass lynchings of Communists. But those Nato reinforcements were only available because of the last-minute rearmament plans pushed through by a new female British Prime Minister, named Mrs Plumber, evidently modelled on Mrs Thatcher. When the book was published, and swiftly became a best-seller on both sides of the Atlantic, Mrs Thatcher was still leader of the Conservative opposition.[34]

Hackett's book was written to bring about a revival of Nato defence spending that was, in fact, already under way. The Committee on the Present Danger, similarly, were not mistaken in arguing that Soviet strategic forces were now at least a match for the US. But the implication that Hackett and the Committee on the Present Danger drew from this, that the West was staring defeat in the face, was more questionable. The underlying reality was different. Even as the fall of the Shah of Iran and the weakening dollar inspired OPEC to another dramatic rise in the price of oil, the creaking Soviet economy was beginning to sink under the strain of imperial overstretch. In China, the aftermath of the Red Guards and Mao's chaos had brought the Soviet Union a new strategic enemy, and the West a potential friend. If the unified new state of Vietnam was seen as a Soviet client, extending its sway over Laos and Cambodia, China was tilting to the West. In January 1979, as President Carter was about to give a formal White House banquet for Deng Xiao-ping, the Chinese leader asked for a confidential session. He described China's plans for the punitive military strike across the border into Vietnam which did take place later that year. Deng went on to suggest to the Americans a very loose form of alliance.

'He said he was not opposed to the SALT II agreement, that it may be necessary,' Carter later confided to his diary.[35]

> But he felt that this fourth negotiation was destined to have the same result as the other three – that is, not to restrain Soviet strategic military buildup. Deng pointed out that the PRC [People's Republic of China] does not want war. The Chinese need a long period of peace to realize their full modernisation. The Soviets will launch war eventually. But we may be able to postpone war for twenty-two years [until the end of the century]. He did not think we ought to have a formal alliance between the US, PRC and India, but we should coordinate our activities to constrain the Soviets.

The Nato allies had already begun to gear up for the new tension. The Helmut Schmidt speech of 1977, on Europe's fear of being decoupled from the US nuclear umbrella, led to the plan from Nato's High Level group for the Soviet SS-20s to be matched by the deployment of 572 new US missiles in Europe. The plan called for 108 Pershing and 96 Cruise missiles in West Germany, 160 Cruise missiles in Britain and 112 in Italy, and 48 each in the Netherlands and Belgium.[36] It caused furious outcries and mass demonstrations throughout Western Europe, the women's peace camps at the Greenham Common airbase in Britain, and damaging divisions within the German SDP and the British Labour Party. The irony was that the Nato rearmament programme had already begun in 1977, the last coordinated strategic decision of the social democratic consensus which had dominated Nato since its birth. General Hackett had written a powerful fantasy, but in the hard reality of 1970s politics it was a Democratic President, a Labour Prime Minister and a Social Democratic Chancellor who agreed to increase their defence budgets by 3 per cent a year, to increase US forces in Europe by 35,000 men, and to deploy the Cruise and Pershing missiles.

The West's rearmament before the coming of the Reagan presidency was sharply intensified by the Soviet occupation of Afghanistan. In his State of the Union address in January 1980, President Carter announced the renewed registration of young men for the draft, and an increase of 5 per cent in real terms for the next defence budget. Under the Carter plan, this would have taken the defence budget to $165 billion in 1981, and to $265 billion in 1985 (in constant dollars). In short, the dramatic rearmament of the Reagan years was largely envisaged by the Carter Administration. Carter announced the formal doctrine that would bear his name: 'An attempt by any outside force to gain control of the Persian Gulf region will be regarded as an assault on the vital interests of the United States of America and such an assault will be repelled by any means necessary, including military force.'[37]

The perception of US humiliations in Iran and Afghanistan was intensified by the scale of the West's economic troubles. The new OPEC price rise of 1979, after the fall of the Shah of Iran, had combined with the deliberate policy of 'benign neglect' of the value of the dollar on the exchange markets to produce some bizarre financial effects. In 1980, the US inflation rate was 17 per cent, and the prime rate for US bank interest, set by the Federal Reserve Bank, climbed to 20 per cent. In the six weeks between 10 December 1979 and 21 January of the next year, the period of the Afghan invasion, the price of gold very nearly doubled, from $431 an ounce to $850. It was less than ten years since President Nixon had dismantled the Bretton Woods system. It had been a miserable decade for America. The gold value of the US dollar dwindled by an extraordinary 96 per cent.

In reality, the situation was nothing like so bad. Rearmament was under way, and the speculation in gold was soon to collapse. The United States had established a new stability in the Middle East, with the Camp David agreement bringing peace between Israel and Egypt and firmly removing Egypt from the Soviet camp. In Western Europe, Helmut Schmidt in Germany and James Callaghan in Britain had declared their readiness to keep up the nuclear guard and challenge their domestic critics by deploying Cruise and Pershing missiles on their soil to confront the new threat of the Soviet SS-20s. Above all, the Western economies were responding to the challenge of high energy prices with a new industrial revolution to recover from the damaging recession which paved the way for the long boom of the 1980s.

These deeper trends were brought into focus by what seemed at first a dramatic new proof of the Soviet Union's grasp for strategic mastery with the invasion of Afghanistan. On small-scale maps, the warm-water ports of the Indian Ocean and the oil supplies of the Persian Gulf seemed only a few days' tank-ride away from Soviet domination. In retrospect, it was the high watermark of Brezhnev's ambition, the last doomed flailing of an exhausted system falling into a trap of its own making. The key basis of Soviet expansion, the special strategic relationship of arms control with the United States, was stopped in its tracks when the invasion of Afghanistan killed off any prospect of the US Senate ratifying the SALT II Treaty. But to the troubled, and some said defeatist West of 1980, it was overshadowed by the new humiliation of America with the seizure of the US diplomats in the Teheran Embassy in Iran, and the hideous failure of the attempt to free them. Once again, a decade ended with the West obsessed with intimations of strategic defeat. And just as the young Jack Kennedy opened the 1960s with a promise to 'bear any burden' in the Cold War, so his contemporaries, Ronald Reagan in Washington and Margaret Thatcher in London, embarked on the 1980s resolved to fend off defeatism, to rebuild the West's defences, and roll back the Soviet advances of the previous decade.

Chapter 11
The New Cold War

> It is with nations as with men,
> One must be first. We are the mightiest,
> The heirs of Rome.
>
> *John Davidson, from 'War Song'*

The leaders of the Soviet Union never wanted to invade or to occupy Afghanistan. The recent opening of the Politburo archives makes it clear that the initial pleas for Soviet military assistance, from the pro-Soviet Afghan Communists who seized power in April 1978, were rejected. That coup, led by Soviet-trained Afghan officers, against the neutralist government of Mohammed Daoud, had taken the Kremlin by surprise. But once its Marxist–Leninist loyalties were proclaimed, Brezhnev's Politburo felt a forced and unhappy duty of limited solidarity with the new regime, offering financial aid and technical assistance. And in that process of seduction and dependence which has characterised relations between superpowers and their client states, the Soviets, rather like the Americans in Vietnam, were drawn ever deeper into a full-scale military commitment.

A year after the 1978 coup surprised the Kremlin, the pro-Soviet regime was in desperate trouble. Its Communist party had split, along broadly tribal lines, into Khalq and Parcham factions. The country's second city of Herat briefly fell to an uprising of the Shi'ite Muslim armed opposition, backed by a mutiny of the Afghan 17th infantry division, who slaughtered around one hundred Soviet military personnel and their families. Their bodies were mutilated, and their severed heads paraded round the city on pikes.[1] According to the Politburo archives, the formal appeal for Soviet ground troops followed immediately, and was first delivered by the Afghan leader Mohammed Taraki on 18 March 1979.

'The situation is bad and is getting worse. We need practical help in both men and weapons,' Taraki told Soviet premier Alexei Kosygin by telephone. Two days later, Taraki arrived in Moscow to deliver his plea 'to save the situation' in person.[2] His first meeting was with Kosygin, defence minister Dmitri Ustinov and foreign minister Andrei Gromyko.

> We will do everything in our power to help you with advisers and military material, but we believe it would be a fatal mistake to commit ground troops [Kosygin said]. The entry of our troops into Afghanistan would outrage the international community, triggering a string of extremely negative consequences in many different areas . . . Our common enemies are just waiting for the moment when Soviet troops appear in Afghanistan. This will give them the excuse they need to send armed bands into the country. If our troops went in, the situation in your country would not improve. On the contrary, it would get worse. Our troops would have to struggle not only with an external aggressor, but with a significant part of your own people. And the people would never forgive such things.

Taraki was able to haggle his way to serious support, of helicopter gunships with Soviet pilots and technicians, and 300,000 tons of grain on credit (which the Soviets purchased from the United States). The buildup continued throughout the summer of 1979, including 700 Soviet paratroops, disguised as aircraft technicians, to defend the airport. Military advisers were assigned to each Afghan field command, down to battalion level. But the Soviet leadership held back from full engagement, and the final reason was explained to Taraki at the end of those talks in March 1979, by Brezhnev himself. 'We have examined this question from all sides, weighed the pros and cons, and I will tell you frankly: We must not do this. It would only play into the hands of enemies – both yours and ours,' Brezhnev said.

The Soviet aid in food and weapons helped to stabilise the situation temporarily, at least in the main city of Kabul, and to enable the recapture of the city of Herat.* But in September, Taraki was overthrown by his chief aide, Hafizullah Amin. According to US diplomatic reports from Kabul, this followed a confused incident in which Taraki had tried to have Amin shot at a meeting which Amin only attended under a safe-conduct from the Soviet Ambassador. Both men

* The author drove into Afghanistan from Pakistan through the Quetta Pass to Herat, to Kabul, and then back into Pakistan through the Khyber Pass, in April/May 1979. There was fighting in the countryside around Herat, and the Khyber Pass was intermittently closed. Soviet military advisers were a common sight in Kabul, and so were air strikes around the capital. But for the most part, the country was in a state of acute tension, marked by sporadic military operations, rather than wholesale war.

were members of the dominant Khalq faction of the party. Amin's eventual success in toppling and later killing Taraki was accepted by the Soviet Ambassador in Kabul, Alexander Puzanov, who urged Moscow to recognise the new regime. The KGB station in Kabul, according to the account of its deputy chief, Alexander Morozov, was strongly opposed to Amin. His coup would lead to 'harsh repressions, and as a result, the activation and consolidation of the opposition . . . The situation can only be saved by the removal of Amin from power and the restoration of unity,' the KGB reported to Moscow.[3]

The clear implication of the KGB report was that Soviet military intervention would be required to overthrow Amin and replace him with a pro-Soviet government able to command broader popular support. In Moscow's eyes, this should not have been difficult. Afghanistan was a semi-feudal country, crying out for those basic reforms at which Communist regimes in the past had proved at least partially successful. Land reform, literacy programmes, rural health and school systems, roads and bridges, and measures to improve the lot of the rural population and the women should have, in principle and over time, made the new government more popular. But the time was too little, and the strength of tradition too great, once the Soviet occupation of December 1979 gave the war against the Russian invaders a patriotic cast.

After Amin's coup, the Soviet Politburo established a special committee on Afghanistan, composed of defence minister Ustinov, the KGB chairman Yuri Andropov, and Boris Ponomaryev, the Central Committee secretary who ran relations with fraternal parties. On 29 October, they concluded that Amin was conducting a purge of his opponents, warned that he was moving towards a 'more balanced' foreign policy and that his protestations of loyalty to Moscow were 'insincere'. The 'balance', in this context, referred not only to the West and the United States, but far more to the tangled regional balance of power in South Asia.

The American view that the Afghan venture symbolised an aggressive, confident Soviet Union marching towards the Indian Ocean would have seemed outlandish in Moscow. The Soviet Union was alarmed at the implications of the fall of the Shah of Iran, and his replacement in 1979 by the militant Islamic regime of Ayatollah Khomeini. Moscow's nervousness at the vulnerability of its southern Muslim Republics to religious appeals was to increase throughout the 1980s. But of greater strategic weight was Moscow's endemic fear of China, and China's traditional friendship with Pakistan. Moscow's closest friend in South Asia was India, whom it supplied with arms and economic aid. The tension between India and Pakistan was endemic. They had gone to war over disputed Kashmir in 1948 and 1965, and in 1971 India declared war again to help win independence from Pakistan for Bangladesh.

Moscow feared that Amin was seeking a *rapprochement* with Pakistan, and thence with China. Amin's links with a shadowy Afghan with American nationality, Zia Nassery, obsessed Soviet officials, who claimed that he was the linchpin of an anti-Soviet alliance that was arming Afghan rebels through Iran and Pakistan, all orchestrated by the CIA. The Chinese hand had also been detected in the operations of Chinese-armed Tadzhik and Kazakh guerrillas in the thin Wakhan corridor which connected Afghanistan, China and Pakistan. The completion of the direct Pakistan–China road connection through the Karakoram Pass in 1979 added to Moscow's nervousness.[4]

A decision was taken to put in place the forces required to overthrow Amin, if that was eventually judged necessary. In the meantime, the KGB's Eighth Department infiltrated a Pushtu-speaking Azerbaijani agent, Lieutenant-Colonel Mikhail Talabov, who could pass as an Afghan, into Amin's kitchen staff, where he tried and failed to poison the Afghan leader.[5] During November 1979, the KGB's élite foreign operations paramilitary force, the Zee Group, was sent to Kabul, under the guise of an Embassy guard. A Soviet motorised infantry battalion was assigned to help guard Amin's residence.

On 12 December, at a full session of the Soviet Politburo, the formal decision was taken to use Soviet troops to overthrow Amin, and to keep them there to stabilise the country while a new and more broadly based pro-Soviet government was installed. Its first symbolic act would be to abandon the red flag, and replace it with the traditional flag of Afghanistan. The final document of authorisation was drafted by hand by Konstantin Chernenko, and spoke only of 'measures' to be taken in a country described only as 'A'. All of the full members of the Politburo were required to sign this document. Defence minister Ustinov formally conveyed the orders to the chiefs of staff the following day. The deputy chief of staff, Marshal Sergei Akhromeyev, later told the Supreme Soviet investigation committee in 1989 that the generals had counselled against the invasion, on the grounds that the troops were not ready. Indeed, there were severe morale, disciplinary and logistical problems with the local Uzbek and Tadzhik units who were initially deployed from the local regional command, before being swiftly replaced by Slavic divisions.

On 23 December, the KGB's élite Alpha anti-terrorist squad was flown into Kabul. And on 27 December, as Soviet tanks and motorised infantry divisions invaded from the north, the Alpha team, the Zee group and Soviet paratroops supported by infantry stormed Amin's palace, and shot him dead. Amin was replaced by Babrak Karmal, leader of the outcast Parcham faction, with Khalq deputies. The Soviets deployed a further 50,000 ground troops in the country, and Moscow's allies in Eastern Europe, Cuba, Africa and Vietnam were told: 'Things were developing in such a way that the achievements of the revolution and their democratic, progressive regime were in danger of liquidation.' One further precaution was taken in Moscow. To preclude his vocal opposition, the decision was taken to exile the human-rights campaigner Andrei Sakharov to the closed city of Gorky.

Moscow's fears of the Chinese connection in its Afghan crisis were sharpened when the United States, in addition to its other economic sanctions, sent Defense Secretary Harold Brown to Beijing in the month after the invasion. The US and China could respond with 'complementary actions in the field of defence as well as diplomacy', Brown said on his arrival in January 1980. Brown proposed that the US and China cooperate on supplying arms to the Afghan rebels, and in a clear indication that Washington as well as Moscow was thinking in a far broader South Asian context, suggested they discuss joint action in the event of a Vietnamese invasion of Thailand. China was responsive up to a point, publicly cancelling the Sino-Soviet negotiations which had been agreed the previous year. But while agreeing to increase the covert flow of arms through Pakistan, China was not ready to embark on a full-blooded alliance with the Americans. Beijing's interests were best served by an end to the US–Soviet *détente*, enabling China to play off the two superpowers while maintaining complete freedom of action.[7]

President Carter's National Security Adviser, Zbigniew Brzezinski, developed at this time a complex theory of Soviet strategic intentions. In his view, Moscow was deploying 'a two-pronged offensive strategy, one pointing through Afghanistan at the Persian Gulf and one through Cambodia at the Straits of Malacca'. He unveiled this thesis before China's vice-premier Geng Biao during his visit to Washington in May, accompanied by Liu Huaquing, deputy chief of staff of the Chinese People's Liberation Army. China was at this time removed from the Warsaw Pact section of the Munitions Control List, and reassigned to a category of countries which qualified for US construction of defence plants and military sales.[8]

The strength of the American reaction to the invasion of Afghanistan was not matched by a similar reaction by the European allies, who saw the affair as something of a sideshow that was taking place within the traditional Soviet sphere of influence. In Britain, although Mrs Thatcher pledged full support of the US position, there were complaints from House of Commons committees of lack of consultation before the US applied sanctions. And when France's President Giscard d'Estaing and Germany's Helmut Schmidt met in Paris, they refused to declare *détente* dead. It had become 'more difficult . . . *Détente* would probably not be able to withstand another shock of the same type,' said their joint declaration.

This was the more infuriating to the Carter Administration in Washington in that it reflected some of the more cautious views of the Secretary of State Cyrus Vance, when Brzezinski in the White House, the Pentagon and President Carter all agreed that the Afghan invasion had finally revealed the Soviets in their true colours. In an election year, with the Republicans already challenging the 'weakness' of President Carter's policies, the White House reaction was politically almost inevitable. But it also echoed the mood in Congress, where the House Foreign Affairs Committee issued an admonitory report which concluded that 'the reactions of the allies have been found wanting'.[9]

In May, the French President visited Moscow, followed the next month by the West German Chancellor. The Europeans were in no mood dutifully to follow the American declaration of sanctions against the Soviet Union. Indeed, to American horror, France, Italy, West Germany and Japan all embarked in summer 1980 on bilateral trade talks with Moscow. A $350 million contract for a speciality steel mill and a $100 million aluminium plant were shifted from American to European firms.[10] The Soviets were keen to maintain the sense of momentum in the European theatre of *détente*, announcing a unilateral withdrawal of 20,000 troops and 1,000 tanks in July, and offering for the first time to apply vague 'confidence-building measures' of limited inspections and notifications of exercises on their own territory.

The Soviet Union had hoped to divide the West, locking the Europeans into a regionalized *détente* process while the Americans railed in isolation. The plan was jolted by the decision of the Polish government to raise food prices in that summer when Moscow hosted its truncated and much-boycotted version of the Olympic Games. The consequent strikes at Poland's Gdańsk shipyard, and the formation of the Solidarity movement, amounted to the sharpest challenge to the Soviet system in Eastern Europe since the Prague Spring of twelve years earlier. The power of Solidarity lay in its threefold objectives. The opposition to higher food prices rallied widespread support. The two demands for legalising strikes and allowing the broadcast of the Roman Catholic mass over state radio each Sunday, rallied the working class, the Church and the large Catholic laity. These twin demands of Gdańsk, an imaginative simultaneous appeal to God and Mammon, were successfully imposed upon the Polish government in the agreement negotiated at the end of August.

The readiness of the Polish government to compromise, and the unwillingness of the Soviet government to worsen its relations with the West after Afghanistan, gave Solidarity room to mobilise. The Soviet army held some threatening military manoeuvres, and the jamming of the Voice of America resumed, for the first time since 1974. The KGB, which was seriously alarmed, launched a characteristically unpleasant anti-Semitic propaganda effort to discredit the intellectual group KOR, the Workers Defence Committee, as a Zionist organisation. But Stanisaw Kania, the new head of the PZPR, the Polish Communist Party, assured Moscow that control could be retained. The KGB reported otherwise, and indeed at the PZPR conference in July 1981, the old central committee was thoroughly purged of more than 80 per cent of its members. The new central committee, the KGB concluded, was composed of 20 per cent open backers of Solidarity, and another 50 per cent of more or less discreet sympathisers.[11] The Soviets were rather more reassured by Kania's appointment of General Wojciech Jaruzelski as prime minister, having greater confidence in the Polish army than in the Polish party. But in March 1981, when Kania and Jaruzelski visited Moscow, the Soviet government issued a plain warning, that 'the socialist community is indivisible and its defence is the concern not just of each individual state, but of the socialist coalition as a whole'.[12]

That socialist coalition had never looked so formidable, at least on the map, as in the last year of the Carter presidency. The world seemed to be erupting into a series of crises, each one of which served to undermine America's global position. Vietnam was establishing control over the rest of Indo-China, and Moscow's troops had advanced to the Hindu Kush. America's traditional ally Iran had been replaced by a fanatical enemy who saw the United States as the Great Satan. The European allies were lukewarm, the American economy was in disrepair, and then new alarms sounded in the American backyard.

Ironically, Jimmy Carter's approach to Central and South America had been liberal and thoughtful. One of the achievements of his

Administration was the Panama Canal Treaty, which began the process of returning the canal and its surrounding, US-occupied zone to the government of Panama. This treaty, which had been supported by leading Republicans including former President Ford, dismayed American conservatives who saw the same expansion of Soviet influence into Africa, with Cuban surrogates, now spreading into their own hemisphere.

In March 1979, the rather woolly Marxist Maurice Bishop seized power in the tiny Caribbean island of Grenada and quickly established friendly relations with Cuba, and subsequently with Moscow, which provided some arms. Four months later, and partly in response to President Carter's rhetoric on human rights, the long dictatorship of the Somoza family in Nicaragua was overthrown by a genuine popular revolution, which was not in the beginning anti-American. But even if an anti-American trend had not been established, Fidel Castro, the Cuban leader, sought to characterise these two events as a new wave of liberation as he hosted the Non-Aligned summit in Havana in September, in the immediate wake of the Nicaraguan revolution. Castro flew almost directly from the summit to the United Nations in New York, to deliver an impassioned and lengthy speech on the new global division between the rich North and the poor South. He concluded with a demand that 'the rich imperialists' transfer and invest some $300 billion to the developing world during the 1980s.[13]

Carter tried to maintain relations with the new Sandinista government of Nicaragua, sufficient at least, 'to keep it from turning to Cuba and the Soviet Union'.[14] But the situation was not to be so easily contained. The squalid dirty war of the El Salvador military against their guerrillas, and a spasmodic war and bombing campaign in Guatemala, made for very little room for the third way that Carter sought. He tried to establish a democratic space between pro-Cuban revolutionaries and the ruthless military regimes which were at least nominally loyal to the United States. It was not a hopeless task; Costa Rica was a successful example of just such a third way. But in an election year, confronted by the twin dramas of Soviet expansion in Afghanistan and American humiliation in Iran, such a compromise course was more than difficult. The efforts by America's European allies to support the Sandinista regime, even after it backed the Soviet invasion of Afghanistan, added to the complexities.

In the election of November 1980, Jimmy Carter was voted out of office and replaced by President Ronald Reagan, who promised from the beginning a much firmer line towards the Soviet camp. To a degree, Reagan's rhetoric was based on his conviction that part of the American problem at the start of the 1980s was psychological. 'America had lost faith in itself . . . We had to recapture our dreams, our pride in ourselves and our country . . . If I could be elected President, I wanted to do what I could to bring about a spiritual revival in America.'[15]

Reagan did not know it, but on that same election day when he had defeated Carter, the then-President had written in his diary a note which illustrated Reagan's concern. Looking at grim opinion poll figures which suggested that American voters did not think the American diplomatic hostages in Teheran were going to be freed soon, Carter wrote:[16]

> This apparently opened up a flood of related concerns among the people that we were impotent, and reminded them all of the negative results of OPEC price increases, over which we had no control – and the hostages being seized, over which we had no control – and the Soviets' invasion of Afghanistan, the Cuban refugee situation, the high interest rates, attributable at least in part to the huge OPEC oil price increase.

Impotent, no control; these depressing admissions of weakness scribbled in the Oval Office point to the demoralisation of a President, and the way in which once again a decade was ending amid gloom about the West's prospects. The West, in the form of the Nato alliance, had been able to muster the traditional solidarity when the threat was in Europe, in the shape of the deployment of the Soviet SS-20 missiles. The governments of Britain, West Germany, Italy, the Netherlands and Belgium were to show considerable political courage in facing down their domestic opposition to proceed with the counter-deployment of Cruise and Pershing missiles. But the threats which worried the Americans were global in character. Afghanistan was far from European concerns, and the sudden wave of alarms which began to excite American conservatives in Central America in 1979–80 stressed even further the divergence of interest and approach between the United States and its mainland European allies.

There was one outstanding exception. In Britain's Margaret Thatcher, Reagan found a triple ally. First, she shared his ideological belief in free markets and an unleashed capitalism as the path to prosperity, and as the buttress against socialism at home and abroad. 'Each time you go further along the socialist road, nearer and nearer to the Communist state, then the consequences of the Communist state will follow,' she warned, even before taking office.[17]

Second, while accepting the commercial implications of Britain's membership of the European Common Market, Mrs Thatcher's strategic loyalty was rooted in the Atlantic Alliance, and in the old 1940s' perception of the world which held that the ambitions of the Soviet Union would only be kept in check by a full revival of the old special relationship between London and Washington. 'An enduring alliance with the United States is fundamental to our beliefs and to our objectives,' she emphasised, in her first official visit to the Reagan White House, the month after his inauguration. In what was to be the first of a series of public occasions when the ideological loving cup was passed between them, Reagan responded: 'People will stay free when enterprise remains free . . . There is one element that goes without question: Britain and America will stand side by side.'[18]

Third, Mrs Thatcher shared one key aspect of the Reagan temperament, a belief in the importance of morale in public life. He spoke of the American spirit, she of the national soul. She too talked in terms of spiritual revival, of the bracing effects of freedom on both the economic and above all the moral fibre of the nation. 'Economics are the method; the object is to change the heart and soul of the nation.'[19]

By the time that Reagan took office, Mrs Thatcher had been prime minister for twenty months. She had already earned her Soviet nickname of the Iron Lady. But she was to be only the first of a remarkable political generation of Western leaders in the 1980s who between them revitalised the alliance. Mrs Thatcher was elected in 1979. Reagan took office in 1981. Later in that year, François Mitterrand was elected President of France. While a socialist, who embarked on two financially disastrous years of public spending and social and welfare reforms which saw repeated devaluations of the franc before France returned to a strict fiscal orthodoxy, Mitterrand was the most supportive member of the Atlantic alliance France had elected since the years before Suez. Under Mitterrand's leadership, France slid slowly but perceptibly back into the military part of the Nato alliance, coordinating its communications and air defence systems with the other Nato allies. Immediately after his election, Mitterrand was assured by the US Ambassador Arthur Hartman that the long-standing covert US technical assistance for the French nuclear programme would remain in force. Mitterrand responded by directing the French general staff to work out joint military plans with Nato, which would move French forces to central Europe if a war was felt to be imminent and come under Nato operational control.[20]

Two years later, in 1983, the conservatives were returned to power in West Germany, under the leadership of Helmut Kohl. This was the same year that saw Mrs Thatcher's second election victory, largely because of the triumphant success of her resolve to reconquer the Falkland Islands from the Argentine invaders in 1982. But her election victory, in spite of the lingering economic recession, was scored over a Labour opposition which was committed to a nuclear-free Britain. Labour fought on a platform of scrapping Britain's independent nuclear deterrent, and removing US nuclear bases from Britain. The Labour programme amounted to a repudiation of Mrs Thatcher's economic and strategic policies. Her reaffirmation of the American alliance had secured another generation of Britain's 'independent' nuclear deterrent, the provision of the American Trident ballistic missile system to replace the elderly Polaris submarine force.

This amounted to a dramatic increase in the size and destructive power of the British nuclear arsenal. The four Polaris boats initially deployed 64 nuclear warheads, later in the 1970s upgraded with the Chevaline triple-warhead to a theoretical maximum of 192 warheads (but many of these were designed to be decoys). The far more advanced Trident force, equipped with multiple-warhead missiles, could deliver as many as 960 nuclear weapons on Soviet targets. At the same time, the Mitterrand government in France was planning a similar expansion of their own indigenous nuclear submarine force. This was to come in two stages, first with the modernisation of the existing *Redoutable* submarines to take the M4 missile, which carried six separate warheads. The second phase, scheduled for deployment in the 1990s, was for five new *Triomphant*-class submarines, equipped with M5 missiles, each capable of carrying twelve warheads.

The full deployment of the British Trident and French *Triomphant* forces would therefore involve a transformation of the European strategic nuclear deterrent into a major force capable of delivering well over 2,000 nuclear warheads on to Soviet targets. This was the equivalent of the US capability in 1960, or the Soviet capability as late as 1972. It represented a dramatic shift in the balance of nuclear power, and Soviet defence planners and arms-control negotiators understandably began to insist that this be taken into account in future discussions of arms control.[21]

The four years between the election of Mrs Thatcher and the election of Helmut Kohl in Germany saw a decisive shift in the balance of political forces in the West. In the four leading Western countries, domestic and economic issues probably played the predominant part in bringing about the elections of Thatcher, Reagan, Mitterrand and Kohl. But the widespread alarm at the behaviour of the Soviet Union, in Afghanistan and in Poland, also played an important role. Thatcher, Reagan and Kohl had campaigned openly and powerfully on the theme of the Soviet threat, and the need for Western rearmament. In Mitterrand's 1981 campaign, the theme was less vociferously stressed, but he criticised the readiness of his rival President Giscard d'Estaing to play an independent, almost Gaullist role in East–West relations, and was particularly outspoken on Soviet human-rights violations.

Mitterrand's strategic shift towards the Western alliance was the easier in that he had little domestic peace movement with which to contend. In Britain, in West Germany and in the Netherlands, and to a lesser but still significant degree in the USA, domestic politics in the early 1980s were often dominated by the marches and protests of the peace movement. Their anti-nuclear policies took over the British Labour Party, and in November 1983 became the official policy of the defeated German Social Democratic Party. Helmut Schmidt had striven mightily to hold his party together, within Nato, and was committed to deploy the Cruise and Pershing missiles against the Soviet SS-20s. But defeat in the 1983 elections broke Schmidt's control, and in the following year the still charismatic Willy Brandt announced that he would campaign for all the European socialist parties to fight the next Euro-elections on a policy of European strategic independence from both powers.[22]

Although eventually unsuccessful, Brandt's was the most striking and genuinely internationalist appeal to have been made to a peace movement that was too divided, and usually too nationally introspective, to respond. The strength of the peace movement was its size – able to mobilise some 300,000 Europeans in public demonstrations on a single weekend. The great weakness of the peace movement was the range of its demands. In Britain, it was aimed partly against the expansion of the British nuclear deterrent with Trident, partly against the principle of a British nuclear force, and partly against the American bases. In Germany, it was aimed against the American bases, but also against nuclear power stations, and divided further over the degree to which it should also embrace the cause of German unification. In the United States, the movement for a nuclear freeze became the broadest coalition, with powerful support in Congress. On 5 August 1982, a formal proposal for a nuclear freeze, of no new weapons deployments by either side, was defeated in the House of Representatives by the narrowest of margins, 204 votes to 202.

But the issue of nuclear disarmament was itself complex. Many opposed the Cruise and Pershing missiles, rather fewer wanted to scrap the British nuclear deterrent, and still fewer wanted to surrender Nato's nuclear umbrella altogether. There was constant suspicion, both within the peace movement and among its opponents, of the role of Soviet intelligence. And while the peace movement was wholly home-grown, the supportive speeches from Soviet officials and the Soviet Peace Committee, and the constant proud claims for their role in its campaigns that were sent back to Moscow by KGB agents in the West, reinforced the suspicions of Western intelligence agencies and their governments of the Soviet role.[23] If the peace movement's adherents knew broadly what they were against, they were never able to rally around a single cause they could agree to be for. The majority of its supporters came from the political left, where the suspicion of the European Community as a rich man's club made it difficult to rally around the EC as a new neutralist grouping. There were divisions between the Church-based wing of the peace movement and the left, and in Britain the women's peace camp at the Greenham Common Cruise missile base added a radical feminist component to what was already a loose and unstable coalition.

Constant distractions were tossed into the debate by the flurry of disarmament or arms-cuts proposals from both Moscow and Washington. In 1981, President Reagan proposed a 'zero option', scrapping both the SS-20s and the Cruise and Pershing deployments, and moving towards a Europe without nuclear missiles. The Soviets responded that this failed to take the French and British nuclear forces into account. The next year in his Eureka College speech, Reagan suggested cutting each side's missiles by one-third, which would have cut the missile-heavy Soviet arsenal far more than that of the United States, with its triad of land- and sea-based missiles, backed up by manned bombers. These proposals were often highly technical, not easy for the layman to understand, and eroded some of the peace movement's potential support by suggesting that the various governments themselves were in theory committed to the general principle of arms control.

The politics of arms control, and of the Atlantic Alliance in the early 1980s, were a confused mess. There were constant irritations between the USA and the Europeans, which suggested to Moscow that the alliance was in serious danger of erosion and splitting. The fervent anti-Communists within the Reagan Administration helped this process by denouncing the Europeans for failing to support the American line at the United Nations, whether over Resolutions on Israel or Central America. Jeane Kirkpatrick, the US Ambassador to the UN, was particularly strident in her denunciations of the Franco-Mexican

Resolution calling for a negotiated settlement in El Salvador. The Resolution was co-sponsored by five Nato members, and by all of the EC members except Britain, which abstained in the vote. Kirkpatrick claimed to have been 'abandoned by our allies on this issue of great importance to us'. And then she delivered a sombre warning. 'Obviously, Europe cannot insist on American support against the Soviet Union in Europe while at the same time supporting pro-Soviet forces outside Europe that may endanger US security [as in Central America].'[24]

The imposition of martial law in Poland in December 1981 sharpened the tensions within Nato, as the European allies simply refused to support the American demands for wholesale sanctions against the Soviet Union. The Europeans pointed out that the United States was continuing to sell grain to the Soviet Union, which had not in fact taken part in what amounted to a coup by the Polish Army, partly designed to preclude a Soviet military intervention. The main feature of the US sanctions was to prevent the sale of Western technology which could help the Soviet Union exploit its oil and gas reserves, and build the pipeline which was intended to export them to Western Europe. With Europe in recession, the $15 billion pipeline project was economically tempting. Some 450,000 West German jobs depended on trade with the East, which produced an annual surplus of $1.5 billion.

On the night the Polish Army struck against Solidarity, West German Chancellor Helmut Schmidt was sleeping in an East German hunting lodge, as the guest of Erich Honecker, and continued his talks the next day as if nothing had happened. His foreign minister, Hans-Dietrich Genscher, simply refused to discuss sanctions with the American officials who flew to Bonn to coordinate the Nato response. The argument simmered on across the Atlantic until the G7 summit in Versailles in June. Reagan insisted on sanctions, and was isolated. Two weeks later, Reagan announced that the sanctions would be extended to overseas subsidiaries of American firms, or those using US licences – an immediate threat to contracts worth over $1 billion held by British, French and Italian companies.[25]

'For all practical purposes, US policy has taken on a form that suggests an end to friendship and partnership,' declared Helmut Schmidt.[26] The Europeans bluntly refused to accept this overbearing exercise of American leadership. The Council on Foreign Relations, the voice of the American foreign-policy establishment, announced that a sea change had taken place in the alliance: 'The days of the old

"Atlantic" system, based on US predominance and its corollary, European reluctance to take wider responsibilities, are over.'[27]

The recession, and its implications, underpinned and deepened this crisis for the Alliance. In Britain and in the United States, the Reagan–Thatcher doctrine of increased defence spending, but sharp cuts in other domestic programmes, sharpened the choice between guns and butter. And the deliberate use of high interest rates in both countries, to help defeat inflation, deepened the recession, bankrupted large sectors of manufacturing industry, and sucked available investment capital from Europe to British and US banks where it could earn high interest rates. The dollar rose steadily in value against the franc and the Deutschmark as a result, a process intensified by the blithe acceptance of sharply increased deficits of over $100 billion a year by the Reagan Administration, to pay for its rearmament programme. 'How can we defend our alliance with the United States when critics say American policy is making us bankrupt?' exploded the French finance minister Jacques Delors.[28]

Under Reagan, the Pentagon was granted almost every new weapons system it wanted, the new MX missile and the B1 bomber programme which Carter had scrapped, a 600-ship navy with new aircraft-carriers, replenished ammunition stocks and new tanks and other conventional weapons. The Reagan rearmament boom represented a dramatic reallocation of resources. In constant (1985) dollars, defence spending rose from $181.5 billion in 1976 to $242.3 in 1982, and to $270 billion in 1984. Under the first term of the Reagan presidency, defence spending increased by 40 per cent in real terms, and from 5.2 to over 7 per cent of GDP.[29] In 1980, when Reagan was elected, the USA was the world's largest creditor, and its national debt was just over $1 trillion. By 1992, after two terms of President Reagan and one of President Bush, the United States was the world's largest debtor and the national debt had reached $4 trillion. The difference – $3 trillion, or $3,000 billion – is roughly equivalent to the accumulated defence budgets of those years.

Reagan's rearmament programme was a classic example of Keynesian deficit-spending, public investment to lift the economy out of recession. It certainly achieved that result, and the Reagan economic boom of the mid- and later 1980s was a triumphant endorsement of Keynes's economic theories. The recession after 1989 points, however, to the folly of public investment in the economically fruitless field of weapons. A similar pumping of an extra $100 billion a year of public investment into education and infrastructure might have shown a greater economic return. But that was not the point. Reagan's rearmament was an investment in national security. It was also the test of Reagan's private conviction that the United States could afford an arms race, while the Soviet Union could not. The Soviet Union would either have to renounce the arms race, or bankrupt itself into collapse in the vain effort to keep up. 'I think there is every indication and every reason to believe that the Soviet Union cannot increase its production of arms,' Reagan explained to the editorial board of the *Washington Post* during his 1980 election campaign. 'Right now, we are hearing of strikes and labour disputes because people aren't getting enough to eat. They've diverted so much to military [spending] that they can't provide for the consumer needs. So far as an arms race is concerned, there's one going on right now, but there's only one side racing.'[30]

This Reagan theory had one serious flaw. There was a third choice for the Soviet government. Faced with the grim alternatives of bankruptcy or surrender, they could launch a pre-emptive nuclear strike. And as the European allies were uncomfortably aware, they could well be the first targets. The European level of distress at Reagan's policies was intensified by the President's blithe conviction that a nuclear exchange need not lead to a general war.

'You could have an exchange of tactical weapons against troops in the field without it bringing either one of the major powers to pushing the button,' Reagan suggested at a question-and-answer session with a group of news editors in Washington in his first year in office.[31] The following month, his Secretary of State Al Haig told a Congressional hearing that Nato had a contingency plan for a 'demonstration' nuclear blast in the event of a Soviet conventional attack.[32]

Statements such as this were a gift for Soviet propagandists, who had the evidence to portray the American President as a dangerous cowboy, ready to shoot nuclear bullets from the hip. Naturally, the US Defense Department had contingency plans to wage a nuclear war; they would have been derelict in their duty if they had not thought the matter through. But in the tense atmosphere of the early Reagan years, the revelation of such plans added to the alarmist mood. Each year, the Pentagon produces a 'Defense Guidance Statement', a loose assessment of likely threats and responses. The 1982 version was leaked to the press, where the cool statement that 'protracted nuclear war is possible' provoked a furore. A subsequent Pentagon press briefing explained that such a war could last up to six months, and was winnable. 'American nuclear forces must prevail and be able to force the Soviet Union to seek earliest termination of hostilities on terms favourable to the United States.'[33]

The mood in the West suddenly recalled those earlier tremors of nuclear dread, the air-raid-warning rehearsals in schools in the 1950s, or the nuclear-shelter panic of the early 1960s. In Britain in 1982, the government issued less than reassuring pamphlets on how to build emergency bomb shelters, which included ludicrous drawings on how to take cover by lying in ditches with a coat wrapped around the head. In the United States, T. K. Jones, the deputy Under Secretary of Defense, with responsibility for Strategic Theatre Nuclear Forces, suggested that survival lay in digging a hole and climbing in. 'If there are enough shovels to go around, everybody's going to make it,' he said, a phrase which caught the popular imagination, although not in the comforting way its author had intended.[34]

Among those infected by the mood of serious alarm was the Kremlin. Irritated by the vacillations of the Carter presidency, they had finally come to treat him with contempt. Carter's final message over the hot line, warning against Soviet intervention in Poland in December 1980, was simply ignored by Brezhnev.[35] And on the principle that it took an anti-Communist like Nixon to have the freedom to go to China, there were some early hopes, according to Georgi Arbatov, that President Reagan might prove more predictable and pragmatic. These were quickly dashed. In his first press conference as President, Reagan was blunt:[36]

> I know of no leader of the Soviet Union since the revolution, and including the present leadership, that has not more than once repeated in the various Communist congresses they hold, their determination that their goal must be the promotion of world revolution and a one-world Socialist or Communist state . . . the only morality they recognize is what will further their cause, meaning they reserve unto themselves the right to commit any crime, to lie, to cheat, in order to attain that.

It was not until two years later that Reagan used the term 'the evil Empire' to define the Soviet Union, a phrase which has come to characterise his vision. It came in a speech to the National Association of Evangelicals, a religious group whose support Reagan sought against the peace movement and against the attempts in Congress to impose a nuclear freeze. Before such an audience, it was tempting to portray the Cold War in moralistic terms, and to describe the Soviet Union as 'the focus of evil in the modern world'. Reagan went further, in a direct appeal to the peace movement:[37]

> In your discussions of the nuclear freeze proposals, I urge you to beware the temptation of pride – the temptation of blithely declaring yourself above it all and label both sides equally at fault, to ignore the facts of history and the aggressive impulses of an evil Empire, to simply call the arms race a giant misunderstanding and thereby remove yourself from the struggle between right and wrong and good and evil.

This was to declare the Cold War to be a Manichean struggle, a crusade against an enemy with whom there could be no quarter, and no ending short of defeat. It was the more dramatic since it was delivered to a new Soviet leadership, one which had already embarked upon a 'peace offensive' in the attempt to mark a new departure from the Brezhnev period. In November 1982, the four new leaders of Great Britain, the United States, France and West Germany, were joined by the first new Soviet General Secretary for eighteen years. The succession of Yuri Andropov was swift. The immediate reaction in the West was grim; Andropov was known as having been the head of the KGB during the past decade of repression of dissidents, and as the Soviet Ambassador in Hungary in 1956: one of the key figures responsible for the brutal suppression of the Budapest uprising.

But the profiles which began to emerge in the Western press were more hopeful. They spoke of Andropov's liking for American jazz, for Scotch whisky and of English spy novels in his bookshelves. These comforting tales were inspired by Andropov's private brains-trust, the *Izvestiya* journalist Alexander Bovin and Georgi Arbatov, the head of the main think-tank on the West, the US and Canada Institute. Two leading figures among that handful of Soviet officials who were licensed to deal with Western journalists in Moscow, Bovin and Arbatov had worked in the Central Committee and had come to know Andropov well. They shared the common view among many Soviet intellectuals that the corruption and stagnation which had been endemic in the Brezhnev years were about to be swept away by Andropov's new broom.[38]

This was not an unreasonable assumption. In the context of Brezhnev's era, Andropov did indeed appear as a brisk reformer, although his first measures were focused more on discipline than on substantive change. Bathhouses and bars were raided in working hours, in highly publicised police swoops on absentee workers. The KGB's specialised anti-corruption task forces intensified their work. But they had been operating for some years, striking mainly in individual Republics like Azerbaijan and Georgia, where the corruption had become legendary and well protected by the Brezhnev family and its extended and highly personalised power structure.

Vassily Mzhavanadze ran Georgia for a gloriously corrupt nineteen years, a period still known as the Victorian era, after his wife. She had a great fondness for diamonds, and the largest of them all, given her by the underground businessman Otari Lazishvili, later found its way to Brezhnev's own daughter. Victoria's seven country villas and her bacchanalian parties, and the cut which the local party hierarchy took from the sale of cars routinely stolen in Moscow and shipped to Tbilisi, became too much even for the relaxed standards of Brezhnev's Soviet Union. With Andropov's essential support, the Georgian police chief Eduard Shevardnadze, later to find fame as Gorbachev's foreign minister and president of an independent Georgia, assembled the evidence. Lazishvili was arrested in the office of his friend Roman Rudenko, chief procurator of the Soviet Union. Victoria fled to the protection of her sister, who was married to Petr Shelest, the party boss of the Ukraine.[39]

Brezhnev's own private collection of sports and vintage cars, including the armoured Lincoln limousine which Nixon had given to him, and in which he had terrified the American President by driving at high speed around the hilly forest bends of Camp David, symbolised the way in which the Soviet leadership enjoyed the fruits of power. The affairs and high life of Galina, Brezhnev's daughter, were so much the stuff of gossip that bitter jokes were widespread in Moscow. Perhaps the most characteristic was the tale of Brezhnev proudly showing his mother and daughters around his luxurious dachas, his hunting lodge at Zavidovo, his vast garage. 'It's wonderful, Leonid,' the mother is said to have muttered. 'But what happens if the Communists come back to power?'

The corruption of privilege in the lifestyle of the Communist Party's *nomenklatura*, those who qualified for the state and party jobs for which Central Committee approval was required, was only one part of the social sickness at the heart of the state. At one level, the party operated as a system of extortion, a form of protection racket. On another, it sought to act as an ideological priesthood which established a firm body of doctrine to which all must adhere, or at least pay lip-service. The enforcement of this mental, and indeed spiritual, discipline was the responsibility of Andropov's KGB. And by contrast with the ruthless slaughter of Stalin's years, the KGB under Khrushchev and Brezhnev had been a somewhat constrained body.

Deportation, the prison camp and the mental tortures of the psychiatric hospitals were on hand as more serious sanctions. But more usually the KGB after Khrushchev's reforms operated through manipulation of ordinary life. The privilege of foreign travel, the chance of good jobs and promotions, and access to universities and special institutes were the standard means by which the KGB maintained its social discipline. While rightly condemned as inhuman by dissidents and by the country's critics, this was, by Soviet standards, or indeed by the traditions of tsarist Russia, a soft repression.

But those who ran it were uniquely placed to comprehend the sullen mood of the country at the end of the Brezhnev era. Andropov's KGB had contained what the West called the Dissident movement, a loose label for a series of distinct and small groups. There were Baltic nationalists and Jews who wanted to leave, human-rights reformers and liberal Marxists, activists for ethnic minorities like the Crimean Tartars and religious believers who could not tolerate the constraints imposed upon a compliant Church by the Soviet authorities. They had never come together into a coherent opposition, and presented little threat to the Soviet state.

They were, however, the tip of a vast iceberg of resentment, a kind of closet dissidence that merged imperceptibly into a widespread constituency for reform which included army generals, top scientists, most of the intelligentsia and large swathes of the younger party hierarchy. This was fuelled in part by yearnings for more cultural and political freedom, but also by a widespread disgust at the way Soviet life had developed under the stagnant hand of Brezhnev. There was a mood of shame at the economic and technical backwardness that was visible to those members of the élite who travelled abroad, a shame reinforced by the West's taunts on human rights.

As the head of the KGB, Andropov was perhaps ideally situated to appreciate these deep weaknesses in Soviet society. An amateur poet, Andropov also paid more regard to the intellectuals and to cultural life than most Politburo members. His son wanted to become an actor, and join the adventurous Taganka theatre company run by Yuri Lyubimov. When Lyubimov advised the boy against an acting career, Andropov called him to the Lubyanka, the KGB headquarters, to thank him. The Taganka enjoyed a special licence thereafter. And in his dealings with his own advisers, Andropov could deploy a certain earthy charm. Witness the poem he wrote to Arbatov and Bovin and Georgi Shakhnazarov, after they had sent him a get-well madrigal while he was in hospital in 1965:[40]

I'll tell it like it is.
I'll cross my heart, alas.
We understand life a lot better
When we land right on our ass.
I warm myself in the balcony sun
And sometimes I sit on the lavatory throne.
And though there's nothing new about that,
At least it's a seat of your own.
And you don't have to be Socrates in order to know:
You want to think? Get down on your ass.

Not what one might have expected from the head of the KGB, this modest doggerel helps explain the deep loyalty Andropov inspired among those party intellectuals and reformists who invested such hopes in him in 1982. Among them were Mikhail Gorbachev and Eduard Shevardnadze, promoted and favoured by Andropov as a new generation who could help haul the country from Brezhnev's stagnant legacy. But the hopes which greeted Andropov's succession were blighted, in part by his illness and the stubborn grip on power of Brezhnev's surviving cronies, but also by the reluctance of the West to respond to a series of Andropov's urgent signals that change was on offer.

Andropov's first months in power were marked by what the Soviet called a 'peace offensive', a blizzard of speeches and interviews and calls for a new East–West summit and proposals for arms reductions. In his first six weeks in office, he made three important new proposals, in addition to his suggestion of a summit with President Reagan. The first was to cut back the SS-20 missiles in Europe to the same number of warheads that Britain and France then deployed, in return for a Nato undertaking not to deploy the Cruise and Pershing missiles. The second, in an interview with the US-based Hearst newspaper group, suggested a 25 per cent cut in the strategic arsenals of both the USA and the Soviet Union, combined with a nuclear freeze on any new deployments. At the Warsaw Pact meeting in Prague, in January 1983, Andropov went considerably further. He proposed nuclear-free zones in the Mediterranean, and in parts of Europe, cuts in naval deployments, and a nuclear-test ban. He also suggested that the US and Soviet Union agree to stop arms sales to the developing world, and to agree to use their savings on military budgets to increase foreign aid.[41]

This was wrapped up in the usual Soviet propaganda prose, which helped the West to dismiss it. But to the intense frustration of Andropov's advisers, the proposals he put forward at the Warsaw Pact meeting contained one dramatic novelty, which the West failed to comprehend. He had suggested a non-aggression pact, in which members of both Nato and the Warsaw Pact would agree not to use force against any member of the other bloc, nor any third country, but above all not to use force against any member of its own alliance. His adviser Georgi Arbatov later described this as 'a crucial breakthrough . . . a break with the Hungarian syndrome that had so plagued him. Of course, it was also a break with what was known throughout the world as the Brezhnev doctrine.'[42]

The renunciation of force against fellow Warsaw Pact members by the Soviet Union could have been presented as Solidarity's charter, a promise not to intervene militarily in the internal affairs of Poland or the other Eastern European countries. But while this suggestion was not taken up by the West, the overall impact of Andropov's flurry of new proposals seized the initiative in East–West relations, and among much of the Western European public. Britain's *The Economist* ran on its cover the picture of a Soviet dove with Andropov's face crushing underfoot a small American eagle with the face of President Reagan.[43]

Andropov's proposals were timed to have maximum impact on the West German elections in March, when the choice was plain: between the Social Democrats, who were deeply unhappy at the escalation involved in deploying Cruise and Pershing missiles; and the Christian Democrats, who supported Reagan's Zero Option. The Social Democrat government had collapsed in November 1982, in the month of Brezhnev's death, when the Free Democrats left the coalition. The Christian Democrats under Kohl formed a caretaker government, but the stage was set for an election as crucial for Nato as that which had brought Thatcher to power in 1979, and Reagan to the White House in 1980. The election campaign formed the high-water mark of the European peace movement, and Andropov's proposals must be considered in the light of the political opportunity this represented. But in spite of European alarm at Reagan's policies, and in spite of the clumsy bullying of the European allies over the Siberian pipeline sanctions, the traditional loyalties of Nato held firm. Kohl was returned to power with a mandate to proceed with the Cruise and Pershing deployment.[44]

Reagan's response to Andropov's proposals came at the time of the German elections, in his celebrated speech about the evil Empire. And that was followed within days by another Reagan speech which transformed not only the technological balance, but the very arena of the Cold War. On 23 March, Reagan announced the Strategic Defence Initiative, a vastly ambitious research project to develop an anti-missile system based both in space and on the ground. It was instantly dubbed Star Wars. While it appeared to flout the basic principle of the Anti-Ballistic Missile Treaty of 1972, that keystone of the arms control process, Reagan insisted that it was 'consistent with our obligations under the ABM Treaty'.[45] There is no doubt that he was wholly genuine in his belief that such a defensive system, which he suggested might be made available to the Soviets too, was far preferable to the perils of deterrence. Reagan had always been appalled by the hair-trigger implications of the nuclear balance, the system of restraining each side by the threat of Mutual Assured Destruction. But his proposal was both destabilising and threatening in a world where the Soviets could have little confidence in the Americans sharing such an advanced technology. If successful, SDI would nullify the Soviet nuclear arsenal and restore that effective monopoly of nuclear threat which the United States had enjoyed in the brief years after Hiroshima.

'All attempts at achieving military superiority over the USSR are futile,' Andropov responded four days after Reagan's announcement, with all the bitterness of a man who had seen his own tentative olive branch brusquely spurned. 'The Soviet Union will never allow them to succeed. It will never be caught defenceless by any threat, let there be no mistake about this in Washington. It is time they stopped devising one option after another in the search for the best ways of unleashing nuclear war in the hope of winning it. Engaging in this is not just irresponsible. It is insane.'[46]

SDI certainly scared the European allies, who suddenly realised that a defensive shield over the USA would leave them uniquely vulnerable to a Soviet nuclear arsenal which might have no other target. Even if the idea worked and was deployed, the thinking behind it was to the Europeans deeply and frighteningly isolationist. Its objective was an American invulnerability, which seemed to strike at the heart of the Nato alliance. Even Reagan's staunchest ally, Margaret Thatcher, was troubled enough to persuade him to modify the plan to include the allies, and not to begin any deployment before consultation.

The more the Soviet and Western scientists examined the grand theory, the more problems they saw in making it work. It would actually tempt the Soviets to build even more missiles, trusting that, with enough of them, a massed attack could overwhelm the SDI defences. The prospect of space-based laser beams was little threat. It took only a minor modification to impart a spin to Soviet missiles on launch, which would make it more difficult for a laser to burn through. The Soviets also took note of those American officials who seemed to cast doubt on Reagan's generous offer to share the technology. The intellectual father of SDI (and of the H-bomb), Edward

Teller of the White House Science Council, was clear on the timing involved: 'We can openly discuss our defensive systems with the Soviets when we have developed a fool-proof system.'[47] One of the most influential of the Pentagon officials, Assistant Secretary of Defense Richard Perle, the author of the Zero Option plan, was even more blunt: 'If it were up to me, I would discourage scientific exchange with the Soviet Union.'[48]

The alarm which Reagan's anti-Communist rhetoric had already inspired in Moscow had one important institutional result. In May 1981, Brezhnev had attended a secret KGB conference in Moscow to condemn Reagan's policies, and he was followed by Andropov, who announced that for the first time the KGB and the GRU military intelligence would cooperate in an unprecedented worldwide effort. It was dubbed RYAN, the Russian acronym for *Raketno-Yadernoye Napadeniye*, which meant simply Nuclear-Rocket Attack. It was a heightened state of intelligence alert, instructing all foreign stations to conduct a constant watch for tell-tale signs of the buildup to a Western nuclear strike.[49]

Soviet agents in the West were instructed to watch for sudden appeals for blood donors, to monitor defence installations at night to check for unusual activity, to see if American civilian personnel were suddenly being withdrawn, and to monitor military radio channels and air bases for any evidence of alerts. The publication, for example, of the British civil-defence pamphlet on ways to protect oneself in the event of a nuclear attack, was the kind of sign that RYAN was looking for. Fear fed fear. A British response to what was perceived as a heightened Soviet threat was interpreted in Moscow as a heightened British threat. Andropov's peace offensive was aimed at scaling down some of these fears. Reagan's response, and the 1983 election victories of Helmut Kohl in West Germany and Mrs Thatcher's Conservatives in Britain, served to increase the fear in Moscow. It reached a new peak on 1 September 1983, when the Soviet air defence forces shot down the Korean airliner, KAL-007, which had strayed over the Sakhalin peninsula in what now seems to have been an innocent navigation error.*

* Although several books and TV investigations into the KAL-007 incident produced substantial indications that Korean and US intelligence had played a role in the flight, a long investigation into the Soviet evidence by *Izvestiya*, from 1990 until 1992, finally concluded that the affair had been a dreadful accident, and an overreaction by a bumbling and panicked Soviet Air Defence Command.

The appalled reaction in the West, and the changing Soviet version of events, led to three *Molnya* (flash) messages being sent from KGB Centre to its offices in the Embassies in the West. Two of them were orders for countermeasure propaganda, allegations that this was a Western spy plane. But the first was a warning to secure all Soviet premises, ships, aircraft and personnel against possible Western attack.[50]

'The world situation is now slipping towards a very dangerous precipice,' Soviet foreign minister Gromyko warned on 8 September: 'Problem number one for the world is to avoid nuclear war.' Andropov, now confined to his kidney-dialysis machine at the Kuntsevo clinic outside Moscow, was desperately depressed, brooding on the imminence of war and what he called the 'outrageous militarist psychosis' of the Reagan Administration.[51]

Andropov's dread was the deeper because the KGB suspected that an imminent Nato exercise, Able Archer 83, could be the occasion for a full-scale nuclear strike against the Soviet Union. Scheduled to be held on 2–11 November, Able Archer was designed to practise command coordination for nuclear-release procedures. The sense of tension was heightened by the award of the Nobel Peace Prize to the Polish Solidarity leader Lech Waeşa on 6 October, and the sudden alert of US forces in the Middle East after the bombing of the US Marine barracks in the Lebanon on 23 October. This was followed almost immediately by another alert in the continental US on 25 October, presaging the brisk invasion of the island of Grenada in the Caribbean. This military assault was accompanied by an intense burst of ciphered communications between London and Washington, as the Queen and Mrs Thatcher protested furiously at the invasion of a Commonwealth member, of which the Queen was nominal head of state, by Britain's closest ally. That can hardly have been the interpretation put on the sudden flood of cable traffic by nervous analysts in Moscow.

The Able Archer exercise might almost have been calculated to trigger a Soviet panic. It involved a brief radio silence, the moving of the command HQs of Nato forces through the various stages of alert, and a change in the codes and frequencies of Nato communications as the alerts shifted from conventional to nuclear levels. The original plan for Able Archer had been even more realistic, calling for President Reagan and Vice-President Bush, and the joint chiefs of staff of the Pentagon, to take part in this test of Nato and US procedures for unleashing nuclear war. The sudden disappearance of such figures, the disruption of usual schedules and the swift movement of the military high command around Washington, were precisely the signs the Soviet intelligence had been told to look for under RYAN. Aware of Soviet nervousness after the KAL-007 incident, the US National Security Adviser Robert McFarlane decided that such high-level involvement could be provocative, and Reagan, Bush and the joint chiefs were not brought into the exercise.[52]

It was just as well. The Soviets went on to heightened alert too, with US electronics intelligence noting nuclear-capable aircraft being placed on stand-by at East German air bases. On the night of 8–9 November, KGB Centre sent another flash message to its stations in Europe, warning that US bases had been placed on alert. This was mistaken, but Soviet nerves were evidently close to screaming pitch. The end of the exercise was met with profound relief in a Moscow which had been convinced by its own propaganda that Reagan's America was capable of a pre-emptive nuclear attack.

Chapter 12

Taking the Enemy Away – Gorbachev and the End of the Cold War

None have saved others as Russians have.
None destroy themselves as Russians do.

'Letter to Yesenin', Yevgeny Yevtushenko

Mikhail Gorbachev did not suddenly emerge from nowhere. He, or some similar Soviet reformer, may even have been inevitable. He was the most prominent of that extraordinary generation of democratically minded reformers who suddenly broke through to the top of the Communist Party *apparat*. Eduard Shevardnadze from Georgia, Boris Yeltsin from Sverdlovsk and Alexander Yakovlev from Yaroslavl swiftly joined him in the Kremlin, and an entirely logical and almost predictable process of generational succession was under way.

For a period of forty monstrous years, from the start of the First World War in 1914 until Stalin's death in 1953, the Soviet Union suffered a series of wars, famines, purges and blood-lettings without cease and without parallel. The war of 1914–17 cost Russia some ten million casualties. It was followed by the disruptions of the Revolution and the civil war between the Bolsheviks and the Whites, and then by famine and by the first organised Terror of Lenin's Cheka, the first Soviet secret police. A brief return to normality in the 1920s was followed by more famines which attended the collectivisation of agriculture, and then by Stalin's purges. The First World War, the Revolution and the civil war had effectively wiped out or deported the tsarist aristocracy, the officer corps and the governing classes. They were replaced by the Old Bolsheviks, who were in their turn almost entirely liquidated by the Purges. The new officer corps of the Red Army then fell in their turn as Stalin's Terror shifted to the military.

So Russia beheaded itself twice over, destroying both tsarist and revolutionary ruling, administrative and military élites. And then the nation ripped out its soul as Stalin's purges extended to the dreaming classes, to the poets, writers and artists. The Revolution slaughtered even its most devoted friends, those hapless Communists in exile from half the countries of the world who were installed at the Hotel Luxe on Moscow's Gorky Street. They dined together each evening, never knowing which of them would still be there at breakfast as the witch-hunters came each night to sniff out the Trotskyists, deviationists and imperialist spies. The Old Bolsheviks died in Eastern Europe, in the Ukraine, in the old Muscovy heartland and above all they died in Siberia. In Central Asia, a bloody colonial war was fought to establish Soviet power to the foothills of the Himalayas. Then came the incomparable slaughter of the Great Patriotic War against Hitler's invasion, followed by Stalin's renewed Terror once victory was won. The four decades of war and revolution, purge and another war, cost the country some sixty million lives.

But then the bloodshed stopped. When Yuri Andropov took power in 1982, the Soviet Union had known almost thirty years of peace, and while there had been repression, there had been no wholesale purges. After losing more than a quarter of the population, the body politic slowly healed from the four decades of devastation. For a young man like Mikhail Gorbachev, whose home in Privelnoye in the lush north Caucasus farmlands had been briefly occupied by the Germans, the war was a brutal memory. His elder brother went into the Red Army, and was killed, along with three of his uncles, and his father was wounded in Poland. But the contrast between Gorbachev's violent, disrupted boyhood and the calm of his adult life was dramatic.

He was born in 1931, into the nightmare of collectivisation. Peasants slaughtered their livestock and ate them rather than surrender this form of wealth to the collective farms. Grain was collected at gunpoint to feed the hungry cities. In the famine and violence that followed, the official Soviet history says, 'Some kolkhozes in the north Caucasus and the Ukraine ceased to come under the organising influence of the party and the state', a euphemism for outright rebellion.[1] One of Gorbachev's grandfathers was sent to Siberia for failing to plant enough seeds in the year of famine, even though half the family had died of starvation. The other grandfather was imprisoned for fourteen months as 'an enemy of the people'.[2]

But after 1945, as Gorbachev came of age and went to Moscow University to study law, he was part of the only Soviet generation to mature in a period of peace. They enjoyed the fruits of a growing economy, became the most educated generation the country had ever produced, and with Khrushchev's Thaw enjoyed more cultural innovation and excitement than Russia had known for a generation. The party was still a hard school, but not the killing field it had been under

Stalin. Under Khrushchev, the principle had been established that defeat in party struggles did not lead to death. Gorbachev rose through the ranks of the party machine until in 1961, he attended his first party congress, where he joined in the unanimous vote to evict Stalin's corpse from its place of honour alongside Lenin in the Red Square mausoleum. It was the best of times to be a young, ambitious Soviet Communist. Yuri Gagarin had just become the first man in space, the most dramatic symbol of the achievements of the Soviet state and the promise of its new generation.

The twenty years of peace which followed this event should have seen the enrichment of the Soviet Union through the bonanza of Siberian gas and oil. They saw instead the diversion of wealth and brains and manpower into the arms race, as the country strained every nerve to reach strategic parity with the United States. Those years also saw the heavy outflows of aid, trade credits, arms and oil-price subsidies. The Soviet empire was expensive, and while the total figures remain elusive, the cost of Soviet aid and trade credits, subsidies and arms shipments ranged between $15 and $20 billion a year after 1980. To put this sum into perspective, annual Soviet hard-currency export earnings over the same period ranged between $27 and $32 billion.[3]

Cuba alone received over $4 billion in aid and oil subsidies each year from 1981 to 1986. Vietnam received over $1 billion each year, and Mongolia almost as much. Non-Communist developing countries received $2.6 billion in 1980, half of it going to India and Afghanistan alone, with Peru, South Yemen, Algeria and Ethiopia accounting for most of the rest.[4] The costs of arms shipments are harder to assess. But between January 1976 and December 1980, at least $4 billion in arms were shipped to sub-Saharan Africa, almost wholly to the new satellites of Ethiopia, Angola and Mozambique.[5] In 1981, $1.5 billion in credits were granted to Iraq alone to pay for arms exports. Subsidised oil prices to Eastern Europe represented not so much a cash drain, as a voluntary renunciation of hard-currency earnings. In 1974, the year that the oil price first jumped dramatically, the Soviet Union exported 60 million tonnes of oil and petroleum products to Eastern Europe at a price ranging from $16 to $20 per tonne. In the same year, it sold 40 million tonnes to Western countries for the world price of $70 a tonne – which meant an annual subsidy of $3 billion to the Warsaw Pact allies in energy supplies alone.[6]

Yuri Andropov came to power in 1982 hoping for a resumption of *détente* with the United States, and dreaming of a transformed relationship with an increasingly neutralist Western Europe: a Labour government in Britain, Social Democrats in West Germany, and Socialists in France. His hopes were utterly confounded. The elections in Britain and Germany in 1983 returned conservatives, and the French socialists proved so loyal to the Atlantic alliance that President Reagan concluded of Mitterrand, after his first G7 summit: 'His resoluteness with regard to the Soviet threat could have sounded like me or anyone else.'[7]

Andropov's death at the beginning of 1984, after a long illness which left him less and less able to promote the domestic economic reforms he had planned, continued the sense of stagnation in Moscow that appeared to be governed from the Kremlin's geriatric ward. He was followed by the third elderly invalid in a row, Brezhnev's old crony, Konstantin Chernenko. He lasted just fourteen months, wheezing his way through Politburo meetings, spitting periodically into the kind of bottle issued to Soviet TB patients. This was the last gasp of the Old Guard, and even before Chernenko's death, in March 1985, there were unmistakable signs of a new course being prepared both at home and abroad. These indications had little to do with Chernenko; they had begun in the brief period between Andropov coming to power and the worsening of his illness.

Andropov had authorised a series of seminars and reports on economic reform, of which the most detailed and the boldest was coordinated at the Siberian think-tank city of Akademgorodok, and led by a leading sociologist, Dr Tatiana Zaslavskaya. Her group, in which the young Politburo member Mikhail Gorbachev took a personal interest, included staff from the Central Committee and Gosplan, the state planning board, as well as academics.[8] It began with a blunt attack upon the core principle of central planning. 'The complexity of the economic structure has long since overstepped the threshold of its efficient regulation from a single centre,' she argued.[9] She went on to attack 'the inhibition of market forces . . . the administrative limitations imposed on all kinds of formalised economic activity by the population in the spheres of production, service and distribution'. The report concluded with an analysis of the forces of opposition to reform, the bureaucratic layers which 'have sprouted like mushrooms in recent years'.

The Soviet economy, which had according to plan outproduced the West in the sinews of the old industrial revolution, in coal and steel and iron, was with enormous effort able to keep pace in the ultimate high-tech area of missiles and weaponry. But faltering Soviet performance in the space race illustrated the way in which the Soviet system was better at exploiting muscle than brains. The Energiya remained the world's most powerful rocket, and the SS-18 was the world's heaviest missile. But in guidance systems, the ability to miniaturise components, and in high-speed computers the Soviets were never able to match the West. They lacked the vast demand network of a sophisticated consumer market which spurred Western technology and innovation. Still, Siberia's vast reserves of raw materials, in oil and gas and metallic ores, cushioned the impact of the decline in technological competitiveness.

According to the highly suspect national statistics, the Soviet national income grew by 62 per cent during the decade of the 1970s. If true, this was better than the American or EC economies. But even according to the official figures, this was the worst decade of Soviet performance since 1945. Moreover, by its own doctored statistics the Soviet economy was running faster and faster to stay in the same place. Each extra 1 per cent in national growth required an increase of 1.4 per cent in national investment, and an increase of 1.2 per cent in output of raw materials.[10]

What made the economy look far more efficient than the reality was the OPEC price rises of 1973–4 and 1979, which for the first time permitted Soviet planners the option of almost unrestrained imports of Western products, both grain and high technology. In the seven years after 1975, the country was able to become a significant market for the West, importing machinery and technology worth over $50 billion. In December 1982, the CIA declassified the 401-page report into the Soviet economy it had delivered to Congress the previous month. Suggesting that the attempted embargo on materials for the Siberian pipeline had been of little effect, the CIA concluded that the Soviet economy was far from collapse. Indeed, the CIA declared it to be 'in good shape', capable of taking the strain of the arms race without cuts in living standards, and developing more rapidly than the US economy.[11]

While the Brezhnev period had produced modest prosperity by Soviet standards, the gap between ever higher inputs of investments for ever lower results in GNP growth was desperately vulnerable to the world oil-price level. This meant it was also at risk to the kind of US pressure which tried to block the introduction of the Siberian gas pipeline to Western European markets. So part of the argument for a return to *détente* was economic, the need to resume normal trading relations with the West. This in turn required a resumption of diplomatic business-as-usual with the American government, and a return to the Geneva arms talks. The long Soviet refusal to negotiate while Cruise and Pershing missiles were deployed was quietly forgotten.

Accordingly, the three years of official silence in US–Soviet relations ended in December 1984, shortly before Gorbachev became General Secretary, when Secretary of State George Shultz and Foreign Minister Anatoly Gromyko met for inconclusive talks in Geneva. In the same month, the Kremlin heir Mikhail Gorbachev made his first top-level trip to the West, where he charmed Mrs Thatcher into announcing that here at last was 'a Communist I can do business with'.[12] Her praise was not only for Gorbachev's unusual openness in Britain, but also because of a speech Gorbachev had delivered to Soviet intellectuals shortly before leaving Moscow in which he first unveiled his concept of glasnost and spoke in veiled but prophetic terms of a new Soviet democracy. It reads in retrospect like a manifesto by a politician running for higher office, a firm platform of reform.

'Profound transformations must be carried out in the economy and the entire system of social relations, and a qualitatively higher standard of living must be ensured for the Soviet people,' he declared, to a characteristically Soviet audience, assembled for the Moscow All-Union Scientific and Practical Conference.[13] 'Only an intensive, fast-developing economy can ensure the strengthening of the country's position in the international arena, enabling it to enter the new millennium appropriately, as a great and prosperous power.' Gorbachev talked of the need to use modern economic mechanisms, like profit and credit, and for the first time talked of the need for a wholesale restructuring, a perestroika. And he also, for the first time, used the other word which entered the international vocabulary as a symbol of the Gorbachev revolution – glasnost, or openness:[14*]

> We particularly need a serious study of the theoretical problems of the development of socialist self-government by the people [Gorbachev went on]. Our contemporary is a person of developed culture and education, with a wide range of spiritual interests, who has seen and experienced a great deal . . . We must speak to him only in the language of truth . . . Glasnost is an integral part of a socialist democracy. Wide, prompt and frank information is evidence of confidence in the people and respect for their intelligence and feelings, and for their ability to

* This address was not given the customary prominence accorded an important policy speech by a Politburo member. *Pravda* published a truncated version of it: the discussion of 'our contemporary' was omitted, although the term 'glasnost' as a herald of reformism was quickly apparent, spread by word of mouth, and by sympathisers inside the Central Committee staff, who ensured that full texts were swiftly made available to Western journalists in Moscow, including this author.

> and for their ability to understand events for themselves. It enhances the resourcefulness of the working people. Glasnost in the work of party and state organs is an effective means of combating bureaucratic distortions and obliges us to be more thoughtful in our approach to the adoption of decisions.

Sweeping economic reform with the profit motive, moves towards political democratisation, and a much greater freedom for the Soviet press and media – these three characteristics of Gorbachev's domestic agenda were publicly announced even while Chernenko was still nominally running the country from the Kremlin hospital's oxygen tent. And in foreign policy too, a fundamental debate had been developing under the grimly immovable image that the Soviet Union had been presenting to the world.

The Institute of World Economy and International Relations (IMEMO), part of the vast intellectual agglomeration of the Soviet Academy of Sciences, was the country's largest and most respected research centre in the field. Under the leadership of Alexander Yakovlev, it was to become the main think-tank of perestroika. But even in the final days of the Brezhnev period, it was a seed-bed of new thinking. One of the oddest examples was Donald Maclean, the KGB spy in the British Foreign Office who had defected to Moscow in 1951. He died in Moscow in 1983 as a rebel against the system he had served, actively campaigning for political dissidents and against the 'irrational' introduction of Soviet SS-20 missiles into Europe. In 1981, while on the IMEMO staff, he produced a long paper titled 'Some Reflections of a Communist', which forecast the coming of perestroika:[15]

> The present authoritarian and oligarchical political superstructure bears little relation, in peacetime at any rate, to the needs of an advanced industrial society. The next five years, owing to favourable changes at the top, will see an improvement in the political, cultural and moral climate in the Soviet Union and the introduction of a complex of reforms affecting most major aspects of the life of the Soviet people. [This would] follow a long-term shift within the power-structure of a leadership group.

Maclean identified 'the spread of a feeling of unease, a critical mood, among the 100,000, say, men and women who have direct responsibility for day-to-day decision-making, the political, industrial, financial, agricultural, scientific, educational, military and other senior managers of all areas of Soviet life'.

Maclean was right. Within five years, Mikhail Gorbachev was in office, and launching perestroika. Identifying himself as a Communist, but of the Italian Euro-Communist variety, and as a supporter of Dubček's attempt to introduce 'socialism with a human face' in the Prague Spring of 1968, Maclean energetically promoted his reformist views within the Soviet system. His IMEMO colleagues later revealed that he wrote 'numerous appeals to the Central Committee of the Communist Party and to the KGB' on behalf of imprisoned dissidents. He campaigned on behalf of the anti-Stalinist historian Zhores Medvedev and the dissident scientist Vladimir Bukovsky, complaining at their mistreatment in psychiatric prisons.

'Indifferent to considerations of expediency, and ignoring the threat of personal difficulties, Donald Maclean was guided by his understanding of moral and political duty to take a principled stand in these cases, as in others,' his colleagues wrote in a 1990 IMEMO edition of Maclean's paper. Maclean's memorandum of 1981 reads like many of the dissident documents of the day, and adds to the growing evidence that the frustrations of the Brezhnev era saw the emergence of a loyal opposition within the Communist Party élite. Maclean attacked both stagnant domestic politics and what he saw as a self-defeating militarisation of foreign policy. He argued:

> At certain crucial turning points in policy-making, the views of the military authorities, with their natural, professional interest in maximising the armed strength of the country, have with the support of the top leadership, prevailed over the views of those who are called upon to assess the overall influence of military policy upon the international interests of the country. It is even rather doubtful whether there is now anyone at the top level who combines a sufficiently profound understanding of the dialectics of world politics with the necessary political authority (and courage) to ensure that the leadership has been and is offered an informed choice between differing priorities.

'The record of the present leadership [Leonid Brezhnev] and its penumbra shows a persistent, regressive tendency to substitute the aim of preserving its own power for the aim of finding ways of realising the energy of the society which they rule,' Maclean went on, in the essay which he bravely circulated among the Soviet élite. 'What has fallen into discredit is not the socialist mode of production on which the entire Soviet structure rests, but the political apex of that structure, the small group of men who make all the decisions on how Soviet society is run.'

There were other signs of change. In the year before Gorbachev came to power, Anatoly Gromyko, the son of the foreign minister and head of the Africa Institute, published (with the diplomatic journalist and later foreign ministry spokesman Vladimir Lomeiko) a book entitled *New Thinking in the Nuclear Age.*[16] This went some way beyond the usual propagandist trumpetings of Soviet commitment to disarmament being flouted by an aggressive imperialism, and put in question for the first time in public the original decision to install SS-20 missiles in Europe. Yevgeny Velikhov, who was to become Gorbachev's personal scientific adviser and a member of his negotiating team at the Reykjavik summit, had also in 1983 established a private study group in the Academy of Scientists which included Roald Sagdayev, director of the Institute of Space Research. They built on the 1982 Rome declaration, which had stressed the need for a nuclear-free world, and the impossibility of nuclear superiority or of a realistic defence against such weapons. Velikhov had been a co-author of this declaration, and Gorbachev had studied the text. By 1984, Velikhov's group were developing a striking proposal for both the USA and Soviet Union to reduce their nuclear arsenals to a minimum deterrent force of some five hundred mobile missiles each.[17]

This thinking about a new foreign policy among the intellectuals was being given force by Gorbachev even before he became General Secretary. In the summer of 1984, when Chernenko was convalescing from a renewed attack of the lung disease that was to kill him, Gorbachev was acting General Secretary, and used his temporary chairmanship of the Politburo to push forward two striking new measures. The first was in a speech at Smolensk in June which called for a reopening of the superpower dialogue with the United States, and the second was a decision that Foreign Minister Gromyko should take advantage of the United Nations General Assembly meeting in September to do this.[18]

Gorbachev was pushing against an open door. The US intelligence analyses of the great panic about an imminent US nuclear strike which had hit Moscow in the autumn of 1983, between the shooting down of the Korean airliner and the Nato Able Archer exercise, had sobered President Reagan. 'I don't see how they could believe that, but it's something to think about,' Reagan told his NSC adviser, Robert McFarlane. Reagan's surprise stemmed from his understanding that the superpower dialogue had already begun in secret, through the veteran Soviet Ambassador to the USA, who was discreetly spirited into Reagan's private quarters in the White House in February 1983.[19]

The dialogue gained the release of a family of Pentecostalists who had taken sanctuary in the US Embassy basement in Moscow, and sealed the negotiations which secured a five-year, $10-billion agreement for Soviet purchases of American grain. But neither the Dobrynin talks in 1983, nor the meeting between Reagan and Foreign Minister Gromyko in September 1984, did anything more than reopen communications that had broken off when the Soviet negotiators walked out of the Geneva disarmament talks in 1982. The renewal of the Cold War in the 1980s reached its deepest point at this period, with the extraordinary tension in Moscow over the Nato Able Archer exercise, and the emergence of what was dubbed by conservative enthusiasts 'the Reagan Doctrine'.[20] This was a grandiose phrase for the spasmodic effort by the Reagan Administration to win back the gains the Soviet Union was perceived to have made during the *détente* period of the 1970s. Certainly in Afghanistan, a large covert operation was mounted to arm the Mujaheddin rebels through Pakistan. It was, however, only in Reagan's second term, after 1985, that the crucial Stinger anti-aircraft missiles were provided. Easily portable and fired by a single soldier, the Stingers turned the tide of the Afghan war by challenging the Soviet command of the air.

In Grenada – where the bombastic quasi-Marxist regime was brusquely swept away by the American invasion in 1983 – and in Nicaragua the Reagan Doctrine had some force. In Nicaragua, a prolonged covert effort to destabilise and overthrow the Sandinista government, along with the US-trained and equipped force of some 30,000 Contra troops, was pressed by the CIA under William Casey. Congress having forbidden the use of US funds to support the Contras, the eventual attempt to use the proceeds of covert arms sales to Iran for the Contras developed into a constitutional crisis when the ploy was uncovered. The last two years of the Reagan Administration were wrapped in this scandal, as the extent of the illegal operation which had been run from the National Security Council of the White House became apparent. In this instance, the Reagan Doctrine clearly did American policy far more harm than good.[21]

In so far as there was an authoritative statement of the Reagan Doctrine, it was promulgated in the month before Gorbachev came to power, in Reagan's State of the Union address. 'We must not break faith with those who are risking their lives on every continent from Afghanistan to Nicaragua to defy Soviet-supported aggression and secure rights that have been ours since birth . . . Support for freedom-fighters is self-defence,' the President declared.[22]

Beyond Nicaragua and Afghanistan, the Reagan Doctrine had little force. In Angola, the anti-Marxist guerrillas of Jonas Savimbi's Unita movement enjoyed a covert support operation of some $15 million a year. But in Mozambique, the US supported the Marxist government against the South African-backed Renamo guerrillas. There was little US participation in the Chinese operations against Vietnamese influence in Cambodia, and none against the gruesome Marxist regime of Mengistu Haile Mariam in Ethiopia.[23] Covert operations to help the Solidarity movement in Poland and the beleaguered Charter 77 human rights activists in Czechoslovakia probably owed more to private, religious and trade-union groups than to the US government. The AFL–CIO American trade-union confederation, and international labour groups like Britain's TUC and the Geneva-based International Metalworkers' Federation, played important roles. Joint action to support Solidarity (and on occasion to restrain it) was discussed between President Reagan and Pope John Paul, and in far greater detail between CIA Director William Casey and Archbishop Pio Laghi, the Apostolic delegate in Washington. In May 1982, the Reagan Administration agreed the still-secret National Security Decisions Directive 32, a broad study of national security strategy which authorised economic, diplomatic, cultural and some covert measures to 'neutralise efforts of the USSR' to maintain its hold on Eastern Europe. In reality, the main official US effort was through radio propaganda, diplomatic isolation of Poland, and support for the Church and human rights.[24]

Considered as a whole, the Reagan Doctrine, and the Manichean vision of the crusade against the Evil Empire, had a spasmodic, even capricious character. But from the standpoint of the Soviet Union, it must have looked concerted, threatening and relentless. Certainly public statements from the Kremlin took this view. 'Rather than pursue negotiations and display a desire to seek agreements, the US Administration has set out to upset the existing correlation of forces. Its aim is to acquire military superiority over the Soviet Union, superiority of Nato countries over Warsaw Pact countries through a massive build-up of its nuclear armaments,' Foreign Minister Gromyko told the Stockholm conference in January 1984. 'New missiles, bombers and aircraft carriers are being churned out in some kind of pathological obsession. New means of mass destruction are being experimented with. In short, the present US Administration is an Administration thinking in terms of war and acting accordingly.'[25]

Yet in a curious way, the Cold War began to end when two elderly gentlemen discovered that they shared a common difficulty with their bladders. Reagan faced re-election in 1984, and his Democratic opponent Walter Mondale was making some stir with his claim that Reagan was the only American President since the Cold War began who had not met his Soviet counterpart. Mrs Nancy Reagan and her astrologer agreed the moment was propitious for a thaw, and Secretary of State George Shultz insisted that there was serious business to be done with the Kremlin. Gromyko was invited to the White House, to see if the arms-control dialogue could be resumed.

President Reagan had been briefed by his staff to raise one crucial issue in complete privacy, when the two men were left alone in the Oval Office before the formal lunch. Their two old heads were seen close together and nodding in conversation through the windows that overlooked the Rose Garden. After lunch, State Department officials asked their Soviet counterparts what their reaction was to the top-secret point Reagan had raised with Gromyko. The Russians looked blank. What secret point? Deputy Secretary of State Mark Palmer checked with the White House security staff, who had observed the encounter through a secret peephole which looks into the Oval Office. Reagan, seventy-three, had asked Gromyko, seventy-five, only if he would like to use the private Presidential lavatory. Indeed Gromyko would. Very much. He went first, Reagan went second. They washed their hands and, much relieved, the two old fellows strolled in to lunch. Arms control was forgotten, but a certain rapport had been forged among the faucets.[26]

The dialogue once resumed, Gorbachev was determined not to make it his first priority immediately he took office. He made a point of telling *Pravda* in his first formal interview that the USSR did not see the world 'solely through the prism of our relations with the US, important as that is'. But with America's allies the pace of the new Soviet diplomacy was furious. The Italian premier Craxi was his first Western visitor. He was told it was time for formal trading links to be established between the European Community and Comecon, the Warsaw Pact's trading bloc. West Germany's Willy Brandt was summoned for five hours of talks on the need for a special relationship between Moscow and Europe's social democratic parties. Gorbachev's first foreign trip as Soviet leader was to Paris. A new dialogue was reopened with the Chinese, and the world's two largest Communist parties agreed once more to address one another as 'Comrade'. Gorbachev's new foreign minister Eduard Shevardnadze began his term by preparing a trip to Tokyo, and the fortieth anniversary of Hiroshima was celebrated by the announcement of a unilateral Soviet ban on nuclear tests. Gorbachev later told a visiting group of US

Congressmen that this decision had been 'a personal risk', taken against the advice of his generals.[27]

But plans for a first summit with Reagan were put in train, the way cleared by an interview Gorbachev gave to *Time* magazine. The new Soviet leader drew a distinction between research into the Strategic Defence Initiative, which he hinted was acceptable, and development of weapons systems, which was not.[28]

Gorbachev's 'Novoye Myshlenniye' or New Thinking in international affairs was first spelt out at the Geneva summit with President Reagan in October 1985, when they agreed in principle to work towards a Strategic Arms Reduction Treaty to cut their nuclear arsenals in half. It was amplified in January 1986, with Gorbachev's detailed scenario for nuclear disarmament by the year 2000. The policy was placed squarely within the framework of a modernised Marxist–Leninist concept of peaceful coexistence in Gorbachev's speech to the twenty-seventh Party Congress in February 1986. That speech also promised a new deal for the Eastern European satellites, signalling an end to the Brezhnev Doctrine of the Soviet right to intervene by force in Eastern European affairs with the declaration that 'no country enjoys a monopoly of the truth'.[29]

Such speeches had been heard before, but not since Khrushchev had they issued from a domestic context of cultural thaw and increasing political relaxation. The unmistakable reality of glasnost emerging in the Soviet press and the growing ferment of blueprints for political and economic reform slowly convinced even the sceptical Reagan Administration that the Gorbachev revolution represented a unique opportunity for a new relationship. Long-banned films and poems and plays and novels suddenly poured forth upon a Soviet intelligentsia which had been excited by the Khrushchev thaw and the promise of Brezhnev's *détente*, and suddenly found one of their own generation in the Kremlin. There was heady talk of a Soviet Kennedy in his own Camelot-on-ice who both signalled and represented a new cultural renaissance. The unprecedented frankness over the Chernobyl nuclear disaster in April 1986 (after a long weekend of silence and stonewalling) emphasised the new readiness to confront the grim realities of Soviet failure at home.

But so far, Gorbachev was covering the kind of ground which had already been charted on domestic reform by Nikita Khrushchev, and rebuilding a mood of *détente* which was familiar from the early Brezhnev period. This was all hopeful and reassuring, rather than electrifying. A new *détente*, the uneasy slackening of confrontation and increase in trade and diplomacy and acceptance of one another's spheres of interest, was what the diplomatic establishments of both sides were hoping to achieve in the mid-1980s. But for the extraordinary coincidence of two extraordinary men, Reagan and Gorbachev, that might well have been what the world got, a replay of the *détente* era of the 1970s. Neither the diplomats nor the arms-control experts were prepared for the quantum leap in the nuclear relationship that Reagan and Gorbachev were about to make. US Secretary of State George Shultz and Shevardnadze, and the professionals at State Department and MID, the Soviet foreign ministry, were equally unready for what was about to hit them.

There had been two signals that the superpowers were led by men with revolutionary ideas about the nuclear balance. Most of the attention paid to Reagan's 1983 announcement of SDI had focused on the technological vision and the threat to East–West stability. Underpinning it was a fundamental principle, that Reagan believed the system of a hair-trigger balance of nuclear terror to be morally wrong. At their Geneva summit, Reagan had tried long and hard to make Gorbachev see his point: 'If our research succeeds, nations could defend themselves against missile attack, and mankind, at long last, escape the prison of mutual terror. And this is my dream.'[30]

The nuclear age was forty years old when they met. The world had grown accustomed to it. The foreign policy and military establishments of both countries had all grown up with the nuclear balance as part of the furniture, indeed part of the very structure of diplomacy. Reagan's 'dream' – like the call for complete nuclear disarmament by the year 2000, which Gorbachev was to make just six weeks after the Geneva summit – was widely dismissed as so much cynical propaganda. But each man believed in what he was saying, even if their advisers did not. The clue to the philosophical underpinning behind Gorbachev's position, which was far more coherent than Reagan's visceral revulsion at nuclear terror, came in February 1986, in his speech to the twenty-seventh Party Congress.

These showcase events were of fundamental political importance to the Communist Party. They were occasions for great and formal statements, like Khrushchev's denunciation of Stalin at the twentieth Party Congress in 1956. Accordingly, they were carefully prepared, and drafts of Gorbachev's six-hour address had already been published in the previous year. Among several departures from that draft, and in the course of a deeply radical list of domestic reforms, Gorbachev spelt out his own sense of the way the world was changing. This passage began:[31]

> The course of history, of social progress, requires ever more insistently that there should be constructive and creative interaction between states and peoples on the scale of the entire world. Such interaction is essential in order to prevent nuclear catastrophe, in order that civilisation should survive . . . [and] that other worldwide problems that are growing more acute should also be resolved jointly in the interests of all concerned . . . The prevailing dialectics of present-day development consist of a combination of competition between the two systems (capitalist and socialist) and a growing tendency towards interdependence of the countries of the world community. This is precisely the way, through the struggle of opposites, through arduous effort, groping in the dark as it were, that the controversial but interdependent and in many ways integral world is taking shape.

In the eleven months between the Geneva summit and their next meeting at Reykjavik, Reagan and Gorbachev explored this 'interdependent and in many ways integral world'. They embarked on a long and private correspondence which explored in great detail their evolving thinking on disarmament, and their occasionally sharp differences over human rights, and regional conflicts like Afghanistan and Nicaragua.[32] In the course of these private letters, interspersed with public statements throughout the year, the building blocks of what were to become both the INF (Intermediate Nuclear Forces) and the START (Strategic Arms Reduction) treaties were prepared. On 15 January, in a public statement, Gorbachev offered to scrap all intermediate-range missiles in Europe (Soviet SS-20s and Nato's Cruise and Pershing missiles). He offered also to move towards the elimination of all nuclear weapons by the year 2000, in exchange for an end to 'the development, testing and deployment of space-strike weapons'.

On 22 February, Reagan, in a handwritten letter of seven pages, gave a private reply to this initiative. He wrote: 'It would be necessary as we reduce nuclear weapons towards zero, that we concurrently engage in a process of strengthening the stability of the overall East–West security balance, with particular emphasis on redressing existing conventional imbalances'. He then went on to propose reducing the strategic arsenals on each side to a maximum of 6,000 warheads: 4,500 each on missiles, and 1,500 on Cruise missiles and bombers. (This was to be the eventual outline of the START treaty which four years later was to be signed by his successor, President Bush.)

The correspondence proceeded, in spite of a series of suddenly erupting crises in the relationship, from the Chernobyl nuclear accident in April 1986, to the US air strike against Libya the following month, and the arrest of the American journalist Nicholas Daniloff in Moscow on espionage charges in September. The main obstacle continued to be Soviet opposition to SDI. In July, Reagan's letter proposed a sweeping response to Gorbachev's January proposal of complete nuclear disarmament. The US President suggested scrapping all ballistic missile systems, while continuing research on SDI. 'If and when such research should indicate that such a defence weapon is possible, both of us would observe tests, and we would agree jointly that deployment must follow elimination of all ICBMs and then the defence be made available to all,' Reagan suggested.

Gorbachev's reply, on 15 September, was frosty, seeing this as 'a bypass route to securing military superiority'. But again he offered a compromise elsewhere, removing intermediate missiles in Europe without demanding compensation for the planned expansion of the British and French nuclear forces, along with on-site verification on Soviet territory. Gorbachev offered to propose 'a mutually acceptable formula' to deal with Reagan's new concern that SS-20 missiles removed from Europe could then be relocated in Asia.

The two men met at the summit in Reykjavik in October 1986 with the theoretical skeleton of a far-reaching deal already in place, at least in the minds of Reagan and Gorbachev. But their advisers, accustomed to summits which were carefully prepared, with the agreements already drafted and ready for the final haggling and signatures of the two leaders, did not expect this hastily arranged session on almost neutral ground to produce any substantive result. They were to be stunned by the extraordinary progress the two men made.

On the first day, Gorbachev and Reagan agreed in principle to the Zero Solution on intermediate-range missiles in Europe, and on Reagan's July proposal to eliminate all ballistic missiles over a ten-year period. On the morning of the second day, Reagan agreed to cut and eventually eliminate other nuclear delivery systems too, including bombers. Then they turned to tactical and battlefield nuclear weapons, and in order to eliminate them, Gorbachev pledged dramatic cuts in Soviet conventional forces. 'For a day and a half, Gorbachev and I made progress on arms reduction that even now seems breathtaking,' Reagan recalled. 'George [Shultz] and I couldn't believe what was happening. We were getting amazing agreements. As the day went on, I felt something momentous was occurring.'[33]

A new situation had been created in the course of that heady conversation. Gorbachev told Reagan: 'Our meeting cannot produce one winner, we both either win or lose.'

In effect, the two men had agreed on a target of a nuclear-free world, along with swingeing conventional-force reductions. Reagan's aides felt they were caught up in a whirlwind for which they were unprepared, even by the long exchange of letters they had read. They scrambled through the night to put the historic agreements into words on paper, squatting in bathrooms and on lavatory seats in the cramped confines of the Hofdi House, scribbling historic accords on to yellow pads.

In the absence of a photocopier, the Americans borrowed carbon paper from the Russians. In the cramped confines of a shared sitting-room for the staff, the veteran professionals of arms control and diplomacy on both sides experienced a bizarre weekend of bonding. Alexander Yakovlev reminisced about his student days at New York's Columbia University. Marshal Akhromeyev told National Security Adviser John Poindexter what it was like to be 'the last of the Mohicans', the last senior Soviet officer to have been a combat veteran in World War Two. He talked of eating American spam and riding to war in American Studebaker trucks supplied under Lend-Lease.

Assistant Secretary of State Rozanne Ridgway began telephoning the European allies to inform them a deal was being reached which would remove the Cruise and Pershing missiles that they had nerved themselves to install. Some old habits died hard. When Soviet deputy foreign minister Viktor Karpov began a standard declaration of the Soviet view, chief of staff Marshal Sergei Akhromeyev simply laid a hand on his arm to stop it. Both teams of negotiators, who had deep doubts about the wisdom of the direction and speed the negotiations were taking, were held back by a mutual code of discipline and deference to their leaders.

'I really felt that he's the President. He got elected twice. He has made no secret of his view on nuclear weapons. So who am I to stop him from saying what he believes and what he's campaigned on,' Secretary of State Shultz commented.[34]

The Reykjavik summit failed, in the sense that it produced no breakthrough agreement. But it succeeded beyond the limited horizons of diplomats and arms controllers in that it shocked the US–Soviet negotiations into a wholly new dimension. The old ground rules of superpower poker, of incremental gains and minimal concessions, had been ripped up. Gorbachev wrote:[35]

> Reykjavik marked a turning point in world history. It tangibly demonstrated that the world could be improved. A qualitatively new situation had emerged. Now no one can act in the way he acted before. The East–West dialogue has now broken free of the confusion of technicalities, of data comparisons and political arithmetic . . . Reykjavik mapped out a route by which humankind can regain the immortality it lost when nuclear arms incinerated Hiroshima and Nagasaki.

Gorbachev's readiness to deliver fundamental change inside the Soviet Union was suddenly being matched by an American readiness to deliver a parallel revolution in international relations. Without Reagan, this would never have been possible.

The Reykjavik proposal to abolish nuclear weapons tumbled at the last fence, at Gorbachev's insistence that Reagan abandon his cherished SDI, or at least confine the research to the laboratory. This was matched by Reagan's stubborn insistence that the United States be allowed to develop and test these new and still theoretical new weapons in space. This was the price of Reagan's naïve idealism; for Gorbachev to join Reagan's vision of a world without nuclear weapons, he had also to buy Reagan's starry-eyed faith in the anti-missile umbrella. In the event, Gorbachev was right to balk, accepting his advisers' judgement that the US Congress would control SDI for him. So it proved. Three weeks before Gorbachev arrived in the United States for the first time, for the Washington summit of December 1987, Congress completed a defence bill that cut the SDI budget by one-third, and prohibited any tests of SDI in space. Three days before Gorbachev arrived for the summit which would sign the formal treaty to abolish the intermediate-range missiles in Europe, Reagan sadly signed the defence bill into law.

The Washington summit was a thundering success, largely because it was built on the foundations laid at Reykjavik. The agreement to scrap medium-range nuclear missiles in Europe changed the traditional diplomatic agenda from arms control to arms reduction. It also began the process of unlocking the European stasis by holding out the prospect of a nuclear-free Eastern and Western Europe. A heady Western mood of Gorby-mania swept the American capital. Gorbachev's astute understanding of Western political ploys, of plunging into crowds and deploying his attractive wife Raisa on to the public-relations circuit, allowed the hungry American media to convey the excitement of this startling summit. Gorby-mania blended the West's lust for celebrity with a widespread conversion to the belief that this

Soviet leader genuinely embodied an astonishing change in the way the world had been organised for a generation.*

The evidence from Moscow was unmistakable in the new press freedoms of glasnost, and the momentum of a peaceful revolution was maintained. Gorbachev's release of Andrei Sakharov from exile in Gorky, just after the Reykjavik summit, and eventually tens of thousands of political prisoners, convinced much of the West of his sincerity. Mrs Thatcher went to Moscow, to trounce her combative interviewers in an unprecedented long live interview on Soviet TV, and to allay one abiding suspicion. At her final press conference in Moscow, she was asked why it was in the West's interests to see Gorbachev succeed in making a more efficient, more prosperous, and thus a stronger Soviet Union.

'A more open society, with more open discussion and wider freedoms, and an economy based more on incentives, is in the long-term interest not only of the Soviet Union but of the West as well,' Mrs Thatcher replied. She spoke with the weight of President Reagan's ideological soulmate, and as the first Western leader who had spotted Gorbachev's potential even before he rose to supreme power: 'Anything that helps make the Soviet Union a more open society will help to strengthen trust and confidence.'[36]

Mrs Thatcher had another issue on her mind, the tremor of alarm that had swept through the unconsulted European allies when they first learned that President Reagan had at Reykjavik come within an inch of abandoning nuclear weapons altogether. For the British prime minister, this would have stripped the nuclear core not only from the Nato alliance, but from the Anglo-American relationship itself. The most potent symbols of that relationship, the Polaris and Trident weapons, were at risk. Like all the Western European leaders, Mrs Thatcher was alarmed at the sudden exposure this implied to Soviet conventional forces. The simple demographic imbalances of population meant that the Soviet Union's 280 million people would always produce more conscripts for conventional armies than Britain, France and West Germany, each with fewer than 60 million people. But her particular concern was what a nuclear-free world would do to the emergent new Europe, which Gorbachev liked to call 'our common European home'.

* The author was present in Washington during the summit, and witnessed the extraordinary crowd scenes as the Amerian public thrilled at Gorbachev's plunge into the throng.

Mrs Thatcher had a simple view of the European Community: it was all very well in its place. That place was purely economic. For a woman almost viscerally suspicious of foreigners who spoke a different language, and whose strategic instincts were Atlanticist, Mrs Thatcher proved to be one of the best Europeans of the 1980s. The sudden revitalisation of the European idea in the late 1980s owed more to her, and to Lord Cockfield, her appointee to the European Commission, than to any other European leader. Lord Cockfield's inspiration of Western Europe as a genuinely single market, with common manufacturing standards and common professional qualifications and trade regulations, was given a riveting focus by his insistence on a target date. Europe 1992 became a vogue phrase for the most energising burst of activity the community had known since the heady days of the 1950s, when the Treaty of Rome was put together. The concept, the target date, and Europe's economic boom all rode high together, in one of those bursts of self-confidence which can at certain times become historical forces in themselves.

Europe as a single market appealed to Mrs Thatcher's belief in the free market. But Europe decoupled from the American nuclear umbrella, learning to live with its looming eastern neighbour in a nuclear-free world, would have to look to its own security. A Western Europe united in a common defence would be a Western Europe that began to look increasingly like a federal state, forced by the circumstance of geography to become a superpower in its own right. And this in turn would give a truly military cast to that metaphor of 'Fortress Europe' which worried American exporters were already beginning to employ.

Mrs Thatcher grasped swiftly that what Gorbachev had achieved at Reykjavik and was to seal at the Washington summit, the eradication of the intermediate-range missiles in Europe, ended the New Cold War which had begun when she and President Reagan came to power. The SS-20 missiles and the invasion of Afghanistan had created the New Cold War, and suspended the slow divergence between European and American interests which had developed in the 1960s and 1970s. Gorbachev's eradication of those missiles, and his undertaking to withdraw from Afghanistan, opened the way for that Atlantic divergence to resume, with Europe far more self-confident and ebullient that it had been in 1979. For that reason, Mrs Thatcher set herself two more specific targets. The first was to lock in the transatlantic nuclear relationship with a new generation of American nuclear weapons, the Lance short-range battlefield missiles and the TASM (tactical air-to-surface missile) which British and US warplanes would deploy from British bases. The second was to convince Gorbachev that it was in the Soviet interest to maintain an American military presence in Europe. The old saw about Nato's role being to keep the Americans in, the Russians out and the Germans down, had new force when the West German economy already dominated the EC. Western Europe was becoming potentially unstable, just when it was starting to look most safe. For that reason alone, Gorbachev too could see the merit in keeping American troops on the continent.

The decision to abolish the SS-20s altogether had strategic implications that went far beyond Europe. The weapon had originally been designed with Chinese targets in mind. Gorbachev's patient wooing of China was already bearing fruit. Beijing had set three conditions for normalising relations with Moscow: withdrawal from Afghanistan; *détente* on the heavily militarised Sino-Soviet border; and restraining the Vietnamese ally in Cambodia and Indo-China. Progress was being made on all three fronts, and by the time Gorbachev made his official visit to Beijing in the summer of 1989, all three had been effectively settled, and commerce between the two states was booming. Sino-Soviet trade doubled to over $4 billion between 1985 and 1989, and negotiations had begun for a special Sino-Soviet free-trade zone to be established near Vladivostok, similar to the booming Guangzhou province by Hong Kong.[37] Gorbachev's decision to scrap the SS-20s, and leave none in Asia, reinforced this policy, just as both Beijing and Moscow were quietly abandoning the ideological baggage which had bedevilled their relations since the Sino-Soviet split.[38]

It was the more striking, therefore, that Japan should choose the year of the Reykjavik summit, 1986, formally to abandon its long constitutional doctrine that defence spending should remain at less than 1 per cent of GDP.[39] This came after Gorbachev's speech in Vladivostok, asserting the Soviet Union's right to be seen as a Pacific Ocean power, although focused mainly on the economic potential of regional cooperation.[40] But it also followed the completion of Japan's rearmament programme, launched in 1976, which established the Japanese Self-Defence Force as a military establishment of 12 army divisions plus six brigades, 55 destroyers, 214 naval combat aircraft and an air-defence force of 415 planes. Even 1 per cent of Japan's booming GDP could purchase a military establishment that was already overtaking that of Britain. 'Japan must possess defence capabilities commensurate with our national power,' Prime Minister Noboru Takeshita told the National Defence Academy in March 1988.[41]

Even with the presence of US troops and the reassurance of the American alliance, the Japanese could justify their armaments by pointing out that with the tension relaxing in Europe, their part of East Asia was poised to replace it as the most tense and heavily armed region on earth. China and the Soviet Union maintained a nuclear balance of their own, North Korea glowered at South Korea (which also had an American garrison) across an Asian version of the Iron Curtain. It was understandable if Japan felt like a vulnerable and pacifist millionaire in a particularly dangerous neighbourhood. Economically, Japan was by far the dominant power of the region, and during the 1980s its GDP outpaced that of the Soviet Union to become the second largest economy on earth.

Militarily, Japan remained relatively feeble. But as Japan's leaders began to improve its defence capabilities, they turned to MITI, the strategic trade and industrial investment ministry which had played a central role in planning Japan's post-war growth. MITI had originally been born as a munitions ministry in pre-war Japan. Under a law enacted in 1953, MITI has always been at the heart of Japan's defence industries, with powers to regulate their design, manufacturing and investment plans. Under this law, companies are required to share their technology and production processes with MITI, which has more than returned the favour by insisting that Japan must be almost self-reliant in defence procurement. In 1979, 85.2 per cent of Japan's military requirements were produced domestically. By 1987, the proportion had risen to 91.1 per cent, which was higher than that of the United States, which was buying Harrier jump-jet technology and artillery from Britain, ammunition from Belgium, and semiconductors from Japan.[42] Of these, by far the most important were the semiconductors. The Pentagon's Defense Science Board concluded in 1987: 'US military forces depend heavily on technological superiority to win. Electronics is the technology that can be leveraged most highly. Semiconductors are the key to leadership in electronics. US defense will soon depend on foreign sources for state-of-the-art technology in semiconductors. This is an unacceptable situation.'[43]

The strategic implications were rammed cruelly home by the publication (in Japan) of a combative book, *A Japan That Can Say No*, by Akio Morita, the president of Sony, and a Liberal Democratic Party prime ministerial candidate, Shintaro Ishihara. Japan's economic and technological prowess, they argued, dictated a more prominent global role. They went further, provoking serious alarm in the USA when they suggested: 'If, for example, Japan sold chips to the Soviet Union and stopped selling them to the US, this would upset the entire military balance.' The Japanese edition of the book was unofficially translated by DARPA, the Pentagon's Defense Advanced Research Project Agency, and bootleg copies swiftly circulated around Washington in 1989.[44]

American nervousness increased in January 1990, when Japan joined the United States and Soviet Union in that exceptional league of countries able to launch satellites into lunar orbit. Japan's new H-2 rocket, scheduled for first launch in 1993, will increase Japan's space capacity. The equivalent of the American Titan 34D, the H-2 has obvious military applications. While Japan's experience at Hiroshima and Nagasaki has given the country a strongly principled anti-nuclear tradition, there is little doubt that Japan has the technology to become a nuclear power virtually at will.[45]

The growing economic power of Japan, and of the East Asian region as a whole, and the apparently irreducible American trade deficit with them, sparked off flutters of alarm that rose in the United States as its traditional fears of the Soviet Union were allayed by Gorbachev's policies. It was not that the Cold War in Europe was being replaced by a new one in the Pacific. Far from it. But the evidence of Japanese prowess, combined with the new self-confidence of a European Community moving towards the single market of 1992, brought home an American realisation that the end of the Cold War did not leave the United States in permanent security. Beset by its mounting trade and budget deficits, the USA in 1987 was nervous enough to make a best-seller of Professor Paul Kennedy's serious tome, *The Rise and Fall of the Great Powers*, which suggested that the Soviet Union and the US were both suffering from that imperial overstretch which had sent seventeenth-century Spain and nineteenth-century Britain down the inexorable slope of decline.[46]

As the American capital thrilled to the Gorbachev visit at the end of 1987, and the signing of the INF Treaty signalled an end to the New Cold War, there was an underlying gloom in the American mood. It came partly from a Reagan Administration besieged by the Iran–Contra scandals, and partly from the sudden, sharp collapse of the Wall Street stock exchange in October. But its real basis was the suspicion that if Gorbachev had ended the New Cold War, then with the Soviet Union still a nuclear equal in strategic terms, the old one was far from done. Moreover, the new economic power of Europe and Japan suggested that an even older form of cold war might be looming. The United States was becoming merely first among equals in a world of four great powers in which it was joined by Europe, Japan, and the Soviet Union. China's pace of economic growth, and China's nuclear capacity, suggested the four might soon see a fifth, in a twenty-first-century re-enactment of that long strategic minuet the great powers of Europe had danced between the Congress of Vienna, which ended the Napoleonic Wars in 1815, and the catastrophe of old Europe in 1914.

Chapter 13
The Year of Miracles and Its Aftermath

> The good old rule
> Sufficeth them, the simple plan,
> That they should take, who have the power,
> And they should keep, who can.
>
> *'Rob Roy's Grave', William Wordsworth*

The early summer of 1988 was the high point of the Gorbachev reform process, bringing together three crucial events. The first was the 1,000th anniversary of the founding of the Orthodox Church in Russia, formally celebrated by the Soviet state in what amounted to a peace treaty with a Church it had persecuted for so long. The second was the Moscow summit in May 1988, which saw President Reagan mobbed in the capital of the 'evil Empire' and enthralling the students of Moscow University with a speech on their golden prospects in a new Soviet Union of free enterprise and free thought. And the third was the nineteenth Communist Party conference of the following month, which firmly established political liberalisation and accepted the principle of non-Communist political organisations.

This crucial and deliberate interplay between international and domestic reform lay at the heart of Gorbachev's policy, using his global prestige to pressure the party conservatives into accepting the subversive implications of his liberalisation at home. For the West, Gorbachev was able to point to glasnost and perestroika as the justifications for an end to the Cold War. And as his domestic reforms ran into increasing resistance from an entrenched Soviet and party bureaucracy, he was able to point to his unique and indispensable role in easing international tensions.

But there was another, more troubling equation at work. The more Gorbachev reformed the system, the more he destabilised it. The more he convinced the West that the Soviet Union was genuinely ready to accept perestroika in the Eastern European empire, the less he was able to control events there. Gorbachev's hesitant efforts to reform the Soviet economy, which were easily nullified by an entrenched, baffled and suspicious bureaucracy, led to a growing imbalance between the soaring political hopes in the Soviet Union, and the creeping despair about the economy. The more that Gorbachev's international prestige transformed the diplomatic prospects, the narrower became his options at home. Ironically, Gorbachev was grappling with the one great achievement that the Soviet system could claim. Stalin's brutal priority of industrialising a backward and largely rural continent within two decades had succeeded, at least to the point of withstanding the furious German onslaught of 1941, and then outproducing the advanced German economy in tanks, guns and warplanes. And while the US economy before 1914 was built on foreign capital, and the post-war German and Japanese economies depended on floods of American money, the Soviet state had to finance its industrial revolution alone. The peasantry was conscripted into the collective farms to provide the food and the surplus labour force for the new factories. The living standards of workers and peasants alike were ground down to provide the resources for yet more investment. The secret police and the state Terror became an institutionalised part of the system to enforce the rigid discipline which sacrificed everything on the altar of industrialisation. The only other state which industrialised on its own resources was nineteenth-century Britain, and the agonies of transition its rural population suffered as the first industrial proletariat became the textbook of Marxism. For all his rejection of Stalin's crimes and of the Terror, Gorbachev never questioned that it had all, in a dreadful way, been worth it.

> The whole of Europe had been unable to stop Hitler, but we smashed him. We defeated fascism not only due to the heroism and self-sacrifice of our soldiers, but also due to our better steel, better tanks and better planes. And all this was forged by our Soviet period [he maintained]. Yes, industrialisation and the collectivisation of agriculture was indispensable. Otherwise, the country would not have been rehabilitated.[1]

So in order to reform the Soviet economy, to dismantle the central planning system and introduce a market system with profits and incentives, perestroika had to succeed in two separate revolutions, economic and political. Each struck at the very essence of the Soviet state. In reforming the economy, it had also to reform the militarised social system which was an integral part of it. The mechanism of discipline had to give way to the mechanism of profit, and this meant undoing much of what the old system had already achieved in its blunt and brutal way. To give one central example; in the old Soviet system, land was owned by the state and was assigned no intrinsic value. If the state wanted electricity, then one way to provide it was to build hydroelectric dams on mighty rivers like the Volga. The fact that this meant flooding high-value farmland was of no more economic importance than a decision to flood a barren high-mountain valley in Kirghizia, because the loss of fertile farmland was not a cost that the system could factor in to the eventual cost of the electricity.

This kind of false economy spread throughout the system. Once that electricity was produced, at a low theoretical cost (but a high practical cost), it was delivered to factories at a subsidised price. The manager of an aluminium plant, which requires huge energy inputs, barely had to include the cost of power in his budget. Nor was there any rational cost calculation in the price the central planners said he should pay for raw materials or for labour. In this context, Gorbachev's first attempt at reform, through a system called 'Khozraschyot', or self-financing, simply had to fail. It called for a factory manager to assign realistic costs to the production factors he bought. But to devise a realistic cost for his energy supply, he had to call on the energy suppliers to provide him with a realistic assessment of their own costs. Using subsidised oil and gas, or 'free' land to produce hydroelectric power, this was impossible for the electricity stations to do. The cost disciplines which threw Western nuclear power stations into economic chaos, once they tried to include a fair estimate of the unknown costs of eventual decommissioning of a nuclear reactor, suggest how difficult this process can be in a Western economy which has the discipline of world market prices. In the Soviet system, to change one element in the complex structure meant changing everything else.

This quickly became apparent to Soviet economists. In June 1987, Academician Leonid Abalkin convened a conference which tried to grapple with this problem, in the light of earlier attempts at economic reform in the 1960s. The participants concluded that economic reform was not possible without political democratisation: 'Deep transformations in the management of the economy cannot be realised without corresponding changes in the political system and in the social and spiritual spheres.'[2]

The essence of Gorbachev's mandate was to bring about fundamental reform by consent. There were limits to his ability to force the party to share the power it had monopolised, and while he was able to achieve a consensus for economic transformation, once the degree of political change involved became clear a serious political struggle became inevitable, and public. Yegor Ligachev, the party boss from the western Siberian oil-producing region of Tyumen, had been brought on to the Politburo by Gorbachev almost as soon as he took power. Ligachev stood for many in the party who favoured economic reform, but not at the price of political democratisation. The market system of the West had its own failings, Ligachev argued, producing unemployment, homelessness and social stratification.[3]

The most adventurous of Gorbachev's supporters on the Politburo, Alexander Yakovlev, believed that political democratisation was desirable in itself. But he also challenged Ligachev directly for the logical inconsistency of supporting the move to the system of self-financing, but not accepting the market disciplines this would have to impose. 'The market has historically been formed as an objective and social reality, a natural, self-regulating mechanism,' Yakovlev argued, in a *Pravda* article that might almost have been penned by an American free marketeer.[4]

But this party debate was only one feature of the obstacles to reform. In the factories and in the Soviet and the 800-odd Republican ministries which assigned investment and credits and raw materials, sat a vast managerial and bureaucratic class.[5] In so far as they knew how they were meant to change, and there is scant evidence that they did, they saw the reform as a threat to their jobs and positions, and blocked it. 'We are encountering direct attempts to distort the essence of the reform, and to fill new forms of management with old content,' Gorbachev complained to the nineteenth Party Conference. 'This is nothing but the result of arbitrariness by ministries in the absence of proper control and also with the connivance of Gosplan [the state planning board] and the permanent bureaux of the Council of Ministers of the USSR.'[6]

As politicians across the world and across all systems have learned, foreign policy is far more tractable and capable of new direction from the top than domestic reform. Gorbachev's difficulty was that he slowly realised that reform itself was not a viable course; he had to destroy the system in order to save it. And the clearer this became, the more Soviet intellectuals cast around for a model they could usefully examine. In the mid-1980s, the Soviet press and theoretical journals began to teem with discussions of other societies which had charted a course that perestroika might follow. Broadly, they suggested European social democracy, with a preference for the Swedish system. But by the late 1980s, the debate had shifted, looking for other countries which had made the transition from an authoritarian system to a market economy and democratised politics.

There was the Spanish scenario, the bumpy but successful transition from Franco's fascist state to the prospering democracy of the 1980s. But that model was not really available: Franco had left the structures of private capital and property intact. Nor could the Soviet Union expect the kind of surge in foreign capital that had come with Spain's tourist boom of the 1960s and 1970s. There was the Chile scenario, which suggested that economic growth could take place under an authoritarian political system, and that a free-market economy could prosper in a police state. Soviet commentators looked at Mrs Thatcher's apparent success in browbeating an entrenched bureaucracy into accepting fundamental change. But these were models which did not have to face the core problem of the Soviet Union's lack of a system of private property, of commercial banking and credit, and of a negotiable currency.[7]

The examples of reform in states which shared the Soviet structure of central planning were Hungary and China. Although Hungary's economy was small, and weighed down by foreign debt, it was the main model for the reform measures announced in 1987, and which the Soviet bureaucracy found so easy to evade. China was a vastly different kind of state, far less educated and industrialised, far more rural and yet also more ethnically and culturally coherent than the sprawling multi-ethnic Soviet Empire. But some distinctive features of the Chinese reforms, notably the free-enterprise zones and the privatisation of small-scale agriculture, found enthusiastic advocates in Moscow.[8]

The cautious faction in the Politburo, around Yegor Ligachev, had a point. In Chile and in the Asian 'tigers' of South Korea, Taiwan and Singapore, and above all in China, economic growth had been achieved while maintaining social stability through authoritarian political control, which could eventually be relaxed. Moreover, the Asian 'tigers' provided an example of a kind of schizoid economic system, taking advantage of the world's free market for their export trade, while maintaining many features of central planning and autarky in their domestic economies. The Soviet dilemma was plain enough: should economic reform or political democratisation be the priority? The Soviet burden was that the delicacy of their international role, the way that Gorbachev had won Western goodwill by dismantling the Gulags and so much of the authoritarian state, virtually foreclosed the models of Chile or the Asian tigers. A return to authoritarian ways in the name of economic growth, with dragooned trade unions and dissidents being hauled back to labour camps, would reignite the Cold War and force the Soviet Union to maintain the ruinous arms race.

Not only was political reform the path of least resistance for Gorbachev; it was also the path being seized by the forces of democratisation, whatever the Kremlin tried to do. By giving the Kremlin's broad approval to the ideals of a free press and democracy, Gorbachev had unleashed a force which was already building beyond his control. By the time of the nineteenth Party Conference, in June 1988, its power was plain to see. The Baltic delegations to the conference were seen off at the train stations in Riga, Tallin and Vilnius by enthusiastic crowds waving the long-suppressed national banners and singing patriotic songs. Three months before the conference, the new Democratic Union had already been founded in Moscow, and had begun holding public demonstrations in the capital. Gorbachev's authorisation for the historians to start filling in the 'blank spots' of the Soviet past had unleashed a flood of revelations about Stalin's years which publicly discredited the entire system, as public lectures at Yuri Afanyasev's Archival Institute drew gasps as the grim litanies of endless lists of slaughtered names were read out loud, crying at last from their graves in the Gulag. Afanysaev brought a petition with 54,000 names to the nineteenth Party Conference, demanding that a national monument be built to Stalin's victims, and Gorbachev endorsed the plan on the conference's final day.[9]

The nineteenth Party Conference took the crucial decision to plunge ahead with dramatic political reform, while hoping that somehow the economy would be able to follow. It endorsed the Theses, or constitutional proposals, which Gorbachev had submitted, which included a Soviet version of the American Bill of Rights:[10]

> creating the material and legal conditions for the realisation of constitutional freedoms (freedom of speech, freedom of the press, freedom to assemble and hold rallies, street processions and demonstrations, freedom of conscience, and others). It also has to do with strengthening guarantees of the citizen's personal rights (the inviolability of the individual and of the home, the right to privacy in correspondence and telephone conversations and others).

Gorbachev's Theses promised to dismantle the *nomenklatura* system, by which the party structure had maintained a monopoly of all important posts in the economy and society. Secret ballots, with a choice among candidates, were to become the standard method of selecting leading party officials. The congress also agreed to hold in the following year the Soviet Union's first free elections for a legitimate national legislative body. In this new Congress of People's Deputies, only one-third of the seats were to be reserved for the party and other 'social organisations'.

The irony of the Soviet system was that even to bring about democratisation, Gorbachev had to rule in the old, authoritarian way. Ligachev and his conservative supporters, including the KGB chief Viktor Chebrikov, had to be removed from the Politburo during closed-door meetings in the Kremlin, taking advantage of Ligachev's absence on holiday. It remained a tense time, with the Moscow military district being placed on alert, and Eduard Shevardnadze cancelling meetings at the UN sessions in New York to fly back for the emergency plenum.[11]

This cleared the way for Gorbachev's own visit to the United Nations in December 1988 to deliver the speech which, more than any other single statement, spelled out the end of the Cold War. Hitherto, his foreign-policy agenda had largely undone the overreaching policies of Brezhnev. The INF Treaty had agreed to dismantle the SS-20 missiles which Brezhnev had deployed to cow Western Europe. The withdrawal of Soviet troops from Afghanistan had begun, along with the negotiations that would lead to the withdrawal of Cuban troops from Angola. US and Soviet negotiators at Geneva were haggling over the terms of the START Treaty to cut back the strategic nuclear arsenals to some 6,000 warheads each, the level the United States had achieved in 1971.

In his UN speech on 7 December 1988, Gorbachev broke new ground. There were three dramatic features to his address, and any one of them could be seen as a turning-point. In combination, they amounted to a revolution that went far beyond *détente*, ripping up the post-1945 settlement of Yalta, and trying also to end the ideological conflict which had gripped the world since 1917. That first Soviet revolution should now be seen as an event rather like the French Revolution of 1789, Gorbachev said. It belonged to history, rather than having any real relevance to the present day.

'We are entering an era in which progress will be based on the common interests of the whole of humankind. The realisation of this fact demands that the common values of humanity must be the determining priority in international politics,' he said. 'This new stage requires the freeing of international relations from ideology.'[12]

The second breakthrough was his elaboration of the statement he had been making since the Geneva summit of 1985, that

> Force or the threat of force neither can nor should be instruments of foreign policy . . . The principle of the freedom of choice is mandatory. Refusal to recognise this principle will have serious consequences for world peace. To deny a nation the freedom of choice, regardless of the pretext or the verbal guise in which it is cloaked, is to upset the unstable balance that has been achieved . . . Freedom of choice is a universal principle. It knows no exception.

This principle, Gorbachev stressed, applied to 'both the capitalist and socialist system'. This was not simply to rip up the Brezhnev Doctrine, which had reserved the Soviet prerogative to intervene in Eastern Europe to maintain its authority and the post-Yalta balance of power. It was to accept that the citizens of Eastern European countries had the right to choose their own social and political course and governments, irrespective of Soviet interests. This endorsed not only Dubček's attempt to build, in the Czechoslovakia of the 1960s, a socialism with a human face; it accepted the principle of a Czech or Slovak or Polish face without any socialism at all.

The third breakthrough of Gorbachev's speech was to announce, 'A new historic reality: the principle of excessive stockpiling of arms is giving way to the principle of reasonable sufficiency for defence.' This was to withdraw from the arms race and, by implication, to renounce the attempt to maintain a force powerful enough to maintain the offensive option. To make his meaning clear, Gorbachev announced a unilateral cut of 500,000 men from the Soviet Army, and a withdrawal of 50,000 men and 5,000 tanks from the Soviet forces in Eastern Europe. More could follow by negotiation, he went on, but these forces were being brought home whether or not the West followed suit. This was not just to consign the Yalta settlement to the history books along with the French Revolution. It was also an attempt to remove from the geopolitics of Europe that threat of a massive invasion from the East which had overshadowed the continent since tsarist Russia had first hurled back Napoleon's armies in 1812.

Gorbachev's UN speech was the precondition for 1989, Europe's Year of Miracles which followed. It began badly, with a wave of 800 arrests in Prague after demonstrators gathered at the site where the young student Jan Palach had burned himself to death twenty years earlier, protesting at the Soviet invasion. Among those imprisoned was the playwright Vaclav Havel, who was by the end of the extraordinary year to be the head of state. The new administration of President George Bush began almost frostily, with National Security Adviser Brent Scowcroft stressing, in January 1989, 'The Cold War is not over.' Scowcroft then accused Gorbachev of being 'interested in making trouble within the Western alliance. And I think he believes the best way to do it is a peace offensive, rather than to bluster the way some of his predecessors have.'[13] An evidently sceptical President Bush announced a lengthy policy review on relations with the Soviet Union, and American foreign policy was almost placed on hold until this was completed in April. But the main impact of Gorbachev's UN speech was not on the Western Alliance, as the White House assumed, but on the Eastern Alliance, which was not to survive the year.

Hungary began the process, its parliament enacting freedom of assembly and association in January, and its Communist Party accepting a multi-party system the following month. In March, 100,000 Hungarians marched through Budapest to demand the withdrawal of Soviet troops. And on 2 May, Hungarian troops began removing the barbed wire along the frontier with Austria, a hole ripped in the Iron Curtain through which another Eastern European nation was to find its way to freedom as East Germans later in the year began to pour through this back door to the West. In the same month of May, the new legislatures in Lithuania and Estonia declared the pre-eminence of their own laws over those of the Soviet Union, a declaration of sovereignty which Latvia followed in June.

These were probes, testing the implications of Gorbachev's promise of 'freedom of choice', and exploring the parameters of the new Europe he had invoked. The White House too was trying to comprehend it, but was still locked in the perception of a bipolar relationship with Moscow in which the two superpowers could define their course. 'The Marxist–Leninist threat is over as an ideological and economic challenge. We won that one,' Scowcroft told his NSC staff, as they worked on the policy review. 'It's still a considerable military threat, but even that is changing. So it's not good enough just to have four more years, modifying the basic approach we inherited. There's a new world out there. We've got to ask where we'd like to be at the end of the century and what policies will get us there.'[14]

The vaunted policy review proved to be a modest disappointment, even when dressed up in the formal grandeur of National Security Directive-23. Its main theme was that America could now move 'beyond containment', a striking illustration of that continuity which had gripped US policy towards the Soviet Union since George Kennan first formulated the concept of containment in 1946. NSD-23 involved tests of Gorbachev's sincerity by asking for Soviet readiness to abandon its old allies and clients in Central America and Afghanistan. But it also inspired the slogan which won the cheers of President Bush's German audience in Mainz on his European trip in May.

'Germany whole and free in a Europe whole and free,' Mr Bush declared. This ringing restatement of what had been a bedrock of American policy for over forty years masked the delusion that the superpowers were still able to define Europe's future between them. The Year of Miracles was to prove otherwise. Once Gorbachev had opened a space for the peoples of Eastern Europe to exploit, they poured into it and through it, seizing the chance of determining their own destiny for the first time since 1939.[15]

There was some striking American arrogance on display that summer. President Bush's official spokesman Marlin Fitzwater scoffed at Gorbachev's repeated attempts to nudge the United States out of its caution, as 'throwing out in a kind of drugstore cowboy fashion one arms control proposal after another'. In Poland, the White House chief of staff John Sununu bridled at suggestions that the modest amounts of US aid on offer were mere tokens, mocking that the Poles would be 'lacking self-discipline like a young person in a candy store'. At their meeting in Gdańsk, the Solidarity leader Lech Waçsa appealed to President Bush for serious economic help of some $10 billion over the next three years. Without such support, he warned, Poland could plunge into civil war. Bush was noncommittal. The Americans did not seem at all in tune with the passions of Eastern Europe that year. Adam Michnik, the Polish intellectual who had been one of the founders of Solidarity, suggested that the Bush Administration was 'sleep-walking through history'. When Boris Yeltsin arrived in the White House in September, this proved literally true. Brent Scowcroft fell fast asleep during their meeting.[16]

The first real test came in Poland, where the Solidarity movement slowly but successfully negotiated with General Jaruzelski to hold the country's first free elections for a generation on 4 June. Solidarity won triumphantly, and after a long telephone call in August between Gorbachev and Mieczysaw Rakowski, the leader of the Polish Communist Party, the Soviet leader persuaded the Communists to agree to take a minority role in a new Solidarity government. The party had voluntarily given up power, and accepted the verdict of an election, with the explicit backing of the Kremlin.

'The political and moral choice that we faced was formulated after Tienanmen Square,' explained Gorbachev's Central Committee aide for international affairs, Andrei Grachev.[17] Having been in Beijing when the pro-democracy students gathered in Tienanmen Square around their plaster model of the Statue of Liberty, Gorbachev shared the world's revulsion at the brutal reimposition of state and party authority which the elderly Chinese leadership unleashed. The Chinese model had never looked less appealing. And Gorbachev had also lived through the extraordinary experience of the Soviet Union's own first free elections, and the twelve intense days of Soviet democracy which were televised nationally after the new Supreme Soviet first met on 25 May. The contrast between the Moscow model, where democracy was enjoying passionate debate in a constitutional forum and doing so publicly on national television could hardly have been more chilling, set against Beijing's choice of economic liberalisation at the price of tanks and machine-guns imposing martial law in the streets of the capital.

But in that heady summer of 1989, there was no knowing whether the Soviet Union would revert to type, lashing out in a final brute spasm of despair. In the Georgian capital of Tbilisi, in the Azerbaijani capital of Baku, in Riga and in Vilnius, the passing of Soviet power in its own domestic empire was to be marked by sudden outbursts of military repression. Eastern Europe reached for its independence in that uncertain space between hope in Gorbachev's promises and bitter memories of the Soviet record. The West, in what was to become the pattern for President Bush's prudent stewardship of foreign policy, was of little help. Gorbachev's attempt to reach out to the G7 summit of the main industrial economies, meeting in Paris in July 1989, met with a cool response.

The East Germans voted with their feet, flooding into Hungary and then through the vast gaps opened in the frontier that led to Austria and the West. The Hungarians declined to stop them, and when the East German government sealed its borders with Czechoslovakia, their people took to the streets of their own cities. With the slaughter of Beijing in mind, the panicked and divided East German government could not summon the authority to order its troops to shoot them down. Four days after the order to seal the Czech frontier, Gorbachev visited East Berlin, to hear the crowds chant, 'Gorby, Gorby, help us.' It was a stunning reversal of the age-old roles, for the Kremlin's chieftain to be hailed as a liberator against the very system the Kremlin had imposed.

Gorbachev's message to the East German satraps was clear: 'Life itself punishes those who delay,' he declared. Asked to make the Soviet garrison available to restore order, he refused. Within ten days, Erich Honecker had fallen, and three weeks later, on 10 November, the Berlin Wall itself toppled. Then after days of demonstrations in

Prague, the Czechoslovak Parliament formally ended the 'leading role' of the Communist Party under the constitution, and on 30 November announced free elections.

As if in reward for his acquiescence in the collapse of Stalin's empire, Gorbachev was then promised American economic help and support for Soviet applications to join the institutions of the capitalist world by President George Bush at the shipboard summit in Malta. The GATT world trade system, the World Bank and International Monetary Fund, all those bodies which had been established at the end of World War Two to become the structures that helped build the West as an economic system to fight the Cold War, became the symbolic mechanisms to seal its ending. After a year of entirely characteristic hesitation, at the Malta summit of December 1989 President Bush seemed finally convinced that the long confrontation was indeed over. Although nothing was sealed, Bush and Gorbachev agreed in principle to the sweeping cuts in conventional forces in Europe that were finally to be signed as an international treaty in Paris in the following year.

The heroic phase of the Gorbachev era in international relations ended with the fall of the Berlin Wall in November 1989, a development he had neither anticipated nor was able to prevent. In spite of intense pressure from conservatives in his own Soviet party, he abided by the course he had established in the speech to the United Nations the previous year. And he did so even as the great spasms of freedom unleashed violence in his own country, with open war between Armenia and Azerbaijan. On his return to Moscow, Gorbachev faced bitter attacks in the Central Committee plenum, and finally threatened to resign, leaving the party to the fate of its comrades in East Germany or Poland.[18] A few days later, he might have pointed to the grisly fate of the last relic of the old regime, Nicolae Ceauşescu in Romania, shot by his own troops after failing to put down a national uprising.

In that speech to the United Nations which had opened Europe's Year of Miracles, Gorbachev had spoken of the impossibility of closing frontiers to the modern media, and of the way the steady seepage of news and views and ideas meant that 'Nowadays, it is virtually impossible for any society to be "closed" '.[19] But simply because the news comes from a society that insists on its freedom, this is no guarantee that the information will be right.

The seductions of the West that had flowed across the old Iron Curtain were not simply high-minded appeals to democracy and civic rights. Part of the charm of the West lay in its glitter, in its glossy magazines and advertising culture, its promise of the citizen as consumer, just as much as its promise of the citizen as a democratic participant in a free society. The moment that the former Communist states positioned themselves to join the West at capitalism's abundant table, the bills fell due.

The cruellest irony of the Year of Miracles was in its timing. Eastern Europe and its old Soviet masters turned to the Western economic model and to the promise of free markets at the moment when the great boom of the 1980s was reaching its peak. That boom had been launched by the Reagan rearmament programme, and the huge budget and trade deficits which the US economy shouldered in order to finance it. Much of the money was provided by investors from Japan and the confident new European Community, riding the crest of the expansionist enthusiasm that followed its decision to plunge ahead with the creation of a single market with free movement of goods and labour across all twelve states.

But by 1990, Britain and the United States had slipped into recession, and Japan's stock market had begun its long, slow crash. Western Europe's unemployment had started to climb again, towards 10 per cent of the labour force, the same levels which had made its countries so much less inviting a model at the beginning of the 1980s, when the vogue phrase was Euro-sclerosis. The Western investment in perestroika that had been so confidently expected, failed to materialise. Europe might have become, in Gorbachev's pungent phrase, 'our common home', but the ideological distinction which had divided the continent by force was replaced, in the absence of any swift levelling, by an economic distinction which divided it by class. The Iron Curtain which had proved so porous was replaced by a Golden Curtain which was all the more solid in being so intangible. Poverty under Eastern European socialism had been tantalised in the Gorbachev years by the prospect of hope; under Eastern European capitalism, it was just poverty.

The Soviet Empire fell, just at the moment when the Soviet heartland plunged into political and economic crisis. By the end of 1989, with the fall of the Berlin Wall and the sudden liberation of Eastern Europe, the world knew it was living through the age of miracles. But the miracles had begun much earlier, when the bizarre idealisms of Gorbachev and Reagan first collided. After the marvellous year of 1989, the miracles ended, and the recession began.

Great empires seldom die well. The Soviet Union died messily, beset by indecision and faction. In the summer of 1990, a group of Soviet economists, led by Professor Nikolai Shatalin and Mr Grigori Yavlinsky, prepared a 500-day plan for a transition to a semi-free market containing a welfare state and akin to the social democracies of Western Europe. The 500-day plan was based on the expectation of Western economic support and investment, and a Soviet budget balanced by sharp cuts in defence spending. This plan provoked a sharp reaction among the senior ranks of the Soviet military and the party technocrats who directed the defence industries, the dominant sector of the Soviet economy.[20] The threat of the 500-day plan rallied opposition in the party, in the bureaucracy and in the ranks of the Soyuz faction in the Supreme Soviet. It gave a focus to the inchoate resentment at the breakdown of law and order, the mounting shortages of food and economic dislocations, the threat of Baltic separatism and the low-intensity guerrilla war between ethnic groups in the Caucasus. It also gave a rallying point to the army, the veterans, and considerable sectors of the Soviet public who complained in their letters to the press and in their angry denunciations of Shevardnadze that the acceptance of a united Germany remaining in Nato represented not just a strategic retreat, but a reversal of the great victory of Stalin's time. This opposition was unable to mount an alternative programme. There was little support for a return to the centrally planned economy of the Brezhnev years, and even less stomach for the reimposition of the authoritarian political control of Stalin's time. This opposition became serious because it won the adherence of relatively moderate party officials like Premier Nikolai Ryzhkov who had been early supporters of perestroika. Their support strengthened the ranks of the internal opposition, even as it weakened their resolve.

In October 1990, this opposition blocked the Shatalin plan, and tried to impose its own emergency programme, a compromise which sought to reduce state subsidies to industries and foodstuffs, while retaining central control. In December, one of Gorbachev's leading liberal supporters, foreign minister Eduard Shevardnadze resigned, warning of an imminent coup. Soviet troops seized the press and TV facilities and shot sixteen civilian protesters in Lithuania and five in Latvia. Disarmament talks with the West began to stall as the military dragged its feet over implementing the Treaty signed at the European summit to slash conventional forces in Europe. Gorbachev tacked to the right to buy time, and redoubled his attempt to play his trump card of Western support in the increasingly tense game of Soviet politics.[21]

In the course of 1991, the leaders of the West were given a series of opportunities to bring the stricken Soviet Union into a new and productive relationship with the old, capitalist enemy. In April, President Gorbachev visited Japan, amid intense speculation in the Soviet press that Moscow's eastern booty from 1945 could be sold. The Kurile Islands, off the northern tip of Japan, had become an important Soviet base, guarding some of the exit channels through which the Pacific fleet at Vladivostok could penetrate Japan's island barrier and reach the open sea. Tokyo insisted on their return, and hinted that up to $24 billion in economic aid could follow. After a hysterical campaign in the Soviet Army newspaper *Krasnaya Zvezda* suggesting that Japanese extremists were planning an armed invasion of the Kuriles, the Soviet General Staff turned against any such exchange, and the Japanese government failed to offer Gorbachev the expected aid.[22]

This was followed by a prolonged debate among Western governments on the merits of a Grand Bargain, drafted by Harvard-based academics and the influential Soviet economist Mr Grigori Yavlinsky. The proposal suggested some $30 billion a year of Western support in return for sweeping structural changes in the Soviet economy. The changes required were similar to the terms that might be imposed upon a defeated nation after a gruelling war. They envisaged a wholesale transformation of the Soviet Union into a free-market economy, with the privatisations of land, housing, the retail trade and industry, and dramatic cuts in the defence budget. It involved a historic transfer of strategic authority over the Soviet economy and currency from the central organs of the state to the vagaries of a global market dominated by Western banks and corporations. Since the consensus of the Soviet economists advising Mr Gorbachev was reaching the conclusion that such a transition to the free market had to be made, the Grand Bargain was not rejected out of hand in Moscow. Indeed, it became one of the crucial battlegrounds of a political confrontation within the Soviet leadership that was reaching the dimensions of a civil war.[23]

'Among the conditions is the implementation of fundamental reforms in the country not as they are envisioned by us but as they are dreamed up across the ocean,' was the complaint of the KGB chief Vladimir Kryuchkov in his address to the Supreme Soviet on 17 June. This was the occasion of what became known in Moscow as the constitutional coup attempt, launched in a curious speech to the Supreme Soviet that day by the prime minister Valentin Pavlov, who suggested that Gorbachev's health was failing and that many of the Presidential powers be transferred to him. This was followed by a sudden panic when the Moscow mayor Gavril Popov went to see the

US Ambassador at his home, and fearful of microphones, scribbled down that a coup was being prepared to topple Gorbachev. Popov named Kryuchkov, defence minister Yazov, and Gorbachev's old law-school classmate and Supreme Soviet chairman Lukyanov as the organisers. Ambassador Jack Matlock sent a top-secret cable to Washington, where President Bush informed Boris Yeltsin, who was visiting the White House at the time. Bush also arranged for Soviet foreign minister Alexander Bessmertnykh to inform Gorbachev. To Popov's horror, Bush later incautiously informed Gorbachev that Popov had been the source of the information.[24]

In the event, Gorbachev beat off this attempt to seize power through the Supreme Soviet, in part because he was able to convince some waverers that a rather lesser version of the Grand Bargain was in prospect, a START Treaty in return for major infusions of Western aid. The START Treaty was indeed achieved, and agreed between Bush and Gorbachev in their private meeting after the G7 summit in London, which opened the way for a formal signing at the Moscow summit that followed. Gorbachev must have felt that the worst was over. He had finally negotiated a new Union Treaty with the main Republics in April, which laid the basis for the Soviet state to be maintained by consent. The Treaty agreed to transfer taxation and economic planning powers to the individual Republics. But the opposition was almost ready to move.[25]

Gorbachev welcomed President Bush to the Moscow summit and signed the START Treaty, whose provisions had been virtually agreed at Reykjavik five years earlier. But there was no bargain. Gorbachev had gone to the G7 summit in London in July desperate for Western economic support. As he received his Nobel Peace Prize in Oslo in June, Gorbachev had declared that perestroika 'had the right to count on large-scale assistance to assure its success'. He returned from the London summit with the West's leaders, where he had been accorded a form of country membership which excluded him from the main sessions, bearing effusive statements of goodwill and assurances of support. But that was all. Having acquiesced in every demand the West had made, in withdrawing from Afghanistan and from Eastern Europe, and in seeing East Germany join both Nato and a resurgent Germany as the dominant new power of Central Europe, Gorbachev had little to show in exchange. He returned to Moscow empty-handed.[26]

President Bush was prepared to do almost anything for Gorbachev except offer him the financial lifeline which the Grand Bargain had always envisaged. After signing the START Treaty in Moscow, Bush flew on to the Ukrainian capital of Kiev, to shore up Gorbachev's attempt to hold the Union together. 'Freedom is not the same as independence,' Bush warned the Ukrainians, who were holding signs which posed (in English) the unanswerable question, 'If Being Part of an Empire is So Great, Why Did America Get Out of One?'

'Americans will not support those who seek independence in order to replace a far-off tyranny with a local despotism. They will not aid those who promote a suicidal nationalism based on ethnic hatred,' Bush declared.[27] He was doubtless under the influence of his last conversation with Gorbachev, who had spoken darkly of the prospects of the Soviet Union plunging into an ethnic bloodbath akin to that which was already under way in Yugoslavia. Bush flew home leaving Gorbachev to the worst of both worlds, bereft of Western economic support, but with Gorbachev and his critics both convinced that the American President would swallow a great deal of tough action from Moscow in order to hold the Soviet Union together. And almost without realising it, Bush had neutralised Gorbachev's trump card. If Gorbachev could not translate his moral and verbal support from the West into concrete support, then he became a dwindling asset in the Kremlin.

The decisive political shift followed, as the generals, unhappy with the loss of Eastern Europe, and the Old Guard of the party *apparat* managed to broaden their support. They won over key members of the moderate technocrats in the massive defence industries who saw the economic situation becoming catastrophic, sufficient to overcome their doubts and requiring desperate measures. Convinced that the food shortages and surging inflation and unemployment would bring the country's grimly silent majority to their side, the Emergency Committee of generals, KGB, party men and technocrats of the military–industrial complex announced they had seized power in the early hours of 19 August.

There were no illusions about the ambitions of the old regime to cling on to its power and privileges. Yeltsin's people had plans for emergency broadcasts and appeals for a general strike, even if the White House were seized and Yeltsin arrested. Even as the tanks were rolling into place on the coup's first day, Yeltsin's foreign minister Andrei Kozyrev was in Paris, armed with Yeltsin's written authority to set up a Russian government in exile.

But all the expectant coup watchers were wrong about one thing. They all thought that if and when it came, the coup would come in winter, following the usual seasonal pattern of Russian revolts, when the shops are empty and the food supplies are down to potatoes and cabbages and the grim cold subdues the spirit. Back in 1825, the liberal aristocrats and officers who tried to change tsardom into a constitutional monarchy are remembered as the Decembrists, after the month they chose. In the abortive revolution of 1905, Bloody Sunday took place in January. In 1917, the revolutions came in February and November.

Summer, when fruits and vegetables fill the markets and people luxuriate as the days stretch out towards midnight, has not proved auspicious for Russian coups. Lenin was forced into hiding, and into temporary exile in Finland, after a botched attempt by the Bolsheviks in June 1917. The desperate fling by the Gang of Eight forgot Lenin's lesson. And mercifully, they also forgot the example of Stalin. It is hard to tell why the coup leaders were dubbed 'the hard-liners'. It was a feeble effort they mounted, evidently intended to be bloodless, but in the end merely incompetent.

The coup leaders left Yeltsin to become a focus of resistance. They left the Metro running and the streets open so that the popular resistance could gather. They failed to close the independent radio stations, failed to jam the Western broadcasts that Mikhail Gorbachev was hearing down in his Crimean detention. They failed to comprehend the way that networks of fax machines and photocopiers enabled part of the free press to continue. They assumed they were still in the Soviet Union of 1964, when Khrushchev fell, and that the new society shaped by six years of perestroika would fall dutifully into line and obey. They were not altogether wrong. In spite of hundreds of thousands of people who went on to the streets to protect their fledgeling democracy, the bulk of the factories ignored Yeltsin's call for a general strike. There remained a silent majority in the Soviet Union which dully waited to see what would happen, and which may well have sympathised with the coup leaders' complaints about the economic and social chaos gripping the country.

Such was the gamble of the coup plotters, and they were wrong. In the big cities, the roots of democracy had sunk too deep. The ill-organised and curiously squeamish coup failed to seize power effectively, and left Boris Yeltsin to provide a focus of resistance around which the people could rally. For the first time in Russian history, the political decisions came not from the Kremlin, to be imposed upon the inert masses. As they braved the tanks around the Russian Parliament building, the people of Moscow took their fate into their own hands. The army split, the coup lost its nerve, and the people imposed their will upon the rulers. Tsars and Commissars alike must have spun in the Kremlin graves, and from his detention in the Crimea, Gorbachev saw his promise of Soviet democracy fulfilled. The revolution came from below – and the West now had another chance to throw its economic support beyond a Soviet democracy which Gorbachev built, which Yeltsin led, and which at once had to grapple with the economic chaos and national separatism that was the legacy of seventy-four years of Soviet rule.

The six years of perestroika did not end in August 1991. The great experiment which Mikhail Gorbachev launched when he won a bitterly contested Politburo election to become General Secretary in March 1985, became heroic with the defeat of the coup. The scale of the popular resistance to the coup stands as an inspiring monument to Gorbachev's reforms, even as Gorbachev himself fell victim to the vengeance and fear of the party machine. And there is a second achievement of Mikhail Gorbachev which only became apparent with the great drama in Moscow. Over the previous two years, Gorbachev had lost much of the popularity he once enjoyed, and much of the respect of the liberal intellectuals who were the spearhead of his reform process. But after the coup, Gorbachev's political manoeuvres, his flirtation with the right wing over the bloody winter in the Baltics, appeared in a new light. They had bought time for the roots of democracy to sink more deeply into the populace, time for the elections to take place which gave Boris Yeltsin the mandate he deployed so bravely.

In retrospect, Gorbachev's greatest achievement may have been the way in which he managed to delay this coup until the late summer of 1991. A year earlier, before so many of them voted for Yeltsin, those soldiers who joined the defences around Yeltsin's Russian Parliament building might never have dared defy their orders. The hero of the barricades, the man of the hour, Yeltsin performed magnificently in a crisis which might have been scripted for his gifts. His raw courage, his populist instincts, and that sometimes disturbing hint of demagoguery were precisely what the dramatic moment required. The irony of the coup is that the Russian people defended democracy before they had built it. They rallied to protect a future which was yet to be defined. And the nature of the Russia that is coming will be determined by its ability to reconcile a society so utterly divided between urban and rural realities, between quasi-European modernity and a surreal, almost Asian backwardness.

The most glaring feature of the Soviet Union for any foreign observer in recent years has been its schizoid nature, the gap between its military and space technology and the brilliance of much of its cultural life, set against its Third World civilian economy. One way to try to grasp this was to think of the Soviet Union as two distinct societies. A rough comparison of the economic statistics suggests that it included a reasonably advanced industrial economy about the size of West Germany, and a southern slice of the traditionally Muslim Republics with the population and economic performance of Iran, all wrapped up in a vast and backward rural pudding that is rather like Romania. And everything that mattered during the week of the coup took place in the German part, in the big urban centres. And it all depended on the technology the German sector produced, from the tanks to the radios, from the factories to those buses that made up the bulk of the impromptu barricades.

By the time of the coup, the ever-present black market had swollen to vast proportions which suggested that a form of raw capitalism was already in place. The dollar and the barter trade, and the imported technology of fax machines and personal computers, had spread throughout that industrial and educated sector of the Soviet economy that we may think of as Germany. And it was this German sector, the military–industrial complex and the organised state and party machine, that was so thumpingly defeated in the Cold War. That vast and miserable Romania out there in the provincial countryside was largely untouched by this process. And until the economic reforms progress to the point at which the peasants are given back their land and allowed to sell their crops for what they are worth, this separation of the urban and rural economies, and the gulf between urban and rural ways of life, is likely to remain.

What the world saw in the streets of Moscow was a kind of civil war within the German sector. The coup was a confrontation between the old administrative class which failed adequately to transform and modernise the industrial economy, and that mass of educated urban dwellers they had misruled for so long. So the most hopeful sign for the future was the way that the Soviet peasantry had made the urban resistance possible by voting so strongly for Yeltsin in the Russian Presidential elections in June 1990. Yeltsin's mandate, the political base for his dramatic resistance, came from the Germany and the Romania alike. Oddly enough, the one time in its seventy-three years that the Soviet system ever functioned triumphantly saw another such coming together of the urban and rural sectors that had been at odds since Stalin regimented the Soviet peasantry into collective farms to feed the industrial workers. It was the alliance of the armaments factories and the Red Army's conscripts from the farms and cities that defeated Hitler, and established the Soviet state's sustaining myth. In the great political event of 1991, the rallying behind the Boris Yeltsin they had elected, that urban and rural alliance was reborn.

But the Soviet Union had died. Even when he returned to Moscow, freed from his detention in the Crimea, Mikhail Gorbachev appeared as a figure from another, already distant time. Having not shared in the drama of the Moscow streets, he failed to understand its power. He failed to visit the Russian White House, or to congratulate the crowds. He spoke instead over national television, as if nothing had changed in the previous four days, and promised to 'work for the renewal of the party', even as the crowd began to topple the statue of Felix Dzerzhinsky, the founder of the party's sword and shield, the secret police.[28]

On the following day, Gorbachev and Yeltsin appeared before the Russian parliament, and in a moment of humiliation and shift of power that was transmitted by TV around the world, Gorbachev was given a list of decrees to read out. They effectively stripped what was left of power from the party Gorbachev had vowed to renew. He protested he had not yet read them. 'Well, read them now,' snapped Yeltsin, wagging an authoritative finger, and sovereignty was visibly transferred.

Before taking Holy Communion in the Russian Orthodox Church, it is customary to ask forgiveness of one's neighbours. In *Boris Godunov*, that most Russian of operas, the great scene roots its power in this tradition, as the dying Tsar begs forgiveness from his people. And with the coup just defeated, and Mikhail Gorbachev and Boris Yeltsin briefly united at the funeral of the three young martyrs of the barricades, this ancient open vein was tapped once more. 'Forgive me, your President, that I was not able to defend and save your sons,' Yeltsin told the parents and the weeping crowd, massed in the Kremlin's shadow. And as James Billington, the American Librarian of Congress and Russian scholar, recorded the scene, it was if a great wound healed. The aftermath of the coup was overwhelmed by the panoply of a far older Russian and religious tradition. For Billington, the leading Western scholar of Russia's cultural past, it was 'a carnival of hope at the heart of the last of the empires, and covered with flowers on the Feast of the Transfiguration'.[29]

Within a week of the coup leaders sending the tanks into Moscow, the new Union Treaty they had determined to stop had already been overtaken. Eight of the fifteen Republics, including the Slavic heartlands of Byelorussia and the Ukraine, had declared full independence. The European Community formally recognised the Baltic states and even the Republic of Kazakhstan declared that the central government of the Soviet Union had died, and could be replaced only by something as politically loose as the British Commonwealth, but as economically coherent as the European Community.

The Cold War ended as it had begun, with the death of an empire, and an attempt to keep its name alive through a resort to that same polite fiction which had maintained a Commonwealth long after the British Empire had collapsed through the impoverishment of its homeland. Just as Britain endured to find a new international presence through her special relationship with the USA and her eventual, reluctant absorption into Europe's economic family, the relics of the Soviet Union sought a similar escape to a new future. But Britain had embarked on that shrunken course in a period of global economic growth, its diminution sweetened by prosperity. Russia and her neighbours faced a colder and a sadly meaner world, without even the Ruritanian pomp and parades of the British monarchy to mask reality with fading splendour.

Chapter 14
Superlosers

Where is the world of eight years past? 'twas there –
I look for it – 'tis gone, a globe of glass,
Cracked, shivered, vanished, scarcely gazed on, ere
A silent change dissolves the shivering mass.
Statesmen, chiefs, orators, queens, patriots, kings
And dandies, all are gone on the wind's wings.

Don Juan, George Lord Byron

After every great war comes a peace conference, which traditionally contains the promise of a new crisis as Europe's diplomats display their legendary skill at bringing the seeds of a new war from the very jaws of peace. The Congress of Vienna in 1815 sought to contain the dangerous new passions of liberalism and nationalism by crushing them in the name of the short-lived Holy Alliance. After the resurgent nationalisms reached their hideous climax with the First World War, the Versailles Peace Treaty of 1919 sought to satisfy those disparate nationalisms at Germany's expense. The result was World War Two, which was ended by the Yalta summit which in turn launched the Cold War.

The pan-European summit in Paris in November 1990 formally ended the Cold War, but left behind a great uncertainty in a European vacuum from which the Warsaw Pact had disappeared. Nato was suddenly bereft of the enemy it was born to confront. From the old East German frontier to Siberia, there was more than an echo of a wasted battlefield as the dreadful reality of ecological disaster wrought by central planning became plain. As in 1945, a new human tide of refugees began to flow from the impoverished East to a West which was beginning to slide into recession, without the prospect of another bout of arms race-Keynesianism to restore the boom.

It had been a marvellous peace, a V-Day across Eastern Europe as they rejoiced in a revolution which had taken nine months in Poland, nine weeks in East Germany, and nine days in Czechoslovakia. But the delirious hopes of 1989 gave way to the increasing gloom of the succeeding years, in spite of the swingeing cuts in troops and tanks in the Conventional Forces in Europe Treaty (CFE) which was signed in Paris. The Treaty of Paris reduced Soviet conventional forces to the west of the Urals by about forty per cent, to a new level equal to the reduced Nato force levels. The Warsaw Pact cuts alone were the equivalent of sixty heavy tank divisions. Soviet air force cuts were equivalent to forty-five air combat wings of seventy warplanes each.[1]

The tradition of breeding new wars from the peace conferences of the old was dutifully maintained by Nato, which arranged to ship 2,000 surplus tanks and other heavy weapons to Greece and Turkey. These weapons, removed from Nato's central front under the CFE Treaty, were the major component of a new regional rearmament programme for the two Nato members most closely involved in the Yugoslav civil wars to their north. The Nato operation was known as 'Cascading', and its was defended as an economy measure, since giving the tanks to Greece and Turkey was cheaper than destroying them. Turkey was assigned 1,057 M60 and Leopard main battle tanks from Germany, the USA and the Netherlands, and Greece received a total of 916 tanks. Each country was also given seventy-two M110 artillery pieces. Greece was also provided with 150 M113 armoured combat vehicles, and Turkey with 600 of them.[2]

The irony, that weapons to be scrapped to seal the peace in central Europe were being shipped to the fringes of a real war zone in the Balkans, was lost on the Nato planners. The Cascading of armoured vehicles was simply the land component of a major rearmament drive by Greece and Turkey, traditionally the most hostile of the Nato allies. Germany agreed to provide Turkey with another thirty-two F-4 fighters, in addition to Turkey's $2.8 billion from the United States to help manufacture eighty F-16 fighter jets. Greece also acquired twenty-eight F-4 fighters and sixty-two A-7 bombers from the USA. As well as pursuing its long-standing dispute over Cyprus, Turkey was openly supporting the Bosnian fellow-Muslims in the Yugoslav imbroglio, while Greece glowered at the former Yugoslav province of Macedonia over its very choice of name.

Immediately east of the Balkans, Russian troops fought a freelance war to help establish the Russian Republic of Trans-Dniester against the forces of the former Soviet Republic of Moldavia. On Turkey's eastern flank, the former Soviet republics of Armenia and Azerbaijan were at war, with Turkey openly backing Azerbaijan. Immediately north of this conflict, the former Soviet Republic of Georgia fought intermittently with its former province of Abkhazia and the Muslim Chechen–Ingush clans of the north Caucasus.

All around Russia's perimeter, the guns thundered in the wars of the Soviet succession. To the east, China learned the lessons of Gorbachev and clamped down in Tienanmen Square before its own economic perestroika toppled the party's control. To the south, India and Pakistan mobilised for a new and potentially nuclear confrontation over disputed Kashmir. In the Gulf, an Iraq freed of Soviet guidance invaded Kuwait, and to the west, a new and vicious ethnic war convulsed the Balkans. The disciplines of both the Soviet state, and of the Cold War itself, began to wither even while the Soviet Union remained nominally in place.

It took some time to die. Gorbachev's failure to grasp the challenge of economic reform brought the hunger winter of 1990–1, with its humiliating appeals to the West for food aid. Leningrad, shelled and besieged by the Germans in World War Two, was fed by the old enemy in the new peace. The tanks that were brought home from Eastern Europe were delivered to the expanded paramilitary forces of the Interior Ministry, and the last Soviet commander of the doomed war in Afghanistan, General Boris Gromov, was placed in charge of the Soviet Army's new mission – preventing civil war.

The West celebrated their victory by bickering over the economic foundations of the New World Order, with a new cool conflict looming over trade between the fast-congealing economic blocs of the European Community, North America and the Japanese-dominated Pacific rim. The last legacy of the old Cold War had been the great boom of the 1980s, which made the free markets of the West so tantalisingly attractive to Mikhail Gorbachev's unravelling empire. But that boom had been financed on American deficits, as the Reagan Administration risked its own economic stability to finance the final spasm of the arms race which exhausted the Soviet Union.

The Cold War ended with the United States and Britain in recession, the Japanese stock market tumbling by 40 per cent, with the wealth of Germany devoted to the rescue of its reunited compatriots, and the world poised for war in the Persian Gulf. There was a glimmer of hope in the rallying of the revitalised United Nations against Iraqi aggression. But that aggression was made the more nightmarish by the way the Cold War's talismanic weapons had spawned their own dragon's teeth, with Israel already a nuclear power and Iraq straining every nerve to become one. In the long term, the prospects should be bright. The enrichment of the West in the forty years after World War Two had stemmed in large part from the way the impoverished Europeans and Japanese had become prosperous new consumer markets. Within a similar period, the 400 million people of Eastern Europe and the former Soviet Union and Vietnam should in principle offer a similar new quantum leap in global trade and prosperity, made the more stable by the comforting argument that democracies have never yet gone to war against one another. The lessons of the recovery of Western Europe and Japan were plain. A far-sighted American decision to invest in the former enemies with the Marshall Plan had built a new alliance of democracies and free markets for the common good. But the spur to that great strategic decision by the United States of the late 1940s had been the Cold War. The threat to national survival had summoned extraordinary reserves of American statesmanship. The passing of that threat left the West too indecisive, and its leaders too worried by the vengeance of their voters, to respond with equal vision.

As the old regime died, two of the essential concepts which sustained the post-war world, and the foreign policy of the American superpower, also ceased to exist. 'The Free World' lost the essential oxygen of its forty-seven-year confrontation with the ideology which imploded on that stretch of the Moskva riverbank that is now named Free Russia Square. The Free World had always embraced, for the morally messy reasons of *realpolitik*, much that was less than free. It was an American phrase used to define its global reach and justify its influence, while acknowledging that its allies enjoyed far more autonomy, and proved far less tractable, than those in the unfree Soviet Empire. But here too the Cold War produced one of its many ironies. The unfree Soviet colonies proved consistently far more rebellious. China was able to break away from Soviet influence, and in 1989, the Kremlin's acquiescence dismantled what was presumably the Unfree World by consent.

The defeat of the Moscow coup also threw into question the future of 'The West', that useful phrase of such geographical imprecision that embraced Germany and Japan alike, that extension of the old Atlantic alliance to include the Cold War's front lines along the River Elbe and the Yellow Sea. Since post-war Germany and Japan owed so much to their American founding fathers and financiers, the West indeed shared many common values. But political theory had to be stretched to include the one-party state of Japan's Liberal Democratic Party within the embrace of Western democracy. By 1992, 'The West' was too ungainly a strategic coalition to be sustained, without the traditional glue of the Soviet threat. Politically, the burgeoning economies of South Korea and Taiwan had little in common with the free press and party democracies of Western Europe and North America.

Economically, the domestic free markets of the United States and of Europe were far more open than the protected systems of the Asian tigers. Even so, the European Community and the United States were engaged in trade skirmishes that looked uncomfortably close to a trade war, and the GATT world trading talks were stalled. The United States, Canada and Mexico began building a trading bloc of their own, while the EC bickered over French farmers. The bold attempt to establish a federal Europe with the Maastricht Treaty threatened to founder over Danish objections, British doubts, and the punitive costs of high German interest rates.[3] The end of the Cold War had thus restored economic issues to that primacy which they tend to enjoy in the absence of war, the threat of war, or confrontations between the great powers. For over four decades, the East–West tension and the long post-war boom of Europe, Japan and North America had tended to overshadow the more mundane matters of getting and spending. But while the missiles and the armies held the brittle peace, the fate of the Cold War was really decided by the West's far greater efficiency at sustaining the costs of permanent militarisation while also offering their citizens a steadily improving standard of living. There were interruptions, recessions and sudden panics, but on a scale of the almost forty-seven years from Yalta to the abortive coup in Moscow, the graph of American, West European and Japanese growth rates rose steadily, and far more consistently than it felt to those living through the changes.

The great dips in the ascending graph came in 1974, and in 1979–81, when the OPEC oil-price rises suddenly savaged the Western economies. By contrast, the increase in the value of its energy exports helped the Soviet economy look as if it was performing rather better than it was. And while the West benefited from the need to adapt to high energy costs, the Soviet economy had no such incentive. As the great economic strains of the arms race, the Afghan war and the Warsaw Pact aid budget all intensified in the 1980s, the deceptive advantage of the high oil price suddenly turned against Gorbachev's strategy of perestroika. It may well have been the largest single economic factor in its eventual failure. For not only did the centrally planned structure of the Soviet economy prove stubbornly resistant to reform, the advantage of high oil prices which it had enjoyed for the decade after the OPEC price rise of 1973–4 came to an end in the year that Gorbachev came to power. After peaking at $35 a barrel in 1981, the oil price fell below $30 a barrel in 1983, and while averaging $26 a barrel throughout 1985, collapsed in December of 1985 and January of 1986 to around $15, and thereafter traded in the volatile range of

$12 to $20 a barrel until the Iraqi invasion of Kuwait in 1990. The expectations of foreign earnings on which Gorbachev had based his planning were more than halved.[4]

Worse still, those foreign hard-currency earnings were halved in rapidly devaluing US dollars, in which the world oil price was set. This dealt a grievous, and possibly decisive blow to Gorbachev's economic reform strategy. But the fate of the US dollar in the 1980s also played a decisive part in the shifts of global economic power which had been the constant companion of the unfolding Cold War. The Reagan Administration had a devastating effect on the American economy. Between the third quarter of 1980, just before he was elected, and the first quarter of 1985, the US dollar rose by 63 per cent according to the index of the International Monetary Fund, and 83 per cent by the index of the US Federal Reserve.[5] This helped reduce the US inflation rate, and to finance a boom which was spurred by the growth of foreign capital entering the USA. The price the US economy paid was a monstrous trade deficit, which began to exceed $150 billion a year in 1986. To put this into perspective, the US trade deficit was slightly larger than the entire economic output of Belgium.[6]

For President Reagan, the boom was an unalloyed delight, an endorsement of the tax-cutting policies and the unrestrained capitalism he had promised. 'In Europe, they are calling it the American miracle. Day by day we are shattering accepted notions of what is possible,' the President enthused in his State of the Union address in January 1985.[7]

Abroad, while sharing in his joy, Reagan's sympathisers took a rather less simplistic view of his success. One of the more astute perceptions was delivered to Britain's House of Lords by Harold Macmillan, the former prime minister now elevated to the peerage as the Earl of Stockton, who discussed the Reagan miracle in his maiden speech.[8]

> I rejoice at what Reagan is doing. He has broken all the rules, and all the economists are furious. Five million new jobs, and at the same time, inflation has been kept quite low. It is a miracle; the House should know how it has been done. I think I know how it has been done; it is because they have had the sense to make other people pay for it. In a word, Reagan, to reverse Keynes, has called in the resources of the old world in order to finance the expansion of the new.

Reagan's strategy, first explained in 1980, to crack the Soviet economy by forcing it into an arms race it could not sustain, was working. But it worked at dreadful cost. The US economy could not afford it either. The Reagan rearmament programme was financed by budget deficits, which were in turn financed by borrowing of foreign capital. This foreshadowed the rather cruder development which was to take place in 1990–1, when the United States financed its military venture against Iraq in the Persian Gulf by getting its cash-rich allies in Germany, Japan and Saudi Arabia to pay for it. The real lesson of the US economic dislocations of the 1980s was clearly understood by those with practical responsibilities for the stewardship of the US currency. 'The stability of our capital and money markets is now dependent as never before on the willingness of foreigners to continue to place growing amounts of money in our markets,' America's central banker, Paul Volcker of the Federal Reserve, explained to Congress in 1985. 'We are in a real sense living on borrowed money and time.'[9]

One of the more illuminating coincidences of the modern age is that the year which brought Gorbachev to power also saw the public humbling of the American economy. The admission that it could no longer afford to lead the global economy, and had to share the responsibility for its stewardship with Europe and Japan, should have been a cause for great pride. The real achievement of the American system in the four decades of the Cold War had not been the eclipse of its Soviet rival, but its creation of something far more magnificent and far more positive: the building of the West. Without it, the Cold War might have ended differently, or never ended at all.

The new economic power of Japan and the European Community was unmistakably on display as US Treasury Secretary James Baker met the European and Japanese finance ministers at the Plaza Hotel in New York in September 1985. That meeting established the principle and the strategy of a concerted approach to the global economy and its currencies. The Plaza Accord saw an agreement for a managed fall in the value of the US dollar, with the West's central banks acting as one.

It was the moment of the US economy's supreme effort, to impose an acceleration on the arms race which the Soviet Union could not match. And if the Soviet economy broke, the US economy bent under the strain. The support of other G7 nations was summoned to help sustain the great strategic effort. Japanese investment flooded into the United States, buying such emblematic American institutions as the Rockefeller Center in New York, and the Pebble Beach golf club in California. America's dreams were on sale, as the Japanese bought Hollywood's Columbia Studios and CBS records. The British, by far the largest foreign investors, bought Burger King. The Germans bought Doubleday. Between 1977 and 1987, the foreign-owned share of US manufacturing more than doubled from 5.2 to 12.2 per cent. But this one-eighth of American manufacturing output was achieved with only 7.9 per cent of American manufacturing employment, which suggests the degree to which the foreigners were investing in the high-productivity and capital-intensive rather than labour-intensive part of the economy. The foreigners were buying into the economy of the future, and leaving the American owners to the past.[10]

A historic change had come with extraordinary speed. In 1972, the value of US direct investment stock abroad was six times higher than that held by foreigners in America. Within sixteen years, the proportions were even. An American dominance in foreign ownership had become a parity. Twenty per cent of the assets of all US banks were owned by foreigners by 1988, and half of this was held by Japan. The two leading American scholars in the field concluded in a special survey for the Institute of International Economics that 'Japan has also been the principal exporter of portfolio capital in the 1980s – in effect the principal source of financing for the US current account deficit'. Britain remained the largest single investor in the USA, with 31 per cent of all foreign holdings in 1988, followed by Japan with 16.2 per cent, the Netherlands with 14.9 per cent and Canada with 8.3 per cent.[11] But as well as buying companies, stock and real estate, they all bought T-bonds, the US Treasury Securities which directly financed the US budget deficit. In 1990, the US Treasury paid out $248 billion in interest on this public debt, of which $38 billion, almost 15 per cent, went to foreign bond-holders.[12]

The Japanese bought more T-bonds than the rest of the outside world's investors combined. And it cost them heavily. The decline of the dollar after the Plaza agreement of 1985, and the parallel rise in the yen, meant that the dollar assets held by Japanese investors were mechanisms for losing money on the exchange rates. Having paid over 200 yen for each dollar in 1985, Japanese investors found that a dollar could be bought for 140 yen by April–May of 1987, which represented a loss of a third of the original investment.[13]

A curious equation now emerges. If the United States prevailed in the Cold War through rearmament, and if that rearmament was financed by budget deficits, and those deficits were sustained by foreign investors who lost money in doing so, then the foreigners financed the American success. The 1980s saw a triumphant return on that American altruism of the immediate post-war period, when its generous vision financed the recovery of those European nations and Japan who were to be their economic competitors. But to put the argument in that way is to miss the essential accomplishment of the Cold War. The objective may have been to contain the Soviet Union. The achievement was to build the West, the global economy which was greater than the sum of its American, European and Japanese parts, and whose creative economic energies were the true victors of the Cold War.

To consider the new global economy which emerged in the 1980s purely in terms of national trade figures, as some nationalist version of profit-and-loss accounts, is to miss the essential point. The global economy no longer operated on such archaic presumptions. For example, the announcement by the US Commerce Department that the Japanese had enjoyed a $31-billion trade surplus in 1984 provoked massive complaints from the US Congress. But in that year, Japanese consumers bought products worth $43 billion from US corporations operating in Japan. Moreover, a significant fraction of those 'Japanese' sales to the US were from Japanese subsidiaries of US-owned multinationals. Japanese-owned multinationals operating in the USA sold another $12 billion to American consumers. When these figures are included, then a rough balance emerges between US and Japanese trade in that year.[14]

Did the US role as a world trader suffer from its monstrous budget deficits and its trade 'imbalances' with Japan? Not at all. The United States enjoyed a 12.9 per cent share of world trade in 1970, which rose to a 14.5 per cent share in 1985. Did the Japanese become the dominant world traders in that period, by exploiting the American market? Not much. The Japanese share of world trade between 1970 and 1985 rose modestly, from 5.9 per cent to 7.7 per cent. The Japanese increase is explained almost entirely by the fall in Britain's share of world trade from 6.4 to 5.4 per cent, and by that of Canada from 4.6 to 3.9 per cent. And much of the British decline in world trade share is explained by the bonanza of North Sea oil, which sharply reduced energy imports.[15]

A myth has developed that Japan's success was the result of an economy ruthlessly dedicated to exporting. This is not and never was the case. Japan never exported as much in value, nor as a share of its economy, as did West Germany. Japan's wealth lay in the extraordinary speed with which it built its home market, which had reached 120 million people by 1987. Indeed, even by British standards, Japan had not seriously geared its economy to exports. Britain was exporting 20 per cent of GDP in 1986, and Japan barely 10 per cent, a pattern which has been maintained since.[16] The distinction which Japan enjoyed, and which had attracted the interest that Gorbachev displayed in his Vladivostok speech in 1986, was to be at the centre of the fastest-growing region on earth. In 1960, the Asian economies accounted for just 4 per cent of global GNP. By 1990, they represented almost twenty-five per cent of global output, and were still growing at a rate which promised to produce one-third of global output by the year 2000. The Japanese economy made up some two-thirds of the larger regional economy of Asia, and so while exports were not essential to the region's surge in prosperity, much of the expansion came from the ability to exploit the growth in world trade as a whole.

Between 1981 and 1991, total world trade increased by 48 per cent. Much of Europe's renewed self-confidence stemmed from the fact that trade among the four largest EC economies, Germany, France, Britain and Italy, increased by almost 60 per cent. But as Dr Kenneth Courtis has pointed out:[17]

> For all of Asia, it doubled. For Singapore, Hong Kong, Korea and Taiwan, trade today [in 1992] is four times larger than it was just ten years ago. In this expansion of trade, Japan and North America have played opposite, but complementary roles. Through direct investment, and its own finely targeted trade expansion, Japan has supplied the region with capital and intermediate goods . . . In contrast, the US has played the role of market for Asia.

The rest of the world also played the role of market for the United States, when the components that made up the American economy are considered as a whole. Once again, one has to look beyond the national trading figures, and enter the far more illuminating statistics of the global economy. In 1988, total US exports of manufactured goods amounted to just over $250 billion. But sales abroad by majority-owned US subsidiaries in manufacturing totalled $465 billion. And sales abroad by US subsidiaries in distribution totalled $180 billion. This produced a grand total of $895 billion in total overseas sales that can be attributed to the US economy. Consider, by way of contrast, Japan, whose exports of manufactured goods at $230 billion were a little way behind the American achievement. But sales abroad by Japanese subsidiaries in distribution were a striking $380 billion, and sales abroad by Japanese subsidiaries in manufacturing amounted to only $140 billion, for a total overseas sales performance of $750 billion. The important feature of these figures is not that Japan was significantly behind the US performance, although it was, but that the fundamental organisation of each country's penetration of foreign markets was so different. The Americans focused on manufacturing abroad, the Japanese on sales through distribution. The global economy was growing so fast that there were all sorts of ways of exploiting it.[18]

For future historians, the Reagan–Thatcher era will be noted less for its decision to renew the West's military will and prosecute the New Cold War than for the liberalisation of financial markets they set in train. The global economy had passed through a long gestation in the nineteenth century, a feeble infancy before 1939, and a sturdy childhood from 1945 to 1974. But it exploded into the furious and barely controllable growth of adolescence after 1980. In that year, the total of international bank lending (domestic lending denominated in foreign currencies plus cross-border lending) stood at $324 billion. By 1991, it had reached $7.5 trillion, a twenty-fold growth. (The economies of the twenty-four leading nations which made up the OECD had grown by a factor of 2.5, from $7.6 trillion to $17.1 trillion over the same period.)[19]

The degree of interdependence of the leading Western economies intensified at an astonishing rate. By 1990, foreigners held almost 20 per cent of America's debt, and 34 per cent of Germany's debt. In 1980, American transactions of securities with foreigners amounted to 9 per cent of American GDP; by 1990 they had increased to 93 per cent of a much larger GDP. In Japan, the comparable figures were 7 per cent in 1980 and 119 per cent in 1990. In the United Kingdom, where the City of London played a very much larger role in this global economy than its domestic economy would warrant, cross-border securities transactions were seven times larger than the entire British GDP in 1990. This was the global economy with a vengeance, financed and spurred on by the collapse of the old Bretton Woods system of stable currencies, and a total foreign-exchange turnover of some $900 billion a day by 1991. Each week, the world's currency markets traded sums equivalent to the total value of the American economy's output for a year.

National governments found themselves helpless before this new global juggernaut called 'the markets'. The European countries poured $20 billion into trying to sustain its Exchange Rate Mechanism in September 1992. This was a matter of overriding EC policy. The ERM was the essential stepping-stone on the path to the single European currency, which the Maastricht Treaty had declared to be the next goal of a Europe that was expecting to expand to include Austria, Switzerland and Sweden. But the markets brushed aside this $20-billion barrier with ease, forcing Italy and Britain out of the ERM and then forcing devaluations by Spain and Sweden. The markets equally refused to swallow the US Federal Reserve's attempts to cut long-term interest rates. The Fed was able throughout 1992 to reduce short-term interest rates to their lowest rates for over twenty years, but the markets ensured that the long-term rates remained stubbornly high.

By all traditional standards, the victory he declared in the Cold War, and the battlefield success that was indeed won in the Gulf War, should have guaranteed the re-election of President George Bush in 1992. But the world had moved on. With America as the unique and militarily unassailable superpower, these strategic considerations were of little concern to an electorate which focused instead on the state of its economy. President Bush had wrapped himself in the American flag to win the election in 1988, and been deeply sceptical of perestroika throughout that election year. 'Gorbachev is not a freedom-loving friend of democracy, but an orthodox, committed Marxist,' he declared at the start of the campaign in January, and in the first Presidential debate, Bush insisted that 'the jury is still out on the Soviet experiment'.[20] His attempt to re-enact this success in 1992, with a patriotic appeal which condemned the Democrat Bill Clinton's avoidance of the draft in the Vietnam War, proved a failure. The voters had shifted their perspective from foreign affairs to domestic worries, from strategic security to job security.

By global standards, the United States had suffered a very moderate recession, which was ending as they went to the polls in 1992. Inflation was down to 3 per cent, the stock market traded near its all-time high, unemployment at 7.5 per cent was modest by European standards, the USA was once again the world's leading exporter and the US economy was still growing. The last GDP figures released before the election suggested that the recession had indeed ended and the economy was growing at 2.7 per cent a year. But the mood was dreadful, and as the 1992 election approached the opinion polls suggested that the malaise was swelling like the Federal budget deficit, even though the total Federal debt is still a smaller proportion of GDP than the economy managed quite comfortably in the peak years between 1943 and 1957.[21]

Like Britain after 1945, American sense of achievement at having 'won' the Cold War was overshadowed by the perceived economic costs of that victory. And like Britain in the entire post-war period, when the average economic growth rate of around 3 per cent a year surpassed the growth rates of the supposedly golden age of economic dominance in the nineteenth century, the USA frets at the perception of relative decline. Britain and the USA have grown far richer and more prosperous, runs the popular argument, but less quickly than their former enemies, Germany and Japan. This may be true of Japan, but it is demonstrably false of Germany. In the 1970s, the West German and US economies averaged annual growth of 3.1 per cent. In the 1980s, West German growth averaged 1.8 per cent, a worse performance than the US growth rate of 2.6 per cent over that decade.[22]

The 1992 American Presidential election was the first to be fought after the end of the Cold War. And while foreign affairs played little direct part in the political debate, the leitmotif of the Cold War ran through the year. President Bush justified his re-election with the claim that 'We won the Cold War', while the Democrats tended to take their text from their early candidate, former Senator Paul Tsongas, who complained that 'The Cold War is over – and Japan won'.[23]

Beyond the slogans, a far deeper debate was taking place. In the course of 1992, to observe the American foreign-policy establishment thinking aloud was rather like getting a bird's-eye view of a grand naval engagement in the great days of sail. As the reports dropped from the think-tanks and institutions of the great and the good, the image of a stately fleet of galleons tacking as one to the new prevailing wind was irresistible. The common theme among them was that the world of geopolitics, in which national virility was measured in missiles and megatonnes, has been replaced by a world of geofinance, in which power comes out of the export industries and the currency markets. And because of this, runs the new thinking, the United States had better see to its sails and its rigging and restive crew, scour the weeds and barnacles from its fouled hull, and make its economy shipshape for the fray.

'Our foreign policy must be founded on a renewal of our domestic strength; rebuilding our economic base is now our highest priority,' began the report from the prestigious Carnegie Commission.[24]

> To advance our interests abroad we must get our own house in order. An America that lacks economic strength and social cohesion will lose respect abroad . . . Greater economic parity among North America, East Asia and Europe has caused a sea change in world trade and finance. We have no choice but to move from what was formerly the hegemony of a single country to collective management by the industrial democracies.

The Carnegie Commission was composed of men who could claim to have manned the general staff of America's last great effort of the Cold War. They included Reagan's former Defense Secretary Frank

Carlucci, former chairman of the Joint Chiefs of Staff Admiral William Crowe (also a Clinton adviser), Barber Conable, the former head of the World Bank, and a group of former assistant secretaries of state, Senators, Congressmen and bankers, and Tom Donahue, secretary-treasurer of the AFL–CIO, the main trade-union organisation. Their chairman was Winston Lord, a former aide to Dr Kissinger and a former US Ambassador to China, who launched the report in Washington with a blistering critique of President Bush's performance: 'The treatment of foreign policy seems somewhere between distressing and appalling,' Lord told a press conference. 'We see no coherent vision here or abroad.'[25]

The Carnegie Commission offered two main proposals. The first was that the world needed a new Dumbarton Oaks conference, to reconsider the structure of the United Nations, the Security Council and other international organisations. The second was that the G7 group of leading industrial nations should become the G3, of the United States, Japan and the European Community. They should reorder the structures of the global economy, to 'review the present institutional arrangements, including the division of responsibilities among the World Bank, the IMF, other international financial organisations and the UN'. This is evidently an agenda for a new Bretton Woods, the 1944–5 conference at which Britain and the United States laid out the post-war economic order, based on the dollar and the pound sterling as the international reserve currencies, at fixed exchange rates. The new focus on the G3 makes it clear that the new world economic order will be based on the dollar, the yen and the Ecu (or Deutschmark), and the objective will be to establish some ground rules for the competitive fray of the new global economy.

In addition to these grand declarations, a number of books and essays were published by various commentators (many of whom expected influential posts in a Clinton Administration), which also explore the need for a dramatic reassessment of the American course. Harvard's Professor Robert Reich, an intimate friend of Governor Clinton since the young Arkansan held the seasick Reich's head over the side of the ocean liner taking them to Oxford and their Rhodes Scholarships, put the American dilemma with characteristic force:[26]

> The next president of the United States either will lead the world into an era of unprecedented peace and growth, in which virtually all nations are knitted together into a seamless economic web, or will watch the world fragment into three trading blocs of advanced and rapidly developing nations and a fourth vast territory – stretching from South America through central Africa, eastern Europe and central and

> southern Asia – largely characterised by deepening poverty, ethnic strife, and civil chaos.

Mr Michael Mandelbaum, formerly of the Council on Foreign Relations (CFR) and then helping coordinate Mr Clinton's foreign policy from the Johns Hopkins School of Advanced International Studies, found that: 'The post-Cold War international agenda is beginning to take shape. It is not likely to be dominated by military confrontation between great nuclear powers, or even by crises like the one in the Persian Gulf. Instead, economic issues will predominate, particularly as former Communist Europe and countries in other regions move toward market institutions and practices.'[27]

Mr Robert Hormats of Goldman Sachs, the trading house which proved the most generous single contributor to the Clinton campaign coffers, and a former assistant Secretary of State for Economic Affairs, took this econocentrism yet further, and more stridently:[28]

> If America's economy does falter, so will the underlying source of its international power. Thus the nation's central foreign policy priority in the coming years and its central domestic priority must be the same: strengthening the American economy. Unless the United States reinvigorates in this decade the economic roots of its international power, it risks an erosion of self-confidence and of its international leadership at the turn of the century. With a weak economy and society in conflict over how to allocate slowly growing resources, this nation would find it increasingly difficult to achieve its essential global objectives . . . The danger for the United States at the end of this century is not imperial overstretch but domestic underperformance.

Mr Hormats's imperial echo recalls a final parallel with Britain which has been little noticed. Just over forty years ago, a Princeton undergraduate submitted as his final thesis an extraordinarily long paper on Ernest Bevin, the former trade-union boss who became Britain's legendary Foreign Secretary from 1945 to 1951.[29] The young James Baker, who was to become President Bush's Secretary of State and later the White House chief of staff and campaign tsar, was fascinated by Bevin's skill at masking the implications of British economic decline. Bevin's trick was to lock the British long-term international role into a series of institutions which would extend the country's influence far beyond its economic merits. The UN Security Council, the World Bank and IMF, Nato and a series of other pacts were Bevin's vehicles to defend British interests far into the declining future.

Mr Baker's subsequent career suggests that he learned Bevin's lesson well. As Treasury Secretary under President Reagan, he established with the Plaza and Louvre Agreements an institution of the industrial world's central banks to manage exchange rates and the orderly decline of the dollar. While maintaining Nato as the institution which gave the United States an automatic leadership in the Atlantic Alliance, he extended it to Eastern Europe with the North Atlantic Consultative Council. In Asia, Baker tried in 1987–8 to establish a Pacific version of the G7 group of industrialised nations which he dubbed P7. To his intense frustration, he found that Hong Kong's colonial status, and difficulties over Taiwan, prevented its fruition. In compensation, Baker built up the Asia–Pacific Economic Cooperation Process, bringing in China, Hong Kong and Taiwan at the third ministerial meeting in Seoul. He also defined it in notably grandiose terms:[30]

> To visualise the architecture of US engagement in the region, imagine a fan spread wide, with its base in North America, and radiating west across the Pacific. The central support is the US–Japan alliance, the key connection for the security structure and the new Pacific partnership we are seeking. To the north, one spoke represents our alliance with the Republic of Korea. To the south, others extend to our treaty allies – the Association of Southeast Asian (ASEAN) countries of the Philippines and Thailand. Further south, a spoke extends to Australia – an important, staunch economic, political and security partner. Connecting these spokes is the fabric of shared economic interests now given form by the Asia–Pacific Economic Cooperation Process . . . Similarly, the emerging North American Free Trade Area will support both APEC and the global, multilateral systems for trade and financial flows.

Mr Baker's fondness for international institutions to sustain America's global role did not always meet with success. His suggestion before the House foreign affairs committee in September 1991 that the most sensible way to guard against any future Iraqi threats was for a security pact between the United States and its allies in the Gulf, was instantly mocked as 'Gulfo', Middle East child of Nato, in the *New York Times*. Mr Baker, ever sensitive to his image and his press relations, dropped the idea like a hot brick. But this was all a part of the global vision of American foreign policy under new and straitened circumstances which Mr Baker spelt out in the policy paper he delivered to the US Senate for his confirmation hearings as Secretary of State:[31]

> We enter a new era characterized especially by the greater strength of our friends. We live in a world of increasingly influential allies whose cooperation is essential if we are to surmount common problems. There are new global dangers, such as terrorism, the international narcotics trade, and the degradation of the world's environment, that cannot be managed by one nation alone – no matter how powerful. These realities will not permit a blind isolationism or a reckless antagonism.

Since the signing of the INF Treaty in 1987 and the announcement of Soviet withdrawal from Afghanistan in 1988, there really has not been a coherent American foreign policy, in spite of Mr Baker's spasmodic conceptualisations before House and Senate committees. The world's only superpower has been floundering about its role ever since Georgi Arbatov first made his prescient warning from his office at Moscow's old US and Canada Institute. 'We are going to do the worst thing we possibly can to America – we are going to take away their enemy,' Arbatov predicted back in 1987. So it proved. The main organising principle of American policy for nearly fifty years, opposition to the Soviet Union, slowly disappeared.[32] Since then, there has been grandiose talk of President Bush's 'New World Order', which seems in retrospect to have been a phrase looking around vaguely for a policy. In the Persian Gulf, it meant collective international action against aggression, led by America. In what used to be Yugoslavia, the New World Order did not seem to mean anything at all. If there were a common thread to the post-Gulf foreign policy, then in both Bosnia and Somalia it seemed to be inspired by the degree of misery portrayed through American TV screens, with the crisis defined by CNN, the media network, and the Administration's response calibrated according to the interest of TV current-affairs programmes.

The Bush Administration was extraordinarily ready to enjoy the fruits of America's uniquely global military reach as the end of the Cold War removed the customary restraint which the Soviet Union had provided, both in a military sense and at the United Nations. There was the brisk little invasion of Panama, whose main result seems to have been the incarceration of General Manuel Noriega in an American gaol. Panama's role as a major drugs trans-shipment centre was not long interrupted, and the hapless economy continued to suffer from the long American embargo.

There was Operation Desert Storm, in which, aside from the expulsion of Iraqi troops from Kuwait, the rest of its desired results drifted off into what we may call Operation Desert Sands. We can hardly speak of the liberation of Kuwait, more of the reinstatement of an authoritarian system which had the one merit of being familiar. Saddam Hussein remained in power. The Gulf remained a dangerous region, with the threat from Iraq's once-swollen army replaced by the swift and massive rearmament in Iran. Saudi Arabia remained the last, best hope of the American defence industries. The region after President Bush's splendid little war looked most remarkably as it did before it.

There were other military forays in the Bush years. The US Marines deployed swiftly and efficiently into Liberia in 1991 to evacuate American and other Western nationals from a horrid civil war which still sputtered on. And the 1992 operation in Somalia was Mr Bush's second bite at this particular cherry. The Marines were deployed briefly in 1991 to evacuate the American Embassy from the galloping anarchy. The Somali relief operation did not come as much of a novelty to the US forces. They learned about this kind of mission in Operation Provide Comfort, helping to guard and feed the hundreds of thousands of Kurdish refugees in northern Iraq.

The Bush record of six military interventions in four years is remarkable. Two wars, two armed evacuations, and two armed relief efforts in which the troops went in with guns cocked. This is not to mention the domestic deployments in the Los Angeles riots in the spring of 1992, 'to win back the city, block by block and street by street', in Pat Buchanan's pungent phrase to the Republican Party convention later that year.[33] The end of the Cold War was not a quiet time for the US armed forces. The Marines had rarely been so busy as under President Bush, even if they had started to become a form of mercenary. Their overseas operations had become contingent on the liquidity of foreign paymasters; the deployment of America's troops in the inner city of Los Angeles spoke of another form of humiliation.

In the aftermath of the Cold War, in the final months of the Bush Presidency, the United States seemed to be stumbling rather painfully through its own Brezhnev era. A remote and privileged political élite inside its Beltway-Kremlin remained obsessed with the lure of global grandeur and the weaponry and military reach. And beyond that bureaucratic fortress, an increasingly alienated public grappled with the besetting sense of economic decline, sought escape in damaging drugs, and almost half the eligible voters declined to encourage its discredited rulers by participating in the electoral system.

At the end of the twelve years of Republican Presidencies under Reagan and Bush, the concept of the West as a series of liberal-capitalist democracies sharing common values and a broadly similar social system was hardly tenable. In its attitudes to the death penalty, to the penal system, to the acceptance of violence, to abortion, to fundamental criteria of civilisation like health care for all, and in the wide disparity of incomes, the United States was sharply distinct from its European and Japanese allies. By December 1992, a total of 186 Americans had been legally executed since the death penalty was resumed by the Supreme Court in 1976.[34] No other Nato member used the death penalty. The homicide rate among young males between the ages of fifteen and twenty-four was twenty times higher in the USA than in Britain, West Germany or France, and forty times higher than in Japan.[35]

The similarities between Moscow in the early 1980s and Washington in the early 1990s became eerily acute to one who had lived through both. The contrast between the former Soviet Union's release of its prisoners, and the way that the USA had over one million of its citizens incarcerated, summoned the bizarre, dismaying thought of an America Gulag. It was inhabited by criminals rather than dissidents, but America in 1992 boasted 426 prisoners per 100,000 population, well ahead of South Africa (333 per 100,000) and the Soviet Union (268 per 100,000). And the American prison population was rising at 13 per cent a year.[36]

Stalin's Gulag was remarkable, not only for its persecution of dissidents, but for its victimisation of entire social classes, like the kulaks, or of racial groups. This was also a chilling feature of the American penal system, in which a black American male was four times more likely to be in prison than a black South African. One in four black Americans aged twenty to twenty-nine is either in prison, on probation, or on parole (compared to one in sixteen for whites). The number of black men in this age group under the control of the criminal justice system, 609,690, was greater than the number of black men in college, 436,000.[37]

The devastating health statistics which showed that Brezhnev's Soviet Union was failing its people found a grim resonance in George Bush's America. Life expectancy for black men began to decline in the 1980s, and in Harlem was worse than Bangladesh.[38] The Centre for the Study of Social Policy in 1991 released a report which compared the life of American children at the start and at the end of the 1980s. The percentage of children in poverty was 22 per cent worse, the juvenile custody rate (age ten to fifteen years) was 10 per cent worse, the violent death rate for the ages fifteen to nineteen was 11 per cent worse.[39]

The pattern of income distribution in the United States was also sharply different from that of its allies. In 1992, the Worldwatch

Project analysed the household-income statistics of the 1980s to establish the proportion of rich (those in the most affluent 20 per cent of households) against poor (those in the least affluent 20 per cent). In the United States, there were twelve times as many poor as rich. In Britain and Germany, there were only four times as many poor, and in Japan and the Soviet Union, only three times as many poor. The startling conclusion is that the income distribution patterns of America's allies looked very much more like the Soviet enemy than they resembled the American friend.[40]

The end of the Cold War brought the price that had been exacted from America and its institutions and social structures into furious focus with the Los Angeles riots of 1992. The Presidential campaign of Bill Clinton, and the grand statements of national direction which emerged from the think-tanks, were rooted in an admission of domestic failure as the cost of global success. The Soviet Union had paid with its very existence for the attempt to sustain the Cold War, and then to reform itself along more humane lines while keeping up the gross military burden. But the United States too had suffered grievously in the epic confrontation. The costs of the Cold War, and the distortions it inflicted upon the social systems of what had been the world's two most powerful economies, suggested that the superpowers had become superlosers during the Cold War's final decade. The USSR had broken, and the USA had bent under the strain. If they did not quite copy Sherlock Holmes and Dr Moriarty in their final struggle, plunging over the Reichenbach Falls together in a deadly embrace, then the USA was left clinging perilously and exhausted to the rim while the Soviet Union crashed down to the rocks below.

But with that resilience and readiness to change which has always distinguished the American way, the battered survivor stumbled to its feet and began searching around for remedies. The Committee for Economic Development, harking back to its 1945 papers which helped make the case for the World Bank and International Monetary Fund, published its own prescription for the future in *The United States and the New Global Economy: A Rallier of Nations*. The intellectual trend to global and national planning was even more marked in the CED study. It offered six principles: the first three were collective security, free trade, and promoting growth in the developing world. But the other three principles were rooted in the severe domestic challenge.

'America's effective performance as a leader is not a foregone conclusion. Our economy and society are plagued with a number of serious problems, ranging from social welfare to education to huge budget deficits to inadequate investment in our own future, that threaten to erode our competitiveness and stability,' the CED report argued. The US should accordingly 'shift its emphasis from military strength to industrial strength', and should do so through explicit and planned social engineering. 'The government should shift federal policy away from encouraging consumption and toward favoring productive saving and investment . . . The US should pursue a comprehensive human investment strategy that begins before each citizen's birth and continues throughout his or her working life.'[41]

The overwhelming impression given by the CED report, by the Carnegie Commission and by the success of the Clinton campaign in 1992, is that the intellectual hegemony enjoyed by the free-marketeers in the Reagan–Thatcher era of the 1980s had withered. Free markets were praised, and their magical effects recommended to the Eastern European and former Soviet nations. But the real thrust of the new American consensus was for state intervention to restore a damaged socio-economic fabric, and global planning based upon international agreement.

The other remarkable feature of America's new econocentric consensus was that it represented a return to the values of what any European would recognise as social democracy. The lesson which sank in after the 1980s is that those nations which America perceived to be doing better were either classic social democracies themselves, like Germany, or those East Asian countries which cleaved to free-market principles in their export trades, while running their domestic economies with a great deal of central planning, *dirigisme* and explicit social engineering.

The common theme of America's new consensus was that while they may claim to have won the Cold War, the free-market theories of the Reagan–Thatcher era of the 1980s amounted to a damaging Anglo-Saxon delusion. The sense of domestic crisis helps to explain why the American foreign-policy establishment shifted the weight of its support to the revamped Democratic strategies of the new President Bill Clinton. The Clinton health-reform plan was based on public regulation of private provision, a deliberate echo of the German system. Clinton's plan for lifetime education and job training was based on the Swedish model. His belief in government's role in strategic planning for the economy was borrowed partly from the French system and partly from Japan.

'We need to create a partnership among government, business, labor and education – just as our competitors do,' said Clinton's manifesto, *Putting People First*, most of which could have been inserted wholesale into either the Carnegie or the CED reports.[42] Modelled on the Pentagon's Defense Advanced Research Projects Agency, he called for 'a new civilian agency bringing businesses and universities together to develop cutting-edge products and technologies . . . The only way America can compete and win in the 21st century is to have the best-educated, best-trained workforce in the world, linked together by transportation and communications networks second to none,' the Clinton–Gore manifesto went on. And that is where government comes in.

During the 1980s hegemony of Reagan–Thatcher free-market economics, that would have been a losing philosophy for the Democrats. But Reagonomics were discredited, and the conservative movement was exhausted, just as the old Democratic welfare policies were exhausted after Lyndon Johnson's bold Great Society programmes in the 1960s. After their triumphs of the 1980s, the Republicans (and Britain's Conservatives) were similarly bereft of any strategy but to defend old ideas which demonstrably no longer worked. Clinton's Democrats were by contrast energised with the prospect of regaining power, and this time with a purpose that looked new to American eyes. But it was all deeply familiar to anyone who studied Willy Brandt's SDP, or Gaullist France, or even Harold Wilson's permissive Britain with its vaunted 'white heat of the technological revolution' from the perspective of the young Bill Clinton, Rhodes Scholar, at his Oxford college in 1969. And significantly, much of the new consensus was also rather familiar to that member in good standing of the American foreign-policy establishment, that great political survivor and early student of the implications of British decline, Mr James Baker.

There is an extraordinary contradiction here. Few diagnoses of the American decline would find automatic agreement among America's friends, or her former enemies. What Joseph Nye astutely called the 'soft power' of American cultural influence and her political values had never been stronger than at the Cold War's end. One had only to ask a Moscow black-marketeer which currency he worked in, or Mexican entrepreneurs why they supported the North American Free Trade Agreement, or a member of Japan's reformist New Party what kind of democracy she sought. The text that the victorious Czech dissidents read aloud during their velvet revolution was Thomas Jefferson. The symbol the Chinese students hauled into Tienanmen Square was the Statue of Liberty.

The collapse of the Communist Party in its heartland reinforced the verdict of the Cold War. The global dominance of US military power, and its subtle ideology of free markets, democratic institutions and American culture, appeared to be beyond challenge. The ability of other nations to conduct an independent foreign policy, or of Third World countries to adopt a different development model, had never been more constrained. And yet America's foreign policy beyond the Cold War will be resting uneasily upon the irony that the American international triumph sits upon an enfeebled domestic base, ill-suited to the trading challenges which lie ahead. The passing of the Cold War implied equally the passing of the historic justification for America's global stewardship. The revolution in Moscow and the final resolution of the Cold War left an America curiously bewildered about the shape of President Bush's New World Order for a lonely superpower which had lost her familiar crusade and had yet to find a role. It left a Russia shorn of the empire accumulated by tsars and commissars, while confronted with the flotsam of that empire in large and worried Russian minorities in the new neighbour states.

Like defeated Germany and Japan in 1945, the exhausted successor states to the Soviet Union represented at once a reproach, a potential threat, and an enormous opportunity. The remarkable generation which had steered American foreign policy to the creation of the West after 1945 found, sadly, no echo in the politics of pygmies which afflicted the West in 1992. Having failed to steel himself to invest in Gorbachev before 1991, President Bush offered little more than palliatives to Boris Yeltsin in 1992. The disgraced former President Nixon returned to Washington to make a moving plea for Western support and investment in the hope of Russian democracy. In a speech to an audience which included President Bush, and simultaneously in a privately circulated memorandum entitled *How to Lose the Cold War*, Nixon accused Bush of

> failing to seize the moment to shape the history of the next half-century . . . If Yeltsin fails, the prospects for the next fifty years will turn grim. The Russian people will not turn back to Communism. But a new, more dangerous despotism based on Russian nationalism will take power. If a new despotism prevails, everything gained in the great peaceful revolution of 1991 will be lost. War could break out in the former Soviet Union as the new despots use force to restore the 'historical borders' of Russia.[43]

The failure, and indeed the inability, of the exhausted America of 1992 to invest in the building of a vast new market of some 400 million people who were hungry for capitalism was all the odder, because financial power and far-sighted investment had been the key to the West's success. Every time the West fought after 1945, it lost or at least failed to win. But while suffering reverses on the battlefields of Korea, Dien Bien Phu, Suez and Vietnam, the West managed to build up regional economic bases in Europe and in Asia which were to prove decisive in the long run, when the rising yen and a resurgent Europe came to the rescue of the reeling dollar after 1985. They were returning the great service that the post-war generation of Americans had provided by building up the Japanese and Western European economies four decades earlier, when the United States had been ready to use its economic strength as a strategic weapon.

The great question about the America of the 1990s was whether it still could muster the national will to think about its economic priorities in such strategic terms. It could easily afford to do so. The US economy had throughout the 1950s and 1960s devoted over 7 per cent of GDP to its defence budget each year, and at the peaks of the Korean and Vietnam wars, far, far more. In the 1990s, that defence share fell from barely 5 per cent of GDP in 1990 to 4 per cent by 1993. One per cent of American GDP was $50 billion; such a sum, invested in a new Marshall Plan for Eastern Europe, was easily manageable. Two per cent would not have been a great strain. But the America which failed to seize the opportunity of the peace after the Cold War was an America which had failed to invest in its own infrastructure and in its own economy throughout the 1980s. It was, in short, a country which had lost sight of the strategic implications of economic choices. The America of the 1990s was a country living off the strategic capital piled up by wiser and thriftier forebears.

'If the United States is to increase its investment ratio significantly, that increase will have to come primarily from the 75 per cent or more of the GNP devoted to consumption, not from the less than 7 per cent committed to defence,' warned Harvard Professor Samuel Huntington, as the Cold War ended. 'Consumerism, not militarism, is the threat to American strength. The declinists have it wrong; Montesquieu got it right: "Republics end with luxury; monarchies with poverty." '[44]

Epilogue
Transcending the Nation State

This Birth was
Hard and bitter agony for us, like Death, our death.
We returned to our places, these Kingdoms,
But no longer at ease here, in the old dispensation,
With an alien people clutching their gods,

'Journey of the Magi', T. S. Eliot

During the international economic summit at Houston in 1990, the leaders of the G7 nations still basked in the tail-end of the 1980s boom and the conviction that the West had prevailed in the Cold War. One bemused French diplomat confided that he felt he had suddenly been transported to an alternative universe, in which World War Two had ended in a negotiated peace early in 1943.[1] In that year, Japan's Greater East Asian Co-Prosperity Sphere had been largely intact, and it dominated Korea, Hong Kong and Shanghai, eastern China, Indo-China, the Philippines and what are now the ASEAN countries. Germany held sway from the Atlantic Ocean to the River Volga, from Norway's North Cape to Crete and Sicily. Allowing for the gross difference between brutal militarism and benign economic influence, the Frenchman's point was clear enough. Japan and Germany had secured through their economic exertions during the Cold War much of what they had sought, and failed to attain, in the hottest war the world has yet endured.

But there is a larger truth to the Frenchman's thought, taking the perspective further back in history than the conventional starting-point of the Cold War in 1945. American and Soviet interests first visibly clashed, after the Yalta conference, over the corpse of a conquered Nazi Germany. Indeed, the Cold War can be seen as just the latest skirmish in Europe's long, long war over the German question. Throughout the nineteenth-century, France exhausted herself in the doomed effort to prevent Germany from uniting, and then from becoming the dominant power in Europe. Unable to sustain the burden alone, France summoned tsarist Russia and Britain to her aid in the twentieth century, and they too exhausted themselves in the process. In 1917–18, and in 1941–5, it took the new energies of the United States and the ferocious discipline of Stalin's Soviet Union to subdue the German beast. And once the Soviet state had fallen, no power on the Eurasian mainland could prevent Germany from rising again.

To see the Cold War as the latest resolution of the German question is to impose once again that Eurocentrist perspective on global affairs which for so long encouraged historians to see world history in terms of the endless warfare of the European tribes. Nearly thirty years ago that perspective was dramatically shifted by the British historian Geoffrey Barraclough, who suggested that the Cold War had really begun in the Pacific Ocean in the first years of this century. Russia and the United States had throughout the nineteenth century tended to support one another against Britain's global sway.[2]

> Now, as England's power passed its zenith, they came face to face across the Pacific. This began a conflict of interests which was eventually to spread to Europe, to south-east Asia and the Middle East, until in the end it divided the world into two hostile camps. What today we too easily simplify as an ideological conflict – the so-called 'cold war' – had its origins in the new power constellation which began to take shape at the beginning of the twentieth century.

That new power constellation was thrust into a new dimension by the clash of ideology. The nature of war was changed in the twentieth century not only by the advance of technology, bringing the prospect of nuclear annihilation, but also because the implications of defeat became more dreadful. From the terrible evidence of their conquests, defeat at German or Japanese hands in World War Two did not simply mean the loss of provinces and the change in ruling personnel. Such adjustments had been the characteristics of European warfare since the end of the Crusades and the later civil wars of the Christian religion. Defeat for Slavs at Hitler's hands meant servitude and slave labour, the death camp and the fate of Untermensch, a lesser form of human. And the prospect of ideological defeat by the Soviet Union involved the threat of wholesale transformation, the levelling of the rich and powerful, the suppression of the Church and the expropriation of property. The century of total war brought the logical consequence of total defeat.

Communism also sought to hold out the alternative of total liberation, a seductive promise for the poor and exploited, and a threat of domestic revolt for the established authorities. In the developed world, that seduction became steadily less potent as the successes of post-war capitalism and its welfare states became more apparent. In the colonised lands of Asia and Africa, and those in Latin America who felt themselves to be economic colonies, Communism was able to hold out a new prospect of liberation by embracing the causes of national independence and of racial equality. As the Western European heartland of the classic industrial working class held firm, this second wave of Marxism–Leninism shifted the ideological focus to the developing world. While professing support for national independence, America found itself in Indo-China sucked into opposing nationalism, and suffered a severe local defeat as a result.

Even as that defeat was being inflicted, and the colonial empires of France and Britain had been replaced by a range of more or less successful and more or less representative local governments, the Soviet suppression of the Prague Spring in 1968 helped shift the colonial argument back again. In the twenty years after the invasion of Czechoslovakia, the Soviet Union was vulnerable to the charge that it was the last of the nineteenth-century colonial empires. For a Hindu, an Uzbek, a Cambodian or an Ndebele, what white folk called the Cold War might with justice have been interpreted as the era of global liberation from white rule.

There are sound historical arguments for playing down the role of ideology in the Kremlin's relations with the outside world from 1917 until the formal ending of the Communist Party's 'leading role' in the state in 1991. For the ten years after the 1917 October Revolution, a period which saw invasion by the capitalist powers, and attempted Communist revolutions in Germany and Hungary, the ideology was central. Once the Soviet Union had adopted the policy of 'socialism in one country' in Stalin's day, ideology played little role in Soviet relations with the United States – at least until the two systems came into direct contact after 1945. Ideology had been central to Soviet relations with Europe in the cockpit of the Spanish Civil War, even though Stalin signed the non-aggression pact with Hitler in 1939 for reasons of *realpolitik*. After 1945, the United States and Soviet Union confronted one another on a series of fronts, from the United Nations to central Europe, in divided Korea and divided Vietnam, under the banner of the Free World on the one side and class and colonial liberation on the other.

The labels were important. The concept of the Free World was not simply useful, it took on real force after the admission of Stalin's Terror and the crushing of Budapest in 1956, and the erection of the

Berlin Wall in 1961. It also reflected the skill with which the countries of the West had modified the failed capitalism of the 1930s into the far more productive social democracies of the 1950s. By the last decade of the Cold War, the supreme irony had emerged of the Soviet Union steadily diluting its ideological commitment, while the Reagan and Thatcher government promoted their own counter-ideology of free markets and private property with proselytising fervour.

These ideological statements constantly harked back to another era, the interwar years of 1921–39 when Fascist Italy and Nazi Germany did claim to be offering an alternative form of state mobilisation to Soviet Communism. Successive Soviet propagandists hurled accusations of neo-Fascism at their Western antagonists after 1945, while the West denounced the spasmodic and diluted repressions of the Soviet system under Khrushchev and Brezhnev as if it were still in the dreadful grip of Stalin's Terror. The Europe of the 1930s remained a constant reference point because two historical accidents had made the old continent appear far more central to world affairs than it really was. The Soviet Union from exhaustion, and the United States from choice, in effect turned their backs on Europe in the interwar years of 1919–39.

Europe was then suffering the political crisis of the imperial successions. The Hohenzollern Empire had fallen in Germany along with the Austro-Hungarian Empire, and the Italian monarchy was swiftly rendered a nullity by the rise of Mussolini's Fascism. In the absence of US and Russian involvement, the sudden emergence of eight new national states and new ideologies rendered interwar Europe extraordinarily vulnerable to the new dislocations that came with the Great Depression. The political stability imposed by the Cold War thus offered a happy opportunity for the quarrelsome Europeans to establish a new order of their own. This was the political objective that always lay beyond the economic provisions of the Treaty of Rome which established the European Economic Community.

For Jean Monnet and Robert Schuman, the French founding spirits of the EC, economic integration was the way to avert future European wars. Their strategy seemed to succeed in Western Europe. But in the east, the end of the enforced stability of the Cold War led to a vicious war between what had been the constituent republics of Yugoslavia. And if the EC had produced peace and prosperity among its members, the forty years of subservience to American strategic priorities had eroded the Europeans' capacity to act decisively on the continent's own behalf. As Bosnia died, Europe did little more than watch, relieved that Russia's renewed withdrawal from European affairs meant that the Sarajevo of 1992 was not the Sarajevo of 1914; that it would not be the occasion of another clash between the great powers, like the one set in train by the assassination of Archduke Franz-Ferdinand of Austria.

The end of Europe's forty years of enforced peace was followed by war in the Balkans, by the division of Czechoslovakia, by neo-Nazi violence in Germany and political crises in Britain, France and Italy. Without that adult supervision imposed by the Soviet and American military presence, Europe showed dismaying signs of reverting to its familiar squabbles. In this sense, the Cold War was but an interruption in the endless contentions which the white tribes had pursued when there was no dominant authority to keep their irrepressible aggressions in check. The only one to have done so with prolonged success had been the Roman Empire, but then the America of the Cold War itself possessed some of the attributes of Rome. For the old Roman roads that held the Empire together, substitute the airline routes and the global data networks that are the arteries of the modern world. The political system of ancient Rome began as a republic founded on principles of civic virtue and evolved into what we might call an imperial presidency.

It is difficult to think of any other nation, at any other time in history, that could within six weeks have deployed an army of 150,000 men some 5,000 miles from their bases, with tanks and guns and warplanes to match, and without denuding any of its other outposts around the world. The United States did so with ease in the autumn of 1990. From a standing armed force of 2,100,000 troops, and a ready reserve of another 1,650,000, Operation Desert Shield represented less than 5 per cent of President Bush's deployable military force. The US could have lost the lot in a devastating chemical attack, and awful though it would have been, the US military machine would not have been seriously damaged by a loss of fighting power equivalent to the whole of the British Army. Even without that technological superiority which was displayed in the air war against Iraq, the world had not seen this kind of global power since the days of Imperial Rome.[3]

This gave a piquancy to the briefly fashionable notion at the high point of Euro-optimism that the EC was a modern revival of the old Holy Roman Empire. The most elegant expression of this view came from the Polish intellectual and dissident Adam Michnik. He suggested to an audience in Moscow late in 1989 that the rich, white world of the northern hemisphere was coming to resemble medieval Christendom. A number of different principalities were then held loosely together by a single faith, by the élites' shared language of Latin, and by the common enemy of Islam, while new forms of commerce and capital organisation sapped at a moribund social and political structure. Substitute the free market for Christianity, American–English for Latin, the transnational corporations for the Lombard bankers, and allow for considerably more erosion of the modern nation state, and Michnik's point is clear.[4]

It is the durability of the nation state as an institution that will provide the key to the world which will finally emerge from the aftermath of the Cold War. The nation state had begun as a form of social organisation to sustain an eternal preparedness for war. In Tudor England and then in seventeenth-century France, the Europe-wide power of Imperial Spain was challenged and overcome by monarchies which were able to impose a bureaucracy and a taxation system that could provide for a standing armed force. This proved so popular that by the eighteenth century, every European nation and principality could boast one, and several had followed England's example of building a professional navy. The maintenance of the Royal Navy, through its dockyards and ordnance factories, its provision of masts and spars from the Baltic forests, and its training of a permanent officer corps, was probably the most advanced and coherent example of industrial organisation the world had hitherto seen.

The next step in this process came when the French Revolution after 1789 proved capable of defeating the professional standing armies of other states through the *levée en masse*. This conscription of the entire nation into a far larger army was the key to Napoleon's success, and the rest of the mainland powers of Europe swiftly followed. This carried interesting political implications: a conscript army was a citizens' army, less liable blindly to carry out the monarch's bidding than a purely professional force. The great Napoleon's nephew, Emperor Napoleon III, based his rule upon the spasmodic consultation of the popular will through plebiscites.

Bismarck's Germany was to advance this symbiosis of state and military by deepening the state's involvement in the social and industrial organisation which sustained the army. The Second Reich became the world's first welfare state, with a parliamentary democracy based on universal manhood suffrage. It was, in effect, the prototype of the modern industrial state. A social insurance and national education system were combined with an industrial policy to build the economic, social and political base for state power. From 1870, when the successful war against France established the new and united German Empire, to 1914 when the organised military power was unleashed, French defence spending doubled, British defence spending tripled, and that of Germany grew tenfold.[5]

'The continent has been converted into a series of giant armed camps, within each of which a whole nation stands in arms,' noted *The Economist* of 1879.[6] In such a condition of tense peace, a prototype of the later Cold War emerged, complete with alliances, arms races, peace movements, propaganda, secret wars between intelligence agencies, and domestic repression in the name of national security. The naval arms race between the British and the German fleets in the years before 1914, vying for technological advances and numerical superiority, bears a striking resemblance to the arms race of missiles later in the century. The similarity extended even to a reluctance to use the Grand Fleets, for as Winston Churchill noted of Admiral Jellicoe, he was 'the only man who could lose the war in an afternoon'.

The pattern is clear: the development of the modern nation state proceeding in step with the organisation of an increasingly complex society for an increasingly devastating war. The Cold War was to push that double development to its logical limit, in the organisation of one society to be able to inflict utter extermination upon another, while bracing itself to live under the constant threat of annihilation by the other side.

But the Cold War took the process one essential step further than the best that Victorian and Edwardian social engineers had been able to achieve before 1914. By extending the nuclear threat and the nuclear umbrella over their allies, both the United States and the Soviet Union pushed the structural organisation for war beyond the nation state and extended it to entire continents. And while Britain and France had fought their eighteenth-century wars in Asia and in North America as well as in Europe, the Cold War conscripted large tracts of the world into the great rivalry. The scale of the war which could now be organised had far outgrown the old nation states. It required the development of superpowers, whose strength lay in the combination of unprecedented military, scientific, technological, industrial and economic power. Failure to keep pace in any one of these fields spelt defeat, even when the superpower was never tested on the field of battle.

The theme of this book has been that if the Cold War can be said to have been 'won', then success was achieved not by the military and diplomatic achievements of the United States, but by its rallying of a wholly new international economic structure to the cause. When the American economy faltered, the European and Japanese economies which American policy had cultivated were able to take up the slack. In the process, and barely understanding what was accumulating before their eyes, the three components of the West created like Dr Frankenstein a new and self-generating force which was beyond their power to control. We can already say that the real significance of the Cold War, which has dominated the lives of most people now alive, has been to play the role of catalyst in the creation of the extraordinary global economy which will dominate our future.

What is now to be the role of the nation state? The cardinal principle of sovereignty in international affairs, the right to declare war, had been constrained by nuclear caution and alliance responsibilities. The cardinal principle of sovereignty in domestic matters, the right to regulate the currency, to decree taxation and to manage the economy in order to establish social priorities, is now constrained by the enforcement mechanism of the new global economy, the markets. In 1981, the people of France elected a socialist President and government with a clear mandate to embark on social reforms. Within two years, the pressure upon the franc had forced a reversal of course. In the 1980s, the most powerful economy of all was repeatedly forced to cut and then to extend its money supply by global market pressures. The Plaza Agreement of the G5 finance ministers in 1985 provides one emblematic moment when the fate of the American economy passed out of Washington's control.

There were others. On 13 February 1982, the US Federal Reserve was obliged to relax its strategy of grinding down inflation to prevent a Mexican default on its $80 billion debt, which would have had devastating consequences for the US and global banking system.[7] In October 1987, the full resources of all the G7 central banks were barely enough to maintain the liquidity of a global finance system devastated by the sudden collapse of Wall Street's Dow Jones by 22.6 per cent of its value on 'Black Monday'. That in turn had been triggered by the plunge in the Japanese bond markets the previous month, and the attempt by US Treasury Secretary James Baker to talk down the dollar while blaming the German banks.[8] The immediate result was to force American policy to change course, with a $76 billion cut in the US budget, and Mr Baker had to announce his encouragement for the dollar to continue its fall.[9]

Like the nature of superpower war, the global economy has grown beyond the capacity of nation states to control it. It is increasingly difficult even to talk coherently of national economies, when so much of the world's growth potential is now locked in offshore and multinational structures that are designed to avoid any single state's direction. Just as the coming of total war created the need for superpowers with the capacity both to wage and to control it, so the coming of the global economy is creating the need for economic superpowers. The USA has pioneered the way, and Japan and Germany are both growing into the roles. But they do so less on their own terms than as the linchpins of their respective regional trading and currency blocs.

Margaret Thatcher noted at the Houston economic summit in 1990 that the world was becoming organised into three currency zones, of the dollar, the yen and the Deutschemark.[10] In that year, global economic output surpassed $20 trillion, of which the United States accounted for just over 25 per cent, the EC for not quite 30 per cent, and Japan for around 10 per cent. Include the other Asian economies of South Korea, Hong Kong, Taiwan and Singapore, which are increasingly dependent on Japanese trade and investment, and what can loosely be called the yen block contributed 20 per cent of global product.[11]

These three economic superpowers bore an uncanny resemblance to the three warring geographic units of Eurasia, Oceana and Eastasia which George Orwell saw conducting a permanent war in *1984*, a novel which caught the implacable tone of the first years of the Cold War. There is no guarantee that great powers who trade profitably among themselves will never go to war. In 1914, Britain was Germany's best customer. The Britain and Germany of 1914 were parliamentary empires, sufficiently dependent on electoral support to cast some doubt on the fashionable nostrum that democracies never go to war against one another.[12] But in 1993, the prospect of major war between the three great currency blocs, which are still a long way from becoming hostile trading blocs, looks more than remote.

It was at the lower levels of geopolitics, among the tribes and provinces and nation states, that war persisted in the 1990s as an endemic feature of the human condition. The wars of the Soviet Succession in the Caucasus and the Balkans, and in Africa's formerly 'Marxist' states of Angola, Mozambique, Ethiopia and Somalia, could trace their origins to the Cold War. But the spasmodic violence between Hindu and Muslim in India, between Israelis and Palestinians in the Middle East, or between Catholic and Protestant in Northern Ireland, had their roots much deeper in history. These enduring conflicts pointed to the power of two not entirely contradictory trends in human affairs which became apparent in the final years of the Cold War. On the one hand was the centripetal momentum as the nations of Europe and many of the rich world's economies merged into larger blocs, and on the other was the centrifugal force which spun tribes and provinces away from their allegiance to traditional states and empires. In the European Community, regions like Lombardy in Italy, Catalonia in Spain, and Scotland in Britain, pressed for ever more local autonomy from the traditional capital, even while stressing their devotion to the European idea. And in formerly Soviet Central Asia, both forces coincided, spinning the traditional Muslim republics away from Moscow, while simultaneously attracting them towards a new agglomeration under Turkish influence.

In modern China, the extraordinary rates of economic growth which more than doubled the size of the economy between 1980 and 1992 held out the promise of superpower status, an economy on track to surpass that of Germany by the year 2000, that of Japan by the year 2010, and to match that of the United States by the year 2030. But at the same time, the concentration of that economic growth in the coastal provinces around the traditional trading centres of Canton and Shanghai carried its own threat of regional autonomy growing into separatist ambition.[13]

The element which both centrifugal and centripetal forces had in common was the traditional form of social organisation from which the tribes and superpowers each departed, the old nation state. To suggest its death would be ridiculously premature; to question its continuing relevance is natural. Beyond cultural and linguistic affinities, the nation state had emerged as a supremely efficient machine for organising society into a tax and resource base for the purpose of war. That role was far from over, but for the structures of taxation, the old nation states of Europe had a new rival in the embryonic federal authority in Brussels. And for the purposes of war, the role of the nation state had long blurred into alternative structures, everything from the Nato alliance to the United Nations, whose authority was deemed essential for the multinational operations in the Gulf War and the Yugoslav and Somalian relief and peace-keeping efforts.

Peering ahead, there are inevitably far more questions than answers. Without the threat of global war, does the world or the American taxpayer still need the lonely American superpower of the traditional, military form? Or are Asians, Europeans and Americans from Alaska to the Guatemalan border exploring a new form of economic superpower for the new world of geo-finance? Has the nation state been transcended by the new superpower structures, or simply curtailed by the rise of regional ambitions? And are the economic superpowers of the European Community, the North American Free Trade Area and emergent East Asia, themselves simply way-stations on the road to a form of global political organisation which will reflect the dominant new financial presence of the global economy to which the long, long trial of the Cold War had given birth?

In 1993, there were signs that the G7 process, the international economic summits of the seven leading industrial powers, might be growing into such a role. Pressed by President Boris Yeltsin, who wanted Russia to be included in a new G8, the governments of the USA, Japan, Germany, France, Britain, Italy and Canada began laboriously and with doubts and hesitations to cobble together an international rescue fund for the Russian economy. And finally starting to fulfil the grand ambitions that its Bretton Woods founders had envisaged back in 1944, the International Monetary Fund assumed the main coordinating role for the mammoth task. There was a historical elegance to this tantalising prospect: that the global economy which had been the main result of the Cold War should see its first serious attempt at stewardship dedicated to the repair and democratisation of the Cold War's imploded empire.

But the Russian challenge was monstrous in its proportions, and the distractions of the West's domestic recessions and the rash of post-Soviet wars were in themselves compelling. The West had been forged together after 1945 by a communal mood of fear and by an American leadership that was newly self-confident of its power and wealth. The West's new challenge, at a time of American introspection and self-doubt, was to live up to the vision of their fathers who constructed Nato, the Marshall Plan and the global financial institutions after 1945. The key to their success had been the wisdom shown in rebuilding West Germany and Japan as economies and as allies.

Today's case for a similar magnanimity in victory towards Russia almost transcends argument. A prolonged commitment, a reliable and unwavering partnership, an openness of Western markets as much as their treasuries; all these will be required, along with a very far-sighted patience as Russia and Ukraine and Eastern Europe plod at the various and querulous paces through the challenges and opportunities ahead. More than just treasure, the West will have to proceed with faith, with hope and with charity. To phrase matters in those biblical terms is to illuminate the difficulty, perhaps the unlikelihood, of success. Like T. S. Eliot's Magi, we are 'no longer at ease here, in the old dispensation', and have all become in this mysterious world after the Cold War, so many 'alien people clutching their gods'. The old rituals and loyalties are losing their force, and the new are yet to be defined.

Notes

Introduction

1. Senator D. P. Moynihan, 'Letter to New York', 20 April 1990, Washington DC.
2. D. Acheson, *Present at the Creation* (New York: 1969), p. 490.
3. W. Chambers, *Witness* (New York: 1952), p. 25.
4. *New York Times*, 28 November 1956. Khrushchev's remark was made at a Kremlin reception and Soviet officials subsequently complained of a misinterpretation of a Russian metaphor, which should have been translated as, 'We will be present at your grave' or, less provocatively, 'We shall outlive you'.

Chapter 1

1. Nigel Nicolson, *Alex* (London: 1973), p. 276.
2. Robert Sherwood, *Roosevelt and Hopkins* (New York: 1948), p. 867.
3. ibid., p. 850.
4. Martin Gilbert, *The Second World War* (London: 1989), pp. 638–41.
5. ibid., pp. 745–6; see also Theodore Ropp, *World War II*, vol. 21 (Chicago: World Books, 1985), pp. 380–411.
6. Arthur Schlesinger Jr, 'Origins of the Cold War', *Foreign Affairs* (NY), October 1967.
7. Winston S. Churchill, *Triumph and Tragedy* (Boston: 1953), p. 353.
8. Churchill to Eden, 8 May 1944 (PREM 3-399-6) (Public Records Office, London).
9. Churchill, op. cit., pp. 226–8.
10. *The Foreign Office and the Kremlin: British Documents on Anglo-Soviet Relations, 1941–5* (Cambridge: 1984), p. 174.
11. Sir John Colville, *The Fringes of Power: Downing Street Diaries* (London: 1985), entry for 23 January 1945.
12. Andrei Gromyko, *Memories* (London: 1989), p. 59.
13. Isaacson and Thomas, *The Wise Men* (New York: 1986), p. 231.
14. Louis Halle, *The Cold War as History* (New York: 1967), p. 38.

15. Isaacson and Thomas, op. cit., p. 238.
16. ibid., p. 239.
17. Milovan Djilas, *Conversations With Stalin* (Harmondsworth: 1969), pp. 90–1.
18. Sherwood, op. cit., p. 848.
19. ibid., p. 866.
20. ibid., p. 858.
21. Gromyko, op. cit., p. 89.
22. US Department of State, *Foreign Relations of the United States*. (The conferences at Malta and Yalta, 1945.)
23. Sherwood, op. cit., p. 852.
24. US Department of State, op. cit.
25. V. I. Lenin, *Collected Works*, vol. VIII (Moscow: 1964), pp. 233–4. For the kind of use made in the West of this common quotation, see Schlesinger, op. cit.
26. *New York Times*, 3 March 1945.
27. *Time* magazine, 5 March 1945, pp. 36–7. See also W. A. Swonberg, *Luce* (New York: 1972), pp. 229–31.
28. Harriman's report cited in Schlesinger, op. cit. For Vyshinsky's unpleasant behaviour, see *Foreign Relations of the United States*, vol. V (1945), pp. 485–92.
29. Nikolai Tolstoy, *Stalin's Secret War* (London: 1981), pp. 297–327 passim.
30. *Foreign Relations of the United States*, vol. V (1945), p. 1075. See also Averell Harriman, *Peace With Russia?* (NY: 1959), pp. 3–4. See also Isaacson and Thomas, op. cit., pp. 247–8.
31. Isaacson and Thomas, op. cit., p. 249.
32. *New York Times*, 26 June 1941.
33. David McCullough, *Truman* (NY: 1992), pp. 354–5.
34. Harry S. Truman Library, OSS file dated 2 April 1945.
35. Isaacson and Thomas, op. cit., p. 262.
36. ibid., pp. 263–4. But see also McCullough, op. cit., pp. 370–1, who notes that Stettinius was in attendance at this meeting, in spite of his later grumblings that Harriman was going behind his back; see Daniel Yergin, *The Shattered Peace* (Boston: 1977), p. 77.
37. McCullough, op. cit., p. 374ff, has the most detailed recent account of this crucial meeting. But see also Isaacson and Thomas, op. cit., p. 265ff. Stimson, Forrestal, Bohlen and Harriman give similar versions in their diaries, and Truman's own memoir can be found in *Year of Decisions* (NY: 1955), pp. 77–8.
38. Truman, op. cit., pp. 79–82. See also Gromyko, op. cit., p. 96; McCullough, op. cit., p. 377ff.
39. Sherwood, op. cit., pp. 892–902.

40. See Schlesinger, op. cit., who observes that this incident 'is hard enough even for those acquainted with the capacity of the American government for incompetence to believe'.
41. *New York Herald Tribune*, 31 March 1946. See also Isaacson and Thomas, op. cit., p. 236.
42. William A. Williams, *American–Russian Relations* (1952) p. 274.
43. Howard K. Smith, *The State of Europe* (New York: 1949), p. 88. See also W. F. Kimball, 'Lend-Lease and the open door', *Political Science Quarterly* (1 June 1971). See also Dimbleby and Reynolds, *An Ocean Apart* (New York: 1988), pp. 177–81.
44. *The Economist*, 15 December 1945.
45. This time it had indeed been lost. The British code name for nuclear weapons was 'Tube Alloys', and Roosevelt's naval aide had misfiled it under 'Submarines: torpedo tubes'. See Margaret Gowing, *Independence and Deterrence: Britain and Atomic Energy* vol. 1 (London: 1974), p. 76.
46. McCullough, op. cit., pp. 431–2.
47. Truman, op. cit., p. 416.
48. McCullough, op. cit., pp. 407–8, 415, 432.
49. Truman, op. cit., p. 397.
50. Gilbert, op. cit., p. 702.
51. McCullough, op. cit., p. 443.
52. Nikita Khrushchev, *Khrushchev Remembers* (Boston: 1970), p. 232.
53. For Harriman's delays, see Isaacson and Thomas, op. cit., p. 316. For the delaying role of Byrnes, see his memoir, *Speaking Frankly* (1947), pp. 207–8. For the views of Stimson and Marshall, see Isaacson and Thomas, op. cit., p. 310.
54. Isaacson and Thomas, op. cit., p. 317.
55. Khrushchev, 1970, op. cit., p. 236.
56. Halle, op. cit., p. 101.
57. Truman, op. cit., pp. 525–34. See also Isaacson and Thomas, op. cit., pp. 318–20.
58. Truman, op. cit., p. 526.
59. ibid., p. 534.
60. *International Security* (Harvard University), vol. 15, no. 4 (spring 1991), p. 171.
61. Truman, op. cit., p. 102.

Chapter 2

1. Howe and Coser, *The American Communist Party* (New York: 1962), p. 433.
2. *Life*, 29 March 1943.
3. Swonberg, *Luce and His Empire* (New York: 1972), p. 214.

4. ibid., p. 211.
5. *Look*, 27 June 1944; *Collier's*, December 1943.
6. *Antioch* review, September 1954. See also Howe and Coser, op. cit., p. 432–3.
7. Paolo Spriano, *Stalin and the European Communists* (London: 1985), p. 237.
8. Halle, op. cit., p. 73.
9. Denis Healey, *The Time of My Life* (London: 1989), p. 100.
10. A. J. P. Taylor, *A Personal History* (London: 1983), p. 226.
11. G. F. Kennan, *Memoirs: 1925–1950* (Boston: 1967), pp. 37–40, 49–58. See also Isaacson and Thomas, op. cit., pp. 149, 165, 171–2.
12. ibid., p. 246.
13. Cited in Dimbleby and Reynolds, op. cit., p. 183.
14. D. W. Larson, *Origins of Containment* (Princeton: 1985), pp. 246–7.
15. *New York Times*, 17 December 1945.
16. Truman, op. cit., vol. 1, p. 412.
17. *Novoye Vremya* (Moscow), 14 November 1945.
18. Byrnes, op. cit., p. 110ff.
19. Daniels (ed.), *A Documentary History of Communism*, vol. 2 (Vermont: 1984), p. 124.
20. Spriano, op. cit., pp. 275–8, and for the conciliation by the Greek Communists, ibid., p. 253.
21. E. Varga, 'Democracy of a new type', *Mirovoye Khozyaistvo i Mirovaya Politika* (Moscow), no. 3, 1947.
22. *New York Times*, 6 November 1945.
23. Larson, op. cit., p. 246.
24. Truman, op. cit., vol. 1, pp. 551–2.
25. *Pravda*, 10 February 1945.
26. *Time*, 18 February 1946; W. Millis (ed.), *The Forrestal Diaries*, (New York: 1951), pp. 134–5.
27. Halle, op. cit., p. 105.
28. The text cited is the original cable, republished in K. M. Jensen (ed.), *Origins of the Cold War* (Washington DC: US Institute of Peace, 1991). See also 'X' (the pseudonym used by Kennan), 'The sources of Soviet conduct', *Foreign Affairs*, July 1947.
29. Daniel Yergin, *The Prize* (New York: 1991), p. 451.
30. The full text of Churchill's Iron Curtain speech is contained in the *Congressional Record*, 79th Congress, 2nd session (A 1146–7).
31. *Wall Street Journal*, 19 March 1946. See also McCullough, op. cit., pp. 489–90.
32. R. Best, *Co-operation with Like-Minded Peoples: British Influences on American Security Policy 1941–7* (New York: 1986), p. 121.
33. *Pravda*, 13 March 1946.
34. The full text of the Roberts cables is published in Jensen, op. cit.

35. Truman, op. cit., vol. 2, p. 94. See also *Foreign Relations of the United States*, vol. 7 (1946), pp. 529–32.
36. *Foreign Relations of the United States*, vol. 1 (1941), pp. 366–8.
37. The full text of the Novikov cable, which was released from the Soviet foreign ministry archives in 1990, can be found in Jensen, op. cit.
38. M. Truman, *Harry S. Truman* (New York: 1973), p. 347.
39. Cited in Larson, op. cit., pp. 297–8.
40. *New York Times*, 24 October 1946.
41. V. M. Molotov, *Problems of Foreign Policy, Speeches and Statements, 1945–1948* (Moscow: 1949), pp. 215–16.
42. G. C. Herring, *Aid to Russia, 1941–46* (New York: 1976), p. 284.
43. M. McCauley, *Origins of the Cold War* (London: 1983), p. 59.
44. Sir Richard Clarke, *Anglo-American Collaboration in War and Peace* (Oxford: 1982), p. 156.
45. Dean Acheson, *Present at the Creation* (New York: 1969), p. 291.
46. ibid., p. 292.
47. *The Private Papers of Senator Vandenburg* (Boston: 1952), pp. 338–9, give Marshall and Truman the credit. Neither Vandenburg nor Truman in *Memoirs*, vol. II (New York: 1956), p. 103, mentions the role Acheson dramatically describes for himself in Acheson, op. cit., p. 292.
48. Truman, op. cit., 1956, vol. II, p. 106.
49. Herbert Hoover, *An American Epic*, vol. 4 (Chicago: 1959), pp. 246, 253–5; J. F. Dulles, 'Europe must federate or perish', published in *Vital Speeches of the Day*, vol. 13 (1947), pp. 234–6.
50. *Die Welt*, 14 December 1946.
51. *Foreign Relations of the United States*, vol. 3 (1947), pp. 230–2. See also Acheson, op. cit., p. 304.
52. Walter Lippmann, *Washington Post*, 5 April and 1 May 1945.
53. *Foreign Relations of the United States*, vol. 3 (1947), p. 239.
54. *New York Times*, 6 June 1947.
55. *Foreign Relations of the United States*, vol. 3 (1947), pp. 296–308. See also A. Bullock, *Ernest Bevin* (New York: 1983), pp. 390–406, and C. L. Mee, *The Marshall Plan* (New York: 1984), pp. 130–7, and *The Marshall Plan* (Cambridge: 1987), pp. 51–5.
56. McCauley, op. cit., p. 71.
57. Spriano, op. cit., p. 283.
58. Healey, op. cit., pp. 86–7.
59. H. Brandon, *Special Relationships* (New York: 1988), p. 41.
60. A. A. Zhdanov, 'Report on the international situation', in *Politics and Ideology* (Moscow: 1949), pp. 25–54.
61. Spriano, op. cit., pp. 293–5.
62. Zhdanov, op. cit., p. 54.
63. McCauley, op. cit., p. 73.
64. T. Powers, *The Man Who Kept the Secrets* (New York: 1979), pp. 31–3.

65. ibid., pp. 25, 32. See also R. Cline, *Secrets, Spies and Scholars* (New York: 1976), p. 102.
66. Dimbleby and Reynolds, op. cit., p. 189.
67. *Foreign Relations of the United States*, vol. III (1948), p. 48.
68. Acheson, op. cit., p. 436.
69. Isaacson and Thomas, op. cit., p. 458.
70. Fifty US bombs is the figure cited in the authoritative *Sipri Yearbook, 1991* (Stockholm), table 1.8, p. 25, 'Strategic nuclear weapons arsenals'. For the eventual arrival of the atom bombs, see Dimbleby and Reynolds, op. cit., p. 201.
71. Dimbleby and Reynolds, op. cit., p. 191.
72. Acheson, op. cit., p. 410.
73. See *Bulletin of the Atomic Scientists* (Washington DC) (March 1993), p. 48.

Chapter 3

1. NSC 13/2, cited in J. Williams, *Japan's Political Revolution* (Athens, Ga.: 1979), pp. 101–2.
2. Gilbert, op. cit., pp. 537, 722, 724–5. Also, 'Declaration of Independence of the Democratic Republic of Vietnam', 2 September 1945; (English translation in) *Vietnamese Studies* (Hanoi), no. 24 (1970), pp. 195–9.
3. ibid., pp. 574, 701. See also R. M. Blum, *Drawing the Line: The Origin of American Containment Policy in East Asia* (New York: 1982), p. 7.
4. Tang Tsou, *America's Failure in China* (Chicago: 1963), p. 304. See also A. D. Barnett, *China and the Major Powers in East Asia* (Washington DC: 1977), pp. 24–5.
5. Acheson, op. cit., pp. 272–6.
6. Tang Tsou, op. cit., pp. 355–6.
7. Truman, 1956, op. cit., p. 89.
8. W. LaFeber, *America, Russia and the Cold War* (New York: 1985), p. 34. See also Vandenburg, op. cit., p. 529.
9. Dean Rusk, *As I Saw It* (New York: 1990), p. 157.
10. A. Ulam, *The Communists* (New York: 1992), p. 40.
11. ibid., p. 53.
12. ibid., pp. 50–1. See also *Sino-Soviet Relations, 1917–1957* (Moscow: 1959), p. 216.
13. W. Manchester, *American Caesar* (London: 1979), pp. 469–70.
14. M. Walker, *Powers of the Press* (New York: 1983), p. 198.
15. *The Years of MacArthur*, vol. 2 (Boston: 1975), p. 695.
16. R. J. Barnet, *The Alliance* (New York: 1983), p. 65.
17. For the US figures for Japanese casualties, see Manchester, op. cit., p. 465. The Japanese view is cited in Gilbert, op. cit., p. 746.

18. *Japan Statistical Yearbook* (Tokyo: 1989). See also G. Friedman and F. Lebard, *The Coming War with Japan* (New York: 1991), p. 107.
19. Barnet, op. cit., p. 80.
20. Friedman and Lebard, op. cit., pp. 105–7.
21. *San Francisco Examiner*, 7 January 1948. See also 'Remarks of Secretary Royall', *Proceedings of the Commonwealth Club, 1948* (San Francisco: 1949).
22. Rusk, op. cit., p. 158.
23. *Life*, December 1948; *Time*, 20 June 1949.
24. D. Caute, *The Great Fear* (New York: 1978), p. 38.
25. *Guardian*, London/Manchester, 25 June 1992. For Michael Straight's sad tale, see Healey, op. cit., pp. 123–4, and Straight's own memoir, *After Long Silence* (New York: 1983).
26. W. Chambers, *Witness* (New York: 1952), p. 541.
27. M. Barson, *Better Dead than Red* (New York: 1992), unnumbered pages.
28. ibid.
29. R. M. Nixon, *Six Crises* (New York: 1962), p. 69.
30. Caute, op. cit., pp. 15–19.
31. *I. F. Stone's Weekly* (Washington DC), 2 April 1956.
32. Caute, op. cit., pp. 62–5; *New York Times*, 28 March 1951.
33. Nixon, op. cit., p. 67.
34. *Foreign Relations of the United States*, vol. 1 (1950), passim. See also Isaacson and Thomas, op. cit., pp. 495–504; also LaFeber, op. cit., pp. 95–8.
35. Acheson, op. cit., p. 491; Isaacson and Thomas, op. cit., p. 496.
36. *New York Times*, 2 June 1950.
37. M. Hastings, *The Korean War* (London: 1987), p. 44.
38. Acheson, op. cit., pp. 463–6.
39. *US News and World Report*, 7 July 1950.
40. Rusk, op. cit., pp. 162, 166.
41. Gromyko, op. cit., pp. 101–2.
42. US Senate, Foreign Relations Committee, *Hearings, Military Situation in the Far East* (Washington: 1951), p. 10.
43. Hastings, op. cit., p. 43.
44. Mao Tse-tung, *The Present Situation and Our Tasks* (Beijing: New China News Agency, 1948). The texts of Mao's two cables, first released in a limited edition in Beijing in 1990 for the eyes of Chinese Communist scholars, were leaked to the West and published in the *New York Times*, 26 February 1992, p. A4. The extraordinary tale of General Lobov and the intervention of the Soviet Air Force was published in the *Observer*, London, 5 July 1992. See also, 'The Sino-Soviet Alliance and China's Entry into the Korean War', Jian Chen, Working Paper No. 1, Cold War International History Project, Woodrow Wilson Center, Washington DC, June 1992.

45. Hastings, op. cit., passim. For the Truman–Attlee meetings, see Acheson, op. cit., pp. 618–27.
46. Acheson, op. cit., pp. 491, 570ff. The remark 'Korea saved us' was spoken at a Princeton seminar, on 8 July 1953, and cited in Isaacson and Thomas, op. cit., p. 504.
47. US Department of State, *Indochina: The War in Southeast Asia* (Washington: 1951), pp. 1–7.
48. LaFeber, op. cit., p. 106.
49. *Asahi Shimbun* staff, *The Pacific Rivals* (Tokyo: 1971), p. 193.
50. Yutaka Kosai, *The Era of High-Speed Growth* (Tokyo: 1986), p. 72.
51. G. C. Allen, *Japan's Economic Recovery* (London: 1960), pp. 98–9.
52. Walker, 1983, op. cit., p. 198.
53. Yutaka Kosai, op. cit., pp. 66, 69, 74.
54. Barnet, op. cit., p. 263.
55. A. Besher, *Pacific Rim Almanac* (New York: 1991), pp. 140–1.
56. *Asahi Shimbun* staff, op. cit., p. 194.
57. Besher, op. cit., p. 556.
58. *Foreign Affairs* (New York), vol. 29, no. 2 (1951), p. 180.
59. M. and S. Harries, *Sheathing the Sword: The Demilitarisation of Japan* (London: 1987), p. 213.
60. J. H. Buck, 'The Japanese self-defence forces', *Asian Survey*, vol. 7, no. 9 (1967).
61. Cited in LaFeber, op. cit., p. 108.
62. J. K. Emmerson, *Arms, Yen and Power: The Japanese Dilemma* (New York: 1971), p. 426.
63. L. C. Gardner (ed.), *The Korean War* (New York: 1972), p. 311.

Chapter 4

1. Republican National Committee, *1952 Platform* (Washington DC: 1952). See also Halle, op. cit., p. 270; and J. F. Dulles, 'A policy of boldness', *Life*, 19 May 1952. For the gap between the Eisenhower and Dulles speeches, see Sherman Adams, *Firsthand Report* (New York: 1961), p. 93.
2. M. Walker, *The Waking Giant* (New York: 1987), p. 5.
3. *Pravda*, 9 August 1953. Eng. trans. in *Soviet News* (Moscow), 15 August 1953. See 'US–Soviet Intelligence and the Cold War; the "small committee" of information 1952–53', V.M. Zubok, Working Paper No. 4, Cold War International History Project, Woodrow Wilson Center, December 1992, pp. 16–17.
4. Khrushchev, 1970, op. cit., pp. 394, 429.
5. M. J. Hogan, *The Marshall Plan* (New York: 1987), pp. 393, 415.
6. ibid., p. 393.
7. Mee, op. cit., p. 257.

8. Acheson, op. cit., pp. 425–6.
9. R. Bothwell, *Canada and the United States* (Toronto: 1992), p. 28.
10. Hastings, op. cit., p. 74.
11. Hogan, op. cit., p. 274.
12. ibid., p. 276.
13. Healey, op. cit., p. 211.
14. Jeaneney et Julliard, *Le Monde de Beuve-Méry* (Paris: 1974).
15. *Foreign Relations of the United States*, vol. 4 (1949), pp. 469–72.
16. Hogan, op. cit., pp. 27ff. See also Isaacson and Thomas, op. cit., p. 443.
17. *Le Monde*, 2 March 1949. See also the monumental Bellanger *et al.*, *Histoire générale de la presse française*, tome IV (Paris: 1978).
18. Walker, 1983, op. cit., p. 68.
19. Bevin to Attlee, 12 January 1951 (PREM 8/1439) (Public Records Office, London).
20. G. Bing *et al.*, *Keep Left* (London: 1947), pp. 33, 42. House of Commons, *Debates*, 23 April 1951. For Boothby's sneer, see the 12 December 1945 debate, *Hansard*, 5th ser., vol. 417, cols. 463–5.
21. Acheson, op. cit., p. 446.
22. *New York Times*, 8 November 1949.
23. Kai Bird, *The Chairman* (New York: 1992), p. 326.
24. ibid., p. 340.
25. B. Donoughue and G. W. Jones, *Herbert Morrison* (London: 1973), p. 481.
26. A. Sampson, *The New Europeans* (London: 1968), p. 8
27. J. Monnet (trans. R. Mayne), *Memoirs* (New York: 1978), pp. 316–17.
28. F. Kaplan, *Wizards of Armageddon* (New York: 1983), pp. 98–9.
29. Woodhouse memoirs, cited in *The Nation*, 29 October 1990, p. 478.
30. McGeorge Bundy, *Danger and Survival* (New York: 1988), pp. 260–8. See also P. Glyn, *Closing Pandora's Box* (New York: 1992), pp. 157–63.
31. Dimbleby and Reynolds, op. cit., p. 214.
32. S. Ambrose, *Eisenhower*, vol. 2 (New York: 1983–4), p. 184.
33. D. D. Eisenhower, *White House Years*, vol. 1 (New York: 1963), p. 181.
34. Dulles speech, *Documents on American Foreign Relations* (New York: Council on Foreign Relations, 1954), pp. 7–15.
35. Kaplan, op. cit., p. 112.
36. E. Fursdon, *The European Defence Community: A History* (London: 1980), p. 77.
37. Acheson, op. cit., pp. 707–17, 796–9, 820–9.
38. C. L. Sulzberger, *A Long Row of Candles* (Toronto: 1969), p. 950.
39. Fursdon, op. cit., pp. 321–2.
40. Cabinet minutes, cited in Dimbleby and Reynolds, op. cit., p. 229.
41. K. Kyle, *Suez* (London: 1991), is the outstanding work on the crisis.
42. Dimbleby and Reynolds, op. cit., p. 230. See also Henry Brandon, *Special Relationships* (New York: 1988), p. 127.

43. *Philadelphia Inquirer*, 2 November 1956.
44. H. Macmillan, *Riding the Storm* (London: 1971), p. 164.
45. B. Goldschmidt, *Le Complexe atomique* (Paris: 1980), passim. See also B. Goldschmidt, *The Atomic Adventure* (Oxford: 1964), p. 137.
46. *Die Welt*, 7 November 1956.
47. H. Thomas, *The Suez Affair* (London: 1970), p. 149.
48. McGeorge Bundy, op. cit., p. 240–1.
49. G. Arbatov, *The System* (New York: 1992), p. 43
50. *New York Times*, 12 May 1953. See also A. Seldon, *Churchill's Indian Summer* (London: 1981), p. 400.
51. A. Ulam, *The Communists* (New York: 1992), p. 109.
52. T. Powers, *The Man Who Kept the Secrets* (New York: 1979), p. 51.
53. J. Steele, *World Power* (London: 1983), pp. 30–2.
54. *Pravda*, 2 January 1955. See also Myron Rush, *Political Succession in the USSR* (New York: 1965), pp. 48, 60. Khrushchev evidently believed that the USSR was inherently less vulnerable, emphasising the advantages of sheer size long after the struggle with Malenkov was settled. See, for example, Khrushchev's speech to the Fourth Session in the Supreme Soviet, reported in *Pravda*, 15 January 1960.
55. *Die Welt*, 10 February 1955; *New York Times*, 11 February 1955.
56. R. Medvedev, *Khrushchev* (Oxford: 1982), p. 74.
57. For the bizarre Soviet application to join Nato, see Gromyko, op. cit., p. 166. The Dulles broadcast, 15 May 1955, cited in LaFeber, op. cit., p. 180.
58. Walker, 1983, op. cit., p. 94.
59. Medvedev, op. cit., p. 97.
60. *Moscow News*, 11 July 1990.
61. O *Mirnom Soyushchestvovanii* (On Peaceful Coexistence), collected speeches of N. S. Khrushchev (Moscow: 1961), pp. 6–14.
62. Chen-Enlai (Zhou Enlai) address, 19 April 1955, *Asia–Africa Speaks from Bandung* (Jakarta: 1955).
63. M. Heykal, *Cairo Documents* (New York: 1973), pp. 120–32. See also M. K. Nasser, *Press, Politics and Power* (Iowa: 1979), p. 36.
64. Ulam, op. cit., p. 139.
65. Central Committee of the Polish United Workers' Party, *The October Plenum* (Warsaw: 1957). Address by W. Gomuka, 20 October 1956.
66. Ulam, op. cit., p. 147.
67. Medvedev, 1982, op. cit., pp. 106–7.
68. Ulam, op. cit., p. 154.
69. R. Jeffreys-Jones, *The CIA and American Democracy* (New Haven: 1989), p. 94.
70. Z. Medvedev, *Andropov* (Oxford: 1983), pp. 37–40.
71. Khrushchev, 1970, op. cit., pp. 463–5.
72. D. Irving, *Uprising* (London: 1981), p. 547.
73. E. J. Hughes, *The Ordeal of Power* (New York: 1962), pp. 220–3.

74. Sampson, op. cit., p. 381.
75. Howe and Coser, op. cit., p. 499.

Chapter 5

1. *New York Times*, 5 November 1956.
2. Irving, op. cit., p. 545.
3. *Yugoslavia's Way: Programme of the League of the Communists of Yugoslavia* (trans. S. Pribichevich) (New York: 1958). See also L. Kolakowski, *Responsibility and History*, Eng. trans., *East Europe* (February/March 1958). For the impact upon China, see E. Crankshaw, *The New Cold War: Moscow v. Pekin* (London: 1963), p. 76. See also Ulam, op. cit., p. 155.
4. LaFeber, op. cit., p. 196.
5. A. Troitsky, *Back in the USSR* (London: 1987), pp. 9–11. See also R. Medvedev, op. cit., pp. 76, 111–12, 120–1; and Walker, 1987, op. cit., pp. 9–11.
6. Kaplan, op. cit., p. 135. *New York Times* 5 October 1957. See also J. Killian, *Sputniks, Scientists and Eisenhower* (Cambridge: MIT, 1977), pp. 2–3.
7. *Daily Mirror* (London), 8 December 1957.
8. *Washington Post*, 20 December 1957. The Gaither Report was not declassified until 1973, and not published until 1976.
9. Barson, op. cit., p. 120.
10. Hughes, op. cit., p. 245.
11. Joint Committee on Defense Production, 94th Congress, *Deterrence and Survival in the Nuclear Age* (The Gaither Report) (Washington: 1976), pp. 22–3, 30–1. See also Kaplan, op. cit., pp. 150–2.
12. Kaplan, op. cit., pp. 158–9.
13. S. Talbott, *The Master of the Game* (New York: 1988), pp. 68–9. See also LaFeber, op. cit., pp. 196–7.
14. F. Rudolph, *The American College and University* (New York: 1962), p. 490. See also *Education Directory, 1960–1*, pt 3, *Higher Education*, US Office of Education (Washington: 1960).
15. Chubb and Moe, *Politics, Markets and American Schools* (Washington DC: 1990), p. 7.
16. Dimbleby and Reynolds, op. cit., p. 238.
17. A. Horne, *Macmillan*, vol. 2 (New York: 1989), pp. 5–6.
18. Dimbleby and Reynolds, op. cit., p. 235.
19. Cited ibid., cabinet minute for 8 January 1957.
20. Horne, op. cit., p. 34.
21. Macmillan, 1971, op. cit., p. 14.
22. D. D. Eisenhower, *The White House Years: Waging Peace* (London: 1966), p. 124.

23. McGeorge Bundy, op. cit., p. 471.
24. Horne, op. cit., p. 34.
25. Walker, 1983, p. 71.
26. Jean Lacouture, *De Gaulle*, vol. 3 (Paris: 1986), p. 466.
27. This point was later made by President Kennedy's national security adviser. See McGeorge Bundy, op. cit., p. 473–4.
28. Horne, op. cit., p. 49.
29. G. F. Kennan, *Memoirs: 1950–63* (Boston: 1972), pp. 77–80, 229–66.
30. J. Judis, *Grand Illusion* (New York: 1972), p. 179.
31. *Remarks to US Ambassadors in Europe*, Paris, 9 May 1958. Nato ministerial meetings, Conference dossiers, Dulles papers, Princeton.
32. Horne, op. cit., pp. 196–7.
33. LaFeber, op. cit., p. 201.
34. H. Wilson, *The Labour Government 1964–70* (London: 1971), pp. 3–4.
35. Horne, op. cit., p. 111.
36. T. Prittie, *Konrad Adenauer* (London: 1972), pp. 263–4. See also Khrushchev, 1970, op. cit., pp. 501–2.
37. *Stenograficheskii Otchet, XXII-y Syezd KPSS. Transcript Report, 22nd Party Congress*, vol. 2 (Moscow: 1961), p. 588; R. Medvedev, op. cit., pp. 116–20.
38. Crankshaw, op. cit., p. 70.
39. Deliberately not reported in the Soviet press, Mao's speech was delivered on 8 November 1957. See W. Zimmerman, 'Russia and the international order', *Survey*, no. 58 (January 1966), pp. 209–12.
40. D. Zagoria, *The Sino-Soviet Conflict* (Princeton: 1962), p. 161. See also Crankshaw, op. cit., p. 71.
41. McGeorge Bundy, op. cit., p. 528.
42. *Vremya i Mi* (Time and Us), no. 48 (Tel Aviv: 1979).
43. G. Arbatov, *The System* (New York: 1992), p. 93.
44. W. Griffith, *The Sino-Soviet Rift* (Cambridge: MIT, 1964), p. 351.
45. N. Khrushchev, *Khrushchev Remembers: The Last Testament* (Boston: 1974), p. 269.
46. Crankshaw, op. cit., p. 81. For Soviet force levels, *Sipri Yearbook, 1991*, op. cit., p. 25.
47. *Pravda*, 30 July 1959.
48. McGeorge Bundy, op. cit., p. 359.
49. ibid., p. 267.
50. R. Medvedev, op. cit., p. 182. See also Khrushchev, 1974, op. cit., pp. 500–1. See also Horne, op. cit., pp. 117–20.
51. 'March 11, 1959, press conference', *Public Papers of the Presidency, 1959* (Washington DC: 1960).
52. Ambrose, op. cit., vol. 2, p. 150.
53. General M. Taylor, *The Uncertain Trumpet* (New York: 1959), pp. 5, 178.

54. *New York Times*, 24 September 1960.
55. Cited in M. R. Beschloss, *The Crisis Years* (New York: 1991), p. 28.
56. McGeorge Bundy, op. cit., p. 350.
57. LaFeber, op. cit., p. 206.
58. *Jane's All the World's Aircraft* (London: 1982), p. 401.
59. Horne, op. cit., p. 224.
60. ibid., pp. 228–31.
61. ibid., p. 232.
62. Crankshaw, op. cit., p. 97ff.
63. *O Mirnom Soyushchestvovanii*, op. cit., pp. 144–5.
64. Khrushchev, 1974, op. cit., p. 545.

Chapter 6

1. Horne, op. cit., p. 239.
2. ibid., pp. 283, 286.
3. *Public Papers of the Presidents: D.D. Eisenhower, 1960–1* (Washington DC: 1962), p. 817.
4. *Statistical Abstracts of the US* (Washington DC: 1986), table 540, p. 331.
5. D. Shulman, *If the Cold War is Over, What are the Implications for the Economy and Real Eastate?* (New York: Salomon Brothers, Bond Market Research, 1989).
6. Walker, 1987, op. cit., p. 71.
7. D. Calleo, *Beyond American Hegemony* (New York: 1987), p. 256.
8. Barnet, op. cit., p. 199. The quotation comes from Calleo, op. cit., p. 86.
9. ibid., p. 200.
10. R. Solomon, *The International Monetary System* (New York: 1977), p. 31.
11. 'Annual message to the Congress on the state of the Union, January 30, 1961', in *Public Papers of the President, 1961* (Washington DC: 1962), p. 13. See also Barnet, op. cit., p. 200.
12. *Balance of Payments of OECD Countries, 1960–77* (Paris: 1979), pp. 10–11.
13. Barnet, op. cit., p. 203.
14. A. Sampson, *The New Europeans* (London: 1968), p. 145.
15. The references for the growth of the global economy require a bibliography to themselves. The US export figures come from I. M. Destler, *American Trade Politics* (Washington DC: 1992), p. 13, and from the Office of the US Trade Representative (OUSTR), *Annual Report* (Washington DC: 1992), table 5. The US investment figures have to be accumulated from a variety of sources, including *Survey of Current Business* (New York: 1990), and Graham and Klugman, *Foreign Direct Investment in the US* (Washington DC: 1989), pp. 27–33, and again

from OUSTR, op. cit. Reference should also be made to H. Stein, *The Fiscal Revolution in America* (Chicago: 1969), and for the worried European reactions, J.-J. Servan-Schreiber, *Le Défi Américain* (Paris: 1967), and J. Rueff, *The Age of Inflation* (Chicago: 1964), p. 188. For the growth of the multinational corporation, see also Barnet and Muller, *Global Reach* (New York: 1974), and A. Shonfield, 'Big Business in the late 20th century', *Daedalus* (winter 1968), and C. Tugendhat, *The Multinationals* (London: 1971). The analysis of the role of US multinationals in Europe was made by the Atlantic Institute in 1968, and cited in Tugendhat, p. 32.

16. R. H. Ullman, 'The covert French connection', *Foreign Policy* (Washington DC), no. 75 (summer 1989), p. 3ff.
17. J. D. Steinbrunner, *The Cybernetic Theory of Decision* (Princeton: 1974), pp. 180–1.
18. Beschloss, op. cit., p. 406.
19. ibid., p. 52.
20. ibid., pp. 60–1.
21. *Public Papers of the President, 1961*, op. cit., 20 January 1961, pp. 1–2.
22. ibid., 30 January 1961, pp. 22–3.
23. ibid., 28 March 1961, pp. 232–5.
24. Powers, op. cit., pp. 166, 393.
25. T. Sorensen, *Kennedy* (New York: 1965), p. 292.
26. J. Oberg, *Uncovering Soviet Disasters* (New York: 1988), pp. 159–62.
27. *Pravda*, 17 April 1961.
28. Sorenson, op. cit., p. 296.
29. Powers, op. cit., pp. 121–34. See also Sorensen, op. cit., pp. 294–309.
30. *Le Monde*, 19 April 1961.
31. *Pravda*, 20 April 1961.
32. Walker, 1983, op. cit., pp. 226–7, 252.
33. *New York Times*, 20 April 1961; *Washington Post*, 19 April 1961. Khrushchev's statement is cited in the *Washington Post* of the same date.
34. *Corriere della sera*, 21 April 1961; *Die Welt*, 20 April 1961.
35. *Public Papers of the President, 1961*, op. cit., 25 May 1961, pp. 396–406.
36. ibid., 1 June 1961, p. 428.
37. Charles de Gaulle, *Memoirs: Renewal* (London: 1971), p. 256.
38. Horne, op. cit., p. 293.
39. Beschloss, op. cit., pp. 188–9.
40. ibid., pp. 194–224.
41. Horne, op. cit., p. 303.
42. *Public Papers of the President, 1961*, op. cit., 25 July 1961, pp. 532–40.
43. Bird, op. cit., pp. 510–11. See also Beschloss, op. cit., pp. 262–3.
44. *New York Times*, 3 August 1961.
45. *Pravda*, 8 August 1961; *Izvestiya*, 9 August 1961.

46. R. Garthoff, 'Berlin 1961: The record corrected', *Foreign Policy*, no. 84 (Washington DC: fall 1991), pp. 142–56.
47. Gromyko, op. cit., p. 197.

Chapter 7

1. Cited in LaFeber, op. cit., p. 217.
2. Stevenson's statement: *New York Times*, 9 October 1962. For Trujillo's murder, see The Church Committee, *Assassination Report* (Washington DC: US Senate, 1975) p. 195.
3. *Public Papers of the President, 1961*, op. cit., p. 725.
4. *Public Papers of the President, 1963* (Washington DC: 1964), p. 840.
5. Cited in D. Horowitz, *The Free World Colossus* (New York: 1965), p. 15.
6. A. Toynbee, *America and the World Revolution* (New York: 1961), p. 37.
7. *Basic Petroleum Data Book*, vol. X, no. 3 (Washington DC: American Petroleum Institute, 1990), sect. XII, table 7.
8. Sorenson, op. cit., pp. 629–32.
9. *Public Papers of the President, 1961*, op. cit., p. 306.
10. Walker, 1987, op. cit., p. 143.
11. Beschloss, op. cit., p. 328.
12. Ellsberg, communication to author.
13. Kaplan, op. cit., pp. 277–8.
14. *Department of Defense Public Information Release* (Washington DC: 21 October 1961).
15. 'Back from the Brink: Cuban missile crisis correspondence between J. F. Kenndy and N. S. Khrushchev', declassified texts published jointly by *Mezhdunarodnaya Zhizn* (Moscow), and *Problems of Communism* (US Information Agency), special issue (spring 1992). The Khrushchev letter cited is from 30 October 1962. The original Russian is clear: '*Moia rol bila proshche, chem u vas, potomy chto ya ne imel v svoyem okruzheniyii lyudei, kotorie xhoteli razvyazat voinu.*'
16. H. Kahn, *On Thermonuclear War* (Princeton: 1960), passim. See also Kaplan, op. cit., pp. 227–9.
17. Kaplan, op. cit., p. 246.
18. *Saturday Evening Post*, 31 March 1962.
19. *Pravda*, 31 March 1962. (The *Saturday Evening Post* appeared some days before the publication date announced on the cover; hence *Pravda*'s apparently instantaneous comment.) See also J. Tatu, *Le Pouvoir au Kremlin* (Paris: 1967), pp. 218–19. For the Novocherkassk riots, see G. Hosking, *A History of the Soviet Union* (London: 1985), pp. 389–90, and Walker, 1987, op. cit., p. 40.

20. McNamara speech to Nato, 5 May 1962, cited in Healey, op. cit., p. 310. See also J. E. Stromseth, *The Origins of Flexible Response* (New York: 1988), pp. 3–5, 31–3, 43.
21. R. P. Berman and J. C. Baker, *Soviet Strategic Forces: Requirements and Responses* (Washington DC: 1982), p. 133.
22. Marshal V. D. Sokolovsky, *Voyennaya Strategiya* (Moscow: 1962). See also M. MccGwire, *Military Objectives in Soviet Foreign Policy* (Washington DC: 1987), p. 25; also M. MccGwire, *Perestroika and National Security* (Washington DC: 1991), pp. 21–2, and L. Freedman, *The Evolution of Nuclear Strategy* (London: 1981), pp. 246–7.
23. Rusk, op. cit., p. 245.
24. Khrushchev, 1970, op. cit., p. 547.
25. F. Burlatsky, 'The lessons of personal diplomacy', in *Problems of Communism* (spring 1992), op. cit., p. 9.
26. Sorensen, op. cit., p. 670.
27. R. Garthoff, *Reflections on the Cuban Missile Crisis* (Washington DC: 1987), pp. 138–46.
28. Sorensen, op. cit., p. 673.
29. The author was present at this encounter. A report was carried in the *Guardian*, 21 March 1988.
30. The Cuban missile crisis deserves a bibliography to itself. The starting-point for all researchers is the Kennedy Library in Cambridge, Massachusetts, its oral-history recordings of the participants, and the transcripts of the crucial White House meetings. Russian historians are now preparing, sadly too late for most participants, a similar effort. I have had the benefit of discussions with three Soviet aides to the Central Committee at the time, Fyodor Burlatsky, Georgi Arbatov, and Alexander Bovin, and with Valentin Falin, later Soviet Ambassador to Bonn, and Mikoyan's son Sergo, who accompanied his father to Cuba for the negotiations at the end of the crisis. In ascending order of publication, this chapter also relied upon the following published accounts: Sorensen, 1965, op. cit.; R. F. Kennedy, *Thirteen Days* (New York: 1969); Khrushchev, 1970, op. cit.; A. Gromyko, *1036 Dnei Prezidenta Kennedi* (Moscow: 1971); G. T. Allison, *The Essence of Decision* (Boston: 1971); Garthoff, 1987, op. cit.; S. Talbott, *The Master of the Game* (New York: 1988); *Nikita Khrushchev: Life and Destiny* (Moscow: Novosti, 1989); Horne, op. cit.; McGeorge Bundy, op. cit.; Rusk, op. cit.; Beschloss, op. cit.; *Problems of Communism*, op. cit.; Glyn, op. cit.; Arbatov, op. cit.; J. A. Nathan (ed.), *The Cuban Missile Crisis Revisited* (New York: 1992); L. Chang and P. Kornbluh (eds.) *The Cuban Missile Crisis, 1962* (Washington DC: 1992); R. S. Thompson, *The Missiles of October* (New York: 1992).

    The proceedings of the four conferences on the Cuban missile crisis organised by Harvard's Centre for Science and International Affairs, the Carnegie Endowment and Brown University's Center for Foreign Policy

Development, and by Moscow's USA and Canada Institute, are indispensable. They represent an extraordinary attempt to re-create a historical moment with many of the key participants on all sides of the crisis. They took place at Hawk's Bay in March 1987; at Cambridge in October 1987; in Moscow in January 1989; and Antigua in 1991.

31. Author's notes of McNamara statement at the Novosti meetings, recorded in the *Guardian*, 21 March 1988.
32. Sorensen, op. cit., p. 559.
33. Brandon, op. cit., p. 177.
34. McGeorge Bundy, op. cit., p. 459.
35. Tatu, op. cit., pp. 273–6.
36. *Pravda*, 2 December 1962. See also Walker, 1987, op. cit., p. 211.
37. R. S. McNamara, *The Ann Arbor Speech*, 16 June 1962, Department of Defense press release.
38. Horne, op. cit., pp. 430–2.
39. Cited in Dimbleby and Reynolds, op. cit., p. 256.
40. *Le Monde*, 15 January 1963.
41. H. Macmillan, *At the End of the Day* (London: 1973), p. 367.
42. *Public Papers of the Presidents, 1963*, op. cit. pp. 459–64.
43. Sorensen, op. cit., pp. 741–2.
44. Beschloss, op. cit., p. 652.
45. ibid., p. 649.

Chapter 8

1. *Public Papers of the President, 1963*, op. cit., pp. 524–5.
2. R. Reagan, *An American Life* (New York: 1990), p. 683.
3. Rusk, op. cit., p. 227.
4. *Public Papers of the President, 1963*, op. cit., p. 524.
5. J. H. Buck, *The Modern Japanese Military System* (Beverly Hills: 1975), p. 242. For a recent report on the declassification of the documents which contain the Dulles threat to block the Kurile Islands compromise, see the *New York Times*, 9 September 1992.
6. Adams, op. cit., p. 449.
7. Bank of Japan, *Economic Statistics Annual* (1981), pp. 227–8.
8. Emmerson, op. cit., p. 84.
9. Barnet, op. cit., p. 267.
10. OECD, *Economic Outlook*, no. 1 (July 1967), and no. 17 (July 1978).
11. Memo from Townsend Hoopes, US Defense Under-Secretary to Clark Clifford, Defense Secretary, 14 March 1968, cited in L. Berman, *Lyndon Johnson's War* (New York: 1989), p. 225. See also Wilson, op. cit., p. 459.

12. L. B. Johnson, *The Vantage Point* (New York: 1971), p. 102.
13. H. Y. Schandler, *The Unmaking of a President: Lyndon Johnson and Vietnam* (Princeton: 1977), p. 225. See also Dimbleby and Reynolds, op. cit., p. 265.
14. Wilson, op. cit., p. 433.
15. ibid., pp. 39–40. But note that the British defence secretary of the time, Denis Healey, says that at the peak of the four-year confrontation, Britain deployed only some 17,000 troops in Borneo, most of them Gurkhas: Healey, op. cit., p. 289.
16. R. Crossman, *The Diaries of a Cabinet Minister* (London: 3 vols., 1975–7), p. 95.
17. Dimbleby and Reynolds, op. cit., p. 270.
18. Wilson, op. cit., p. 440.
19. Healey, op. cit., p. 288.
20. J. Prados, *Keepers of the Keys: A History of the National Security Council from Truman to Bush* (New York: 1991), pp. 140–7.
21. Healey, op. cit., p. 323. See also Wilson, op. cit., pp. 625–6.
22. Kennan's conversation cited in LaFeber, op. cit., p. 230.
23. ibid.
24. Rusk, op. cit., p. 432.
25. ibid., p. 433.
26. ibid., p. 427.
27. E. Becker, *America's Vietnam War* (New York: 1992), p. 82.
28. Johnson, op. cit., pp. 117–18.
29. Berman, op. cit., p. 10.
30. Rusk, op. cit., pp. 461–5.
31. Becker, op. cit., p. 88. See also Gromyko, 1989, op. cit., p. 184.
32. Ulam, op. cit., p. 254.
33. Berman, op. cit., p. 12.
34. ibid., p. 15.
35. Rusk, op. cit., pp. 465, 469.
36. R. Morgan, *The US and West Germany: 1945–73* (London: 1974), p. 157.
37. *Papers of the Presidency, 1966* (Washington DC: 7 October 1967).
38. *NATO Final Communiqués: 1947–1970* (Brussels: 1971), pp. 188–92. The formal title Harmel Report, named after Belgian foreign minister Pierre Harmel, is *The Future Tasks of the Alliance: Report of the Council.*
39. Walker, op. cit., 1987, pp. 139–52.
40. 'Report to the President by the Commission on CIA Activities within the US', published as the *Rockefeller Report* (New York: 1975), pp. 130–2.
41. J. A. Schumpeter, *Imperialism and Social Classes* (New York: 1955), p. 51.

Chapter 9

1. Isaacson and Thomas, op. cit., p. 679.
2. ibid., pp. 683–4.
3. Berman, op. cit., p. 223.
4. D. Brinkley, *Dean Acheson: The Cold War Years* (New Haven: 1992), p. 261. See also Berman, op. cit., pp. 196–8.
5. C. Clifford, *Counsel to the President* (New York: 1991), pp. 488–526. See also Rusk, op. cit., pp. 480–1.
6. The Vietnamese military statistics are a result of a compilation of the briefings given by the CIA's George Carver and General Du Puy to the Wise Old Men. See Berman, op. cit., pp. 195, 201–2.
7. *Statistical Abstracts of the US, 1984* (Washington DC: 1983), table 498, p. 315.
8. Cited in Berman, op. cit., p. 225.
9. ibid., p. 193.
10. Barnet, op. cit., pp. 250–3.
11. Johnson, op. cit., p. 455.
12. *Statistical Abstracts of the US*, op. cit., table 498, p. 315.
13. The most entertaining explanation of the CIA's role in subsidising anti-Communist intellectuals in Europe is to be found in the memoir of the plan's author, Tom Braden, *Saturday Evening Post*, 20 May 1967, in an engaging article entitled 'Why I'm glad the CIA is immoral'.
14. M. Mason, *American Multinationals and Japan* (Cambridge: 1992), p. 197.
15. H. Gimlin, 'American investments in European industry', *Editorial Research Reports* (26 January 1968).
16. Dimbleby and Reynolds, op. cit., p. 296.
17. Barnet, op. cit., p. 248.
18. Wilson, op. cit., p. 334.
19. 'West German prosperity', *Editorial Research Reports* (19 January 1969), p. 69.
20. *Sipri Yearbook, 1991*, op. cit., p. 25.
21. R. F. Byrnes (ed.), *After Brezhnev* (Georgetown: Center for Strategic and International Studies, 1983). See 'Military forces', p. 157.
22. A. Isaev, *Kommunist, 5* (Moscow: Central Committee of the Communist Party of Soviet Union, 1989).
23. General V. Zemskov, *Voyennaya Misl* (Military Thought), vol. 7 (1969).
24. L. I. Brezhnev, *Izbrannye Proizvedeniya* (Collected Works), vol. 1 (Moscow: 1981), p. 21.
25. 'Inaugural address of President Richard M. Nixon', 20 January 1969, *Presidential Documents*, vol. 5 (Washington DC: 1969), pp. 152–3. See also H. Kissinger, *White House Years* (Boston: 1979), pp. 50, 127–8.

26. R. Whalen, *Catch the Falling Flag: A Republican's Challenge to His Party* (Boston: 1972), pp. 140–4. Whalen was Nixon's speechwriter at the time.
27. R. Garthoff, *Détente and Confrontation* (Washington DC: 1985), p. 208.
28. *Pravda*, 28 August 1969; *Evening News* (London), 16 September 1969. A former Gulag inmate, later accused by dissidents of having been a *stukach*, or camp stool-pigeon, Viktor Louis was released in the Khrushchev thaw and worked for the veteran American journalist Ed Stevens. He married an English nanny who was working in Moscow, and later became rich through his journalism and his monopoly of the Moscow telephone directory for foreigners. Louis lived in some luxury in a dacha outside Moscow with his collection of classic cars, including a Rolls-Royce and Bentley, until his garage burned down. He sent his sons to Oxford, and went to Cambridge for his own kidney transplant, paying £35,000 in cash. He died in 1992 virtually ostracised by the Western press corps for his role in delivering KGB surveillance film of the Nobel laureate Andrei Sakharov to the West, film calculated to fend off Western speculation that Sakharov was dead. Louis claimed a series of scoops in the 1960s, including the fall of Khrushchev, the defection of Stalin's daughter Svetlana, and the first, doctored edition of Solzhenitsyn's *Cancer Ward*. He was assumed by Western colleagues to be a useful and tolerated tool of the KGB. In the perestroika period, he became an agent for some Western businessmen, including the discredited publishing tycoon Robert Maxwell. (Author's observation and personal acquaintance with Louis.)
29. M. and B. Kalb, *Kissinger* (New York: 1975), pp. 259–60.
30. Kissinger used this phrase in his press conference of 23 December 1975. *State Bulletin* (US Department of State, Washington DC), vol. 74 (1976), p. 70.
31. Chou En-lai (Zhou Enlai), 'Chinese government and people strongly condemn Soviet revisionist clique's armed occupation of Czechoslovakia', *Peking Review*, vol. 11 (August 1968).
32. R. Wich, *Sino-Soviet Crisis Politics* (Cambridge: 1980), pp. 123–40.
33. *Foreign Affairs*, vol. 46 (October 1967), pp. 122–3. See also *Time* magazine, 5 October 1970.
34. R. M. Nixon, *US Foreign Policy for the 1970s*, vol. 4 (Washington DC: 1973), p. 233. Although published under Nixon's name, these volumes were carefully vetted by Kissinger before publication. See Garthoff, op. cit., p. 28, n. 8.
35. Sampson, op. cit., p. 25.
36. Wilson, op. cit., p. 582.
37. J. Ardagh, *Germany and the Germans*, rev. edn (London: 1991), p. 18.
38. Willy Brandt, *People and Politics* (Boston: 1978), p. 205.
39. Wilson, op. cit., p. 554.

40. Calleo, op. cit., pp. 89–90. See also the powerful essay by Robert Bartley, editor of the *Wall Street Journal*, on the twentieth anniversary of Nixon's announcement, *Wall Street Journal*, 15 August 1991.
41. *Wall Street Journal*, ibid.
42. Destler, op. cit., 2nd edn, table 3.1, p. 45.
43. Quoted in Kissinger, op. cit., p. 953.
44. Yergin, op. cit., pp. 581–3.
45. *Basic Petroleum Data Book*, 1990, op. cit., sect. 7, table 2.
46. *Asahi Shimbun*, 17 August 1971.
47. A. Roth, *Heath and the Heathmen* (London: 1972), p. 224.
48. Cited in Bartley, op. cit.
49. W. Greider, *Secrets of the Temple* (New York: 1987), pp. 344–5.
50. Barnet, op. cit., p. 305.
51. W. Isaacson, *Kissinger* (New York: 1992), p. 351.
52. *Final Report of the Committee on the Judiciary, House of Representatives, on the Impeachment of Richard M. Nixon* (New York: 1975), pp. 180–1. See also Isaacson, op. cit., p. 530.
53. Yergin, op. cit., pp. 612–15.
54. *New York Times*, 28 October 1973; *Le Figaro*, 30 October 1973; *Al-Ahram*, 18 November 1973; *Pravda*, 29 October 1973; *Corriere della sera*, 8 November 1973.
55. Cited in Isaacson, op. cit., p. 665.

Chapter 10

1. H. H. Humphrey, *The Education of a Public Man* (New York: 1976), p. 106.
2. M. Davie, *California: The Vanishing Dream* (New York: 1972), pp. 49–52.
3. D. P. Moynihan, *Counting Our Blessings* (London: 1980), p. 260.
4. J. Carter, *A Government as Good as Its People* (New York: 1977), pp. 93, 96.
5. All statistics from *International Economic Indicators, 1988* (Cologne: Institut der Deutschen Wirtshaft, 1988), tables 5, 12 and 35.
6. *SSSR v Tsifrakh, v 1984 Godu* (Moscow: Finansy i Statistika, 1985), pp. 70–9. See also Walker, 1987, op. cit., p. 53.
7. W. W. Rostow, *The World Economy: History and Prospects* (Austin, Texas: 1978), pp. 91–8, 278–9. See also Calleo, op. cit., pp. 147–8.
8. D. L. Bond, 'CMEA growth projection for 1981–5', in *The CMEA Five-Year Plans in a New Perspective* (Brussels: Nato Economic Directorate, 1982).
9. Ed Hewett, 'Near-term consequences for the Soviet natural gas industry, and implications for East–West trade', paper submitted to US Congress

for hearings, in *Soviet Economy in the 1980s: Problems and Perspectives*, vol. 1 (Washington DC: 1983), p. 394. (The strategic implications of the Soviet energy boom were not lost on US policy-makers; by 1991, the author of that report, Mr Ed Hewett, had become President Bush's senior adviser on Soviet and later CIS affairs in the White House National Security Council.)
10. *SSSR v Tsifrakh, v 1984 Godu*, op. cit., pp. 56–7, 112.
11. L. I. Brezhnev, *Following Lenin's Course* (Moscow: 1975), pp. 554–7.
12. ibid., pp. 522–3.
13. ibid., p. 581.
14. Friedman and Lebard, op. cit., p. 136.
15. *International Economic Indicators, 1988* (Institut der Deutschen Wirtschaft), op. cit., table 24.
16. W. U. Chandler, *Increasing Energy Efficiency* (Washington DC: Worldwatch Institute, 1985), pp. 150, 158. (State of the World, 1985.)
17. Barnet, op. cit., p. 391.
18. R. J. Lieber, 'Europe and America in the world energy crisis', *International Affairs* (London) (October 1979), pp. 542–3.
19. Yergin, op. cit., pp. 658–9.
20. W. R. Cline, *International Debt and the Stability of the World Economy* (Washington DC: Institute for International Economics, 1983), pp. 14–15.
21. G. C. Hufbauer, *US Taxation of International Income* (Washington DC: Institute for International Economics, 1992), p. 5.
22. ibid., p. 3.
23. Glyn, op. cit., p. 268.
24. C. Menges, *The Twilight Struggle* (Washington DC: 1990), p. 111.
25. Isaacson, op. cit., p. 611.
26. ibid., p. 679.
27. Garthoff, op. cit., p. 1003.
28. *Guardian* (London/Manchester), 29 October 1977.
29. Z. Brzezinski, *Power and Principle* (New York: 1983), pp. 180–1.
30. C. Vance, *Hard Choices: Critical Years in American Foreign Policy* (New York: 1983), pp. 73–4.
31. Glyn, op. cit., p. 288.
32. For a brief summary of the events leading to the fall of the Shah, see Walker, 1983, op. cit., pp. 342–93.
33. R. Brownstein and N. Easton, *Reagan's Ruling Class* (Washington DC: 1982), pp. 532–4. See also Helen Caldicott, *Missile Envy* (New York: 1984), pp. 193–8.
34. General Sir John Hackett *et al.*, *The Third World War* (London: 1978), passim.
35. J. Carter, *Keeping Faith: Memoirs of a President* (New York: 1982), pp. 204–5.
36. *NATO: Facts and Figures* (Brussels: Nato, 1989), pp. 102–4.

37. 'The state of the Union' (23 January 1980), *Presidential Documents*, vol. 16 (Washington DC), p. 197. See also Garthoff, op. cit., p. 954.

Chapter 11

1. H. S. Bradsher, *Afghanistan and the Soviet Union* (Durham, NC: 1983), pp. 100–1. See also Arbatov, op. cit., p. 198. For the account of the angry response of Soviet military intelligence by the former KGB General Oleg Kalugin, see *Moscow News*, 24 May 1990, p. 11.
2. This account is drawn from the pioneering analysis of the partially opened Politburo archives by Michael Dobbs, and reported in the *Washington Post*, 15 and 16 November 1992. Some of the records were made available by the Constitutional Court of Russia, under its proceedings in the case of President Boris Yeltsin's formal banning of the Communist Party. Others emerged from the newly established Centre for the Preservation of Contemporary Documents.
3. Morozov's account was published in *Novoye Vremya*, Moscow, May 1992. The US Embassy cables on the Taraki–Amin shoot-out are cited in Bradsher, op. cit., pp. 112–13.
4. See, for example, the account of Vadim Zagladin, first deputy secretary of the International Department of the Central Committee, in *Stern* (Hamburg), 31 January 1980. For Soviet fears of China's role, see also Yuri Agranov, 'The Afghan revolution and Peking's treacherous course', *Problemy Dal'nego Vostoka* (Far Eastern Questions) (Moscow), no. 3 (1980). See also Garthoff, op. cit., pp. 921–2.
5. C. Andrew and O. Gordievsky, *KGB: The Inside Story* (London: 1990), p. 480. See also A. Borovik's article in *Ogonyok* (Moscow), no. 46 (1989).
6. Arbatov, op. cit., pp. 197–8. For details of the poor quality of the Soviet Central Asian troops, see A. Cockburn, *The Threat* (London: 1983), p. 114.
7. Garthoff, op. cit., p. 985. See also Z. Medvedev, op. cit., pp. 163–4.
8. Brzezinski, op. cit., pp. 424–5.
9. 'East–West relations in the aftermath of the Soviet invasion of Afghanistan', *Hearings before the House Foreign Affairs Committee*, 96th Congress, 2nd session, 24 and 30 January 1980 (Washington DC: 1980).
10. Garthoff, op. cit., pp. 977–8.
11. Andrew and Gordievsky, op. cit., p. 485.
12. Cited in D. Simes, 'Clash over Poland', *Foreign Policy* (Washington DC), no. 46 (1982), p. 53.
13. T. Szulc, *Fidel: A Critical Portrait* (London: 1987), pp. 533–4.
14. Carter, 1982, op. cit., p. 585.
15. Reagan, op. cit., p. 219.
16. Carter, 1982, op. cit., p. 568.

17. Spoken on BBC-1's television programme *Panorama*, 11 July 1977.
18. *Public Papers of the Presidency, 1981*, 26 February 1981, p. 170.
19. *Sunday Times* (London), 3 May 1981.
20. Ullman, op. cit., pp. 22–3.
21. International Institute of Strategic Studies, *The Military Balance 1989–90* (London: 1989), p. 52.
22. For one of the more thoughtful considerations of Brandt's appeal and its implications, see R. W. Johnson, *The Politics of Recession* (London: 1985), pp. 90–103.
23. See, for example, Andrew and Gordievsky, op. cit., p. 490.
24. 'Problems of the alliance', speech by J. Kirkpatrick to the Committee for the Free World, Washington DC, 23 January 1982, and reprinted in J. Kirkpatrick, *The Reagan Phenomenon* (Washington DC: 1983), pp. 174–82.
25. Barnet, op. cit., p. 432.
26. *Washington Post*, 25 June 1982.
27. K. Kaiser *et al.*, *Western Security: What Has Changed?* (New York: Council on Foreign Relations, 1982), p. 17.
28. *New York Times*, 13 February 1982.
29. Caspar Weinberger, *Annual Report to the Congress, Department of Defense, Fiscal Year 1985* (Washington DC: 1984), pp. 279–80.
30. The *Washington Post* editorial board meeting with candidate Reagan took place on 18 June 1980. The text was published in L. Cannon, *President Reagan: The Role of a Lifetime* (New York: 1991), p. 297.
31. *New York Times*, 18 October 1981, p. 1.
32. *New York Times*, 5 November 1981, p. 1.
33. *Los Angeles Times*, 15 August 1982, p. 1.
34. R. Scheer, *With Enough Shovels* (New York: 1982), p. 18.
35. Carter, 1982, op. cit., p. 585.
36. *Papers of the Presidency, 1981* (Washington DC: 1981), 29 January 1981.
37. *Papers of the Presidency, 1983* (Washington DC: 1984), 8 March 1983.
38. Arbatov, op. cit., pp. 254–86.
39. Walker, 1987, op. cit., pp. 143–4.
40. Arbatov, op. cit., pp. 116–17.
41. *Pravda*, 22 December 1982 and 7 January 1983.
42. Arbatov, op. cit., pp. 276–7.
43. *The Economist* (London), 15–21 January 1983.
44. Ardagh, op. cit., p. 23.
45. *Papers of the Presidency, 1983* (Washington DC: 1984), 23 March 1983.
46. *Pravda*, 27 March 1983.
47. 'Defense as a deterrent of war', *Harvard International Review* (Cambridge, Mass.), January–February 1985.
48. *New York Times*, 1 July 1985.

49. The fullest account of RYAN is to be found in Andrew and Gordievsky, op. cit., pp. 488ff. Oleg Gordievsky was a KGB colonel who defected to Britain in 1985, when he had already been appointed KGB station chief in London. He had in fact been a British intelligence agent since 1974, and his reports of RYAN doubtless helped intensify Western fears, just when the Soviet Union was at its most nervous.
50. Andrew and Gordievsky, op. cit., p. 498.
51. ibid., p. 501. See also the *Guardian*, 9 September 1983 and 29 September 1983.
52. D. Oberdorfer, *The Turn* (London: 1992), p. 65.

Chapter 12

1. Y. Moshkov, *Zernovaya problema v gody sploshnoi kollektivizatsii* (Moscow: 1966), p. 215.
2. *Pravda*, 12 January 1990.
3. *Vneshnaya Torgovlya, SSSR*, vol. 3 (Moscow: 1986).
4. C. Fogarty and K. Tritle, 'Moscow's economic aid programs in less-developed countries: A perspective on the 1980s', in *Gorbachev's Economic Plans*, vol. 2 (Washington DC: Joint Economic Committee, Congress of the US, 1987), pp. 537–8, 540.
5. J. Krause, 'Soviet arms transfers to sub-Saharan Africa', in R. C. Nation and M. V. Kauppi (eds.), *The Soviet Impact in Africa* (Lexington, Mass.: 1984).
6. J. Steele, *World Power* (London: 1983), pp. 91–2.
7. Cannon, op. cit., p. 466.
8. Sometimes known as the Novosibirsk Report, the conclusions of the Zaslavskaya group were leaked to the *Washington Post* in 1983. A full English translation of the Zaslavskaya report was published in *Survey*, vol. 28, no. 1 (1984), from which these quotations are taken.
9. A. Guber, *Intensified Economy and Progress in Science and Technology* (Moscow: Novosti, 1984), p. 5.
10. *SSSR v Tsifrakh, v 1984 Godu*, op. cit., pp. 56–7.
11. For the CIA Report, see the *International Herald Tribune*, 27 December 1982; and see also 'Disussion', by the later CIA Director Robert Gates, in R. Godson (ed.), *Intelligence Requirements for the 1990s* (Washington DC: 1989), pp. 111–19.
12. *Guardian* (London), 17 December 1984.
13. M. S. Gorbachev, *Zhivoye Tvorchestvo Naroda* (Moscow: 1984).
14. ibid.
15. *Mirovaya Ekonomika i Mezhdunarodnye Otnosheniya* (Moscow: November 1990). The original English text of Maclean's document was printed in S. Hirsch (ed.), *Memo 3* (Washington DC: 1992), pp. 195–214.

16. A. Gromyko and V. Lomeiko, *Novoye Myshlenniye v Yaderniy Vek* (Moscow: 1984).
17. S. F. Cohen and K. vanden Heuvel (eds.), *Voices of Glasnost* (New York: 1989), pp. 158–60.
18. C. Schmidt-Hauer, *Gorbachev: The Path to Power* (London: 1984), pp. 104–5.
19. Oberdorfer, op. cit., pp. 17, 67.
20. The term 'Reagan Doctrine' was first coined by conservative columnist Charles Krauthammer, in *Time* magazine, 1 April 1985.
21. See *Iran–Contra Affair*, US Senate report 100–216, House of Representatives Report 100–533 (Washington DC: November 1987).
22. *Papers of the Presidency, 1985*, State of the Union Address, 6 February 1985 (Washington DC: 1985).
23. Cannon, op. cit., pp. 369–72.
24. W. Arkin *et al.* (eds.), *Encyclopaedia of the US Military* (New York: 1990), p. 451. Significantly, the most thorough history of the National Security Council, J. Prados, *Keepers of the Keys* (New York: 1991), contains no reference to NSDD 32, nor to Poland. See also 'The holy alliance', *Time* magazine, 24 February 1992.
25. 'Statement by A. A. Gromyko', 18 January 1984, *Conference on Confidence and Security-Building Measures and Disarmament in Europe: Documents, 1984* (Stockholm: 1984).
26. Oberdorfer, op. cit., pp. 116–17, 121.
27. Walker, 1987, op. cit., pp. 117–18.
28. *Time* magazine, 5 September 1985.
29. The author attended the party congress. See also M. S. Gorbachev, *Political Report of the CPSU Central Committee to the 27th Party Congress of the CPSU* (Moscow: 1986), p. 77.
30. *Papers of the Presidency, 1985*, Address to the Joint Session of Congress, 21 November 1985 (Washington DC: 1986).
31. Gorbachev, 1986, op. cit., p. 23.
32. Extracts from the entire exchange of letters, and full texts of several of them, were published in Reagan's memoirs, *An American Life*, Reagan, op. cit., pp. 642–72.
33. Oberdorfer, op. cit., p. 203. This account rests heavily on Mr Oberdorfer's outstanding reconstruction of the Reykjavik meetings, which in turn relied heavily on Mr Shultz's memory. See also M. S. Gorbachev, *Perestroika* (London: 1987), pp. 236–41. Use has also been made of the author's interviews with Soviet sources who were present at Reykjavik, including deputy foreign minister Karpov, Marshal Akhromeyev, Georgi Arbatov, and the Soviet foreign ministry spokesman Gennady Gerasimov.
34. Oberdorfer, op. cit., p. 203.
35. Gorbachev, 1987, op. cit., p. 240.

36. *Guardian*, 1 April 1987. The question was put to Mrs Thatcher by the current author.
37. A. I. Salitzkiy, 'The foreign economic structure of the People's Republic of China', *Memo* (Moscow) (September 1986). An English edition was published in *Memo* (Washington DC) (1989), p. 154.
38. Ulam, op. cit., p. 412.
39. A. D. Romberg, 'US–Japan relations', in G. Allison and G. T. Treverton (eds.), *Re-Thinking America's Security* (New York: 1992), p. 368.
40. Gorbachev, 1987, op. cit., p. 181. See also V. I. Ivanov and P. A. Minakir, 'On the role of foreign economic relations in the development of the USSR's Pacific coast regions', *Memo* (Moscow) (1988); English edition, *Memo* (Washington DC) (1989), pp. 309–11.
41. T. Kitazume, 'Détente puts Japanese defences in new light', *Japan Times* weekly, 13 January 1990, p. 5. For Japan force sizes, see *Defence of Japan, 1989* (Tokyo: Japan Defence Agency, 1989), and *Japan's Defence Planning in an Era of Global Change* (Tokyo: Japan Economic Institute, September 1990), 35A, p. 4.
42. *Defence of Japan, 1989*, op. cit., p. 321. For US procurement, see 'Armaments co-operation', in *NATO Facts and Figures* (Brussels: 1989), pp. 263–86.
43. *The International Economy* (Washington DC) (December 1989/January 1990), p. 52.
44. *Wall Street Journal*, 7 November 1989, p. 1.
45. Friedman and Lebard, op. cit., p. 353.
46. P. Kennedy, *The Rise and Fall of the Great Powers* (New York: 1987), passim.

Chapter 13

1. Gorbachev, 1987, op. cit., pp. 40–1.
2. *Voprosy Ekonomiki* (Moscow), no. 2 (1988), p. 79. See also A. Aslund, *Gorbachev's Struggle for Economic Reform* (Ithaca, NY: 1989), pp. 180–1.
3. *Pravda*, 6 August 1988.
4. *Pravda*, 11 August 1988.
5. Aslund, op. cit., p. 117.
6. *Pravda*, 29 June 1988.
7. For a brisk discussion of the search for foreign models, see Aslund, op. cit., pp. 182–4.
8. See, for example, Burlatsky and Bogomolov in *Literaturnaya Gazeta*, 11 June 1986.
9. The author attended all sessions of the nineteenth Party Congress. But also see A. Brumberg (ed.), *Chronicle of a Revolution* (New York: 1990), pp. 197–8; and Cohen and vanden Heuvel, op. cit., p. 111.

10. *Theses Presented to the 19th Conference of the CPSU by the Political Bureau of the CPSU* (Moscow: 1988), pp. 14–16.
11. R. Kaiser, *How Gorbachev Happened* (New York: 1991), pp. 220–1.
12. The author was in the hall at the United Nations when Gorbachev spoke. This and subsequent quotations for Gorbachev's UN Address are cited from the *Guardian* (London) and the *New York Times*, 8 December 1988.
13. *Guardian*, 23 January 1989. See also the transcript of ABC TV's *This Week with David Brinkley*, 22 January 1989.
14. M. R. Beschloss and S. Talbott, *At the Highest Levels* (New York: 1993), p. 25.
15. Bush's speech at Mainz was reported in the *Guardian*, 1 June 1989. For NSD-23, see Beschloss and Talbott, op. cit., pp. 68–9.
16. For Fitzwater's 'drugstore cowboy' comment, see the *Washington Post*, 17 May 1989. Sununu's 'candy store' phrase was made to several reporters in Warsaw, including the current author, and was reported in the *New York Times*, 11 July 1989. For Waęsa's meeting with Bush, and the Yeltsin interview with Scowcroft, see Beschloss and Talbott, op. cit., pp. 89, 104. Adam Michnik's comment was made to the current author, during a meeting in Moscow in October 1989.
17. Author's interview with Grachev. See also Kaiser, op. cit., p. 271.
18. *Moscow News*, 9 December 1989.
19. *New York Times*, 8 December 1988.
20. P. Hanson, 'Shatalin plan', *Soviet/East European Report* (Radio Free Europe/Radio Liberty), vol. VIII, no. 2 (10 October 1990). See also E. Teague, 'Soyuz group' (ibid.), vol. VIII, no. 32 (20 May 1991).
21. E. Shevardnadze, *The Future Belongs to Freedom* (New York: 1991), pp. 189–204.
22. *The Economist* (London), 20–5 April 1991, p. 31.
23. G. Allison and R. Blackwill, 'America's stake in the Soviet future', *Foreign Affairs* (New York) (summer 1991). One of the earliest calls for such a trade-off was published by the present author: 'Wrong cause at the wrong time', *New York Times*, 2 February 1991.
24. *Pravda*, 18 June 1991. See also Beschloss and Talbott, op. cit., pp. 393–407.
25. S. F. Starr, 'The Novoye Ogarevo agreement', Testimony before the Subcommittee on Europe and the Middle East, of the House Committee on Foreign Affairs, 16 May 1991 (Washington DC: US Congress, 1991).
26. For Gorbachev's Nobel Prize statement, see the *New York Times*, 6 June 1991.
27. *New York Times*, 2 August 1991.
28. *New York Times*, 23 August 1991.
29. J. Billington, *Russia Transformed* (New York: 1992), p. 175.

Chapter 14

1. *Arms Control Today* (Washington DC), vol. 20, no. 10 (December 1990), p. 3.
2. *Guardian*, 4 December 1992.
3. See *The Economist* (London): 'Europe's Dutch treat', 14–20 December 1991, and 'Half-Maastricht', 26 September/1 October 1992.
4. *Basic Petroleum Data Book*, op. cit., sect. VI, tables 3, 3a, 3b.
5. S. Marris, *Deficits and the Dollar: The World Economy at Risk* (Washington DC: Institute of International Economics, December 1985), p. 14.
6. Greider, op. cit., p. 687.
7. *Papers of the Presidency, 1985*, State of the Union Address, 6 February 1985.
8. *Hansard: Parliamentary Debates* (London: House of Lords, 1984), 13 November 1984.
9. 'US Federal Reserve, Statement of the Chairman', 5 February 1985. The text was delivered on that date by Mr Paul Volcker to the Joint Economic Committee of the US Congress.
10. E. M. Graham and P. R. Krugman, *Foreign Direct Investment in the US* (Washington DC: Institute for International Economics, 1989), p. 13.
11. ibid., pp. 18, 30–1.
12. *Budget of the US Government. Fiscal Year 1990* (Washington DC: 1989), sect. 5, 171. See also C. L. Schultze, *Memos to the President* (Washington DC: 1992), p. 105.
13. C. F. Bergsten and W. R. Cline, *The US–Japan Economic Conflict* (Washington DC: Institute of International Economics, 1985), pp. 41–52. This study is the source of the classic contention that 'the rise in the US–Japanese trade deficit from 1980 to 1984 can be fully explained by changes in the exchange rate and rates of economic growth'. See also M. Moffitt, 'Reaganomics and the decline of US hegemony', *World Policy Journal* (New York: fall 1987), p. 571.
14. Moffitt, op. cit., p. 558.
15. *International Economic Indicators, 1988* (Köln: Institut der Deutschen Wirtschaft, 1989), p. 57.
16. For the comparative 1986 figures, see *International Economic Indicators, 1988*, op. cit., pp. 11, 45. (These German tables are calculated from a Deutschmark base, which gives a more stable model for international comparisons of the highly fluctuating sterling–dollar–yen ratios.) The Bank of Japan figures even for 1991 suggest that Japanese total exports account for 9.7 per cent of GDP; see *Japan 1992: An International Comparison* (Tokyo: Keizai Koho Center, December 1991), table 4:1, p. 30.

17. K. S. Courtis, *Asia in the 1990s: Movement and Contradictions* (Tokyo and Hong Kong: Deutsche Bank Group, Global Strategy Research Papers, September 1992).
18. D. J. Encarnation, *Rivals Beyond Trade* (Ithaca, NY: 1992), p. 22.
19. 'Fear of finance', *'The Economist' Survey of the World Economy*, September 1992, pp. 8–9.
20. Beschloss and Talbott, op. cit., pp. 9–10.
21. *Budget of the US Government. Fiscal Year 1991*, pp. 217–19. Note, however, that higher interest rates mean that the cost of net interest as a percentage of total outlays, at more than 14 per cent since 1988, is higher even than in 1950.
22. *Harvard Business Review* (September–October 1992), p. 164.
23. *New York Times*, 10 August 1992, reporting President Bush's speech in Orange County, California. For Senator Tsongas's remark see P. E. Tsongas, *A Call to Economic Arms* (Boston: 1991), p. 60.
24. *Changing Our Ways* (Washington DC: Carnegie Endowment National Commission, 1992), pp. 4, 12, 35, 85.
25. *Washington Post*, 23 July 1992.
26. R. Reich, 'The great bargain', *The American Prospect*, no. 7 (fall 1991), p. 12.
27. 'The Bush foreign policy', *Foreign Affairs*, vol. 70, no. 1 (winter 1990–1).
28. R. D. Hormats, 'The roots of American power', *Foreign Affairs*, vol. 70, no. 3 (winter 1990–1), pp. 133–4, 137.
29. 'The post-war British Labour Party', J. A. Baker III (senior thesis, 1952 Princeton University archive). It is dedicated 'To Mumo, with love'.
30. J. A. Baker III, 'America in Asia', *Foreign Affairs*, vol. 70, no. 5 (winter 1991–2), pp. 4–7.
31. *Current Policy Paper 1146*, US State Department, 17 January 1989.
32. Arbatov made this comment to several visitors in the early spring of 1987, including the present author. See Arbatov, op. cit., p. vi.
33. *New York Times*, 19 August 1992.
34. *US Executions* (Washington DC: Death Penalty Information Centre, 1992).
35. *Journal of the American Medical Association*, no. 36 (June 1990).
36. *Young Black Men in the Criminal Justice System* (Washington DC: The Sentencing Project, 1990); *Americans behind Bars: A Comparison of International Rates of Incarceration* (Washington DC: The Sentencing Project, 1991).
37. *Americans Behind Bars: One Year Later* (Washington DC: The Sentencing Project, 1992).
38. C. McCord and H. Freeman, 'Excess mortality in Harlem', *New England Journal of Medicine* (January 1990).
39. *Kids Count* (Washington DC: Centre for the Study of Social Policy, 31 January 1991).

40. L. R. Brown, C. Flavin and H. Kane (eds.), *Vital Signs, 1992* (Washington DC: 1992), pp. 110–11.
41. *The United States and the New Global Economy: A Rallier of Nations* (Washington DC: Committee for Economic Development, 1992), pp. 2–3.
42. W. Clinton and A. Gore, *Putting People First* (New York: 1992), pp. 6, 75, 158.
43. *Moscow Times*, 11 March 1992.
44. S. P. Huntington, 'The US – decline or renewal?', *Foreign Affairs*, vol. 67, no. 2 (winter 1988–9), pp. 87–8.

Epilogue

1. A comment to the current author, and cited in M. Walker, 'Victory and delusion', *Foreign Policy* (Washington DC), no. 83 (summer 1991). p. 166.
2. G. Barraclough, *An Introduction to Contemporary History* (London: 1964), pp. 102–5.
3. M. Walker, 'The US and the Persian Gulf crisis', *World Policy Journal* (New York) (fall 1990), pp. 794–5. These figures refer to the initial buildup of Operation Desert Storm. For the eventual assault upon Iraq's main forces, the US deployed over two-thirds of its available tactical aircraft, and some 40 per cent of American front-line strength in main battle tanks.
4. The author was fortunate to be present at Michnik's performance, after an International Press Institute conference in Moscow's Oktyabrskaya Hotel in October 1989.
5. Q. Wright, *A Study of War*, vol. 1 (Chicago: 1965), pp. 670–1.
6. Cited in Glyn, op. cit., p. 5. My debt to Mr Glyn's striking book, and to his original essay 'The Sarajevo fallacy', published in *The National Interest* in 1987, should be apparent.
7. Greider, op. cit., pp. 517–18.
8. *New York Times*, 18 October 1987, and G. Soros, 'After Black Monday', *Foreign Policy* (Washington DC), no. 70 (spring 1988), pp. 65–82.
9. *Wall Street Journal*, 5 November 1987.
10. *The Economist*, 14 July 1990, p. 28.
11. *Changing Our Ways*, Report of the Carnegie Commission (Washington DC: 1992, p. 18. (This emphasises that under a measure of purchasing-power parity, rather than market exchange rates, the US GDP would be larger than that of the twelve nations of the EC.) See also Courtis, op. cit.
12. The classic statement of this beguiling theory can be found in M. J. Doyle, 'Liberalism and world politics', *American Political Science Review*, LXXX (December 1986), pp. 1151–62.
13. R. Keatley, 'Foreign insight', *Wall Street Journal*, 6 November 1992.

Index